# Cracking DES

# Cracking DES
## *Secrets of Encryption Research, Wiretap Politics & Chip Design*

Electronic Frontier Foundation

***Cracking DES: Secrets of Encryption Research, Wiretap Politics, and Chip Design***
by the Electronic Frontier Foundation

Distributed by O'Reilly & Associates, Inc., 101 Morris Street, Sebastopol, CA 95472.

## Printing History:

May 1998:            First Edition.

Many of the designations used by manufacturers and sellers to distinguish their products are claimed as trademarks. Where those designations appear in this book, and the publisher was aware of a trademark claim, the designations have been printed in caps or initial caps.

While many precautions have been taken in the preparation of this book, the publisher and distributor assume no responsibility for errors or omissions, or for damages resulting from the use of the information contained herein.

This book is printed on acid-free paper with 85% recycled content, 15% post-consumer waste. O'Reilly & Associates is committed to using paper with the highest recycled content available consistent with high quality.

ISBN: 1-56592-520-3

# Table of Contents

# Foreword
# by Whitfield Diffie

In 1974 the Stanford computer science community ate at Loui's.[*] As I sat eating one evening in the fall, Butler Lampson approached me, and in the course of inquiring what I was doing, remarked that the IBM Lucifer system was about to be made a national standard. I hadn't known it, and it set me thinking.

My thoughts went as follows:

> NSA doesn't want a strong cryptosystem as a national standard, because it is afraid of not being able to read the messages.

> On the other hand, if NSA endorses a weak cryptographic system and is discovered, it will get a terrible black eye.

Hints that Butler was correct began to appear and I spent quite a lot of time thinking about this problem over the next few months. It led me to think about trapdoor cryptosystems and perhaps ultimately public-key cryptography.

When the Proposed Data Encryption Standard was released on the 17th of March 1975,[†] I thought I saw what they had done. The basic system might be ok, but the keyspace was on the small side. It would be hard to search, but not impossible. My first estimate was that a machine could be built for $650M that would break DES in a week. I discussed the idea with Marty Hellman and he took it on with a vengance. Before we were through, the estimated cost had fallen to $20M and the time had declined to a day.[‡]

---

[*] Louis Kao's Hsi-Nan restaurant in Town and Country Village, Palo Alto

[†] 40 Federal Register 12067

[‡] Whitfield Diffie and Martin E. Hellman. Exhaustive cryptanalysis of the NBS data encryption standard. Computer, 10(6):74-84, June 1977.

Our paper started a game in the cryptographic community and many papers on searching through DES keys have since been written. About three years after the publication of our paper, Robert Jueneman—then at Satellite Business Systems in McLean, Virginia—wrote "The Data Encryption Standard vs. Exhaustive Search."[*] This opus was substantially more optimistic about the chances for DES breaking. It predicted that by 1985 a half-million dollar investment would get you a DES key every hour and that by 1995, $10 million similarly spent would reduce that time to two seconds, an estimate remarkably close to one made fifteen years later.

A decade later, Yvo Desmedt and Jean-Jaques Quisquater made two contibutions, one whimsical, one serious. Using a related "birthday problem" sort of approach, they proposed a machine for attacking many cryptographic problems at a time[†]. Their whimsical suggestion took advantage of the fact that the polulation of China was about the square root of the size of the DES key space.[‡]

The year 1993 brought a watershed. Michael Wiener of Bell-Northern Research (BNR) designed the most solid paper machine yet.[§] It would not be too far off to describe it as a Northern Telecom DMS100 telephone switch, specialized to attacking DES. What made the paper notworthy was that it used standard Northern Telecom design techniques from the chips to the boards to the cabinets. It anticipated an investment of under a million dollars for a machine that would recover a key every three hours. A provocative aside was the observation that the required budget could be hidden in a director's budget at BNR.

Finally, in 1996, an estimate was prepared by not one or two cryptographers but by a group later, and not entirely sympathetically, called the magnificent seven.[‖] This estimate outlined three basic approaches loosely correlated with three levels of resources. At the cheap end was scrounging up time on computers you didn't need to own. In the middle was using programmable logic arrays, possibly PLA machines built for some other purpose such as chip simulation. The high end was the latest refinement of the custom chip approach.

---

[*] R. R. Jueneman, The Data Encryption Standard vs. Exhaustive Search: Practicalities and Politics. 5 Feb 1981.

[†] Yvo Desmedt, "An Exhaustive Key Search Machine Breaking One Million DES Keys", presented at Eurocrypt 1987. Chapter 9 of this book.

[‡] Jean-Jacques Quisquater and Yvo G. Desmedt, Chinese Lotto as an Exhaustive Code-Breaking Machine, Computer, 24(11):14-22, November 1991.

[§] Michael Wiener, "Efficient DES Key Search", presented at the Rump session of Crypto '93. Reprinted in Practical Cryptography for Data Internetworks, W. Stallings, editor, IEEE Computer Society Press, pp. 31-79 (1996). Currently available at ftp://ripem.msu.edu/pub/crypt/docs/des-key-search.ps.

[‖] Matt Blaze, Whitfield Diffie, Ronald L. Rivest, Bruce Schneier, Tsutomu Shimomura, Eric Thompson, and Michael Wiener. "Minimal key lengths for symmetric ciphers to provide adequate commercial security: A report by an ad hoc group of cryptographers and computer scientists", January 1996. Available at http://www.bsa.org/policy/encryption/cryptographers.html.

Exhaustive key search is a surprising problem to have enjoyed such popularity. To most people who have considered the probem, it is obvious that a search through $2^{56}$ possibilites is doable if somewhat tedious. If it a is mystery why so many of them, myself included, have worked to refine and solidify their estimates, it is an even greater mystery that in the late 1990s, some people have actually begun to carry out key searches.

At the 1997 annual RSA cryptographic trade show in San Francisco, a prize was announced for cracking a DES cryptogram*. The prize was claimed in five months by a loose consortium using computers scattered around the Internet.† It was the most dramatic success so far for an approach earlier applied to factoring and to breaking cryptograms in systems with 40-bit keys.

At the 1998 RSA show, the prize was offered again. This time the prize was claimed in 39 days‡ a result that actually represents a greater improvement than it appears to. The first key was found after a search of only 25% of the key space; the second was not recovered until the 85% mark. Had the second team been looking for the first key, they would have found it in a month.

These efforts used the magnificent seven's first approach. No application of the second has yet come to light. This book skips directly to the third. It describes a computer built out of custom chips. A machine that 'anyone' can build, from the plans it presents—a machine that can extract DES keys in days at reasonable prices, or hours at high prices. With the appearance of this book and the machine it represents, the game changes forever. It is not a question of whether DES keys can be extracted by exhaustive search; it is a question of how cheaply they can be extracted and for what purposes.

Using a network of general purpose machines that you do not own or control is a perfectly fine way of winning cryptanalytic contests, but it is not a viable way of doing production cryptanalysis. For that, you have to be able to keep your activities to yourself. You need to be able to run on a piece of hardware that you can protect from unwanted scrutiny. This is such a machine. It is difficult to know how many messages have been encrypted with DES in the more than two decades that it has been a standard. Even more difficult is knowing how many of those messages are of enduring interest and how many have already been captured or remain potentially accessible on disks or tapes, but the number, no matter precisely how the question is framed must be large. All of these messages must now be considered to be vulnerable.

---

\* http://www.rsa.com/rsalabs/97challenge/

† June 17, 1997, See the announcements at http://www.rsa.com/des/ and http://www.frii.com/~rcv/deschall.htm

‡ February 24, 1998, http://www.wired.com/news/news/technology/story/10544.html and http://www.distributed.net.

The vulnerability does not end there, however, for cryptosystems have nine lives. The most convincing argument that DES is insecure would not outweigh the vast investment in DES equipment that has accumulated throughout the world. People will continue using DES whatever its shortcomings, convincing themselves that it is adequate for their needs. And DES, with its glaring vulnerabilities, will go on pretending to protect information for decades to come.

# *Preface*

*In privacy and computer security, real information is too hard to find. Most people don't know what's really going on, and many people who do know aren't telling.*

This book was written to reveal a hidden truth. The standard way that the US Government recommends that we make information secure and private, the "Data Encryption Standard" or DES, does not actually make that information secure or private. The government knows fairly simple ways to reveal the hidden information (called "cracking" or "breaking" DES).

Many scientists and engineers have known or suspected this for years. The ones who know exactly what the government is doing have been unable to tell the public, fearing prosecution for revealing "classified" information. Those who are only guessing have been reluctant to publish their guesses, for fear that they have guessed wrong.

This book describes a machine which we actually built to crack DES. The machine exists, and its existence can easily be verified. You can buy one yourself, in the United States; or can build one yourself if you desire. The machine was designed and built in the private sector, so it is not classified. We have donated our design to the public domain, so it is not proprietary. There is no longer any question that it can be built or has been built. We have published its details so that other scientists and engineers can review, reproduce, and build on our work. There can be no more doubt. **DES is not secure.**

# Chapters

The first section of the book describes the Electronic Frontier Foundation's research project to build a machine to crack DES. The next section provides full technical details on the machine that we designed: for review, critique, exploration, and further evolution by the cryptographic research community. The final section includes several hard-to-find technical reports on brute force methods of cracking DES.

## Technical description

Chapter 1, *Overview*, introduces our project and gives the basic architecture of the Electronic Frontier Foundation's DES-cracking machine.

Chapter 2, *Design Specification*, by Paul Kocher of Cryptography Research, provides specifications for the machine from a software author's point of view.

Chapter 3, *Hardware Specification*, by Advanced Wireless Technologies, provides specifications for the custom gate array chips, and the boards that carry them, from a hardware designer's point of view.

## Technical design details

Chapter 4, *Scanning the Source Code*, explains how you can feed this book through an optical scanner and regenerate the exact source code needed to build the software and the specialized gate array chip that we designed.

Chapter 5, *Software Source Code*, contains a complete listing of the C-language software that runs on a PC and controls the DES-Cracker.

Chapter 6, *Chip Source Code*, contains a complete listing of the chip design language (VHDL) code that specifies how we designed the custom gate array chip.

Chapter 7, *Chip Simulator Source Code*, contains a complete listing of the C-language software that simulates the operation of the chip, for understanding how the chip works, and for generating test-vectors to make sure that the chips are properly fabricated.

Chapter 8, *Hardware Board Schematics*, provides schematic diagrams of the boards which provide power and a computer interface to the custom chips, as well as information on the layout of the boards and the backplanes that connect them.

# *Related Research Papers*

Chapter 9, *Breaking One Million DES Keys* by Yvo Desmedt, is a 1987 paper proposing an interesting design for a machine that could search for many DES keys simultaneously.

Chapter 10, *Architectural considerations for cryptanalytic hardware*, by Ian Goldberg and David Wagner, is a 1996 study that explores cracking DES and related ciphers by using field-programmable gate array chips.

Chapter 11, *Efficient DES Key Search - An Update*, by Michael J. Wiener, revises for 1998 the technology estimates from his seminal 1993 paper, which was the first to include full schematic diagrams of a custom chip designed to crack DES.

Chapter 12, *About the Authors*, describes the foundation and the companies which collaborated to build this project.

# 1

# Overview

## Politics of Decryption

We began the Electronic Frontier Foundation's DES Cracker project because of our interest in the politics of decryption.* The vulnerability of widely used encryption standards like DES is important for the public to understand.

A "DES Cracker" is a machine that can read information encrypted with the Data Encryption Standard (DES), by finding the key that was used to encrypt it. "Cracking DES" is a name for this search process. It is most simply done by trying every possible key until the right one is found, a tedious process called "brute-force search".

If DES-encrypted information can easily be decrypted by those who are not intended to see it, the privacy and security of our infrastructures that use DES are at risk. Many political, social, and technological decisions depend on just how hard it is to crack DES.

We noticed an increasing number of situations in which highly talented and respected people from the U.S. Government were making statements about how long it takes to crack DES. In all cases, these statements were at odds with our own estimates and those of the cryptographic research community. A less polite way to say it is that these government officials were lying, incompetent, or both. They were stating that cracking DES is much more expensive and time-consuming than we believed it to be. A very credible research paper had predicted that a

---

* DES, the Data Encryption Standard, encrypts a confidential message into scrambled output under the control of a secret key. The input message is also known as "plaintext", and the resulting output as "ciphertext". The idea is that only recipients who know the secret key can decrypt the ciphertext to obtain the original message. DES uses a 56-bit key, so there are $2^{56}$ possible keys.

machine could be built for $1.5 million, including development costs, that would crack DES in 3-1/2 hours. Yet we were hearing estimates of thousands of computers and weeks to years to crack a single message.

On Thursday, June 26, 1997 the U.S. House of Representatives' Committee on International Relations heard closed, classified testimony on encryption policy issues. The Committee was considering a bill to eliminate export controls on cryptography. After hearing this testimony, the Committee gutted the bill and inserted a substitute intended to have the opposite effect. A month later, a censored transcript of the hearing was provided; see `http://jya.com/hir-hear.htm`. Here are excerpts:

### Statement of Louis J. Freeh, Director, Federal Bureau of Investigation

> . . . And we do not have the computers, we do not have the technology to get either real-time access to that information or any kind of timely access.

> If we hooked together thousands of computers and worked together over 4 months we might, as was recently demonstrated decrypt one message bit. That is not going to make a difference in a kidnapping case, it is not going to make a difference in a national security case. We don't have the technology or the brute force capability to get to this information.

### Statement of William P. Crowell, Deputy Director, National Security Agency

> . . . I would go further and say there have been people who have said that Louis Freeh's organization should just get smarter technically, and if they were just smarter technically, they would be able to break all of this stuff. I would like to leave you with just one set of statistics, and then I think I am going to close with just a few comments on the bill itself.

> There is no brute force solution for law enforcement. [blacked out ------------ ----------------- ---- ----------------- ---------- -------- --------- ------- --------- -------- ----------- -------- ----- -------- -------- -----] A group of students -- not students -- the Internet gang last week broke a single message using 56-bit DES. It took 78,000 computers 96 days to break one message, and the headline was, DES has weak encryption.

> He doesn't consider that very weak. If that had been 64-bit encryption, which is available for export today, and is available freely for domestic use, that same effort would have taken 7,000 years. And if it had been 128-bit cryptography, which is what PGP is, pretty good privacy, it would have taken 8.6 trillion times the age of the universe.

### Comments made later in the hearing

Chairman Gilman. Would you need added manpower resource and equipment if there is a need to decrypt? And would that add to your already difficult case of language translation in many of your wiretaps?

Director Freeh. We would certainly need those resources, but I think more importantly is the point that was made here. Contrary to the National Research Council recommendation that the FBI buy more computers and Bill Gates' suggestion to me that we upgrade our research and development [blacked out---- --------------------------] American industry cannot do it, and that is decrypt real time encryption over a very minimal level of robustness. [blacked out---------] If you gave me $3 million to buy a Cray computer, it would take me how many years to do one message bit?

Mr. Crowell. 64 bits, 7,000 years.

Director Freeh. I don't have that time in a kidnapping case. It would kill us.

On March 17, 1998, Robert S. Litt, Principal Associate Deputy Attorney General, testified to the U.S. Senate Judiciary Committee, Subcommittee on the Constitution, Federalism, and Property. The subject of the hearing was "Privacy in a Digital Age: Encryption and Mandatory Access". Mr. Litt's whole statement is available at `http://www.computerprivacy.org/archive/03171998-4.shtml`. The part relevant to DES cracking is:

Some people have suggested that this is a mere resource problem for law enforcement. They believe that law enforcement agencies should simply focus their resources on cracking strong encryption codes, using high-speed computers to try every possible key when we need lawful access to the plaintext of data or communications that is evidence of a crime. But that idea is simply unworkable, because this kind of brute force decryption takes too long to be useful to protect the public safety. For example, decrypting one single message that had been encrypted with a 56-bit key took 14,000 Pentium-level computers over four months; obviously, these kinds of resources are not available to the FBI, let alone the Jefferson City Police Department.

## What's Wrong With Their Statements?

Some of the testimony quoted may have been literally true; nevertheless, it is deceptive. All of the time estimates presented by Administration officials were based on use of general-purpose computers to do the job. But that's fundamentally the wrong way to do it, and they know it.

A ordinary computer is ill-suited for use as a DES Cracker. In the first place, the design of DES is such that it is inherently very slow in software, but fast in hardware. Second, current computers do very little in parallel; the designers don't know exactly what instructions will be executed, and must allow for all combinations.

The right way to crack DES is with special-purpose hardware. A custom-designed chip, even with a slow clock, can easily outperform even the fastest general-purpose computer. Besides, you can get many such chips on a single board, rather than the one or two on a typical computer's motherboard.

There are practical limits to the key sizes which can be cracked by brute-force searching, but since NSA deliberately limited the key size of DES to 56 bits, back in the 1970's when it was designed, DES is crackable by brute force. Today's technology might not be able to crack other ciphers with 64-bit or 128-bit keys — or it might. Nobody will know until they have tried, and published the details for scientific scrutiny. Most such ciphers have very different internal structure than DES, and it may be possible to eliminate large numbers of possible keys by taking advantage of the structure of the cipher. Some senior cryptographers estimated what key sizes were needed for safety in a 1996 paper;* they suggest that to protect against brute force cracking, today's keys should have a minimum of 75 bits, and to protect information for twenty years, a minimum of 90 bits.

The cost of brute-force searching also overstates the cost of recovering encrypted text in the real world. A key report on the real impact of encryption on law enforcement† reveals that there are no cases in which a lack of police access to encrypted files resulted in a suspected criminal going free. In most cases the plaintext was recovered by other means, such as asking the suspect for the key, or finding another copy of the information on the disk. Even when brute force is the method of choice, keys are seldom truly random, and can be searched in the most likely order.

## Export Controls and DES

The U.S. Government currently restricts the ability of companies, individuals, and researchers to export hardware or software that includes the use of DES for confidentiality. These "export controls" have been a severe impediment to the development of security and privacy for networked computers, cellular phones, and other popular communications devices. The use of encryption algorithms stronger than DES is also restricted.

In December 1996, the government formally offered exporters the ability to incorporate DES, but nothing stronger, into their products. The catch is that these companies would have to sign an agreement with the government, obligating them to

---

* Minimal Key Lengths For Symmetric Ciphers To Provide Adequate Commercial Security: A Report By An Ad Hoc Group Of Cryptographers And Computer Scientists. Matt Blaze, Whitfield Diffie, Ronald L. Rivest, Bruce Schneier, Tsutomu Shimomura, Eric Thompson, Michael Wiener, January 1996. Available at http://www.bsa.org/policy/encryption/index.html.

† Encryption and Evolving Technologies: Tools of Organized Crime and Terrorism, by Dorothy E. Denning and William E. Baugh, Jr. National Strategy Information Center, 1997. ISSN 1093-7269.

install "key recovery" into their products within two years. Key recovery technology provides a way for the government to decrypt messages at will, by offering the government a copy of the key used in each message, in a way that the product's user cannot circumvent or control. In short, the government's offer was: collude with us to violate your customers' privacy, or we won't let you export *any* kind of secure products.

At the same time, the FBI was let into the group that reviews each individual company's application to export a cryptographic product. All reports indicate that the FBI is making good on the threat, by objecting to the export of all kinds of products that pose no threat at all to the national security (having been exportable in previous years before the FBI gained a voice). The FBI appears to think that by making itself hated and feared, it will encourage companies to follow orders. Instead it is encouraging companies to overturn the regulatory scheme that lets the FBI abuse the power to control exports. Industry started a major lobbying group called Americans for Computer Privacy (http://www.computerprivacy.org), which is attempting to change the laws to completely decontrol non-military encryption exports.

Some dozens of companies to signed up for key recovery, though it is unclear how many actually plan to follow through on their promise to deploy the technology. You will not find many of these companies trumpeting key recovery in their product advertisements. Users are wary of it since they know it means compromised security. If customers won't buy such products, companies know it makes no sense to develop them.

The best course for companies is probably to develop products that provide actual security, in some jurisdiction in the world which does not restrict their export. Some companies are doing so. The government's "compromise" offer discourages hesitant companies from taking this step, by providing a more moderate and conciliatory step that they can take instead. Companies that go to the effort to build overseas cryptographic expertise all use stronger technology than DES, as a selling point and to guard against early obsolesence. If those companies can be convinced to stay in the US, play the government's key-recovery game, and stick with DES, the government continues to win, and the privacy of the public continues to lose.

The success or failure of the government's carrot-and-stick approach depends on keeping industry and the public misled about DES's security. If DES-based products were perceived as insecure, there would be little reason for companies to sign away their customers' privacy birthrights in return for a mess of DES pottage. If DES-based products are perceived as secure, but the government actually knows that the products are insecure, then the government gets concessions from companies, without impacting its ability to intercept communications. Keeping the public ignorant gives the government the best of both worlds.

## *Political Motivations and EFF's Response*

We speculate that government officials are deliberately misleading the public about the strength of DES encryption:

- To encourage the public to continue using DES, so their agencies can eavesdrop on the public.

- To prevent the widespread adoption of stronger standards than DES, which the government would have more trouble decrypting.

- To offer DES exportability as a bargaining-chip, which actually costs the government little, but is perceived to be valuable.

- To encourage policy-makers such as Congressmen or the President to impose drastic measures such as key recovery, in the belief that law enforcement has a major encrypted-data problem and no practical way to crack codes.

As advocates on cryptography policy, we found ourselves in a hard situation. It appeared that highly credible people were either deliberately lying to Congress and to the public in order to advance their own harmful agendas, or were advocating serious infringement of civil liberties based on their own ignorance of the underlying issues. Most troubling is the possibility that they were lying. Perhaps these government executives merely saw themselves as shielding valuable classified efforts from disclosure. As advocates of good government, we do not see that classifying a program is any justification for an official to perjure themselves when testifying about it. (Declining to state an opinion is one thing; making untruthful statements as if they were facts is quite another.)

The National Research Council studied encryption issues and published a very complete 1996 report.* The most interesting conclusion of their report was that "the debate over national cryptography policy can be carried out in a reasonable manner on an unclassified basis". This presumes good faith on the part of the agencies who hide behind classified curtains, though. If it turns out that their public statements are manipulative falsehoods, an honest and reasonable public debate must necessarily exclude them, as dishonest and unreasonable participants.

In the alternative, if poor policy decisions are being made based on the ignorance or incompetence of senior government officials, the role of honest advocates should be to inform the debate.

---

* Cryptography's Role In Securing the Information Society, Kenneth W. Dam and Herbert S. Lin, editors. National Academy Press, Washington, DC, 1996.

In response to these concerns, EFF began a research program. Our research results prove that DES can be cracked quickly on a low budget. This proves that these officials were either lying or incompetent. The book you are holding documents the research, and allows it to be validated by other scientists.

# Goals

The goal of EFF's DES Cracker research project is to determine just how cheap or expensive it is to build a machine that cracks DES usefully.

Technically, we were also interested in exploring good designs for plaintext recognizers. These are circuits that can notice when the result of decryption is likely enough to be correct that specialized software — or a human — should look at it. Little research has been published on them,* yet they are a vital part of any efficient system for cryptanalysis.

Merely doing the research would let EFF learn the truth about the expense of cracking DES. But only publishing the research and demonstrating the machine would educate the public on the truth about the strength of DES. Press releases and even technical papers would not suffice; the appearance of schematics for a million-dollar DES Cracker in Michael Wiener's excellent 1993 paper should have been enough. But people still deploy DES, and Congressmen blindly accept the assurances of high officials about its strength.

There are many people who will not believe a truth until they can see it with their own eyes. Showing them a physical machine that can crack DES in a few days is the only way to convince some people that they really cannot trust their security to DES.

Another set of people might not believe our claims unless several other teams have reproduced them. (This is a basic part of the scientific method.) And many people will naturally be interested in how such a box works, and how it was built for only about $200,000. This book was written for such people. It contains the complete specifications and design documents for the DES Cracker, as well as circuit diagrams for its boards, and complete listings of its software and its gate array design. The full publication of our design should enable other teams to rapidly reproduce, validate, and improve on our design.

---

* But see: David A. Wagner and Steven M. Bellovin, "A Programmable Plaintext Recognizer," 1994. Available at http://www.research.att.com/~smb/papers/recog.ps or recog.pdf.

# History of DES Cracking

DES Crackers have been mentioned in the scientific and popular literature since the 1970's. Whitfield Diffie's Foreword describes several of them. The most recent detailed description was in a paper by Michael Wiener of Bell Northern Research in 1993. Wiener's paper included a detailed hardware design of a DES Cracker built with custom chips. The chips were to be built into boards, and the boards into mechanical "frames" like those of telephone central office switches. A completed design would have cost about a million dollars and would determine a DES key from known plaintext and known ciphertext in an average of 3-1/2 hours (7 hours in the worst case).

Mr. Wiener updated his conclusions in 1998, adjusting for five years of technological change. His update paper is included in this book, thanks to the courtesy of RSA Data Security, which originally published his update.

Ian Goldberg and David Wagner of the University of California at Berkeley took a different approach. Their design used a "field programmable gate array" (FPGA), which is a chip that can be reprogrammed after manufacturing into a variety of different circuits.

FPGA chips are slower than the custom chips used in the Wiener design, but can be bought quickly in small quantities, without a large initial investment in design. Rather than spend a big chunk of a million dollars to design a big machine, these researchers bought one or two general purpose chips and programmed them to be a slow DES Cracker. This let them quickly measure how many slow chips they would need to pile up to make a practical DES Cracker. Their paper is also included in this book.

# EFF's DES Cracker Project

The Electronic Frontier Foundation began its investigation into DES Cracking in 1997. The original plan was to see if a DES Cracker could be built out of a machine containing a large number of FPGA's.

Large machines built out of FPGAs exist in the commercial market for use in simulating large new chip designs before the chip is built. A collection of thousands of relatively incapable FPGA chips can be put together to simulate one very capable custom chip, although at 1/10th or 1/100th of the speed that the eventual custom chip would run at. This capability is used by chip designers to work the "bugs" out of their chip before committing to the expensive and time-consuming step of fabricating physical chips from their design.

EFF never got access to such a chip simulator. Instead, our investigations led us to Paul Kocher of Cryptography Research. Paul had previously worked with a team of hardware designers who knew how to build custom gate array chips cheaply, in batches of a few thousand chips at a time.

Paul and EFF met with the chip designers at Advanced Wireless Technologies, and determined that a workable DES Cracker could be built on a budget of about $200,000. The resulting machine would take less than a week, on average, to determine the key from a single 8-byte sample of known plaintext and ciphertext. Moreover, it would determine the key from a 16-byte sample of ciphertext in almost the same amount of time, if the statistical characteristics of the plaintext were known or guessable. For example, if the plaintext was known to be an electronic mail message, it could find all keys that produce plaintext containing nothing but letters, numbers, and punctuation. This makes the machine much more usable for solving real-world decryption problems.

There is nothing revolutionary in our DES Cracker. It uses ordinary ideas about how to crack DES that have been floating around in the cryptographic research community for many years. The only difference is that we actually built it, instead of just writing papers about it. Very similar machines could have been built last year, or the year before, or five or ten years ago; they would have just been slower or more expensive.

## *Architecture*

The design of the EFF DES Cracker is simple in concept. It consists of an ordinary personal computer connected with a large array of custom chips. Software in the personal computer instructs the custom chips to begin searching, and interacts with the user. The chips run without further help from the software until they find a potentially interesting key, or need to be directed to search a new part of the key space. The software periodically polls the chips to find any potentially interesting keys that they have turned up.

The hardware's job isn't to find the answer, but rather to eliminate most of the answers that are incorrect. Software is then fast enough to search the remaining potentially-correct keys, winnowing the "false positives" from the real answer. The strength of the machine is that it replicates a simple but useful search circuit thousands of times, allowing the software to find the answer by searching only a tiny fraction of the key space.

As long as there is a small bit of software to coordinate the effort, the problem of searching for a DES key is "highly parallelizable". This means the problem can be usefully solved by many machines working in parallel, simultaneously. For example, a single DES-Cracker chip could find a key by searching for many years. A thousand DES-Cracker chips can solve the same problem in one thousandth of the time. A million DES-Cracker chips could theoretically solve the same problem in about a millionth of the time, though the overhead of starting each chip would become visible in the time required. The actual machine we built contains 1536 chips.

When conducting a brute-force search, the obvious thing to do is to try every possible key, but there are some subtleties. You can try the keys in any order. If you think the key isn't randomly selected, start with likely ones. When you finally find the right key, you can stop; you don't have to try all the rest of the keys. You might find it in the first million tries; you might find it in the last million tries. On average, you find it halfway through (after trying half the keys). As a result, the timings for brute-force searches are generally given as the **average** time to find a key. The **maximum** time is double the average time.

## *Search units*

The search unit is the heart of the EFF DES Cracker; it contains thousands of them.

A search unit is a small piece of hardware that takes a key and two 64-bit blocks of ciphertext. It decrypts a block of ciphertext with the key, and checks to see if the resulting block of plaintext is "interesting". If not, it adds 1 to the key and repeats, searching its way through the key space.

If the first decryption produces an "interesting" result, the same key is used to decrypt the second block of ciphertext. If both are interesting, the search unit stops and tells the software that it has found an interesting key. If the second block's decryption is uninteresting, the search unit adds one to the key and goes on searching the key space.

When a search unit stops after finding an interesting result, software on the host computer must examine the result, and determine whether it's the real answer, or just a "false positive". A false positive is a plaintext that looked interesting to the hardware, but which actually isn't a solution to the problem. The hardware is designed to produce some proportion of false positives along with the real solution. (The job of the hardware isn't to find the answer, but to eliminate the vast majority of the non-answers.) As long as the false positives don't occur so rapidly that they overwhelm the software's ability to check and reject them, they don't hurt, and they simplify the hardware and allow it to be more general-purpose. For the kinds of problems that we're trying to solve, the hardware is designed to waste less than 1% of the search time on false positives.

## *Recognizing interesting plaintext*

What defines an interesting result? If we already know the plaintext, and are just looking for the key, an interesting result would be if the plaintext from this key matches our known block of plaintext. If we don't know the plaintext, perhaps the guess that it's all composed of letters, digits, and punctuation defines "interesting". The test has to be simple yet flexible. We ended up with one that's simple for the hardware, but a bit more complicated for the software.

Each result contains eight 8-bit bytes. First, the search unit looks at each byte of the result. Such a byte can have any one of 256 values. The search unit is set up with a table that defines which of these 256 byte values are "interesting" and which are uninteresting. For example, if the plaintext is known to be all numeric, the software sets up the table so that the ten digits (0 to 9) are interesting, and all other potential values are uninteresting.

The result of decrypting with the wrong key will look pretty close to random. So the chance of having a single byte look "interesting" will be based on what fraction of the 256 values are defined to be "interesting". If, say, 69 characters are interesting (A-Z, a-z, 0-9, space, and a few punctuation characters), then the chance of a random byte appearing to be interesting is 69/256 or about 1/4. These don't look like very good odds; the chip would be stopping on one out of every four keys, to tell the software about "interesting" but wrong keys.

But the "interest" test is repeated on each byte in the result. If the chance of having a wrong key's byte appear interesting is 1/4, then the chance of two bytes appearing interesting is 1/4 of 1/4, or 1/16th. For three bytes, 1/4th of 1/4th of 1/4th, or 1/64th. By the time the chip examines all 8 bytes of a result, it only makes a mistake on 1/65536th of the keys ($1/4^8$ keys).

That seems like a pretty small number, but when you're searching through 72,057,594,037,927,936 keys ($2^{56}$ keys, or 72 quadrillion keys), you need all the help you can get. Even having the software examine 1/65536th of the possible keys would require looking at 1,099,511,627,776 keys ($2^{40}$ or about a trillion keys). So the chip provides a bit more help.

This help comes from that second block of ciphertext. If every byte of a result looks interesting when the first block of ciphertext is decrypted, the chip goes back around and decrypts the second block of ciphertext with the same key. This divides the "error rate" by another factor of 65536, leaving the software with only 16,777,216 ($2^{24}$ or about sixteen million) keys to look at. Software on modern computers is capable of handling this in a reasonable amount of time.

(If we only know one block of ciphertext, we just give the chip two copies of the same ciphertext. It will test both copies, and eventually tell us that the block is interesting. The amount of time it spends checking this "second block" is always a tiny fraction of the total search time.)

In the plaintext recognizer there are also 8 bits that lets us specify which bytes of a plaintext are interesting to examine. For example, if we know or suspect the contents of the first six bytes of a plaintext value, but don't know anything about the last two bytes, we can search for keys which match in just those six bytes.

## Known plaintext

The chips will have many fewer "false positives" if the plaintext of the message is known, instead of just knowing its general characteristics. In that case, only a small number of byte values will be "interesting". If the plaintext has no repeated byte values, only eight byte values will be interesting, instead of 69 as above.

For example, if the plaintext block is "hello th", then only the six byte values "h", "e", "l", "o", space, and "t" are interesting. If a plaintext contains only these bytes, it is interesting. We'll get some "false positives" since many plaintexts like "tholo tt" would appear "interesting" even though they don't match exactly.

Using this definition of "interesting", a byte resulting from a wrong key will look interesting only about 8/256ths of the time, or 1/32nd of the time. All eight bytes resulting from a wrong key will look interesting only 1/32nd to the eighth power (1/32nd of 1/32nd of 1/32nd of 1/32nd of 1/32nd of 1/32nd of 1/32nd of 1/32nd) of the time, or 1/1,099,511,627,776th of the time ($1/2^{40}$ of the time). In other words, a search unit can try an average of a trillion keys before reporting that a wrong key looks interesting. This lets it search for a long time without slowing down or bothering the software.

## Speed

Once you get it going, a search unit can do one decryption in 16 clock cycles. The chips we have built can run with a clock of 40 Mhz (40 million cycles per second). Dividing 16 into 40 million shows that each search unit can try about 2.5 million keys per second.

In building the search units, we discovered that we could make them run faster if we used simpler circuitry for adding 1 to a key. Rather than being able to count from a key of 0 all the way up to a key of all ones, we limited the adder so that it can only count the bottom 32 bits of the key. The top 24 bits always remain the same. At a rate of 2.5 million keys per second, it takes a search unit 1717 seconds (about half an hour) to search all the possible keys that have the same top 24 bits. At the end of half an hour, the software has to stop the chip, reload it with a new value in the top 24 bits, and start it going again.

## Feedback Modes

The chip can also decrypt ciphertext that was encrypted in "Cipher Block Chaining" mode. In this mode, the ciphertext of each block is exclusive-OR'd into the plaintext of the next block before it is encrypted. (An "initialization vector" is exclusive-OR'd into the first block of plaintext.) The search unit knows how to exclusive-OR out an Initialization Vector (IV) after decrypting the first cyphertext, and to exclusive-OR out the first cyphertext after decrypting the second one. The software specifies the IV at the same time it provides the cyphertext values.

## Blaze Challenge

In June, 1997 Matt Blaze, a cryptography researcher at AT&T, proposed a different sort of cryptographic challenge. He wanted a challenge that not even the proponent knew how to solve, without either doing a massive search of the key-space, or somehow cryptanalyzing the structure of DES.

His challenge is merely to find a key such that a ciphertext block of the form XXXXXXXX decrypts to a plaintext block of the form YYYYYYYY, where X and Y are any fixed 8-bit value that is repeated across each of the eight bytes of the block.

We added a small amount of hardware to the search units to help with solving this challenge. There is an option to exclusive-OR the right half of the plaintext into the left half, before looking to see if the plaintext is "interesting". For plaintexts of the form YYYYYYYY, this will result in a left half of all zeros. We can then set up the plaintext recognizer so it only looks at the left half, and only thinks zeroes are interesting. This will produce a large number of false positives (any plaintext where the left and right halves are equal, like ABCDABCD), but software can screen them out with only about a 1% performance loss.

## Structure Of The Machine

Now that you know how a single search unit works, let's put them together into the whole machine.

Each search unit fits inside a custom chip. In fact, 24 search units fit inside a single chip. All the search units inside a chip share the same ciphertext blocks, initialization vector, and the same plaintext-recognizer table of "interesting" result values. Each search unit has its own key, and each can be stopped and started independently.

The chip provides a simple interface on its wires. There are a few signals that say whether any of the search units are stopped, some address and data wires so that the software can read and write to the search units, and wires for electrical power and grounding.

Since each search unit tries 2.5 million keys per second, a chip with 24 search units will try 60 million keys per second. But there are a lot of keys to look at. For a single chip, it would take 6,950 days (about 19 years) to find the average key, or 38 years to search the entire key space. Since we don't want to wait that long, we use more than one chip.

Each chip is mounted onto a large circuit board that contains 64 chips, along with a small bit of interface circuitry. The board blinks a light whenever the software is talking to that board. 64 other lights show when some search unit in each chip has stopped. In normal operation the software will talk to the board every few seconds, to check up on the chips. The chips should only stop every once in a while, and should be quickly restarted by the software.

The boards are designed to the mechanical specifications of "9U" VMEbus boards (about 15" by 15"). VMEbus is an industrial standard for computer boards, which was popular in the 1980s. We used the VMEbus form factor because it was easy to buy equipment that such boards plug into; we don't actually use the VMEbus electrical specifications.

9U VMEbus boards are much larger than the average interface card that plugs into a generic PC, so a lot more chips can be put onto them. Also, 9U VMEbus boards are designed to supply a lot of power, and our DES Cracker chips need it.

Since each chip searches 60 million keys per second, a board containing 64 chips will search 3.8 billion keys per second. Searching half the key space would take the board about 109 days. Since we don't want to wait that long either, we use more than one board.

The boards are mounted into chassis, also called "card cages". In the current design, these chassis are recycled Sun workstation packages from about 1990. Sun Microsystems built a large number of systems that used the large 9U VMEbus boards, and provide excellent power and cooling for the boards. The Sun-4/470 chassis provides twelve slots for VMEbus boards, and can easily be modified to handle our requirements. Subsequent models may use other physical packaging.

Each chassis has a connector for a pair of "ribbon cables" to connect it to the next chassis and to the generic PC that runs the software. The last chassis will contain a "terminator", rather than a connection to the next chassis, to keep the signals on the ribbon cable from getting distorted when they reach the end of the line.

Since each board searches 3.8 billion keys per second, a chassis containing 12 boards will search 46 billion keys per second. At that rate, searching half the key space takes about 9 days. One chassis full of boards is about 25% faster than the entire worldwide network of machines that solved the RSA "DES-II" challenge in February 1998, which was testing about 34 billion keys per second at its peak.

Since an informal design goal for our initial DES Cracker was to crack an average DES key in less than a week, we need more than 12 boards. To give ourselves a comfortable margin, we are using 24 boards, which we can fit into two chassis. They will search 92 billion keys per second, covering half the key space in about 4.5 days. If the chips consume too much power or produce too much heat for two chassis to handle,* we can spread the 24 boards across three chassis.

*Table 1-1: Summary of DES Cracker performance*

| Device | How Many In Next Device | Keys/Sec | Days/avg search |
|---|---|---|---|
| Search Unit | 24 | 2,500,000 | 166,800 |
| Chip | 64 | 60,000,000 | 6,950 |
| Board | 12 | 3,840,000,000 | 109 |
| Chassis | 2 | 46,080,000,000 | 9.05 |
| EFF DES Cracker | | 92,160,000,000 | 4.524 |

We designed the search unit once. Then we got a speedup factor of more than 36,000 to 1 just by replicating it 24 times in each chip and making 1500 chips. This is what we meant by "highly parallelizable".

## Budget

The whole project was budgeted at about US$210,000. Of this, $80,000 is for the labor of designing, integrating, and testing the DES Cracker. The other $130,000 is for materials, including chips, boards, all other components on the boards, card cages, power supplies, cooling, and a PC.

The software for controlling the DES Cracker was written separately, as a volunteer project. It took two or three weeks of work.

The entire project was completed within about eighteen months. Much of that time was used for preliminary research, before deciding to use a custom chip rather than FPGA's. The contract to build custom chips was signed in September, 1997, about eight months into the project. The team contained less than ten people, none of whom worked full-time on the project. They include a project manager, software designer, programmer, chip designer, board designer, hardware technicians, and hardware managers.

---

* At publication time, we have tested individual chips but have yet not built the full machine. If the chips' power consumption or heat production is excessive in a machine containing 1500 chips, we also have the option to reduce the chips' clock rate from 40 MHz down to, say, 30 MHz. This would significantly reduce the power and heat problems, at a cost of 33% more time per search (6 days on average).

We could have reduced the per-chip cost, or increased the chip density or search speed, had we been willing to spend more money on design. A more complex design could also have been flexible enough to crack other encryption algorithms. The real point is that for a budget that any government, most companies, and tens of thousands of individuals could afford, we built a usable DES Cracking machine. The publication of our design will probably in itself reduce the design cost of future machines, and the advance of semiconductor technology also makes this cost likely to drop. In five years some teenager may well build her own DES Cracker as a high school science fair project.

## Who Else Is Cracking DES?

If a civil liberties group can build a DES Cracker for $200,000, it's pretty likely that governments can do the same thing for under a million dollars. (That's a joke.) Given the budget and mission of the US National Security Agency, they must have started building DES Crackers many years ago. We would guess that they are now on their fourth or fifth generation of such devices. They are probably using chips that are much faster than the ones we used; modern processor chips can run at more than 300 Mhz, eight times as fast as our 40 Mhz chips. They probably have small "field" units that fit into a suitcase and crack DES in well under a day; as well as massive central units buried under Ft. Meade, that find the average DES key in seconds, or find thousands of DES keys in parallel, examining thousands of independent intercepted messages.

Our design would scale up to finding a DES key in about half an hour, if you used 333,000 chips on more than 5,200 boards. The boards would probably require about 200 parallel port cards to communicate with them; an IBM-compatible PC could probably drive four such cards, thus requiring about 50 PC's too. The software required would be pretty simple; the hard part would be the logistics of physical arrangement and repair. This is about 200 times as much hardware as the project we built. A ridiculously high upper bound on the price of such a system would be 200 times the current project price, or $40 million.

Of course, if we were going to build a system to crack DES in half an hour or less, using a third of a million chips, it would be better to go back to the drawing board and design from scratch. We'd use more modern chip fabrication processes; a higher-volume customer can demand this. We'd spend more on the initial design and the software, to produce a much cheaper and simpler total system, perhaps allowing boards full of denser, faster, lower-voltage chips to use a small onboard processor and plug directly into an Ethernet. We'd work hard to reduce the cost of each chip, since there would be so many of them. We'd think about how to crack multiple DES keys simultaneously.

It would be safe to assume that any large country has DES Cracking machines. After the publication of this book wakes them up, probably more small countries and some criminal organizations will make or buy a few DES Crackers. That was not the intent of the book; the intent was to inform and warn the *targets* of this surveillance, the builders of equipment, and the policy makers who grapple with encryption issues.

# What To Do If You Depend On DES

Don't design anything else that depends on single DES.

Take systems out of service that use permanently fixed single-DES keys, or superencrypt the traffic at a higher level. Superencryption requires special care, though, to avoid providing *any* predictable headers that can be used to crack the outer DES encryption.

Start changing your software and/or hardware to use a stronger algorithm than DES.

Three-key Triple-DES is an obvious choice, since it uses the same block size and can possibly use the same hardware; it just uses three keys and runs DES three times (encrypting each block with the first key, decrypting it with the second, then encrypting it with the third). The strength of Triple-DES is not known with any certainty, but it is certainly no weaker than single DES, and is probably substantially stronger. Beware of "mixed up" variants or modes of Triple-DES; research by Eli Biham[*] and David Wagner[†] shows that they are significantly weaker than the straightforward Triple-DES, and may be even weaker than single-DES. Use three copies of DES in Electronic Code Book (ECB) mode as a basic primitive. You can then build a mode such as Cipher Feedback mode using the primitive ECB 3DES.

The US Government is tardily going through a formal process to replace the DES. This effort, called the Advanced Encryption Standard, will take several years to decide on a final algorithm, and more years for it to be proven out in actual use, and carefully scrutinized by public cryptanalysts for hidden weaknesses. If you are designing products to appear five to ten years from now, the AES might be a good source of an encryption algorithm for you.

The reason that the AES is tardy is because the NSA is believed to have blocked previous attempts to begin the process over the last decade. In recent years NSA

---

[*] "Cryptanalysis of Triple-Modes of Operation", Eli Biham, Technion Computer Science Department Technical Report CS0885, 1996.

[†] "Cryptanalysis of some Recently Proposed Multiple Modes of Operation", David Wagner, University of California at Berkeley, http://www.cs.berkeley.edu/~daw/multmode-fse98.ps. Presented at the 1998 Fast Software Encryption workshop.

has tried, without success, to get the technical community to use classified, NSA-designed encryption algorithms such as Skipjack, without letting the users subject these algorithms to public scrutiny. Only after this effort failed did they permit the National Institute of Standards and Technology to begin the AES standardization process.

# *Conclusion*

The Data Encryption Standard has served the public pretty well since 1975. But it was designed in an era when computation cost real money, when massive computers hunkered on special raised flooring in air-conditioned inner sanctums. In an era when you can carry a supercomputer in your backpack, and access millions of machines across the Internet, the Data Encryption Standard is obsolete.

The Electronic Frontier Foundation hopes that this book inspires a new level of truth to enter the policy debates on encryption. In order to make wise choices for our society, we must make well-informed choices. Great deference has been paid to the perspective and experience of the National Security Agency and Federal Bureau of Investigation in these debates. This is particularly remarkable given the lack of any way for policy-makers or the public to check the accuracy of many of their statements.* (The public cannot even *hear* many of their statements, because they are classified as state secrets.) We hope that the crypto policy debate can move forward to a more successful and generally supported policy. Perhaps if these agencies will consider becoming more truthful, or policy-makers will stop believing unverified statements from them, the process can move more rapidly to such a conclusion.

---

* DES cracking is not the only issue on which agency credibility is questionable. For example, the true extent of the law enforcement problem posed by cryptography is another issue on which official dire predictions have been made, while more careful and unbiased studies have shown little or no impact. The validity of the agencies' opinion of the constitutionality of their own regulations is also in doubt, having been rejected two decades ago by the Justice Department, and declared unconstitutional in 1997 by a Federal District Court. The prevalence of illegal wiretapping and communications interception by government employees is also in question; see for example the Los Angeles Times story of April 26, 1998, "Can the L.A. Criminal-Justice System Work Without Trust?"

# 2

# *Design for DES Key Search Array*

Cryptography Research
and
Advanced Wireless Technologies, Inc.

## *On-Chip Registers*

Each chip contains the following registers. They are addressed as specified in Figure 2-1.

### Ciphertext0 (64 bits = 8 bytes)

The value of the first ciphertext being searched. Ciphertext0 is identical in all search units and is set only once (when the search system is first initialized).

### Ciphertext1 (64 bits = 8 bytes)

The value of the second ciphertext being searched. Ciphertext1 is identical in all search units and is set only once (when the search system is first initialized).

### PlaintextByteMask (8 bits)

The plaintext byte selector. One-bits in this register indicate plaintext bytes that should be ignored when deciding whether or not the plaintext produced by a particular key is possibly correct. This mask is helpful when only a portion of the plaintext's value is known. For example, if the first 5 bytes equal a known header but the remaining three are unknown, a PlaintextByteMask of 0x07 would be used.

### PlaintextXorMask (64 bits = 8 bytes)

This register is XORed with decryption of ciphertext0. This is normally filled with

## *Figure 2-1: Register Addressing*

```
Register(s)     Description & Comments
0x00-0x1F       PlaintextVector
0x20-0x27       PlaintextXorMask
0x28-0x2F       Ciphertext0
0x30-0x37       Ciphertext1
0x38            PlaintextByteMask
0x39-0x3E       Unused (reserved)
0x3F            SearchInfo
0x40-0x47       Search unit  0 key counter (0x40-0x46) and SearchStatus (0x47)
0x48-0x4F       Search unit  1 key counter (0x48-0x4E) and SearchStatus (0x4F)
0x50-0x57       Search unit  2 key counter (0x50-0x56) and SearchStatus (0x57)
0x58-0x5F       Search unit  3 key counter (0x58-0x5E) and SearchStatus (0x5F)
0x60-0x67       Search unit  4 key counter (0x60-0x66) and SearchStatus (0x67)
0x68-0x6F       Search unit  5 key counter (0x68-0x6E) and SearchStatus (0x6F)
0x70-0x77       Search unit  6 key counter (0x70-0x76) and SearchStatus (0x77)
0x78-0x7F       Search unit  7 key counter (0x78-0x7E) and SearchStatus (0x7F)
0x80-0x87       Search unit  8 key counter (0x80-0x86) and SearchStatus (0x87)
0x88-0x8F       Search unit  9 key counter (0x88-0x8E) and SearchStatus (0x8F)
0x90-0x97       Search unit 10 key counter (0x90-0x96) and SearchStatus (0x97)
0x98-0x9F       Search unit 11 key counter (0x98-0x9E) and SearchStatus (0x9F)
0xA0-0xA7       Search unit 12 key counter (0xA0-0xA6) and SearchStatus (0xA7)
0xA8-0xAF       Search unit 13 key counter (0xA8-0xAE) and SearchStatus (0xAF)
0xB0-0xB7       Search unit 14 key counter (0xB0-0xB6) and SearchStatus (0xB7)
0xB8-0xBF       Search unit 15 key counter (0xB8-0xBE) and SearchStatus (0xBF)
0xC0-0xC7       Search unit 16 key counter (0xC0-0xC6) and SearchStatus (0xC7)
0xC8-0xCF       Search unit 17 key counter (0xC8-0xCE) and SearchStatus (0xCF)
0xD0-0xD7       Search unit 18 key counter (0xD0-0xD6) and SearchStatus (0xD7)
0xD8-0xDF       Search unit 19 key counter (0xD8-0xDE) and SearchStatus (0xDF)
0xE0-0xE7       Search unit 20 key counter (0xE0-0xE6) and SearchStatus (0xE7)
0xE8-0xEF       Search unit 21 key counter (0xE8-0xEE) and SearchStatus (0xEF)
0xF0-0xF7       Search unit 22 key counter (0xF0-0xF6) and SearchStatus (0xF7)
0xF8-0xFF       Search unit 23 key counter (0xF8-0xFE) and SearchStatus (0xFF)
```

the CBC mode IV.

### PlaintextVector (256 bits = 8 bytes)

Identifies allowable plaintext byte values (ignoring those masked by the PlaintextByteMask). If, for any plaintext byte P[i=0..7], bit P[i] is not set, the decryption key will be rejected. PlaintextVector is identical in all search units and is set only once (when the search system is first initialized).

### SearchInfo (8 bits)

The bits in SearchInfo describe how the correct plaintext identification function works. Bits of SearchInfo are defined as follows:

### bit 0 = UseCBC

If this bit is set, Ciphertext0 is XORed onto the plaintext produced by decrypting Ciphertext1 before the plaintext is checked. This bit is used when checking CBC-mode ciphertexts.

### bit 1 = ExtraXOR

If set, the right half of the resulting plaintext is XORed onto the left before any plaintext checking is done. ExtraXOR and UseCBC cannot be used together.

### bit 2 = ChipAllActive

If cleared, one or more search units in this chip have halted (e.g., SearchActive is zero). This value is computed by ANDing the SearchActive bits of all search units' SearchStatus bytes. The inverse of this value is sent out on a dedicated pin, for use in driving a status LED which lights up whenever the chip halts.

### bit 3 = BoardAllActive

This pin is the AND of the ChipAllActive lines of this chip and all later chips on the board. This is implemented by having each chip n take in chip n+1's BoardAllActive line, AND it with its own ChipAllActive line, and output the result to chip n-1 for its BoardAllActive computation. This makes it possible to find which chip on a board has halted by querying $\log_2 N$ chips, where N is the number of chips on the board. If BoardAllActiveEnable is not set to 1, BoardAllActive simply equals the BoardAllActiveInput pin, regardless of the chip's internal state.

### bit 4 = BoardAllActiveEnable

If this value is set to 0 then BoardAllActive always equals the BoardAllActiveInput pin, regardless of whether all search units on the board are active. If this bit is set to 1, then the BoardAllActive register (and output) are set to reflect the internal state of the chip ANDed with the input pin.

### bits 5-7 = Unused

### KeyCounter (56 bits)

The value of the key currently being checked  The KeyCounter is updated very frequently (i.e., once per key tested). A unique KeyCounter value is assigned to every search unit. When the search unit halts after a match, KeyCounter has already been incremented to the next key; the match was on the previous key.

### SearchCommandAndStatus (8 bits)

The bits in SearchStatus describe the current search state of a specific search unit. A unique SearchStatus register is allocated for each search unit. Bits of SearchStatus are allocated as follows:

### bit 0 = SearchActive

Indicates whether the search is currently halted (0=halted, 1=active). The computer sets this bit to begin a search, and it is cleared by the search unit if a matching candidate key is found. The host computer checks the status of this bit periodically and, if it is zero, reads out the key then restarts the search. (See also ChipAllActive and BoardAllActive in the SearchInfo register.)

### bit 1 = CiphertextSelector

Indicates whether the search engine is currently checking Ciphertext0 or Ciphertext1. (0=Ciphertext0, 1=Ciphertext1). If this bit is clear, the search engine decrypts Ciphertext0 and either sets CiphertextSelector to 1 (if the plaintext passes the checks) or increments KeyCounter (if the plaintext does not pass). If this bit is set, the search engine decrypts Ciphertext1 and either sets SearchActive to 0 (if the plaintext passes the checks) or sets CiphertextSelector to 0 and increments KeyCounter (if the plaintext does not pass).

### bits 2-7 = Unused

# Commands

In order to be able to address each search unit separately, each can be addressed uniquely by the combination of its location on the chip, the location of the chip on the board, and board's identifier. The BoardID is interpreted off-chip; each chip has a board select pin, which notifies the chip when the board has been selected. Chip ID matching is done inside each ASIC; the ID pins of the ASIC are wired to the chip's ID.

All commands are originated by the computer go via a bus which carries 8 bits for BoardID/ChipID/Register address, 8 bits for data, and a few additional bits for controls.

To do a search, the host computer will program the search units as shown in Figure 2-2. (N is the total number of search units, numbered from 0 to N-1, each with a unique BoardID/ChipID/Register address.)

# Search Unit Operation

Each search unit contains a DES engine, which performs DES on two 32-bit registers L/R using the key value in KeyCounter. Each search unit goes through the process detailed in Figure 2-3, and never needs to halt. If registers are updated during the middle of this process, the output is meaningless (which is fine, since an incorrect output is statistically almost certain to not be a match).

## *Figure 2-2: Example algorithm for programming the search array using host computer*

This is a very simple algorithm intended only as an example. The actual software will use more intelligent search techniques, using the BoardAllActive and ChipAllActive lines.

Load Ciphertext0, Ciphertext1, PlaintextXorMask, PlaintextByteMask,
    PlaintextVector, and SearchInfo into each chip.
For i = 0 upto N-1
    Set SearchStatus in search unit i to 0 while loading the key.
    Set KeyCounter of search unit i to ((256)(i) / N).
    Set SearchStatus in search unit i to 1 to enable SearchActive.
EndFor
While correct key has not been found:
    For i = 0 upto N-1:
        Read SearchStatus from search unit i.
        Check SearchActive bit.
        If SearchActive is set to 0:
            Read KeyCounter from search unit i.
            Subtract 1 from the low 32 bits of the key.
            Perform a DES operation at the local computer to check the key.
                If the key is correct, the search is done.
            Set the SearchActive bit of SearchStatus to restart the search.
        EndIf
    EndFor
EndWhile

# *Sample Programming Descriptions*

This section describes how the system will be programmed for some typical operations.

## *Known ciphertext/plaintext (ECB, CBC, etc.)*

If a complete ciphertext/plaintext block is known, this mode is used. This works for most DES modes (ECB, CBC, counter, etc.), but does require a full plaintext/ciphertext pair.

### PlaintextVector

For this search, there are 8 (or fewer) unique plaintext bytes in the known plaintext. The bits corresponding to these bytes are set in PlaintextVector, but all other bits are set to 0.

## *Figure 2-3: Search unit operation*

1. If CiphertextSelector is 0, then Let L/R = Ciphertext0.
   If CiphertextSelector is 1, then Let L/R = Ciphertext1.

2. Decrypt L/R using the key in KeyCounter, producing a candidate
   plaintext in L/R.

3. If ExtraXOR is 1, then Let L = L XOR R.
   If CiphertextSelector is 0, then
       Let L/R = L/R XOR PlaintextXorMask.
   If CiphertextSelector is 1 and UseCBC is 1, then:
       Let L/R = L/R XOR Ciphertext0.

4. If SearchActive = 1 AND (
   (PlaintextByteMask[0x80] = 0 AND PlaintextVector[byte 0 of L] is 0) OR
   (PlaintextByteMask[0x40] = 0 AND PlaintextVector[byte 1 of L] is 0) OR
   (PlaintextByteMask[0x20] = 0 AND PlaintextVector[byte 2 of L] is 0) OR
   (PlaintextByteMask[0x10] = 0 AND PlaintextVector[byte 3 of L] is 0) OR
   (PlaintextByteMask[0x08] = 0 AND PlaintextVector[byte 0 of R] is 0) OR
   (PlaintextByteMask[0x04] = 0 AND PlaintextVector[byte 1 of R] is 0) OR
   (PlaintextByteMask[0x02] = 0 AND PlaintextVector[byte 2 of R] is 0) OR
   (PlaintextByteMask[0x01] = 0 AND PlaintextVector[byte 3 of R] is 0)) then:
       Let CiphertextSelector = 0.
       Increment KeyCounter.
   else
       If CiphertextSelector is 1 then Let SearchActive = 0.
       Let CiphertextSelector = 1.

5. Go to step 1.

**Ciphertext0**
Equals the ciphertext block.

**Ciphertext1**
Equals the ciphertext block.

**SearchInfo**
UseCBC and ExtraXOR are both set to 0.

**PlaintextByteMask**
Set to 0x00 (all bytes used).

**PlaintextXorMask**
Set to 0x0000000000000000.

Because the plaintext byte order does not matter, there are 8 acceptable values for each ciphertext byte, or $8^8 = 2^{24} = 16.7$ million possible ciphertexts which will satisfy the search criteria. The probability that an incorrect ciphertext will pass is $2^{24} / 2^{64}$, so over a search of $2^{55}$ keys there will be an average of $(2^{55})(2^{24} / 2^{64})$, or 32768 false positives which will need to be rejected by the controlling computer. Because the Ciphertext0 and Ciphertext1 selections are identical, any false positives that pass the first test will also pass the second test. (The performance penalty is negligible; the search system will do two DES operations on each of the 32768 false positive keys, but only one DES operation on all other incorrect keys.)

## ASCII text (ECB or CBC)

A minimum of two adjacent ciphertexts (16 bytes total) are required for ASCII-only attacks.

**PlaintextVector**
Set only the bits containing acceptable ASCII characters. For normal text, this would normally include 55 of the 256 possible characters occur (10=line feed, 13=carriage return, 32=space, 65-90=capital letters, and 97-122=lowercase letters).

**Ciphertext0**
Equals the first ciphertext.

**Ciphertext1**
Equals the second ciphertext.

**SearchInfo**
UseCBC is set to 0 if ECB, or set to 1 if the ciphertext was produced using CBC. ExtraXOR is set to 0.

**PlaintextByteMask**
Set to 0x00 (all bytes used).

**PlaintextXorMask**
Set to 0x0000000000000000 for ECB, to IV for CBC.

The probability that the two (random) candidate plaintexts produced by an incorrect key will contain only the ASCII text characters listed above is $(55/256)^{16}$. In a search, there will thus be an average of $2^{55} (55/256)^{16} = 742358$ false positives which need to be rejected by the computer. For one key in about 220,000, the first check will pass and an extra DES will be required. (The time for these extra DES operations is insignificant.) Idle time lost while waiting for false positives to be cleared is also insignificant. If the computer checks each search unit's SearchActive flag once per second, a total of 0.5 search unit seconds will be wasted for every false positive, or a total of 103 search-unit hours, out of about 4 million search-unit hours for the whole search.

When programming CBC mode, note that the PlaintextXorMask must be set to the IV (or the previous ciphertext, if the ciphertext being attacked is not in the first block).

## Matt Blaze's Challenge

The goal is to find a case where all plaintext bytes are equal and all ciphertext bytes are equal.

**PlaintextVector**
Set only bit 0.

**Ciphertext0**
Set to a fixed value with all bytes equal

**Ciphertext1**
Same as Ciphertext0.

**SearchInfo**
UseCBC is set to 0. ExtraXOR is set to 1.

**PlaintextByteMask**
Set to 0x0F (only left half examined).

**PlaintextXorMask**
Set to 0x0000000000000000.

If the right and left half are equal, as must be the case if all plaintext bytes are the same, then when the ExtraXOR bit's status causes the L=L XOR R step, L will become equal to 0. The plaintext byte mask selects only the left half and the PlaintextVector makes sure the 4 bytes are 0.

False positives occur whenever L=R, or with one key in $2^{32}$. Because this search is not guaranteed to terminate after $2^{56}$ operations, the average time is $2^{56}$ (not $2^{55}$). The number of false positives is expected to be $2^{56}/2^{32} = 2^{24} = 16.8$ million. Each search unit will thus find a false positive every $2^{32}$ keys on average, or about once every half hour. At 1 second polling of search units, $(0.5)(16.8$ million$)/3600 = 2333$ search unit hours will be idle (still under 1% of the total). The host computer will need to do the 16.8 million DES operations (on average), but even a fairly poor DES implementation can do this in just a few minutes.

# Scalability and Performance

The architecture was intended to find DES keys in less than 10 days on average. The performance of the initial implementation is specified in Figure 2-4. Faster results can be easily obtained with increased hardware; doubling the amount of hardware will halve the time per result. Within the design, boards of keysearch ASICs can be added and removed easily, making it simple to make smaller or larger systems, where larger systems cost more but find results more quickly. Larger systems will have additional power and cooling requirements.

## *Figure 2-4: Performance Estimate*

| | |
|---|---|
| Total ASICs | 1536 |
| Search units per ASIC | 24 |
| Total search units | 36864 |
| Clock speed (Hz) | 4.00E+07 |
| Clocks per key (typical) | 16 |
| DES keys per search unit per second | 2.50E+06 |
| Total DES keys per second | 9.22E+10 |
| Search size (worst case) | 7.21E+16 |
| Seconds per result (worst case) | 7.82E+05 |
| Days per result (worst case) | 9.05 |
| Search size (average case) | 3.60E+16 |
| Seconds per result (average case) | 3.91E+05 |
| **Days per result (average case)** | **4.52** |

# Host Computer Software

Cryptography Research will write the following software:

**Simulation**

Cryptography Research will develop software to generate test vectors for the chip for testing before the design is sent to the fab. This software will test all features on the chip and all modes of operation. This program will have a simple command line interface.

**Host computer**

The host computer software program will implement the standard search tasks of breaking a known plaintexts, breaking encrypted ASCII text (ECB and CBC modes), and solving the Matt Blaze challenge. These programs will be written in standard ANSI C, except for platform-specific I/O code. The host program will also have a test mode, which loads search units with tasks that are known to halt reasonably quickly (e.g., after searching a few million keys) and verifies the results to detect of any failed parts. (The software will include the capability of bypassing bad search units during search operations.) Users who wish to perform unusual searches will need to add a custom function to determining whether candidate keys are actually correct and recompile the code.

The initial version of this program will have a simple command line interface and will be written for DOS. A Linux port will also be written, but may not be ready by the initial target completion date. (Because the only platform-specific code will be the I/O functions, it should be very easy to port to any platform with an appropriate compiler.) Software programs will identify the participants in the project (AWT, EFF, and Cryptography Research).

Cryptography Research will also produce a version with a prettier user interface to make the demonstration more elegant (platform-to-be-determined).

All software and source code will be placed in the public domain.

# *Glossary*

**BoardID**
An 8-bit identifier unique for each board. This will be set with a DIP switch on the board. The host computer addresses chips by their ChipID and BoardID.

**CBC mode**
A DES mode in which the first plaintext block is XORed with an initialization vector (IV) prior to encryption, and each subsequent plaintext is XOR with the previous ciphertext.

**ChipID**
A value used by the host computer to specify which chip on a board is being addressed.

**Ciphertext**
Encrypted data.

**Ciphertext0**
The first of the two ciphertexts to be attacked.

**Ciphertext1**
The second of the two ciphertexts to be attacked.

---

Pre-ANSI C can be supported if required. Any GUI code will probably be written in C++.

### CiphertextSelector

A register used to select the current ciphertext being attacked. The selector is needed because a single DES engine needs to be able to test two ciphertexts to determine whether both are acceptable matches before deciding that a key is a good match.

### DES

The Data Encryption Standard.

### ExtraXOR

A register to make the search units perform an extra operation which XORs the right and left halves of the result together. This is used to add support for Matt Blaze's DES challenge.

### Host computer

The computer that controls the DES search array.

### KeyCounter

Each search unit has a KeyCounter register which contains the current key being searched. These registers are each 7 bytes long, to hold a 56-bit key.

### Plaintext

Unencrypted data corresponding to a ciphertext.

### PlaintextByteMask

An 8-bit register used to mask off plaintext bytes. This is used to mask off bytes in the plaintext whose values aren't known or are too variable to list in the PlaintextVector.

### PlaintextVector

A 256-bit register used to specify which byte values can be present in valid plaintexts. It is the host computer's responsibility to ensure that only a reasonable number of bits are set in the PlaintextVector; setting too many will cause the DES search units to halt too frequently.

### PlaintextXorMask

A 64-bit register XORed onto the value derived by decrypting ciphertext 0. Normally this mask is either zero or set to the CBC mode initialization vector (IV).

### SearchActive

A bit for each search unit which indicates whether it is currently searching, or whether it has stopped at a candidate key. Stopped search units can be restarted by loading a key which does not halt and resetting this bit.

### SearchInfo

A register containing miscellaneous information about how DES results should be post- processed and also indicating whether any search units on the chip or on the board have halted.

**UseCBC**

A bit in SearchInfo which directs the search engine to do CBC-mode post-processing after decryption (e.g., XOR the decryption of ciphertext1 with ciphertext0 to produce plaintext1).

# 3

# *Design for DES Key Search Array Chip-Level Specification*

Advanced Wireless Technologies, Inc.
and
Cryptography Research

## *ASIC Description*

Select1
>    Selects Cipher text 1

C0
>    Cipher text 0

C1
>    Cipher text 1

Search
>    Search is active

K
>    Key

Mask
>    Plain text bit mask and DES output

Match=0
>    a Zero is found in any bit position of plain text vector as specified in step 4 of Search Unit Operation (see Chapter 2)

CBC & Extra XOR
>    Perform step 3 of Search Unit Operation (see Chapter 2)

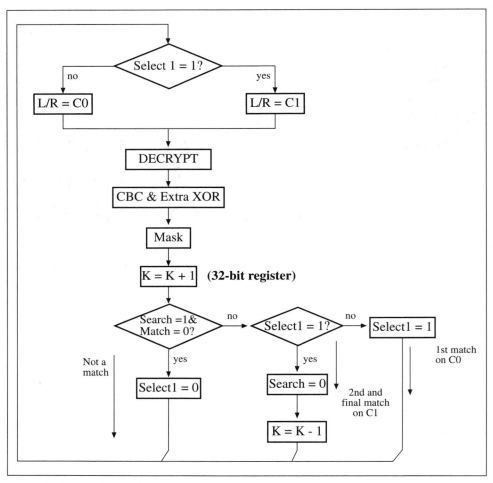

*Figure 3-1: Search Unit Operation Flow Chart*

To determine the maximum number of bit required for the Key:

$$K = \log_2(\text{Maximum combinations/number of chips})$$

$$= \log_2(2^{56}/(24 \text{ cpc} * 64 \text{ cpb} * 24 \text{ boards}) = \log_2(1.95E12) = 42 \text{ bits}$$

If we are going to use 32-bit counters, then it will overflow every:

$$2^{32} * 16 \text{ cycles} * 25\text{ns} = 1.72 * 10^{12}\text{ns} = 1720 \text{ sec} = 28.7 \text{ minutes}$$

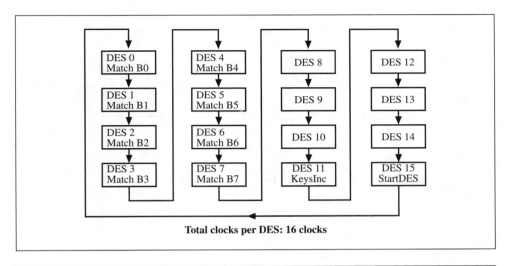

**Total clocks per DES: 16 clocks**

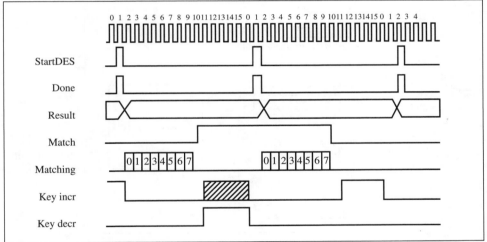

*Figure 3–2: State Diagram for the Search Unit*

# Board description

The PC will interface with the ASICs through a parallel card. The parallel card has three ports, assigned:

> Port A: Address(7:0)
> Port B: Data(7:0)
> Port C: Control, 8 signals

To reduce the routing resources on the boards and ASICs we multiplex the address lines. To access a register on the ASIC, it is required that the software latch the

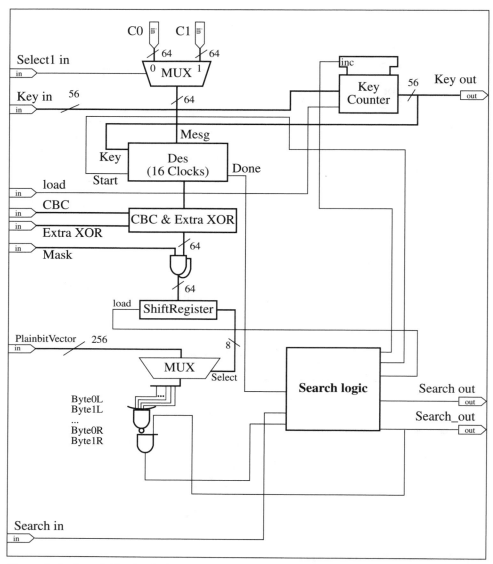

*Figure 3-3: Search Unit's Block Diagram*

address three times: Board-ID(7:0), Chip-ID(6:0) and then Register address.

Having switches on the board makes the design flexible and expandable. Each board has its own unique Board-ID configured on switches: for example a board with an ID of hexadecimal 5F has its board ID switches configured as follows:

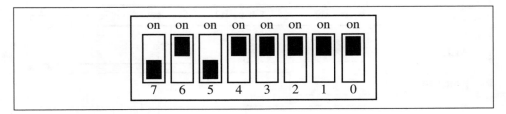

# *Read and Write Timing*

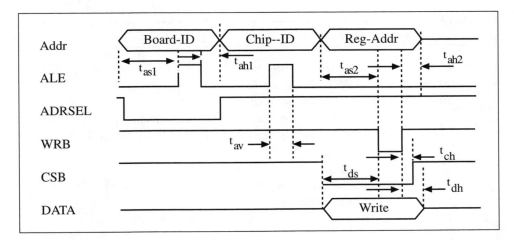

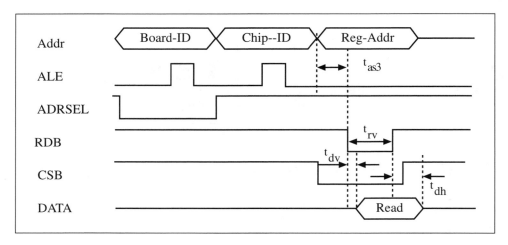

| $t_{as1}$ | 10 ns | Min | Board-ID and Chip-ID Address setup |
|-----------|-------|-----|-----------------------------------|
| $t_{as2}$ | 10 ns | Min | Write Register-Address setup |
| $t_{as3}$ | 10 ns | Min | Read  Register-Address setup |
| $t_{ah1}$ | 10 ns | Min | Board-ID and Chip-ID Address invalid (hold) |
| $t_{ah2}$ | 10 ns | Min | Write strobe trailing edge to Address invalid (hold) |
| $t_{av}$ | 10 ns | Min | ALE valid |
| $t_{ds}$ | 10 ns | Min | Data valid to Write strobe goes low (setup) |
| $t_{ch}$ | 10 ns | Min | Chip select hold |
| $t_{dh}$ | 10 ns | Min | Write strobe goes high to data invalid (Data hold) |
| $t_{rv}$ | 10 ns | Min | Read strobe duration |
| $t_{dv}$ | 100 ns | Max | Read strobe goes low to data valid |
| $t_{dh}$ | 100 ns | Max | Read strobe goes high to data invalid (Data hold) |

# Addressing Registers

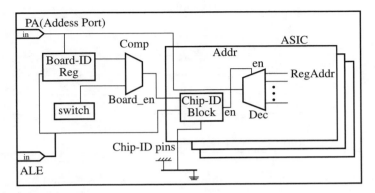

*Figure 3-4: Address Bus Scheme*

# All-active Signal

If low, one or more search unit is halted. This value is the result of ANDing all of the SearchActive bit together. We will place one AND gate per ASIC and cascade them.

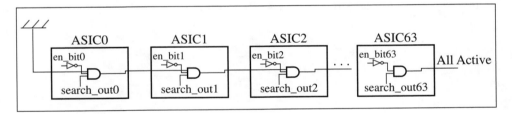

# *ASIC Register Allocation*

| Registers Common to All Search Units | |
|---|---|
| 0x00-0x1f | PlaintextVector |
| 0x20-0x27 | PlaintextXorMask |
| 0x28-0x2f | CipherText0 |
| 0x30-0x37 | CipherText1 |
| 0x38 | PlaintextByteMask |
| 0x39-0x3e | Reserved |
| 0x3f | SearchInfo |
| Additional Registers for Search Units | |
| 0x40-0x47 | Search Unit 0: Key counter (first 7 bytes) and Search Status |
| 0x48-0x4f | Search Unit 1: Key counter (first 7 bytes) and Search Status |
| . . . | |
| 0xf8-0xff | Search Unit 23: Key counter (first 7 bytes) and Search Status |

Number of register required:

58 common registers + 8 * $n$ registers; $n$ = the total number of search units in an ASIC

In this case $n$ = 24, therefore $58 + 192 = 250$ registers

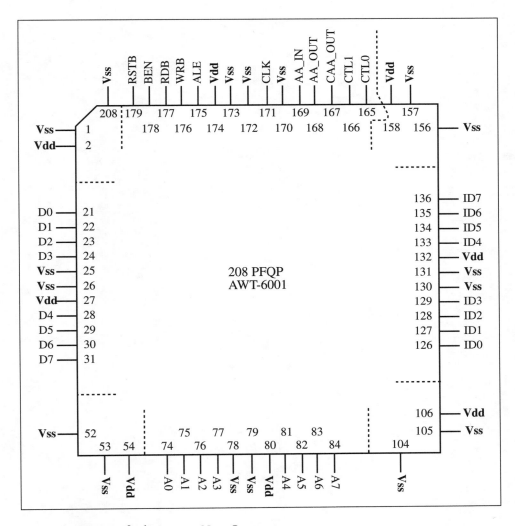

Note: The unspecified pins are Non-Connects

CNTRL0 = ALE = ADDSEL1

CNTRL1 = CSB = ADDSEL2

4

# Scanning the Source Code

The next few chapters of this book contain specially formatted versions of the documents that we wrote to design the DES Cracker. These documents are the primary sources of our research in brute-force cryptanalysis, which other researchers would need in order to duplicate or validate our research results.

## The Politics of Cryptographic Source Code

Since we are interested in the rapid progress of the science of cryptography, as well as in educating the public about the benefits and dangers of cryptographic technology, we would have preferred to put all the information in this book on the World Wide Web. There it would be instantly accessible to anyone worldwide who has an interest in learning about cryptography.

Unfortunately the authors live and work in a country whose policies on cryptography have been shaped by decades of a secrecy mentality and covert control. Powerful agencies which depend on wiretapping to do their jobs — as well as to do things that aren't part of their jobs, but which keep them in power — have compromised both the Congress and several Executive Branch agencies. They convinced Congress to pass unconstitutional laws which limit the freedom of researchers — such as ourselves — to publish their work. (All too often, convincing Congress to violate the Constitution is like convincing a cat to follow a squeaking can opener, but that doesn't excuse the agencies for doing it.) They pressured agencies such as the Commerce Department, State Department, and Department of Justice to not only subvert their oaths of office by supporting these unconstitutional laws, but to act as front-men in their repressive censorship scheme, creating unconstitutional regulations and enforcing them against ordinary researchers and authors of software.

The National Security Agency is the main agency involved, though they seem to have recruited the Federal Bureau of Investigation in the last several years. From the outside we can only speculate what pressures they brought to bear on these other parts of the government. The FBI has a long history of illicit wiretapping, followed by use of the information gained for blackmail, including blackmail of Congressmen and Presidents. FBI spokesmen say that was "the old bad FBI" and that all that stuff has been cleaned up after J. Edgar Hoover died and President Nixon was thrown out of office. But these agencies still do everything in their power to prevent ordinary citizens from being able to examine their activities, e.g. stonewalling those of us who try to use the Freedom of Information Act to find out exactly what they are doing.

Anyway, these agencies influenced laws and regulations which now make it illegal for U.S. crypto researchers to publish their results on the World Wide Web (or elsewhere in electronic form).

# *The Paper Publishing Exception*

Several cryptographers have brought lawsuits against the US Government because their work has been censored by the laws restricting the export of cryptography. (The Electronic Frontier Foundation is sponsoring one of these suits, *Bernstein v. Department of Justice, et al* ).* One result of bringing these practices under judicial scrutiny is that some of the most egregious past practices have been eliminated.

For example, between the 1970's and early 1990's, NSA actually *did* threaten people with prosecution if they published certain scientific papers, or put them into libraries. They also had a "voluntary" censorship scheme for people who were willing to sign up for it. Once they were sued, the Government realized that their chances of losing a court battle over the export controls would be much greater if they continued censoring books, technical papers, and such.

Judges understand books. They understand that when the government denies people the ability to write, distribute, or sell books, there is something very fishy going on. The government might be able to pull the wool over a few judges' eyes about jazzy modern technologies like the Internet, floppy disks, fax machines, telephones, and such. But they are unlikely to fool the judges about whether it's constitutional to jail or punish someone for putting ink onto paper in this free country.

---

* See http://www.eff.org/pub/Privacy/ITAR_export/Bernstein_case/.

Therefore, the last serious update of the cryptography export controls (in 1996) made it explicit that these regulations do not attempt to regulate the publication of information in books (or on paper in any format). They waffled by claiming that they "might" later decide to regulate books — presumably if they won all their court cases — but in the meantime, the First Amendment of the United States Constitution is still in effect for books, and we are free to publish any kind of cryptographic information in a book. Such as the one in your hand.

Therefore, cryptographic research, which has traditionally been published on paper, shows a trend to continue publishing on paper, while other forms of scientific research are rapidly moving online.

The Electronic Frontier Foundation has always published most of its information electronically. We produce a regular electronic newsletter, communicate with our members and the public largely by electronic mail and telephone, and have built a massive archive of electronically stored information about civil rights and responsibilities, which is published for instant Web or FTP access from anywhere in the world.

We would like to publish this book in the same form, but we can't yet, until our court case succeeds in having this research censorship law overturned. Publishing a paper book's exact same information electronically is seriously illegal in the United States, if it contains cryptographic software. Even communicating it privately to a friend or colleague, who happens to not live in the United States, is considered by the government to be illegal in electronic form.

The US Department of Commerce has officially stated that publishing a World Wide Web page containing links to foreign locations which contain cryptographic software "is not an export that is subject to the Export Administration Regulations (EAR)."* This makes sense to us — a quick *reductio ad absurdum* shows that to make a ban on links effective, they would also have to ban the mere mention of foreign Universal Resource Locators. URLs are simple strings of characters, like `http://www.eff.org`; it's unlikely that any American court would uphold a ban on the mere *naming* of a location where some piece of information can be found.

Therefore, the Electronic Frontier Foundation is free to publish links to where electronic copies of this book might exist in free countries. If we ever find out about such an overseas electronic version, we will publish such a link to it from the page at `http://www.eff.org/pub/Privacy/Crypto_misc/DES_Cracking/`.

---

* In the letter at `http://samsara.law.cwru.edu/comp_law/jvd/pdj-bxa-gjs070397.htm`, which is part of Professor Peter Junger's First Amendment lawsuit over the crypto export control regulations.

# *Scanning*

When printing this book, we used tools from Pretty Good Privacy, Inc (which has since been merged into Network Associates, Inc.). They built a pretty good set of tools for scanning source code, and for printing source code for scanning. The easiest way to handle the documents we are publishing in this book is to use their tools and scanning instructions.

PGP published the tools in a book, naturally, called "Tools for Publishing Source Code via OCR", by Colin Plumb, Mark H. Weaver, and Philip R. Zimmermann, ISBN # 1-891064-02-9. The book was printed in 1997, and is sold by Printers Inc. Bookstore, 301 Castro St, Mountain View, California 94041 USA; phone +1 650 961 8500; `http://www.pibooks.com`.

The tools and instructions from the OCR Tools book are now available on the Internet as well as in PGP's book. See `http://www.pgpi.com/project/`, and follow the link to "proof-reading utilities". If that doesn't work because the pages have been moved or rearranged, try working your way down from the International PGP page, `http://www.pgpi.com`.

PGP's tools produce per-line and per-page checksums, and make normally invisible characters like tabs and multiple spaces explicit. Once you obtain these tools, we strongly suggest reading the textual material in the book, or the equivalent README file in the online tool distribution. It contains very detailed instructions for scanning and proofreading listings like those in this book. The instructions that follow in this chapter are a very abbreviated version.

The first two parts of converting these listings to electronic form is to scan in images of the pages, then convert the images into an approximation of the text on the pages. The first part is done by a mechanical scanner; the second is done by an Optical Character Recognition (OCR) program. You can sometimes rent time at a local "copy shop" on a computer that has both a scanner and an OCR program.

When scanning the sources, we suggest "training" your OCR program by scanning the test-file pages that follow, and some of the listings, and correcting the OCR program's idea of what the text actually said. The details of how to do this will depend on your particular OCR program. But if you straighten it out first about the shapes of the particular characters and symbols that we're using, the process of correcting the errors in the rest of the pages will be much easier.

Some unique characters are used in the listings; train the OCR program to convert them as follows:

Right pointing triangle (used for tabs) - currency symbol (byte value octal 244)

Tiny centered triangle "dot" (used for multiple spaces) - center dot or bullet (byte value octal 267)

Form feed - yen (byte value octal 245)

Big black square (used for line continuation) - pilcrow or paragraph symbol (byte value octal 266).

Once you've scanned and OCR'd the pages, you can run them through PGP's tools to detect and correct errors, and to produce clean online copies.

# *Bootstrapping*

By the courtesy of Philip R. Zimmermann and Network Associates, to help people who don't have the PGP OCR tools, we have included PGP's bootstrap and boot-strap2 pages. (The word *bootstrap* refers to the concept of "pulling yourself up by your bootstraps", i.e. getting something started without any outside help.) If you can scan and OCR the pages in some sort of reasonable way, you can then extract the corrected files using just this book and a Perl interpreter. It takes more manual work than if you used the full set of PGP tools.

The first bootstrap program is one page of fairly easy to read Perl code. Scan in this page, as carefully as you can:  you'll have to correct it by hand. Make a copy of the file that results from the OCR, and manually delete the checksums, so that it will run as a Perl script. Then run this Perl script with the OCR result (with check-sums) as the argument. If you've corrected it properly, it will run and produce a clean copy of itself, in a file called `bootstrap`. (Make sure none of your files have that name.) If you haven't corrected it properly, the perl script will die some-how and you'll have to compare it to the printed text to see what you missed.

When the bootstrap script runs, it checks the checksum on each line of its input file. For any line that is incorrect, the script drops you into a text editor (set by the EDITOR environment variable) so you can fix that line. When you exit the editor, it starts over again.

Once the bootstrap script has produced a clean version of itself, you can run it against the scanned and OCR'd copy of the bootstrap2 page. Correct it the same way, line by line until bootstrap doesn't complain. This should leave you with a clean copy of bootstrap2.

The bootstrap2 script is what you'll use to scan in the rest of the book. It works like the bootstrap script, but it can detect more errors by using the page checksum. Again, it won't correct most errors itself, but will drop you into an editor to correct them manually. (If you want automatic error correction, you have to get the PGP book.)

All the scannable listings in this book are in the public domain, except the test-file, bootstrap, and bootstrap2 pages, which are copyrighted, but which Network Associates permits you to freely copy. So none of the authors have put restrictions on your right to copy their listings for friends, reprint them, scan them in, publish them, use them in products, etc. However, if you live in an unfree country, there may be restrictions on what you can do with the listings or information once you have them. Check with your local thought police.

```
--a2b7 000063ee6a780010001 Page 1 of test-file

2e0bc8 This is a test page for OCR training. ·This includes many possible
206b53 glyphs for training purposes.
e4af5a
d96fef ·!"#$%&'()*+,-./0123456789:;<=>?@ABCDEFGHIJKLMNOPQRSTUVWXYZ[\]^_`abcdefghijklmno
f2a107  !"#$%&'()*+,-./0123456789:;<=>?@ABCDEFGHIJKLMNOPQRSTUVWXYZ[\]^_`abcdefghijklmnop
6816d9  "#$%&'()*+,-./0123456789:;<=>?@ABCDEFGHIJKLMNOPQRSTUVWXYZ[\]^_`abcdefghijklmnopq
e998f4  #$%&'()*+,-./0123456789:;<=>?@ABCDEFGHIJKLMNOPQRSTUVWXYZ[\]^_`abcdefghijklmnopqr
050dba  $%&'()*+,-./0123456789:;<=>?@ABCDEFGHIJKLMNOPQRSTUVWXYZ[\]^_`abcdefghijklmnopqrs
5ea3b1  %&'()*+,-./0123456789:;<=>?@ABCDEFGHIJKLMNOPQRSTUVWXYZ[\]^_`abcdefghijklmnopqrst
8d72eb  &'()*+,-./0123456789:;<=>?@ABCDEFGHIJKLMNOPQRSTUVWXYZ[\]^_`abcdefghijklmnopqrstu
333e8c  '()*+,-./0123456789:;<=>?@ABCDEFGHIJKLMNOPQRSTUVWXYZ[\]^_`abcdefghijklmnopqrstuv
68465e  ()*+,-./0123456789:;<=>?@ABCDEFGHIJKLMNOPQRSTUVWXYZ[\]^_`abcdefghijklmnopqrstuvw
84d756  )*+,-./0123456789:;<=>?@ABCDEFGHIJKLMNOPQRSTUVWXYZ[\]^_`abcdefghijklmnopqrstuvwx
e334a8  *+,-./0123456789:;<=>?@ABCDEFGHIJKLMNOPQRSTUVWXYZ[\]^_`abcdefghijklmnopqrstuvwxy
319bd3  +,-./0123456789:;<=>?@ABCDEFGHIJKLMNOPQRSTUVWXYZ[\]^_`abcdefghijklmnopqrstuvwxyz
d8390f  ,-./0123456789:;<=>?@ABCDEFGHIJKLMNOPQRSTUVWXYZ[\]^_`abcdefghijklmnopqrstuvwxyz{
5120a8  -./0123456789:;<=>?@ABCDEFGHIJKLMNOPQRSTUVWXYZ[\]^_`abcdefghijklmnopqrstuvwxyz{|
c29e23  ./0123456789:;<=>?@ABCDEFGHIJKLMNOPQRSTUVWXYZ[\]^_`abcdefghijklmnopqrstuvwxyz{|}
f5152f  /0123456789:;<=>?@ABCDEFGHIJKLMNOPQRSTUVWXYZ[\]^_`abcdefghijklmnopqrstuvwxyz{|}~
e103f5  ·!"#$%&'()*+,-./:;<=>?@[\]^_`{|}~ !"#$%&'()*+,-./:;<=>?@[\]^_`{|}~ !"#$%&'()*+,-
a65757  !"#$%&'()*+,-./:;<=>?@[\]^_`{|}~ !"#$%&'()*+,-./:;<=>?@[\]^_`{|}~ !"#$%&'()*+,-.
3f0d4d  "#$%&'()*+,-./:;<=>?@[\]^_`{|}~ !"#$%&'()*+,-./:;<=>?@[\]^_`{|}~ !"#$%&'()*+,-./
39c2e4  #$%&'()*+,-./:;<=>?@[\]^_`{|}~ !"#$%&'()*+,-./:;<=>?@[\]^_`{|}~ !"#$%&'()*+,-./:
af95c7  $%&'()*+,-./:;<=>?@[\]^_`{|}~ !"#$%&'()*+,-./:;<=>?@[\]^_`{|}~ !"#$%&'()*+,-./:;
bd83ed  %&'()*+,-./:;<=>?@[\]^_`{|}~ !"#$%&'()*+,-./:;<=>?@[\]^_`{|}~ !"#$%&'()*+,-./:;<
616284  &'()*+,-./:;<=>?@[\]^_`{|}~ !"#$%&'()*+,-./:;<=>?@[\]^_`{|}~ !"#$%&'()*+,-./:;<=
27af5a
91caca The following letters are often confused.
ce6e48 C vs. c C c C c Cc cc CCC ccc CcCc cCcC ·O vs. o O o O o OO oo OOO ooo OoOo oOoO
666db7 P vs. p P p P p PP pp PPP ppp PpPp pPpP ·S vs. s S s S s SS ss SSS sss SsSs sSsS
a1d639 U vs. u U u U u UU uu UUU uuu UuUu uUuU ·V vs. v V v V v VV vv VVV vvv VvVv vVvV
3f1e31 W vs. w W w W w WW ww WWW www WwWw wWwW ·X vs. x X x X x XX xx XXX xxx XxXx xXxX
3883cf Y vs. y Y y Y y YY yy YYY yyy YyYy yYyY ·Z vs. z Z z Z z ZZ zz ZZZ zzz ZzZz zZzZ
8bbbae 1 vs. l 1 l 1 l 11 ll 111 lll 1l1l l1l1 ·9 vs. g 9 g 9 g 99 gg 999 ggg 9g9g g9g9
e5035e - vs. _ _ _ _ _ __ __ ___ ___ _-_- -_-_ ·@ vs. a @ a @ a @@ aa @@@ aaa @a@a a@a@
a39025 i vs. ; i ; i ; ii ;; iii ;;; i;i; ;i;i ·% vs. X % X % X XX %% XXX %%% X%X% %X%X
408038 . vs. · . · . · .. ·· ... ··· .·.· ·.·. ·i vs. 7 i 7 i 7 ii 77 iii 777 i7i7 7i7i
406e48 C vs. c C c C c CC cc CCC ccc CcCc cCcC ·O vs. o O o O o OO oo OOO ooo OoOo oOoO
a0af5a
d4a6bb Some normally non-printing characters are printed.
68c3d5          ▷ One space: One tab:▷ One form feed:¥
2ae0c3 ▷ Two tabs:▷              Two spaces: ·Two form feeds:¥
c47e1d ¥
62c06d ▷ Three spaces: ··Three tabs:▷      ▷          ▷ One trailing space:·
71af5a
82fc34 Very long lines are wrapped as follows:
a53f7d !"#$%&'()*+,-./0123456789:;<=>?@ABCDEFGHIJKLMNOPQRSTUVWXYZ[\]^_`abcdefghijklmno■
f7dc06 pqrstuvwxyz{|}~!"#$%&'()*+,-./0123456789:;<=>?@ABCDEFGHIJKLMNOPQRSTUVWXYZ[\]^_`■
c2dace abcdefghijklmnopqrstuvwxyz{|}~!"#$%&'()*+,-./0123456789:;<=>?@ABCDEFGHIJKLMNOPQ■
aa1090 RSTUVWXYZ[\]^_`abcdefghijklmnopqrstuvwxyz{|}~!"#$%&'()*+,-./0123456789:;<=>?@AB■
113f71 CDEFGHIJKLMNOPQRSTUVWXYZ[\]^_`abcdefghijklmnopqrstuvwxyz{|}~!"#$%&'()*+,-./0123■
f2ff02 45678
25af5a
4f751f ▷      ▷      int some_identifiers_look_like_this;
d861db ▷      ▷      #ifdef OTHER_DEFINES_LOOK_LIKE_THIS
5bdb4a ▷      ▷      ▷    for (i = 0; i < 100; i++)
c8f92d ▷      ▷      ▷       if (foo() || bar())
073aae ▷      ▷      ▷      ▷    variable ^= FLAG_ONE|FLAG_TWO|FLAG_THRE■
64c29b E;
4a15b5 ▷      ▷      }
aee89d The following lines have 77 underscores:
2a6438 /*_____
a77cb9 _____*/
dcaf5a
33c707 ▷      ▷      ▷      ▷      Tabs and spaces▷ ···▷     ····▷ Tabs and spaces
977212 ·▷     ·▷     ·▷     ·▷     Tabs and spaces▷ ····▷    ·····▷ Tabs and spaces
f4eca2 ··▷    ··▷    ··▷    ··▷     Tabs and spaces▷ ·····▷   ······▷ Tabs and spaces
c551ac ···▷   ···▷   ···▷   ···▷    Tabs and spaces▷ ······▷  ·······▷Tabs and spaces
18af5a
4354d3 The OCR radix-64 character set:
88cb81 ▷    ABCDEFGHIJKLMNPQRSTVWXYZabcdehijklmnpqtuwy145689\^!#$%&*+=/:<>?@
06af5a
```

```
--b735  00039830fb280010001 Page 2 of test-file

39eaa9 The following pattern contains every pair of adjacent printable ASCII chars:
3eaf5a
36eac9 .  ~!}"¦#{$z%y&x'w(v)u*t+s,r-q.p/o0n1m2l3k4j5i6h7g8f9e:d;c<b=a>`?_@^A]B\C[DZEYFXG
654ed8 ·.!~"}#¦${%z&y'x(w)v*u+t,s-r.q/p0o1n2m3l4k5j6i7h8g9f:e;d<c=b>a?`@_A^B]C\D[EZFYGX
ad9f70 ·!.~"#}$!%{&z'y(x)w*v+u,t-s.r/q0p1o2n3m4l5k6j7i8h9g:f;e<d=c>b?a@`A_B^C]D\E[FZGYH
438a45 !".#~$}%¦&{'z(y)x*w+v,u-t.s/r0q1p2o3n4m5l6k7j8i9h:g;f<e=d>c?b@aA`B_C^D]E\F[GZHY
b20375 !" #.$~%}&¦'{(z)y*x+w,v-u.t/s0r1q2p3o4n5m6l7k8j9i:h;g<f=e>d?c@bAaB`C_D^E]F\G[HZI
5038d1 "!# $.%~&}'¦({)z*y+x,w-v.u/t0s1r2q3p4o5n6m7l8k9j:i;h<g=f>e?d@cAbBaC`D_E^F]G\H[IZ
8bd3e3 "#!$ %.&~'}(¦{*z+y,x-w.v/u0t1s2r3q4p5o6n7m8l9k:j;i<h=g>f?e@dAcBbCaD`E_F^G]H\I[J
9f2301 #"!$ &.'~(}¦{+z,y-x.w/v0u1t2s3r4q5p6o7n8m9l:k;j<i=h>g?f@eAdBcCbDaE`F_G^H]I\J[
67f2c3 #$"!$ '.(~)}+¦{,-z.y/x0w1v2u3t4s5r6q7p8o9n:m;l<k=j>i?h@gAfBeCdDcEbFaG`H_I^J]K\
331559 $#%"$! (.)~*}+¦{-z.y/x0w1v2u3t4s5r6q7p8o9n:m;l<k=j>i?h@gAfBeCdDcEbFaG`H_I^J]K\
8027ee $%#$"!( ).*~+},-{-z/y0x1w2v3u4t5s6r7q8p9o:n;m<l=k>j?i@hAgBfCeDdEcFbGaH`I_J^K]L
9ca861 %$&#!"(!( ).+,*~.}-{-z/y0x1w2v3u4t5s6r7q8p9o:n;m<l=k>j?i@hAgBfCeDdEcFbGaH`I_J^K]L
3d9206 %&$'#("(!)!* +.,-{-.~-}·|/{0z1y2x3w4v5u6t7s8r9q:p;o<n=m>l?k@jAiBhCgDfEeFdGcHbIaJ`K_L^M
a93391 &%'$"(!* !+ ,-.}/|{0{1z2y3x4w5v6u7t8s9r:q;p<o=n>m?l@kAjBiChDgEfFeGdHcIbJaK`L_M^
4da208 &'%($#"#!*!"+! -..·-"/}0¦1{2z3y4x5w6v7u8t9s:r;q<p=o>n?m@l·AkBjCiDhEgFfGeHdIcJbKaL`M_N
d5b793 '&(%)$#*"+!",-..·./"0}1¦2{3z4y5x6w7v8u9t:s;r<q=p>o?n@mAlBkCjDiEhFgGfHeIdJcKbLaM`N_
73959b '(&)%*$+#,"-!.·-/"0}1¦2{3z4y5x6w7v8u9t:s;r<q=p>o?n@mAlBkCjDiEhFgGfHeIdJcKbLaM`N`O
eb9b69 ')(&*%+$,#-"..·/!0"1}2{3z4y5x6w7v8u9t:s;r<q=p>o?n@mAlBkCjDiEhFgGfHeIdJcKbLaMaN`O`
517be6 ()·*&+%,$-#..!/·0"1 1.2~3}4{5z6y7x8w9v:u;t<s=r>q?p@oAnBmClDkEjFiGhHgIfJeKdLcMbNaOaP
4d37bd )(*·+&,%-$.#/·0"1 2.3~4}5{6z7y8x9w:v;u<t=s>r?q@pAoBnCmDlEkFjGiHhIgJfKeLdMcNbObPa
22bd2c )*(·+',&-%.$/#0"1·2 3.4~5}6{7{8z9y:x;w<v=u>t?s@rAqBpCoDnEmFlGkHjIiJhKgLfMeNdOcPbQb
901ab2 *)·(·,'-&.%/$0#1"2·3 4.5~6}7¦8{9z:y;x<w=v>u?t@sArBqCpDoEnFmGlHkIjJiKhLgMfNeOdPcQb
fa9d4d *+),·(-'.&/%0$1#2"3·4 5.6~7}8¦9{:z;y<x=w>v?u@tAsBrCqDpEoFnGmHlIkJjKiLhMgNfOePdQcR
ee5dbe +*,)·(-·.'/&0%1$2#3"4·5 6.7~8}9¦:{;z<y=x>w?v@uAtBsCrDqEpFoGnHmIlJkKjLiMhNgOfPeQdR
ec7999 +,·*-)·.(/'0&1%2$3#4"5·6 7.8~9}:¦;{<z=y>x?w@vAuBtCsDrEqFpGoHnImJlKkLjMiNhOgPfQeRdS
b266a7 ,+·-*·.),'/(0&1%2$3#4"5!6·7 8.9~:};¦<{=z>y?x@wAvBuCtDsErFqGpHoInJmKlLkMjNiOhPgQfReSd
6f131d ,-·+·.·*/)0(1'2&3%4$5#6"7!8 9·:.;~<}=¦>{?z@yAxBwCvDuEtFsGrHqIpJoKnLmMkNjOiPhQgRfSeT
da9cb0 -,·.+/·*01)2(3'4&5%6$7#8!9 :·;.<~=}>¦?{@zAyBxCwDvEuFtGsHrIqJpKoLnMmNkOjPiQhRgSfTe
4cc3fb -.·/,0+1·*2)3(4'5&6%7$8#9!9: ;·<.=~>}?¦@{AzByCxDwEvFuGtHsIrJqKpLoMnNmOkPjQiRhSgTfU
129172 ./-0,1+2·*3(4'5&6%7$8#9"!9:; <·=.>~?}@¦A{BzCyDxEwFvGuHtIsJrKqLpMoNnOmPkQjRiShTgUf
982f4e ·/-0·1,2+3(4'5&6%7$8#9"!9:; <·=.>~?}@¦A{BzCyDxEwFvGuHtIsJrKqLpMoNnOmPkQjRiShTgUf
d7eebc /·0-1,2+3(4'5&6%7$8#9"!9:;< =·>.?~@}A¦B{CzDyExFwGvHuItJsKrLqMpNoOnPmQkRjSiThUgV
baebc1 /0·1-2,3+4·5(6'7&8%9$:#;"<!= >·?.@~A}B¦C{DzEyFxGwHvIuJtKsLrMqNpOoPnQmRlSkTjUiVhW
5a5020 0/1.2-3,4+5*6)7(8'9&:%;$<#=">!? @·A.B~C}D¦E{FzGyHxIwJvKuLtMsNrOpPoQnRmSlTkUjViWhX
a1f664 01/2.3-4,5+6*7)8(9':&;%<$=#>"?!@ A·B.C~D}E¦F{GzHyIxJwKvLuMtNsOrPqQoRnSmTlUkVjWiX
0998b1 102/3.4-5,6+7*8)9(:';&<%=$>#?"@!A B·C.D~E}F¦G{HzIyJxKwLvMuNtOsPrQqRoSnTmUlVkWjXi
b7adac 1203/4.5-6,7+8*9):';<&=%>$?#@"A!B C.D~E}F¦G{HzIyJxKwLvMuNtOsPrQqRoSnTmUlVkWjXjY
a2317d 21304/5.6-7,8+9*:);'<&=%>$?#@"A!B C D.E~F}G¦H{IzJyKxLwMvNuOtPsQrRqSpTmUnVmWlXkYj
bf2f5c 231405/6.7-8,9+:*;)<'=&>%?$@#A"B!C D E.F~G}H¦I{JzKyLxMwNvOuPtQsRrSqTpUoVnWmXlYkZ
8ad4c7 3241506/7.8-9,:+;*<)=>(?'@&A%B$C#D"E!F G.H~I}J¦K{LzMyNxOwPvQuRtSsTrUqVpWoXnYmZk
013dd1 34251607/8.9-:,;+<*=>)?(@'A&B%C$D#E"F!F G.H~I}J¦K{LzMyNxOwPvQuRtSsTrUqVpWoXnYmZk
3e5c3b 435261708/9.:-;,<+=*>)?(@'A&B%C$D#E"F!G H.I~J}K¦L{MzNyOxPwQvRuStTsUrVqWpXoYnZm[l
104fca 4536271809/:.;-<,=+>*?)@(A'B&C%D$E#F"G!H I.J~K}L¦M{NzOyPxQwRvSuTtUsVrWqXpYoZn[m\
4a2737 5463728190/;.<-=,>+?*@)A(B'C&D%E$F#G"H!I J.K~L}M¦N{OzPyQxRwSvTuUtVsWrXqYpZo[n\m
4c12b5 564738291:0;/<.=->,?+@*A)B(C'D&E%F$G#H"I!J K.L~M}N¦O{PzQyRxSwTvUuVtWsXrYqZp[o\n]
f77b32 65748392:1;0</=.>-?,@+A*B)C(D'E&F%G$H#I"J!K L.M~N}O¦P{QzRySxTwUvVuWtXsYrZq[p\o]n
589b18 6758493:2;1<0=/>.?-@,A+B*C)D(E'F&G%H$I#J"K!L M.N~O}P¦Q{RzSyTxUwVvWuXtYsZr[q\p]o^
cae791 768594:3;2<1=0>/?.@-A,B+C*D)E(F'G&H%I$J#K"L!M N.O~P}Q¦R{SzTyUxVwWvXuYtZs[r\q]p^o
f6c12b 78695:4;3<2=1>0?/@.A-B,C+D*E)F(G'H&I%J$K#L"M!N O.P~Q}R¦S{TzUyVxWwXvYuZt[s\r]q^p_
b1a023 8796:5;4<3=2>1?0@/A.B-C,D+E*F)G(H'I&J%K$L#M"N!O P.Q~R}S¦T{UzVyWxXwYvZu[t\s]r^q_p
f58008 897:6;5<4=3>2?1@0A/B.C-D,E+F*G)H(I'J&K%L$M#N"O!P Q.R~S}T¦U{VzWyXxYwZv[u\t]s^r_q`
d4dad0 98:7;6<5=4>3?2@1A0B/C.D-E,F+G*H)I(J'K&L%M$N#O"P!Q R.S~T}U¦V{WzXyYxZw[v\u]t^s_r`q
eb1627 9:8;7<6=5>4?3@2A1B0C/D.E-F,G+H*I)J(K'L&M%N$O#P"Q!R S.T~U}V¦W{XzYyZx[w\v]u^t_s`ra
88e179 :9;8<7=6>5?4@3A2B1C0D/E.F-G,H+I*J)K(L'M&N%O$P#Q"R!S T.U~V}W¦X{YzZy[x\w]v^u_t`sar
a6b1f1 ;:9<8=7>6?5@4A3B2C1D0E/F.G-H,I+J*K)L(M'N&O%P$Q#R"S!T U.V~W}X¦Y{ZzZy[z\y]x^w_v`uatbs
3d31ad ;<:9=8>7?6@5A4B3C2D1E0F/G.H-I,J+K*L)M(N'O&P%Q$R#S"T!U V.W~X}Y¦Z{[z\y]x^w_v`uatbs
32c163 <;=:9>8?7@6A5B4C3D2E1F0G/H.I-J,K+L*M)N(O'P&Q%R$S#T"U!V W.X~Y}Z¦[{\z]y^x_w`vaubtc
749224 <=;:>9?8@7A6B5C4D3E2F1G0H/I.J-K,L+M*N)O(P'Q&R%S$T#U"V!W X.Y~Z}[¦\{]z^y_x`wavbuct
fbd2e2 <=;:>9?8@7A6B5C4D3E2F1G0H/I.J-K,L+M*N)O(P'Q&R%S$T#U"V!W X.Y~Z}[¦\{]z^y_x`wavbucud
8975ad =<>;?:@9A8B7C6D5E4F3G2H1I0J/K.L-M,N+O*P)Q(R'S&T%U$V#W"X!Y Z.[~\}]¦^{_z`yaxbwcvdu
db7126 =><?;@:A9B8C7D6E5F4G3H2I1J0K/L.M-N,O+P*Q)R'S&T%U$V#W"X!Y Z.[~\}]¦^{_z`yaxbwcvdu
c9c2e2 >=?<@;A:B9C8D7E6F5G4H3I2J1K0L/M.N-O,P+Q*R)S(T'U&V%W$X#Y"Z![ \.]~^}_¦`{azbycxdwev
f8cfa9 >?=@<A;B:C9D8E7F6G5H4I3J2K1L0M/N.O-P,Q+R*S)T(U'V&W%X$Y#Z"[![ \.]~^}_¦`{azbycxdwev
5f267a ?>@=A<B;C:D9E8F7G6H5I4J3K2L1M0N/O.P-Q,R+S*T)U(V'W&X%Y$Z#[" \.]~^}_¦`{azbycxdwexf
10c95b ?@>A=B<C;D:E9F8G7H6I5J4K3L2M1N0O/P.Q-R,S+T*U)V(W'X&Y%Z$[#\"]! \.]~^}_¦`{czdzeyfxg
0afa94 @?A>B=C<D;E:F9G8H7I6J5K4L3M2N1O0P/Q.R-S,T+U*V)W(X'Y&Z%[$\#]"^! .a~b}c¦d{ezfygx
943f18 @A?B>C=D<E;F:G9H8I7J6K5L4M3N2O1P0Q/R.S-T,U+V*W)X(Y'Z&[%\$]#^"_! a.b~c}d¦e{fygzhy
965f95 A@B?C>D=E<F;G:H9I8J7K6L5M4N3O2P1Q0R/S.T-U,V+W*X)Y(Z'[&\%]$^#_"`! !a b.c~d}e¦f{gzhy
75fd5c AB@C?D>E=F<G;H:I9J8K7L6M5N4O3P2Q1R0S/T.U-V,W+X*Y)Z([']&\%]$^#_"`!a!b c.d~e}f¦g{hzi
39b879 BAC@D?E>F=G<H;I:J9K8L7M6N5O4P3Q2R1S0T/U.V-W,X+Y*Z)[(\'`]&\%^$_#`"a!b!c d.e~f}g¦h{iz
```

```
--2402  0008e65720980010001 Page 3 of test-file

6783e0  BCAD@E?F>G=H<I;J:K9L8M7N605P4Q3R2S1TØU/V.W-X,Y+Z*[)\(]'^&_%`$a#b"c!d e.f~g}h|i{j
7a0Ø3c  CBDAE@F?G>H=I<J;K:L9M8N706P5Q4R3S2T1UØV/W.X-Y,Z+[*\)]('^_'&`%a$b#c"d!e f.g~h}i|j{
Ø860ab  CDBEAF@G?H>I=J<K;L:M9N807P6Q5R4S3T2U1VØW/X.Y-Z,[+\*])(^_'`&a%b$c#d"e!f g.h~i}j|k
a30f62  DCEBFAG@H?I>J=K<L;M:N908P7Q6R5S4T3U2V1WØX/Y.Z-[,\+]*^)('`a&b%c$d#e"f!g h.i~j}k|
6fd75a  DECFBGAH@I?J>K=L<M;N:09P8Q7R6S5T4U3V2W1XØY/Z.[-\,]+^*_)('a'b&c%d$e#f"g!h i.j~k}l
4845ae  EDFCGBHAI@J?K>L=M<N;0:P9Q8R7S6T5U4V3W2X1YØZ/[.\-],^+_*')a(b'c&d%e$f#g"h!i j.k~l}
81cac2  EFDGCHBIAJ@K?L>M=N<0;P:Q9R8S7T6U5V4W3X2Y1ZØ[/\.]-^,_+'*a)b(c'd&e%f$g#h"i!j k.l~m
4e48f8  FEGDHCIBJAK@L?M>N=0<P;Q:R9S8T7U6V5W4X3Y2Z1[Ø\/].^-_,`+a*b)c(d'e&f%g$h#i"j!k l.m~
81ada4  FGEHDICJBKAL@M?N>0=P<Q;R:S9T8U7V6W5X4Y3Z2[1\Ø]/^.-_,`a+b*c)d(e'f&g%h$i#j"k!l m.n
1c70̄40  GFHEIDJCKBLAM@N?0>P=Q<R;S:T9U8V7W6X5Y4Z3[2\1]Ø^/_.-,`a-b+c*d)e(f'g&h%i$j#k"l!m n.
5fed17  GHFIEJDKCLBMAN@O?P>Q=R<S;T:U9V8W7X6Y5Z4[3\2]1^Ø_/.-,`.a-b,c+d*e)f(g'h&i%j$k#l"m!n o
b6d83b  HGIFJEKDLCMBNAO@P?Q>R=S<T;U:V9W8X7Y6Z5[4\3]2^1_Ø`/.a.b-c,d+e*f)g(h'i&j%k$l#m"n!o.
a3ad8f  HIGJFKELDMCNBOAP@Q?R>S=T<U;V:W9X8Y7Z6[5\4]3^2_1`Øa/.b-c,d+e*f)g(h'i&j%k$l#m"n!o!p
725802  IHJGKFLEMDNCOBPAQ@R?S>T=U<V;W:X9Y8Z7[6\5]4^3_2`1aØb/c.d-e,f+g*h)i(j'k&l%m$n#o"p!
959bd0  IJHKGLFMENDOCPBQAR@S?T>U=V<W;X:Y9Z8[7\6]5^4_3`2a1bØc/d.e-f,g+h*i)j(k'l&m%n$o#p"q
a7ece6  JIKHLGMFNEODPCQBRAS@T?U>V=W<X;Y:Z9[8\7]6^5_4`3a2b1cdØe/f.g-h,i+j)k(l'm&n%o$p#q"
41182d  JKILHMGNFOEPDQCRBSAT@U?V>W=X<Y;Z:[9\8]7^6_5`4a3b2c1dØe/f.g-h,i+j+k*l)m'n&o%p$q#r
cØca81  KJLIMHNGOFPEQDRCSBTAU@V?W>X=Y<Z;[:\9]8^7_6`5a4b3c2d1eØf/g.h-i,j+k*l)m'n&o%p$q$r#
Ø2ff93  KLJMINHOGPFQERDSCTBUAV@W?X>Y=Z<[;\:]9^8_7`6a5b4c3d2e1fØg/h.i-j,k+l*m)n(o'p&q%r$s
6d2e9f  LKMJNIOHPGQFRESDTCUBVAW@X?Y>Z=[<\;]:^9_8`7a6b5c4d3e2f1gØh/i.j-k,l+m*n)o(p'q&r%s$
6e2054  LMKNJOIPHQGRFSETDUCVBWAX@Y?Z>[=\<];:^9_8`.9`8a7b6c5d4e3f2g1hØi/j.k-l,m+n*o)p(q'r&s%t
48b315  MLNKOJPIQHRGSFTEUDVCWBXAYAZ@[>\]=]<^;`:9a8b7c6d5e4f3g2h1iØj/k.l-m,n+o*p)q(r's&t%
3eb1de  MNLOKPJQIRHSGTFUEVDWCXBYAZA[?\>]=<_`;`:a9b8c7d6e5f4g3h2i1j0̄k/l.m-n,o+p*q)r(s't&u
3a0012  NMOLPKQJRISHTGUFVEWDXCYBZA[@\]?>^=<_'`;a:b9c8d7e6f5g4h3i2j1kØl/m.n-o,p+q*r)s(t'u&
a59b13  NOMPLQKRJSITHUGVFWEXDYCZBEA[@]?^>_=`<`a:b;c9d8e7f6g5h4i3j2k1lØm/n.o-p,q+r*s)t(u'v
ba4ad0  ONPMQLRKSJTIUHVGWFXEYDZCE[B\A]@^_?`>a=b<c;d:e9f8g7h6i5j4k3l2m1nØo/p.q-r+s*t)u(v'w
bØfcc9  OPNQMRLSKTJUIVHWGXFYEZDEC\B]A^@_-?`>a=b<c;d:e9f8g7h6i5j4k3l2m1nØo/p.q-r,s+t*u)v(w
Ødab0d  POQNRMSLTKUJVIWHXGYFZED\C]B^A@a_?`>a=b<c;d:e9f8g7h6i5j4k3l3m2n1oØp/q.r-s,t+u*v)w)x
53bd66  PQORNSMTLUKVJWIXHYGZFE[E\D]C^B_A`@a?b>c=d<e;f:g9h8i7j6k5l4m3n2o1pØq/r.s-t,u+v*w)x
a26c65  QPRONSMTULVKWJXIYHZGE[F\E]D^C_B`Aa@b?c>d=e<f;g:h9i8j7k6l5m4n3o2p1qØr/s.t-u,v+w+x)
19511a  QRPSOTNUMVLWKXJYIZHE[G\F]E]^D_C`BaAb@c?d>e=f<g;h:i9j8k7l6m5n4o3p2q1rØs/t.u-v,w+x*y
6c16da  RQSPTOUNVMWLXKYJZIIH\G]F^E_D`CaBbAc@d?e>f=g<h;i:j9k8l7m6n5o4p3q2r1sØt/u.v-w,x+y*
eØf314  RSQTPUOVNWMXLYKZJEIJI\H]G^F_E`DaCbBcAd@e?f>g=h<i;j:k9l8m7n6o5p4q3r2s1tØu/v.w-x,y+z
c6caf3  SRTQUPVOWNXMYLZKEJI\I]H^G_F`EaDbCcBdAe@f?g>h=i<j;k:l9m8n7o6p5q4r3s2t1uØv/w.x-y,z+
de37f4  STRUQVPWOXNYMZLEK\J]I^H_G`FaEbDcCdBeAf@g?h>i=j<k;l:m9n8o7p6q5r4s3t2u1vØw/x.y-z,{
2b2379  TSURVQWPXOYNZME[L\K]J^I_H`GaFbEcDdCeBfAg@h?i>j=k<l;m:n9o8p7q6r5s4t3u2v1wØx/y.z-{'
ede510  TUSVRWQXPYOZNE[M\L]K^J_I`HaGbFcEdDeCfBgAh@i?j>k=l<m;n:o9p8q7r6s5t4u3v2w1xØy/z.{-{'
20eb2e  UTVSWRXQYPZOE[N\M]L^K_J`IaHbGcFdEeDfCgBhAi@j?k>l=m<n;o:p9q8r7s6t5u4v3w2x1yØz/{.{~}
6714a3  UVTWSXRYQZPEO\N]M^L_K`JaIbHcGdFeEfDgChBiAj@k?l>m=n<o;p:q9r8s7t6u5v4w3x2y1zØ{/|.}
fc8685  VUWTXSYRZQEP\O]N^M_L`KaJbIcHdGeFfEgDhCiBjAk@l?m>n=o<p;q:r9s8t7u6v5w4x3y2z1{Ø{/|.}
3750b7  VWUXTYSZREQ\P]O^N_M`LaKbJcIdHeGfEgEhDiCjBkAl@m?n>o=p<q;r:s9t8u7v6w5x4y3z2{1{Ø}/}~
45ee74  WVXUYTZSER\Q]P^O_N`MaLbKcJdIeHfGgEfEhDiCjBkAl@m?n>o=p<q;r:s9t8u7v6w5x4y3z3{2{1}1Ø}~/
64b9b2  WXVYUZTES\R]Q^P_O`NaMbLcKdJeIfHgEgEhFiEjDkClBmAn@o?p>q=r<s;t:u9v8w7x6y5z4{3{2}1~1.Ø
20c748  XWYVZUET\S]R^Q_P`OaNbMcLdKeJfIgHhGiEfEjFkEkDlCmBnAo@p?q>r=s<t;u:v9w8x7y6z5{4{3}2~1.0
bc3d2d  XYWZVEU\T]S^R_Q`PaObNcMdLeKfJgIhHiGjEkFkElDmCnBoAp@q?r>s=t<u;v:w9x8y7z6{5}4}3~2.1`
e6c1a4  YXZWEV\U]T^S_R`QaPbOcNdMeLfKgJhIiHjEkIlElFmDnCoBpAq@r?s>t=u<v;w:x9y8z7{6}5}4~3.2!
7a663b  YZXEW\V]U^T_S`RaQbPcOdNeMfLgKhJiIjHkGlFmEnDoCpBqArAs?t>u=v<w;x:y9z8{7}6}5~4.3 2!
efa2ac  ZY[X\W]V^U_T`SaRbQcPdOeNfMgLhKiJjIkHlGmFnEoDpCqBrAsAt?u>v=w<x;y:z9{8}7}6~5.4 3!2
c198ae  Z[Y\X]W^V_U`TaSbRcQdPeOfNgMhLiKjJkIlHmGnFoEpDqCrBsAtAu?v>w=x<y;z:{9}8}7~6.5 4!3"
97238a  [Z\Y]X^W_V`UaTbScRdQePfOgNhMiLjKkJlIlKmHnGoFpEqDrCsBtAuAv?w>x=y<z;{:}9}8~7.6 5!4"3
aa0ad0  [\Z]Y^X_W`VaUbTcSdRePfQgPhOiNjMkLlKlKmJnIoHpGqFrEsDtCuBvAwAx?y>z=<{;}:}9~8.7 6!5"4#
8cd1ba  \[]Z^Y_X`WaVbUcTdSeRfQgPhOiNjMkLlKmKmJnIoHpGqFrEsDtCuBvAwAx?y>z=<{;}:}~9.8 7!6"5#4
98f7cb  \]Z[^_Y`X`WbVcUdTeSfRgQhPiOjNkMlLlKmMnLoKpJqIrHsGtFuEvDwCxBxAy?z>=<{;}:}~.9 8!7"6#5$
Øc80ce  ]\^[_Z`YaXbWcVdUeTfSgRhQiPjOkNlMmKlLnKoMpLqKrJsItHuGvFwEsDtCuBxAy@z?>=<{;}:}~9!8"7#6$5
dcf8ca  ]^\[_`ZaYbXcWdVeUfTgShRiQjPkOlNmMnKlLoKpMqLrKsJtItHuGvFwEsDtCuBxAya@z{?|}>=~<.; !9"8#7$6%
Ød9748  ^]_\`[aZbYcXdWeVfUgThSiRjQkPlOmNmLnKoLpMqLrKsJtIuHvGwFxEsDtCuBxAyz{a@{?|}>=~<.; !9"8#7$6%
ff5a18  ^_]\`a[bZcYdXeWfVgUhTiSjRkQlPmOnMnLoKpMqLrKsJtIuHvGwFxEsDtCuByzC{a@}?>.= <!;"!#9$8%7&
3fe6b9  _^`]a\[cZbYdXeWfVgUhTiSjRkQlPmOnNmLoKpMqLrKsJtIuHvGwFxEyzDC{@a?>.> =!<"!#9$8%7&'
515664  _`^]a[bZc[dZeYfXgWhViUjTkSlRmQnPoOpNqMrLsKtJuIvHwGxFyEzDC{B}A~a@.> >!=<"#;$:%9&8'
Øf1ce8  `_a^]b]c\d[eZfYgXhWiVjUkTlSmRnQoPpOqNrMsLtKuJvIwHxGyFzE{D}C}B~A.a @ ?!>"=#<$;%:&9'8
d99cbd  `a_b^]c]d\e[fZgYhXiWjVkUlTmSnRoQpPqOrNsMtLuKvJwIxHyGzFzE{D}C~B.A a@ ?!"=#<$%;&:'<
322b4d  a`_b^c]d]e\f[gZhYiXjWkVlUmTnSoRpQqProSnTmUlVkWjXiYhZg{F}E}D~.C B.A !a@"#?$>%=&<';!:(9
ef9c29  ab`c_d^e]f\g[hZiYjXkWlVmUnToSpRqQrProQoPnTmUlWkXjYiZh{G}F}E~.D C!B"A#a@?$>%=&<'(:;
ec74ce  bac`d_e^f]g\h[iZjYkXlWmVnUoToSpRqQrProQpOnUmVlWkXjYi{H}G}F~E!D C"B#A$a@?%>&=<'(;):*
f43761  bcad`e_f^g]h\i[jZkYlXmWnVoUpTqSrRqPoSnToUmVlWkXjYi{I}H}G~F!E D"C#B$A%a@?&>'=<(;):<
b3a479  cbdae`f_g^h]i\j[kZlYmXnWoVpUqTrSsRqPoToUnVmWlXkYjZ{J}I}H~G.F!E"D#C$B%A&a@?'>(=<);:<
cb79f0  cdbeaf`g_h^i]j\k[lZmYnXoWpVqUrTsSrQpToUnVoWmXlYkZj{K}J}I~H.G!F"E#D$C%B&A'a@?(>)=<(;:*<
cc2a87  dcebfag`h_i^j]k\l[mZnYoXpWqVrUsTtSsRqProUnVoWnXmYlZk{L}K}J~I.H!G"F#E$D%C&B'A(a@?)>(=<*;:+
1b4685  decfbgah`i_j^k]l\m[nZoYpXqWrVsUtTtSsRqProSnVoWoXnYmZl{M}L}K~J.I!H"G#F$E%D&C'B(A)a@?*>)=<+*;:=
5dcf03  edfcgbhai`j_k^l]m\n[oZpYqXrWsVtUuTtSsRqProSnToWoXnYm{N}M}L~K.J!I"H#G$F%E&D'C(B)A*a@?+>)=<,*;=
cf0f70  efdgchbiaj`k_l^m]n\o[pZqYrXsWtVuUvUtTsRqProSnToUpXoYn{O}N}M~L.K!J"I#H$G%F&E'D(C)B*A+a@?,>+=<-
8e0d9c  fegdhcibjak`l_m^n]o\p[qZrYsXtWuVvUwVuTtSsRqProSnToUpVqZr{P}O}N~M.L!K"J#I$H%G&F'E(D)C*B+A+a@?,>-
```

```
--6332  000cb2b0f0d80010001 Page 4 of test-file

3eea20  fgehdicjbkal`m_n^o]p\q[rZsYtXuWvVwUxTySzR{Q¦P}O~N.M L!K"J#I$H%G&F'E(D)C*B+A,@-?.
fca03c  gfheidjckblam`n_o^p]q\r[sZtYuXvWwVxUyTzS{R¦Q}P~O.N M!L"K#J$I%H&G'F(E)D*C+B,A-@.?
ec6e74  ghfiejdkclbman`o_p^q]r\s[tZuYvXwWxVyUzT{S¦R}Q~P.O N!M"L#K$J%I&H'G(F)E*D+C,B-A.@/
e46bb2  hgifjekdlcmbnao`p_q^r]s\t[uZvYwXxWyVzU{T¦S}R~Q.P O!N"M#L$K%J&I'H(G)F*E+D,C-B.A/@
233e6e  higjfkeldmcnboap`q_r^s]t\u[vZwYxXyWzV{U¦T}S~R.Q P!O"N#M$L%K&J'I(H)G*F+E,D-C.B/A0
bfc578  ihjgkflemdncobpaq`r_s^t]u\v[wZxYyXzW{V¦U}T~S.R Q!P"O#N$M%L&K'J(I)H*G+F,E-D.C/B0A
9ab11c  ijhkglfmendocpbqar`s_t^u]v\w[xZyYzX{W¦V}U~T.S R!Q"P#O$N%M&L'K(J)I*H+G,F-E.D/C0B1
4d3718  jikhlgmfneodpcqbras`t_u^v]w\x[yZzY{X¦W}V~U.T S!R"Q#P$O%N&M'L(K)J*I+H,G-F.E/D0C1B
53e9a2  kjilhmgnfoepdqcrbsat`u_v^w]x\y[zZ{Y¦X}W~V.U T!S"R#Q$P%O&N'M(L)K*J+I,H-G.F/E0D1C2
7381b2  kjlimhngofpeqdrcsbtau`v_w^x]y\z[{Z¦Y}X~W.V U!T"S#R$Q%P&O'N(M)L*K+J,I-H.G/F0E1D2C
20acf2  kljiminhogpfqerdsctbuav`w_x^y]z\{[¦Z}Y~X.W V!U"T#S$R%Q&P'O(N)M*L+K,J-I.H/G0F1E2D3
152764  lkmjniohpgqafresdtcubvaw`x_y^z]{\|[}Z~Y.X W!V"U#T$S%R&Q'P(O)N*M+L,K-J.I/H0G1F2E3D
49579d  lmknjoiphqgrfsetducvbwax`y_z^{]|\}[~Z.Y X!W"V#U$T%S&R'Q(P)O*N+M,L-K.J/I0H1G2F3E4
ba5335  mlnkojpiqhrgsfteudvcwbxayz`{^¦]}\~[.Z Y!X"W#V$U%T&S'R(Q)P*O+N,M-L.K/J0I1H2G3F4E5
2f2f06  mnlokpjqirhsgtfuevdwcxbyaz`{_¦}^]~\.[ Z!Y"X#W$V%U&T'S(R)Q*P+O,N-M.L/K0J1I2H3G4F5
6a6f06  nmolpkqjrishtgufvewdxcybza{`_¦}_}^~_.] \.[ Z!Y"X#W$V%U&T'S(R)Q*P+O,N-M.L/K0J1I2H3H4G5F
efbf49  nomplqkrjsithugvfwexdyczb{a¦}`_^.] \![ Z!Y$X%W&V'U(T)S*R+Q,P-O.N/M0L1K2J3I4H5G6
3f7c1f  onpmqlrksjtiuhvgwfxeydzc{b¦a}`~_.^ ]!\"[#Z$Y%X&W'V(U)T*S+R,Q-P.O/N0M1L2K3J4I5H6G
bd4c7d  opnqmrlsktjuivhwgxfyezd{c¦b}a~`_.] ^![ ]"\#[$Z%Y&X'W(V)U*T+S,R-Q.P/O0N1M2L3K4J5I6H7
6fa56d  poqnrmsltkujviwhxgyfze{d¦c}b~a.` _!]^"]#\$[%Z&Y'X(W)V*U+T,S-R.Q/P0O1N2M3L4K5J6I7H
47a050  pqornsmtlukvjwixhygzf{e¦d}c~b.a `!_"^#]$\%[&Z'Y(X)W*V+U,T-S.R/Q0P1O2N3M4L5K6J7I8
113535  qprosntmulvkwjxiyhzg{f¦e}d~c.b a!`"_#^$]%\&[']((Z)Y*X+W,V-U.T/S0R1Q2P3O4N5M6L7K7J8I
144d7f  qrpsotnumvlwkxjyizh{g¦f}e~d.c b!a"`#_$^%]&\'[(Z)Y*X+W,V-U.T/S0R1Q2P3O4N5M6L7K8J9
3423b4  rqsptounvmwlxkyjzi{h¦g}f~e.d c!b"a#`$_%^&]'\([)Z*Y+X,W-V.U/T0S1R2Q3P4O5N6M7L8K9J
64762c  rsqtpuovnwmxlykzj{i¦h}g~f.e d!c"b#a$`%_&^'](\)[*Z+Y,X-W.V/U0T1S2R3Q4P5O6N7M8L9K:
f9a617  srtqupvownxmylzk{j¦i}h~g.f e!d"c#b$a%`&_'^(])\*[+Z,Y-X.W/V0U1T2S3R4Q5P6O7N8M9L:K:
5e5771  struqvpwoxnymzl{k¦j}i~h.g f!e"d#c$b%a&`'_(^)](\*[,Z-Y.X/W0V1U2T3S4R5Q6P7O8N9M:L;
85db5e  tsurvqwpxoynzm{l¦k}j~i.h g!f"e#d$c%b&a'`(_)^*]+\,[-Z.Y/X0W1V2U3T4S5R6Q7P8O9N:M;L
c7debb  tusvrwqxpyozn{m¦l}k~j.i h!g"f#e$d%c&b'a(`)_*^+],\-[.Z/Y0X1W2V3U4T5S6R7Q8P9O:N;M<
cbac24  utvswrxqypzo{n¦m}l~k.j i!h"g#f$e%d&c'b(a)`*_+^,]-\.[/Z0Y1X2W3V4U5T6S7R8Q9P:O;N<M
ed7864  uvtwsxryqzp{o¦n}m~l.k j!i"h#g$f%e&d'c(b)a*`+_,^-].\/[0Z1Y2X3W4V5U6T7S8R9Q:P;O<N
32169a  vuwtxsyrzq{p¦o}n~m.l k!j"i#h$g%f&e'd(c)b*a+`,_-^.]/\0[1Z2Y3X4W5V6U7T8S9R:Q;P<O=
79bc26  vwuxtyszr{q¦p}o~n.m l!k"j#i$h%g&f'e(d)c*b+a,`-_.^/]0\1[2Z3Y4X5W6V7U8T9S:R;Q<P=>
45e089  wvxuytzs{r¦q}p~o.n m!l"k#j$i%h&g'f(e)d*c+b,a-`.//[0]1\2[3Z4Y5X6W7V8U9T:S;R<Q=P>O
4ee0e2  wxvyuzt{s¦r}q~p.o n!m"l#k$j%i&h'g(f)e*d+c,b-a.`/_0^1]2\3[4Z5Y6X7W8V9U:T;S<R=Q>P?
f989db  xwyvzu{t¦s}r~q.p o!n"m#l$k%j&i'h(g)f*e+d,c-b.a/`0_1^2]3\4[5Z6Y7X8W9V:U;T<S=R>Q?
869caf  xywzv{u¦t}s~r.q p!o"n#m$l%k&j'i(h)g*f+e,d-c.b/a0`1_2^3]4\5[6Z7Y8X9W:V;U<T=S>R?@
6c9875  yxzw{v¦u}t~s.r q!p"o#n$m%l&k'j(i)h*g+f,e-d.c/b0a1`2_3^4]5\6[7Z8Y9X:W;V<U=T>S?@
1ba50d  yzx{w¦v}u~t.s r!q"p#o$n%m&l'k(j)i*h+g,f-e.d/c0b1a2`3_4^5]6[7Z8Y9X:W;V<U=T>S?@RA
b140c9  zy{x¦w}v~u.t s!r"q#p$o%n&m'l(k)j*i+h,g-f.e/d0c1b2a3`4_5^6]7[8Z9Y:X;W<V=U>T?@SAR
15d133  z{y¦x}w~v.u t!s"r#q$p%o&n'm(l)k*j+i,h-g.f/e0d1c2b3a4`5_6^7[8Z9Y:X;W<V=U>T?@SAB
8eb266  {z¦y}x~w.v u!t"s#r$q%p&o'n(m)l*k+j,i-h.g/f0e1d2c3b4a5`6_7^8]9[:Z;Y<X=W>V?@UATBS
9bde2c  {¦z}y~x.w v!u"t#s$r%q&p'o(n)m*l+k,j-i.h/g0f1e2d3c4b5a6`7_8^9[:Z;Y<X=W>V?@UABTC
21e1c4  ¦{z~y.x w!v"u#t$s%r&q'p(o)n*m+l,k-j.i/h0g1f2e3d4c5b6a7`8_9^:]:Z<Y=X>W?@VABVUCT
41b188  ¦}{~z.y x!w"v#u$t%s&r'q(p)o*n+m,l-k.j/i0h1g2f3e4d5c6b7a8`9_:^;]<[=Z>Y?@XAWBVCUD
ed5a3a  }¦{~.{ z!y"x#w$v%u&t'(s)r*q+p,o-n.m/l0k1j2i3h4g5f6e7d8c9b:a;`<_=^>]?@ZAYBXCWDVE
9cebb3  ~¦{.{ z!y"x#w$v%u&t's(r)q*p+o,n-m.l/k0j1i2h3g4f5e6d7c8b9a:`;_<^=]>[?@ZAYBXCWDVE
e4be9d  ~}.¦ {!z"y#x$w%v&u't(s)r*q+p,o-n.m/l0k1j2i3h4g5f6e7d8c9b:a;`<_=^>]?@ALZBZYCXDWEV
97a297  ~.} ¦!{"z#y$x%w&v'u(t)s*r+q,p-o.n/m0l1k2j3i4h5g6f7e8d9c:b;a<`=_>^?@JA\ACBZCYDXEWF
d43633  .~ }!¦"{#z$y%x&w'v(u)t*s+r,q-p.o/n0m1l2k3j4i5h6g7f8e9d:c;b<a=`>_?@JA\BCCZDYEXFW
b6af5a
44529f  This is random noise with every printable ASCII character:
094411  Qt!d6p07F- faNY*}T[b0 yxW+<"_3W1 Vs<DCSjM=N L(k{ujYQMiLE !M¦$*0X<6/ OSM#?{Ajf* \qJ
165bf0  +=2U_qV kZ8y1Q0@^\ ,_1(}xo&iI 5R2D(q3^ ··5yHf'hBcZN hT?bAELg:^ M B?4"?46Q ^55DWu
05b360  ¦$9e UEvzr^6Nyc < c;=wQn#- 50\+L`A/6w -oEl#sccC ·$9"xgm{ur1 M9n+[}BPPL u6Agy%{wf
1625e6  - e#xT kD._q ¦}!x=NFik: -"w0*lv4}T t/5`SClCef f_[5$B~>&, 6<G#1\~kqs 'QKG>k.&*q b
6f4b1a  %f&$%CØBY j]XG\D6M<= dd;No>Xb!< e?hjbx.:äu x=Q:S~Smz6 6d@T: SSd9 M!SC/md%bZ 4uo0
12983f  IZ+_+B Hs_HG0*]$W Tzk?\n"8.3 {CTSN5^mV$ 3I'DSeE+By .9`¦8x)K$" YU:k2)B6hS lw40=@q
d97aef  4A! "zbx$.y&yS 4<k:_" 0bm t:B5-VS.!U cK+qF.hvg¦ S5pV2!6¦&+ H=E~pP GVc aR6p;.X5?-
343a33  ·0`Z.vW4#o\ 2X2bUV76Fx ]f!h=3(GX5 0@{dT~R.=d OE<#\RIR8$ 6iTFn¢~!!, ¦quyD!7)dc }f
57d159  (MØ[b2rx D=k=<l>F,8 ~2\!Fbb*/a 7/7~o_.h*$ rA@]\fiu~h [fL;JVJ,EL A!+O-tV1wJ 8%-~k
0cda24  #}T)V Rrc&:lHv%i .6Q mbw531 >0&A,WG_my Q}j;FaA1&L TL25DGER^c a&l:JI(EyW aof@.tDZ
598658  :x L.IqTxP8Y3 CJfm0)g$II -i##+^=%bf }Xd 'zY:3} yk. P3FvXT (WicqnDX{J aJ6Y"Ml ,d·
c0598a  :d6J,-0]jU Q6$=ZY:#ex {RLF?LR!2m H8oReM;8\l ](·7B*};Tv ">*Kp,^[o$ \TW'oocY;A BU$
534b45  LP<~H"!! 2LQ;(.(* d TkNAO(\mj ·kLt)K:0I}? OW{Z_#ZAa/ -MV6+D}+hf Zo}t)Go:8? 2z05Rn
8f0eb8  w_x% P88t3@Zzr5 p'e5v}N7mj :r>$ jIM a?4 z/r-s` Wr)UA=@{LZ )aWGa?p,@P TMC`@NT}·
2ce552  , i^0(~,QZxZ Q wmm$.>0b p@&?u$ ~uf #kZ/>2)uKW CBaGQ¦t4fb L"Hq~Ddb#d [sjmy`:NQZ 3
0f4684  ·@0qQvT$a LP0q52qvaM I9b(P.Y+¦l =yylnNpP"; N-3a{*@Gqg Qo1]I9Z6Eu <b{kSLjnJ: ]xrd
8284d9  6:W}z& )c7B<Jd2U" QjB{U/Fl(" zcy28t*?c3 wS<a8Nu7=D `@UodBtc&m ] `q(¦R; K :h"hC9$
aa0c35  ·9d nQ .Fc11++ h}:ePRcx<} >c:Tg8mIVY Ve?:sPB _) vnKG0BcM!" 9VvQB>(x9C UrS'5Pc;NC
3f36cf  ·v#W6f#8e2Q &#XD(R[c.1 ^5h/y%ZU-R de<g>"vL8} q?TDz50*h/ R>6TykaI>C Z)+Y Trz"a S&
cbc063  3fU=0aZ~ pSwZ2AxVMQ U(\+zX-\s] 'D3Btt¦srj jBW)9+Tjg* E5k}?En}#r 624(,){wNc #mP/?
```

```
--7fda  0002a3ecf6580010001 Page 5 of test-file

45283a  8vI)< t7{7#y:v:M NV3T0+#3?' p3=&*d/GA$ =9_5SS0~Yz LP"tP22T.# H&r-67N7ri 0~" K!ZF
fc0cd2  SD R7EaIyoIb9 RCeiozYVK* J*}KaA{$6K [.aRz(51Wd ;KB6&x^-K* IUvjOw!z0Y n-"v?3N%ef·
1abcb9  ({S!\`Ifuo i[eaY^n1d] fT]w _]g.c aa>@,"6{9 ·{^,ZM=@+X$ 3x\sWD~8$] B}#B4 X1QT ]0:
1f7770  wMBPN~d YU¦zT5~2/? 0^B07Q^k>= V2FucrrE;L 8DLMD[Ycii *vV[V?vp9J \Ac04&j`} ·GJF!%'
d6751f  jkFq ¦J7=?%Si%0 f]?L[¦hF 0 F1rNy\th=o Q-SV`:XmF? e-q`u8`#&' yR)SEqp5#B Su nNm5n7
db875e  w )Xk>6nA;}; 'n3y\Ey{gN d:>S0-jD#p n,1ZMLYi8] HT0n0,S}~9 =idGQ&G?!6 0mxYD_q#6; C
9f21f7  ''0Z"Kp7e x*) QH}ds. mhwMWw`oP$ TQOW¦=k`ue ~e=E`"9oR$ KR*C0wp2kF ;zZVf;LL'K AppC
4abf3f  (]v,0? :_i/Q{{w\4 4jVP7$W`0u }9V[-chL<! &0^~,SXACm y>Azr")hP' (c-hLY%Jc) ?(gr^&3
b9783c  L0+ N#WP,=!49& Fn>}qiazE~ *n^.#(;+Li A7;^5Lx<A< \:yFyqhxrp N~gT7rA!~c 7?Jc8f"Rl^
232864  ·f&`VkYF\?t $FowhpsI&+ Qn~5pN"08f y=?Pc{oUUq Efb4Z)7eqh m{?<}kUd?L [¦bTj6*\0M o^
f12495  zxuJg_/V NoV:B9Vn82 xgT,n.<9N, I"n'iK3@$a WxPpP@'_* ·^,1iEJ8N@a _e:WxXXWf- 7{}T#
eecfe5  [[ ·7 .!KV9yvzJ# dWV:-.!:_6 Zg66D34[9? duv^lo&oMk %&Q3%lo8 K 4^DGo!a0^F R#sB)`pt
17809e  &r T&zAv3??3S UzkV\x2!~d o%-Nr Qeu& pE_!d{48ti `=jVLkR/o@ yn'y@ioCR` 3aM,sb!Zs^·
994ff6  ^5BGeQ7&e1 i)2SxU$W<7 fa'GBb;}Xv z>vMR¦0`qz !KcS08ocNT V{A64?n(Pf D1uABV0:>1 ~b0
d471d9  70sb$r6 4L1Q89" \D 0eP$vjB%NA [U5086@L4T B&2Y&/6J=f nj!V*$"Hh] z+3/K_@ Vb h<*tPQ
3f8df9  24[! ]X&aZNG6IC \Rl:olpRmV tK:C]N \JJ M<i{c E$A~ .9Cx'sf]]Y w¦dC¦AjZP8 :4X;V\\U1
f312bf  h T^pHE0&{Rz 7;vU&0&;F> ~Y#Y3VjxC? 1e}]hv1dpE h{$8`?[=lX l2%Cy}c9Vu QPeHaJ:(G ·H
e75df3  5 em;0F,< 1]0->fc1b2 HZDoqL5qM] K@rco60*i~ 9,#¦l5`~t& 6vIc,8.f=V 0:tF{~0$cG dAyv
69371f  ~uk&L" rb&,niFBnV dyb`(cB0p$ gzm]cs'emw p!2WGTG}/) nf¦R&I@*8{ &bhvgLa_o0 "'%VK#c
114cc0  QwR r#?<CJTILW 6Np_0M0_.N 3%03eb)6x{ 55Y_j#-?-@ } {LL\Wz>h Nxc."y'z0: iyxj$8wA$u
a7cb8b  ·!?jZwbx``D ASY8WQEq_/ Uyjnn-oeHp 1HysAWQf/o fn7M^wZHM 09A:*$cw&t !e_X5fQ%]M ]e
774040  U&Z-N%_[ }vC~Z;%LY& :_D]DG9rR` %f0352opNj qi?+nhauxx :Wvapf1Q<7 LGJ\48+~}z :#T!d
ecf923  Jy^y4 ns!U"0o9d9 ,uqA"p<yVT ,U^S0:N~M: KlTz\j\sIh 8+h*Db]x\i 9>zSi\~$.J _CHK <qf
a15cca  &* l13Lo-*YXC Ts^1r_<;N¦ sE[07?3A. ·BM@LTy%wlV Kg\)"tT{PH ,XULksWiDv d@k\C`IyIq·
125920  #zawOZHt{R N{7BS!dK5F ·!#,^I'(9f, H$a#JV{¦"J 6iL7KtLr^J j):n.SU:d} C}fzycyAY0 #DT
9d92b4  xpDT88< R,L#^dg]!, d$PEzq~+w" Jw=niR$cpS :VN~<}¦Eb^ 3$A"#Lw#xB 6.Bh0&Vcrp AmTHjv
9a47e4  (J=8 ^70+/0$NG7 i¦joSKbAc" 5Gw,0BIdm% :0,f1W/E2x yiuCI8$KD: <C?[j$Jo!a *I_^XRnNt
13cf6d  e h)_}.(BEx_ 8;M:b>8B9B E}>tllgS#P _Nggm*`Mpy >1FYIeohN3 l(TWo%Z=^: D~WN`"<WeX -
00334e  /2r z?0^) 3`&58@q0*6 aa-c{dJTJT \D`Tcm3j$D 'VaGH.Q[Z0 gt7I<hspIM +~vu3^yT*! HFQw
faa3af  w-0)E8 \^4ES%o}7w +m.ihbqfjW <L#G¦)l5$G 5lD7Y@NQ>W I>#,-iset. wU//!?A"f37 WN+tyZ3
03b612  Nw\ zewaWJVemN ¦LW<N<0bm$ xy)P*WEdB@ ; "xVgc# a Uz{qG^_KmU v'MNL2njY* Y >>dA<Cnq
997419  ·jcbFa.4uN+ xWD(F/aMv8 2W/Ts0@bj{ MNfYcY(kT! x&f%g1{}_+ k\F<¦&$%LR 0,5i1}>/?4 &9
b8843b  y82wt>J] mvus{w=NIM [5hZPtye*! $5,y'GAbB0 5!U.?!WiX4 >nP3e3=b/? ;6¦bW_#d75 LC#nx
1617d6  lD-lc :v^M2A\N7u 2U<nU"&kes h_%U$2?g(Y f'k&a:=T~L 8<]7?F¦3Re X<tg[Yp36T ~Z{9uM5B
9e56ab  XN 3e{Y`,)F¦^ nG9H5L\ff[ `r8.(WcS4s 0Jw<T;63x% 2Ki^%QB]p ·),S`l'ta;" 0<]LRnEUCW·
35e6cb  .3 \R]MS)S \4Ic"({&2- oYr[{H PC+ Cg4}2g'eAc jEzsB"&0Dr 70#\LT W5C I?N.F10{?8 !,L
5f26ef  #/<D~@Y D6zu70(Wk0 7];E+CKCmL WLXpmW2G'S ~IrLNG5}<M Wodw;(bdQ: *+¦a=Dem#b r/f;Dd
ca8676  Wn>, #!w(c]Yzhc eCA(&/(hD{ (4:ik)&te) ^/V9H0W"JTe ump#uZDq0L f3nm9`S@S/ *E5XH\.+G
314574  ! 6$kmH[:q^" Nl?,@_`M/j BD8~0CDP9Z &Eza_m@^pk 0ximV7y>'< @</`]`w53} .\:xyyicEz /
c942f6  e0C_NK¦/h >Ip{A&/<`; z4pq~T8v.D >=i6uyI2 :.b@;{!Vry cki5!]CC:^ TE:g<12NQL 1jt.
718a76  kK}b4^ zsMY4psoyE 1.NB@yqiQ ·C.>l)!!gP{ {UilGVdir 535-%¦^%Q" ln7nl¦<iR8 =#cpdNZ
7d58c8  WCm VzLSVo"U}o 5^/2wxe16 ·vpuBIMf76= #mero;p_]$ m64cxBvxSn I11vwE-2T. 7!m0oM+sfu
47fe31  ·zY!=@yp=^: o.D29ScGTz BH5lS&SI.N /h@&Ynep;R _e63FZdB $ 6q;9BdGndS 4Z/ =¦;lyw -_
3dcd7e  vgm9hr}{ 95&zJr_1Hp Wq&T-pL&CY 7?¦P(oK$Qd S_sF=#n.hC lu([B.)x:6 7c=%0AStU' FKoI?
2a2790  z0[x¦ !Zp,UfCk¦W :\]Y.R/2"U q¦rj-N`'¦^ jj4N+}KbNc ,:K[F]^x9M )5¦Wu$QDS5 tgGr1+>q
8e36ad  HJ p#0K^Ha*<j 9?3;pdz*"o Fb}N!osHxd H.%mo/'[0> bViGQpFB`j ^9!K+FDloi uUk"YDQw<1·
0ee8b7  &V!wy@Ud?2 @]'d sQflD XGs¦uk9(8= 62RSg8rv11 5uR&G6rlPK DE*-\/BygX ;)pP¦ha+;v jyH
4bb686  }m2N6Co Kz9W=0@s9X *)vrg"+[#u ItCXaW¦14H J FW=:pu5z )kc,v?,jrR 3,¦j8+~4F X}fon\
62f038  %gY/ :8JWD2JtnJ iI'qER$iz\ aIT<rXo- 7d2G,'3g%y )lSXm:TG#3 T0=mBuZMcq s6<zJ!}D/
3bdbde  ·_]xz2@zB2L L:2@t_!cot )pB'kc6oru km\*h 92re "#Ab&&0y!U C\S'0Dvbn` Lj7L$J<fv> 9
a6b96a  !?Jc= L] ]a!V-.7[@# rs :@f/[NH ;d%¦"#F\\@ $_q.j&fB%V "q`i!<8FvQ yN'¦q`V2xW kbYn
9c2f0b  Ixq!9s y]p7s7+B?% C~_$$qy(ae 8R2/D3H8#C pWd<(_'Dbqd Qe2@`;"C$8 6G:GoPJ0A< &AH*c(x
46daf4  HiG ygL2g06 'I >p4k9E-r0 07TW0}?W*9 sK%$^%(%LG `3-#>_.KP] 8&p!RI(kf{ k¦op&t:Jhw
ccaaba  ·r{u0'B!d&$ v"G='3$ DL 4Z 'tJLj#' x0j;.L>/B6 iP5}R5??0Q -XLUBTX#8Q #j<M)Lo<ZY pT
76d9da  @#t\0FW> Bs>vL?-zP0 i]o6J,n%v\ 7_HqmkI,gh $]ICjDpw+Z wn!!Z#x7Z- #~aoFmT/jX 4{TVi
d4f49d  MaB!V ~Wh#P Z^sZ VJ!A!_-UwA Mw9wVXu-ft 0t300nD+Jw H90VC&LeRv hn/Bd9)V{Y 0&{{G$C?
2dcf19  Wi '@y*i\Y`5C Db.]heZ?2@ +`j0%+dn^h Usv3JTEj"i 0D4r~S"cv. b;Jj 6IhB{ 6,%kQoj;;w·
3051d5  Lk\ mAwxfW .B1Ahz`dTw V`CBNL_C=, y)w8Jp{U#* 4K`,*Ca"58 XY+56K0?UG M_G;\z;coM QY7
83e1a5  q;6'Qu\ }oBF<axc{C M\zHw[5Ehc ¦U80\f&7r! 2E@p>%vbCD >i4y{Z`~W] onsWq(Gp,V LDTN;4
29ed6c  q\S0 h(@@h!wC4d %9"-]r91&c Z2nl%I=2i& *C#(8G=zV? UMrHc!NGW' Dp\m.nW2*_*gnQ"i&Bz
ca8989  [ j"PlMuAQMe *SQx,c k6+ "YPh1odV\L *9b [5MATT &N~fKg}S5 ·eigRK!,w67 y4j,_,`4~dz
e9e7e9  K,_I_uGjX S,YQ5QhL`_ KkAUIRQ.3J ?*!~¦EjVS; -lt_U?=2}i <<EnjS"5+A *>:0&m$AJ. =ja\
04586a  )sWols 2bvbe*k$Gu aBHMCfwRu5 WnFHF62:?8 &]);mab`~A GnG/gy%y4Y [~-n2h,S@= }XC_8$^
a415fe  Y%' I6.C8%Tqk0 y¦¦?&N_C$Z H:1IyjN!1w <8L?m;+z&" $AzR};SX1x BCg+ne9dyV Cud^}]d!0e
c223ca  ·K8>cisubd5 L@r2ZT).NL 1+~nm >S@f [HS0;62P:^ *nF^wQ*ER; N',LCLi'SE $gg7$6Q`"X E7
8938cb  Qv9[LFW;t S> =($pJQt 6->L[~K5Np sde`+>x}zJ zgB~VlMK'd C./BZAnKgb N@9L74gaQ_ p[ E7
9a6222  Fbnx& (ETF4!/v/] EJLZ/+)nQy LTQo4@h7;n l5njAcy{x@ EwRP!A~ziH ;8aY~xqjS^ CJ?$A;¦^
479d17  _B /oWQk085¦P ^'FTx1)U/I KM;cJzCiNP $"BS7TPg¦/ CdeUj8a15* Qm&J/lw_C{ bPr5}Z2+GR·
c926e2  +%WCfhVmD( JNh7CHW@$: vLhN^ss2`~ 5B{}uf?zCi )mQU+RmuI ^uvPi&1h:g 3B~zby;IDE /sw
162349  7Ge-m}h q9JwH3/l<C 8;k2V6S{X_ Pv24!¦/ja! )xF=(3VH@n_,};?04w/~F 1W%/fomgnv 51bIg,
b3c963  fSor (0~:%+9K/H 5Wf"BNp6,$ oM-x1^h!+n ')72B_?j`Q GS^sBu¦F;i Hb~$L /;26 FFc&eLc7k
2a22a1  ) H¦'>yMYd;~ :$p;0)JGJp ,sPUUg>^Lf T%R~[78X\R JjiQ2.x x" IWJ.v&[]a- 1,9IDq#tKJ 3
```

```
--1285  001f0024b3880010001  Page 6 of test-file

af9d47  {oAro;taa )mD/F~mS_ .vF~hIs5pME =f]+~Ri^ s A rAnC}n t ~[[omI>34X q`vEKUB<~d q#(2
79d247  }v2p)/ a~:,=M@vD0 8U jt9iVVX [jXS}IY-r< *EGTe;uro/ my;'dqZ:L7 "g$HA.8Z7B ^vcvlVg
314c2f  {¦U 5YU'5oPIuO vwR%-+:0+x kp1@U*=(}O PVs>%=4TN) ~+W*E(2<K{ \<_dVd_&C1 50^R`4~iCz
455427  ·3"881Ta-^; ; ·`#AqJV <&{M"c&¦V: nO.A18¦Jb9 _6+`Wy>+5W 2#4u)/L@(8 6Y~OTI/mtk ¦L
ccd2d2  Ywjd-@s< )2L5[m=t[Q Z} "*jsulp Fe((pH¦-k# 65x!Rm\!74 46) *¦lx=0 E50n/ZW2wm pkw\E
cdc9aa  xsZu% ~"u{nk9{J_ wK>R#NJnr8 jt!aeXWkCS 6MZ"fSJCbB ~qoM9[@Q3) 1g*i<r+o^A 6A"fkBJ+
2bbb58  /F {s3W1aj:#¦ +c;zn,Y.Fl HT;h~CwB=s MHG,0_0-^8 z3]$jhJW8p PY(pNJ.?`X &ewbr#>(q9·
9ed9e0  L:&6e^KSgy pjC;vwy0\¦ Q_%T}-C5Fm I!2%LemCo^ Hv&@mR¦jeO j!FuBX90%b 5hZzS~k/+1 .Rt
a54165  `L\Fx%/ K":!;G&zU8 044,¦C7.GE 9'+uJ!zYxC @AsTEo*JP; bDk#\wJ~U` ]WN_0%Up^c R8W?C6
f18e74  m[%P qSYi~Y<\Yz (Wa+*Rimd9 :YGMG Rw A Z(G1B%j=6p wxxGbg*{hD 0ny-An-`8d \r(a[BuI4
b7c98b  j .3"r:)[[Qh Huk8 IMb0* 8l.[_TlJvw xjttCPC)wk d!¦+N\;Y/Q ;* ovJgo#] tO{Cr%;\"¦ {
e96423  )'XAJgo! ·!pnHU[H03> ,^S/y-.wh* lb<JG-KH$I rnkK5{\S\h .w)8&}}-xj 655@]ZD$p5 Y`&U
815e30  =V0$e; nS¦jR*c=wv *7.aY0Rn!) '^gJkhC'a/ [y+f[H[Oub "D>2s*3¦S: ;wE!8IcG%? 0#wV[GI
aa0a2d  >,K JJSTpM)($A IC5r$Zu@v# nV¦6!<@I{j M=uwF~{d{B 23)i)J`)nL k_[% %~k*I !AI ;.{J4+
effc2b  ·=qvgR}S{[= 7?\9>EDdKE tB?!;¦5DkO _5f]eb6#?J yd[?)AhKEJ a[)[mMG>d% Hb6+v7HAWB 3^
105291  ,TGWv#EX L5JyYh[^6! L-6cRW8q^L g)u@rubKQ/ {'8a_swa3B I#>~<-]eZB PbSCC¦uOWn lN7aF
a7fec7  uqea9 ¦8#*rea5F0 wS<qFkI6@4 Tr(Jdn)}U& U-);n?^~5S NEv7l-W}n) tSU`YQ3_gh n!Y+_U@1
afe035  &k )#@(X>ta/i bJl4]JxC4g jr!A02G{fB 'KUC=7R'G2 5F)_aLs%m\ n}#~B¦eeyi O-Kc]O,o}>·
7406d4  $zQMnV;KI' M&iGkLAVZm #N>RW/Mu@Q q~JH7&o>J: 4a+`#^8m@; ^mtj8g+iV¦ 1Cy435^JWr cP/
390c15  ?hy_$6< (''m0mD*PR Jf]`F(561u @6M7uON2;S @AD.bN_5y' Wg@J}Vks8* cA}0o-KDAk ewF5T[
93e60a  _[U` u;?J(0b28F 6VD@ e_hHE nW2Hcn}E0t L<h\~wtCL( pFyS&`{HAh T1a@,$P!b¦ HV:AI]mNT
db8854  [ O,w-%ANm? ·}=)#m'bgB( \Ie:44kl'8 ~E~@ti_qf[ [Lzs>`6F¦o b*~ssiz,_z ^8DFu6-QCv <
f87f3e  jH¦"nvqYV VJm@Cy >L\ m#IX-zE$%a M[m:R]p&TG ?dq6e-`?`N +PL#vM)U9S %m^b_e4'7S )i06
8fae24  Gksv+{ T ;"&n;Y}= \ %?1)SdrY ?lp(ag3]-d Ef`4 8]=]i _)LeJ/V7Xr I{f/,D<q a ]vUr#pP
3bf707  l,- UpTdGk:7md Ts=v-,snaQ 5Bc&rP/}Gd xG3baGPCX# ryA~j.]9mr QuL#%JGj6A F!pmQ5CTI6
3cfda2  ·k26vpMH]4 U7Y¦[A0yPV BBJTe{}yHf [J¦)@^0T3e lcD/s?\H:~ aSM^0D$6Q_ Nf2*vf:YO( s4
9449a6  /0pTKm<- fhp,L%ZJy& )1%oK^?Py0 &ASZiAssbW QcGV;qMB V %Cxa_J[o,^ _6t!*faaA0 hf^[1
f2f02f  ![gN^ H@jrxW{Wc\ XZt?<SJLsG S AQX&}41F x9JQ2~5nij ^(c0e.$*;T J$`c"trHGh q:pnLJX5
872d32  %5 eE pF+-{2g oH~b;D'%#u pdfK>xPS34 3%</8Kv58 1zXU~ZUutD [ouQAFdR<t V1gkY[~q{0·
77c485  Rci-9\"J5Z (,lOp<hfs? X,N5+=.8%` on3IppCI<d &1DBy(47yl E~Kb+`hk]U p{F^Xox=E~ f?E
a43b93  nP\h:¦. EnE$W.^*fL -+^¦!x?}D' jrmD\(?g?a ae+mD2Tp9^ tXznwx3{3z }@I$_.@Ab# mpI!B;
092ec5  7!5, -wN',K7'86 ^7!LWCOZH; q9j*Ph?Y?M nQ[7h_O{%. &wkFECn`i^ QhD;&}WPMF )Jgi-ak8t
458cb5  n ]6V~"4e]+7 00JJ(zuKy~ ~e4@NJ3>Ep /LSCR2KgVw !^^3SH2E]n ]oDH#_!p10 dP+vxoJp%K;
3cf020  AC!1Rj`Ei f2MF1;WAv9 #.hoXWt~e. &/UYw3~^`e .)~I`A>v1> v.[N!]4/); St3cpqDS`O \v:}
3270c8  51,S4$ lR_GgnE +v ;Zb+¦3hIoE 'DR5M#IQb3 BZf/!f:tXR 8]IKFs8l4? gTXg{+J/*m pyhT1Z-
015fac  c'E QmeE&OVEZ; 4S=K#F6j4 PhA+r#25B` %#&RZH-r?> 3Z@3}Vz/gH &Sg)b¦KD¦N #!~K+okJc{
ed20fa  ·!/}X'-=O C gMbeu$bDIc E/Q5zxvszw xM'$gV$,Vh 7KI8,nao1% _7wX.kq$lG sH7HL@~3v3 @L
3fab58  j,+Z>0Zz OQS;#TxJ!y 8B=X>PLO0i wv$S22+-WZ (r^Zx'[ozp 5IMcryp\rh t<b$DmX~I` )8h0s
0e52d2  X(dg= 2!z-qX)X)q iu:WN6!0&' n4:D<{,W%? ·LEXI]_<oI '}^>{kA$1. KRRE_*J{_J %!n ](p'
21a2cf  ;t v0}bR~s`8= gboq-hNT.Q )Q0&?4>565 2wt1iRI`c1 P p:OEHJxF &l=z=`NxA` 7rWi9[MHB~·
a5eb04  39qY^oO#=R 'm0#:)Dzw[ OC")mJKll_ _6b0bei50m @p;G63?n{k }t}E>j2}kn K<s18)>q*[ B#u
4932b4  V?bR)qM or9X"7DqEo 9}1C9#Jtcj V>29m8);4x MN-bo((\*? <_p<'c qYW hm}"v63mA` L@*HFf
f94ba9  Pb<l -&Ip$<GXL1 H0;^C&!!?M Irb.CEJ-gT 1F5Jjmtx1= LxIRvHrAg9 JDX[nfTAwb -+0w F)!L
186797  V v&(?xI$0[N 5;AxlbmLGw soT:xkgL¦[ %wIK{Y(G,: M3L-}uQuKB ·][lB)fz\h #4kJ93fSo1 <
e27b85  >a/LWZ/:X sB)¦}$VqsY \4=lzp\)Ux 7&4$9+w 5qa6ES{ Td qR*b/35&XJ i7i+8!4.YF <\Fl
a21c97  aCADQ0 Xp#l&&BP/, v5ztI)No)g LR)lpM?"Aw AauH$DT.)H $=i*iY4N J )KoVgnt_^7 T\@u.N·
3278d1  Wn! X)[2=(0w&9 um(d_hCv%u Ekbqh7`g): bL+gY#mpDa LF>2g37]cZ CL0Z-taGeA p)Kps92Uw_
bd7ca2  ·4naD$?(^bL r$5gbzJ$L8 t"`/9T$uQ5 3ViO_H3)P# bhp=0qfI¦Y {efPi] ¦C0 *J0Rm9 pDb 5}
49f3af  g$d.!>[¦ ?Kk¦Ke=X6G Gv$`vr"WF4 .9:9:Vq5W2 C/)&J^=qud vBJfE2.Vg9 ·S(SE=+WzL !R/_o
249b50  }RQdJ @.4R<j;V[8 ckI}v"xCcy oV`m*3PQ"p 6@y}XMVpT: z5Q¦+q]%bM D<cTi5SZqi kdQ6<BjV
3efdb7  ¦f K`t:?wJiQ? 5plGDD9+=# n9,.~`(eJS ?kb7fJe&Mz ;?8\YCy\3e @tt}¦ZHN~d ^y})_!WXto·
f91557  -LQMD+`'~} s{vLABK'Y' W.JXb6MR/W ]%=ibEea>V 2#¦TK!+S"b \8Asbs :l] (D M*aha9{ 6M.
9417d0  7Y^69=s ^d50dM<BiA inqHUPbN3u A.U Ao=2?{ TK[~d{i'cS R!W$\v7RpX CU¦0r/0n$" _!{[j·
33b1c6  <<sl 9pr.%E~Z!B )P#* n."Rr# ~Gk¦a(pN>' .5AQ1xRQ)P )W"tf"wR#s npXt^'0f@? ^p+WCYJpC
3780a5  f ZX/YP^\BVI />o4NVTm04 Wk~.GLi.3B ?{2~YTU#ed Uui,HUX\1. .<lw$x+CJK lGuB¦u(^4] {
49338f  fzQ<WbGym dfeZq)5:E" 9D^/I;A$m= hn%=NI4:+x mPose+:h1S I_Qd!RO;;8 =RVffmoJn] ^Rti
82bb9b  lZT=az 0\<c,7{A?6 r¦Z`l8OHG+ 9rdpD"R?{` wA(-=ILS=< t¦8.I`RQ[k @\h?,(;i!1 &>HLgxf
c5c092  $G\ \jG==uu&;3 !0k*jS(x^/ [CxJC¦B w( <9"3,N<dO MVT!_M`k_e X`g$kB K{@PG]5vIc
575959  ·)a(IBs)%8a }5jb^g-G{X =*jw<^A¦'= /c" l(6Kn4 Vv=;$d8Z%R lJ}Hh{P#[\ ZZPbp¦N"X" u>
cae640  wWSRY#4F 2n3+<7fvzB L"?IQA"P7t ,I?^#BoFl# }.05rF-2tY 4#bU"4is v =R@\CfJCyE FWAid
67bb7f  P^?er HEBY,3W#Qt nQsSx7}>bp "ZXR6w8)7^ V8WjoX9a,( ·X*4#Fvp9x qL^fad{@0R h:CAS&JY
8eef9d  7G >[3dR${IMj )RWnNx{}Ld o#frJ@*qPF `(}d$G/o:6 q%jg!e1c{" ct/!¦}Q@I/ DqJh!7#4Vq·
0f0b01  >W8$hx!g\d hbWg5t1A=U d>5{>F00#m uoQnp9KRs5 H¦G=+iX]¦= /:7VfG4U-* [u0qA_cSq, :GU
f2479f  !¦3z:,( @[6hLhrs+N ;@(z$\L.*$ `"0pzf}#6> L$H5s<=B#X +Pag=oo?BM n><S9<iUt3 =EKVbm
813521  Y8Ke .J#}:B>ga* z]=5Dr*TJE u{\`Sq-9Z8 ^3{}Qc\YgU #jYut.=:&0 _ngRx}-1^h Zds<AM!va
058700  $ 8wQD5hJC¦* a\+_g9<PJv Q0T{2H[6(s V5>?_a:gp{ xY,2uZlil? A8-gs@eLC j_[Iy@:vd0 n
051d76  BCI/*3K%R 2:UP$;¦G4d l.~ErqU@] `'$j;Mpm/ ·dM)}GM2,Q~ P,\Cz/cY$A &-uSz~_weA k?m9
cfad31  NwkM/9 i]0x>&z`c! WQe8.][0$d o{;ggfs!=] iTzoLXQMC) )>*f7Yh¦FU b=JF1[`l8K 08mhi8,
cfd8fc  o12 8uCn^=613u p<JJyJ_Eko VUEk^6]p?5 b$C!7T4*$# aM>,*`ty<H b4+u.{5@_t #rYX%`Y(%8
5c550b  ·@D\!6S>[¦} (s}!&;`z\d 6:pwsxy,H: %8~UV<RQ,W 'XHB6A~w-3 }(#s"/<9Y> :s&VCW_zzc @#
daeff0  fa _k3nf rZ7~sPY/"p "HCW%;Rfko P0i0;y~ 2n FnLvHXs9Yu yJa6yH~j20 y\Rp\R!H+G T<\-0
f00899  vc#R[ 4qH\m3l>Jf }TTMUzUJ2* o5JcuJ3QxH ?"/0kJzOBu tCZoyX~!rn :0*bc[X)¦w ,HwS@Gu6
```

```
--e140 001c21fe2ae80010002 Page 1 of bootstrap

94e666 #!/usr/bin/perl -s
0ea601 #
794467 # bootstrap -- Simpler version of unmunge for bootstrapping
e5a601 #
9f33f9 # Unmunge this file using:
3137c3 # ··perl -ne 'if (s/^ *[^-\s]\S{4,6} ?//) { s/[\244\245\267]/ /g; print; }'
29a601 #
438bb8 # $Id: bootstrap,v 1.15 1997/11/14 03:52:53 mhw Exp $
85af5a
851496 sub Fatal▷        { print STDERR @_; ·exit(1); }
c50a97 sub Max▷▷        { my ($a, $b) = @_; ·($a > $b) ? $a : $b; }
1e36b1 sub TabSkip▷      { $tabWidth - 1 - (length($_[0]) % $tabWidth); }
a1af5a
394cdd ($tab,$yen,$pilc,$cdot,$tmp1,$tmp2)=("\244","\245","\266","\267","\377","\376");
393067 $editor = $ENV{'VISUAL'} || $ENV{'EDITOR'} || 'vi';
d3e7e6 $inFile = $ARGV[0];
d94e2f doFile: {
49e81b ····open(IN, "<$inFile") || die;
095163 ····for ($lineNum = 1; ($_ = <IN>); $lineNum++) {
dfaacd  ▷       s/^\s+//; ·s/\s+$//;▷       # Strip leading and trailing spaces
05b32f  ▷       next if (/^$/);▷▷       # Ignore blank lines
52f118  ▷       ($prefix, $seenCRCStr, $dummy, $_) = /^(\S{2})(\S{4})( .*))?/;
6faf5a
b2b8ac  ▷       # Correct the number of spaces after each tab
a32d31  ▷       while (s/$tab( *)/$tmp1 . ($tmp2 x &Max(length($1), &TabSkip($`)))/e) {}
c33e7b  ▷       s/ ( +)/" " . ($cdot x length($1))/eg;▷ # Correct center dots
a0024c  ▷       s/$tmp1/$tab/g; ·s/$tmp2/ /g; ·# Restore tabs and spaces from correction
8b3cd0  ▷       s/\s*$/\n/;▷       ▷       # Strip trailing spaces, and add a newline
2baf5a
9f2516  ▷       $crc = $seenCRC = 0;▷    ▷        ▷        # Calculate CRC
3f3db3  ▷       for ($data = $_; $data ne ""; $data = substr($data, 1)) {
68e002  ▷       ····$crc ^= ord($data);
342ea8  ▷       ····for (1..8) {
be0b86  ▷       ▷        $crc = ($crc >> 1) ^ (($crc & 1) ? 0x8408 : 0);
ca4d5a  ▷       ····}
5a1aea  ▷       }
264656  ▷       if ($crc != hex($seenCRCStr)) {▷▷        # CRC mismatch
425ba7  ▷       ····close(IN); ·close(OUT);
a04921  ▷       ····unlink(@filesCreated);
e4fc5c  ▷       ····@filesCreated = ();
4fce26  ▷       ····@oldStat = stat($inFile);
b9e5b0  ▷       ····system($editor, "+$lineNum", $inFile);
df1549  ▷       ····@newStat = stat($inFile);
bd93df  ▷       ····redo doFile if ($oldStat[9] != $newStat[9]); ·# Check mod date
68a0de  ▷       ····&Fatal("Line $lineNum invalid: $_");
e71aea  ▷       }
fdaf5a
a97b7d  ▷       if ($prefix eq '--') {▷ ▷        ▷        # Process header line
4d541c  ▷       ····($code, $pageNum, $file) = /^(\S{19}) Page (\d+) of (.*)/;
2e88c3  ▷       ····$tabWidth = hex(substr($code, 11, 1));
c77d01  ▷       ····if ($file ne $lastFile) {
9d1aaf  ▷       ▷        print "$file\n";
e98e77  ▷       ▷        &Fatal("$file: already exists\n") if (!$f && (-e $file));
eaa6b3  ▷       ▷        close(OUT);
db097b  ▷       ▷        open(OUT, ">$file") || &Fatal("$file: $!\n");
4cbd21  ▷       ▷        push(@filesCreated, ($lastFile = $file));
3c4d5a  ▷       ····}
3d4ccd  ▷       } else {▷        ▷        ▷        # Unmunge normal line
e25291  ▷       ····s/$tab( *)/"\t".(" " x (length($1) - &TabSkip($`)))/eg;
47b547  ▷       ····s/$yen\n/\f/;▷       # Handle form feeds
c17ad4  ▷       ····s/$pilc\n//;▷       # Handle continuation lines
019f82  ▷       ····s/$cdot/ /g;▷       # Center dots -> spaces
23af5a
97e546  ▷       ····print OUT;
591aea  ▷       }
4f6fe7 ····}
caca06 ····close(IN); ·close(OUT);
c2efe6 }
```

```
--ac52 001077b880880010003 Page 1 of bootstrap2

94e666 #!/usr/bin/perl -s
0ea601 #
e04352 # bootstrap2 -- Second stage bootstrapper, a version of unmunge
91a601 #
849cbb # $Id: bootstrap2,v 1.4 1997/11/14 03:52:54 mhw Exp $
b4af5a
5dd22f sub Cleanup▷     { close(IN); ·close(OUT); ·unlink(@files); ·@files = (); }
cd2a1e sub Fatal▷       { &Cleanup(); ·print STDERR @_; ·exit(1); }
a136b1 sub TabSkip▷     { $tabWidth - 1 - (length($_[0]) % $tabWidth); }
9a172b sub TabFix▷      { my ($needed, $actual) = (&TabSkip($_[0]), length($_[1]));
735323 ····$tmp1 . ($tmp2 x $needed) . (" " x ($actual - $needed)); }
4b20f4 sub HumanEdit▷   { my ($file, $line, @message) = ($inFile, @_); ·&Cleanup();
0c2db1 ····@old = stat($file); ·system($editor, "+$line", $file); ·@new = stat($file);
bc77e8 ····redo doFile if ($old[9] != $new[9]);▷         # Check mod date
d77c59 ····&Fatal("Line $line, ", @message); }
16af5a
104cdd ($tab,$yen,$pilc,$cdot,$tmp1,$tmp2)=("\244","\245","\266","\267","\377","\376");
f43067 $editor = $ENV{'VISUAL'} || $ENV{'EDITOR'} || 'vi';
4da6f7 ($inFile, $manifest, @rest) = @ARGV;
6bbb70 if ($manifest ne "") {▷  ▷         # Read manifest file
229970 ····open(MANIFEST, "<$manifest") || &Fatal("$manifest: $!\n");
d5e3e3 ····while (<MANIFEST>) { $dir = $1 if /^D\s+(.*)$/;
449857 ▷        $index[$1] = $dir . $2 if /^(\d+)\s+(.*)$/; }
bcefe6 }
954e2f doFile: {
ec779a ····$seenPCRC = $pcrc1 = 0; ·$lastFlags = 1; ·$lastFileNum = 0;
342616 ····open(IN, "<$inFile") || &Fatal("$inFile: $!\n");
d7c787 ····for ($line = 1; ($_ = <IN>); $line++) {
1daacd ▷        s/^\s+//; ·s/\s+$//;       # Strip leading and trailing spaces
75b32f ▷        next if (/^$/);▷▷         # Ignore blank lines
2df118 ▷        ($prefix, $seenCRCStr, $dummy, $_) = /^(\S{2})(\S{4})( (.*))?/;
8e3e5a ▷        while (s/$tab( *)/&TabFix($`, $1)/eo) {} ·# Correct spaces after tabs
dcdb12 ▷        s/($tmp2¦ )( +)/$1 . ($cdot x length($2))/ego;▷ # Correct center dots
fa4668 ▷        s/$tmp1/$tab/go; ·s/$tmp2/ /go; ·# Restore tabs/spaces from correction
5e3cd0 ▷        s/\s*$/\n/; ▷      ▷         # Strip trailing spaces, and add a newline
15af5a
160460 ▷        $crc = 0; ·$pcrc = $pcrc1;▷      ▷         # Calculate CRCs
bc3db3 ▷        for ($data = $_; $data ne ""; $data = substr($data, 1)) {
d860ae ▷        ····$crc ^= ord($data); ·$pcrc1 ^= ord($data);
2d28f0 ▷        ····for (1..8) { $crc = ($crc >> 1) ^ (($crc & 1) ? 0x8408 : 0);
1700f2 ▷        ▷        $pcrc1 = ($pcrc1 >> 1) ^ (($pcrc1 & 1) ? 0xedb88320 : 0); } }
441aea ▷        }
21e7eb ▷        ($seenPLCRC, $seenCRC) = map { hex($_) } ($prefix, $seenCRCStr);
244eda ▷        &HumanEdit($line, "CRC failed: $_") if $crc != $seenCRC;
fd7b7d ▷        if ($prefix eq '--') {▷ ▷         # Process header line
332129 ▷        ····&HumanEdit($line - 1, "Page CRC failed") if $pcrc != $seenPCRC;
98991f ▷        ····($humanHdr, $pageNum, $file) = /^\S{19} (Page (\d+) of (.*))/;
b63710 ▷        ····($vers, $flags, $seenPCRC, $tabWidth, $prodNum, $fileNum) =
d62c3f ▷        ▷        map { hex($_) } /^(\S)(\S\S)(\S{8})(\S)(\S{3})(\S{4})/;
4d0b72 ▷        ····if ($fileNum != $lastFileNum) {
4970bd ▷        ▷        print STDERR "MISSING files\n" if $fileNum != $lastFileNum + 1;
4d6102 ▷        ▷        &Fatal("Missing pages\n") if $pageNum != 1 || !($lastFlags & 1);
7d6aeb ▷        ▷        if ($manifest ne "") {
24fd6f ▷        ▷        ····($_ = $index[$fileNum]) =~ m%([^/]*)$%;
f9ae35 ▷        ▷        ····&Fatal("Manifest mismatch\n") if ($file ne $1);
0f50d2 ▷        ▷        ····($file = $_) =~ s¦/+¦mkdir($`, 0777), "/"¦eg; ·# mkdir -p
e9467a ▷        ▷        }
f98e77 ▷        ▷        &Fatal("$file: already exists\n") if (!$f && (-e $file));
895c6f ▷        ▷        close(OUT); ·open(OUT, ">$file") || &Fatal("$file: $!\n");
0fb066 ▷        ▷        push(@files, $file); ·print "$fileNum $file\n";
969957 ▷        ····} else {
03efb5 ▷        ▷        &Fatal("MISSING pages\n") if ($pageNum != $lastPageNum + 1);
294d5a ▷        ····}
8fba7e ▷        ····($lastFlags,$lastFileNum,$lastPageNum) = ($flags,$fileNum,$pageNum);
3ce809 ▷        ····$pcrc1 = 0;
e14ccd ▷        } else {▷       ▷        ▷         # Unmunge normal line
f61c35 ▷        ····&HumanEdit($line, "CRC failed: $_") if ($pcrc1 >> 24) != $seenPLCRC;
fc65f0 ▷        ····s/$tab( *)/"\t".(" " x (length($1) - &TabSkip($`)))/ego;
c6c825 ▷        ····s/$yen\n/\f/o; ·s/$pilc\n//o; ·s/$cdot/ /go; ·print OUT;
3b1aea ▷        }
206fe7 ····}
07efe6 }
```

# 5

# *Software Source Code*

This chapter contains a complete listing of the C-language software that we wrote to control the DES Cracker hardware. This software provides a simple user interface for testing the hardware, setting up problems to be solved by searching through the possible keys, and running such searches. We're publishing it to show both people and machines how to control the DES Cracker.

This version of the software is fairly rudimentary; it doesn't include a graphical user interface, collaborate with others across the Internet to speed up brute force cracking attempts, etc. By the time you read this book, there will probably be a better version of the software, which you will be able to read about in our web pages at `http://www.eff.org/pub/Privacy/Crypto_misc/DES_Cracking/`.

This software is known to build and run in a "DOS Window" under Windows 95 on a PC using the Borland C++ Compiler, version 3.1. It also compiles cleanly using Microsoft Visual C++ version 5.

The software is documented in the file `readme.txt`.

For details on why these documents are printed this way, and how to scan them into a computer, see Chapter 4, *Scanning the Source Code*.

```
--ffd0 0015103933880020001 Page 1 of MANIFEST

7bf681 1 MANIFEST
ec8ce7 2 readme.txt
05e777 3 autoconf.c
cedb16 4 build.bat
a0056e 5 chipio.c
151f75 6 chipio.h
1a8e30 7 des.c
11db2a 8 des.h
0aac3f 9 initsrch.c
0f78d8 10 keyblock.c
f699dd 11 keyblock.h
ba96cf 12 search.c
5127f6 13 search.h
```

```
--e562 0004451557280020002 Page 1 of readme.txt

e0af5a
1aaf5a
d44c86 ·········README FOR DES SEARCH ENGINE CONTROLLER SOFTWARE
afaf5a
29825e ·······················April 23, 1998
4aaf5a
0eaf5a
fb3fcf Written 1998 by Cryptography Research (http://www.cryptography.com)
216a64 for the Electronic Frontier Foundation (EFF). ·Placed in the public
4ad8d3 domain by Cryptography Research and EFF.
a7af5a
50ff62 This is unsupported free software. ·Use and distribute at your own
e0daf4 risk. U.S. law may regulate the use and/or export of this program.
ffeaa2 Foreign laws may also apply.
f7af5a
b4af5a
34af5a
fa176f -------------------------------------------------------------------
b1a6ff Section 1: ·Compiling the Programs.
79af5a
801f81 Compiling the programs should be easy. ·Using 32-bit Microsoft Visual
a26186 C++ for Windows compile as shown below. ·For Borland C++ or other
1d3a41 compilers, replace "cl" with the compiler name (e.g., bcc). ·On a 16-
7c7812 bit DOS compiler with a large search array, the large memory model
3f769d (Borland's "-ml" flag) is required or the system will run out of
392d57 memory.
62af5a
ce209c ···> cl search.c keyblock.c chipio.c des.c
fcc3fb ···> cl initsrch.c keyblock.c
6b758b ···> cl autoconf.c chipio.c
7057a9 ···> cl testvec.c sim.c des.c
42af5a
b8af5a
1caf5a
ea176f -------------------------------------------------------------------
93e4fb Section 2: ·Auto-Configuring the Search Array.
80af5a
19d9c3 The auto-configuration program is an important part of the DES
2927fe Cracker. ·Because there are a large number of chips in the system, it
9fb6be is inevitable that a few fail. ·By automatically removing defective
0d0b4b units, it is not necessary to repair the system when failures do
4f9dc9 occur.
a8af5a
018826 The program "autoconf.exe" will automatically identify the
6f723b configuration of a search array. ·With the I/O port base address at
cd7d24 210 hex, simply run the program with the command:
5daf5a
75065b ···> autoconf search.cfg -t
98af5a
c7e245 Note that the "-t" flag performs register testing (recommended if the
dfdfea search system might contain defective chips that need to be avoided).
e003e2 If the I/O port is at an address other than 210, specify the address.
ff49ba The "-v" flag provides verbose output. ·For example:
c1af5a
2faf9f ···> autoconf search.cfg 210 -t -v
26af5a
185f44 When autoconf completes, it will print the total number of chips to
bae103 the screen and save the configuration information to the
f44721 configuration file. ·The configuration can be edited (e.g., with
942a9c grep) to remove defective units not caught with autoconf.
8daf5a
70e81e (Note that this first release does not implement search unit testing·
7f1a7b code except for the register tests.)·
74af5a
d9af5a
47af5a
cd176f -------------------------------------------------------------------
2611d1 Section 3: ·Initializing a Search.
40af5a
7c71c4 The search parameters have to be specified before a key can be found.
0b480d The program initsrch creates a "search context" file that contains
443422 these search parameters and a list of the regions of keyspace that
```

```
--8d6f 0009a4c5f7080020002 Page 2 of readme.txt

6d2d23 remain to be searched.
f3af5a
757db9 The search parameters can either be entered into initsrch or
03be37 specified on the command line. ·To enter them manually, run initsrch
b17249 with no parameters:
34af5a
f0a5ad ···> initsrch
d4af5a
83b591 The program will then prompt for the search context file. ·Press
a473ca enter for the default filename ("search.ctx").
98af5a
953b91 Next, the program will prompt for a search mode. ·Five modes are·
096098 supported and are described in the following sections.·
30af5a
45b5a1 ···K - Known plaintext
442856 ···E - ECB ASCII text
019879 ···C - CBC ASCII text
31e1fd ···B - Blaze challenge
ddbb69 ···M - Manual parameter specification
e9af5a
5eaf5a
2edf4c 1. ·Known plaintext searching
ccaf5a
06f1ec This is the simplest (and most common) mode of operation. ·If a
4dd2c9 complete DES plaintext/ciphertext pair is known, this mode can be
0f91b5 used to quickly search for the key. ·When prompted, enter the
c281eb plaintext in hexadecimal form (e.g., "123456789ABCDEF0") and press
95792f enter. ·Next, enter the ciphertext, also in hexadecimal. The program
6fb05a will then create a search context file and exit.
d1af5a
fcaf5a
68cc8f 2. ·ECB ASCII text searching
9aaf5a
6e7074 If your target message is known to be ASCII text and was encrypted
1edff6 using DES ECB mode, enter two different ciphertexts. ·The program
d92df0 will create the search context file and exit. ·The program is
234bf0 configured to include all letters ("a-z" and "A-Z"), numbers ("0-9"),
470b54 and common punctuation (ASCII zero, tab, linefeed carriage return,
0ded96 space, and common punctuation (!"'(),-.^_). ·For other character
98fbc6 sets, use the manual parameter specification option.
f8af5a
bcaf5a
a7fe29 3. ·CBC ASCII text searching
caaf5a
f85465 If your message is ASCII text and was encrypted using DES CBC mode,
bae166 this option lets you specify an initialization vector and two
aa45de ciphertext messages. ·The CBC mode ASCII option uses the same ASCII
6c4548 text characters as ECB ASCII.
09af5a
18af5a
706ad7 4. ·The Blaze challenge
0caf5a
20b2e8 Matt Blaze's DES challenge involves searching for a key such that a
4f29b1 repeated plaintext byte produces a repeated ciphertext byte. ·This
98ce02 option will search for keys that meet the challenge. Simply specify
2851f0 the desired repeated ciphertext byte.
68af5a
6baf5a
fba0ab 5. ·Manual parameter specification
e2af5a
f4f30d The manual parameter mode allows direct control over the search
a1c03a parameters. The manual mode requires entering more data than the
f21978 other modes; it is often easier to pipe input from a script file,
3cab72 e.g.:
6caf5a
114c2d ···> initsrch < search.scr
5baf5a
b6c924 First, enter the plaintext vector. ·This is 64 hex digits long and
984fe4 specifies the bytes that can appear in "valid" plaintexts. The most
caf7a9 significant bit of the left-hand digit specifies whether ASCII 255
ea0906 can appear, and the least significant bit of the last digit specifies
9ad545 whether ASCII zero can appear. For example, the plaintext vector for
```

```
--0018  00065d8074680020002 Page 3 of readme.txt
569be0  the ASCII text modes is:
45af5a
328424  ···00000000000000000000000000000000007FFFFFFC7FFFFFE8FFF738700002601
47af5a
6294a7  Next, enter the initialization vector for the first DES, if any.
6b8f16  This will be XORed onto the first plaintext before its validity is
5587b3  checked.
b6af5a
f4fd67  Next, enter the two ciphertexts (ciphertext 0 and ciphertext 1).
aaf9a7  These may be the same or different.
a2af5a
d4a2dd  Next, enter the plaintext byte mask. ·This sets bits that should be
f36fe4  ignored in the plaintext. ·For example, if the left-hand byte of the
cac85d  plaintext is unknown or can have any value, the plaintext byte mask
379f87  would be set to 80 (hex).
11af5a
9d87cc  Finally, enter the searchInfo byte. Bit 1 of this byte specifies
97a928  whether CBC mode should be used. ·If so, the first ciphertext will be
595ef9  XORed onto candidate plaintexts produced by decrypting the second
2dff09  ciphertext. ·Bit 2 of searchInfo specifies whether the extraXor
13de86  operation should be done. This operation XORs the right half of the
8aac2c  plaintext onto the left half before it is checked. ·(For the Blaze
06de4f  challenge, the desired plaintext has a single byte repeated. ·The
13ab4a  extraXor operation will set the left half of the plaintext to zero if
c6781e  the plaintext is good. ·The plaintextByteMask can then be set to 0x0F
e2b3f0  to ignore the right half and the plaintextVector has only the bit for
521d7e  ASCII zero set.)
39af5a
1baf5a
4c288d  5. ·The search context file
8daf5a
179dcb  The search context file contains a header, the search parameters, and
8f1477  2^24 bits corresponding to the unsearched key regions. ·The search
91edfe  parameters are: plaintextVector (32 bytes), plaintextXorMask (8
55d722  bytes), ciphertext0 (8 bytes), ciphertext1 (8 bytes),
3583fb  plaintextByteMask (1 byte), and searchInfo (1 byte). ·Each search
421808  region includes 2^32 keys. The first bit (the MSB of the first key
c79bf0  region byte) corresponds to the keys 0000000000000000 through
462847  000000FFFFFFFF, in 56-bit notation. ·(To produce the 56-bit form of a
f21751  64-bit DES key, delete the eight parity bits.)
d6af5a
efaf5a
f5af5a
48176f  ----------------------------------------------------------------------
81999d  Section 4: ·Running a Search.
c1af5a
05ae2f  The most common way to run a search is to type:
5caf5a
057f42  ···> search search.cfg search.ctx logfile -q
2faf5a
80edd9  The "-q" flag requests quiet output, which prints less information to
e101f1  the screen. ·The search.cfg file is produced by autoconf, and
2200bc  search.ctx is produced by initsrch. ·The logfile will contain a list
f4a0ec  of candidate keys encountered.
12af5a
223e71  If a search is stopped partway through, work done in partially-
0c0b95  completed key regions is lost, but completed regions are noted in the
a252e6  search context file. ·Note that a complete search will produce a
433e44  rather large amount of data in the logfile. ·If hard disk space is
649464  limited, it may be desirable to stop the search occasionally (for
9ad667  example, daily) to purge the logfile.
c2af5a
5daf5a
1eaf5a
8b176f  ----------------------------------------------------------------------
f98443  Section 5: ·Porting to other platforms.
d9af5a
9aa861  When porting to other platforms, some code changes or additions may
9a17dd  be required. ·The following may not be found on all systems:
49af5a
0946df  ······stricmp: ···This is a case-insensitive strcmp found on many
659051  ···········compilers. ·If it isn't present, you can either use strcmp
```

```
--a334 0019f8825ad80020002 Page 4 of readme.txt

70faf5 ·········(though commands will become case sensitive) or write one.
4daf5a
57970a ······SEEK_SET: ··A constant (equal to zero) used to tell fseek()
bdc708 ·········to go to a fixed offset. ·Usually defined in stdio.h
02af5a
ca5e28 ······kbhit(void): ·Returns true if a key has been pressed. (Used to
662151 ·········check for commands during searches.)
bbaf5a
6d2832 ······getch(void): ·Reads a keystroke from the keyboard.
4daf5a
c13802 ······inportb(unsigned portNum): ·Reads a byte from an I/O port. Used
5c2f71 ·········only by chipio.c. ·On other platforms, inportb may need to
27977e ·········be emulated. ·(For Visual C++, inportb is implemented in
3c461d ·········chipio.c as inline assembly language.)
97af5a
9e58f5 ······outportb(int portNum, int value): ·Sends a byte to an I/O port.
59dbb1 ·········Used only by chipio.c. ·On other platforms, outportb may
3bb05f ·········need to be emulated. ·(For Visual C++, outportb is
0f88ab ·········implemented in chipio.c as inline assembly language.)
a3af5a
1eaf5a
bbaf5a
f7176f -----------------------------------------------------------------
a166bf Section 6: ·Final comments
15af5a
05182b As this code goes to press, there was little opportunity for testing
a3aa2b and the code has not undergone any of the assurance, code review, or
a4419d testing processes we normally use. ·When working on the code, you
57167e you may find a few bugs. ·Feedback, as always, is appreciated.
9baf5a
dba0c7 Paul Kocher, Josh Jaffe, and everyone else at Cryptography Research
969732 would like to thank John Gilmore and the EFF for funding this unique
1930dc project, and AWT for their expert hardware work!
37af5a
9faf5a
```

```
--8884 0008b9a267780020003 Page 1 of autoconf.c
8d2d03 /*******************************************************************************
caf463 ·* autoconf.c ·······················································*
4740b6 ·* ····················Search Engine Controller Program ·····················*
c429eb ·* ···························································*
6c09fc ·* ···Written 1998 by Cryptography Research (http://www.cryptography.com) ···*
938aaf ·* ····and Paul Kocher for the Electronic Frontier Foundation (EFF). ······*
b9caeb ·* ······Placed in the public domain by Cryptography Research and EFF. ······*
184992 ·* ·THIS IS UNSUPPORTED FREE SOFTWARE. USE AND DISTRIBUTE AT YOUR OWN RISK. ·*
2129eb ·* ···························································*
6cc755 ·* ·IMPORTANT: U.S. LAW MAY REGULATE THE USE AND/OR EXPORT OF THIS PROGRAM. ·*
5529eb ·* ···························································*
03489b ·* *******************************************************************************
5129eb ·* ···························································*
3215cb ·* ··IMPLEMENTATION NOTES: ·······································*
f829eb ·* ···························································*
dfa8b8 ·* ··This program automatically determines the configuration of a search ····*
491db9 ·* ··array. ·Additional diagnostic code should be added to detect common ····*
2e87f9 ·* ··chip failures (once these are known). ·······························*
fe29eb ·* ···························································*
26489b ·* *******************************************************************************
3b29eb ·* ···························································*
286eef ·* ··REVISION HISTORY: ···········································*
5429eb ·* ···························································*
4528d9 ·* ··Version 1.0: ·Initial release by Cryptography Research to EFF. ·········*
3b486f ·* ·····················Note: Detailed diagnostic tests not implemented yet. ······*
c829eb ·* ···························································*
34d8c3 ·* *******************************************************************************/
29af5a
05bcd3 #define SOFTWARE_VERSION "1.0"
9aa5c9 #define SOFTWARE_DATE ···"04-21-1998"
86af5a
d7af5a
d4bea3 #include <stdlib.h>
a4feb2 #include <stdio.h>
ddbb5f #include <assert.h>
e5c737 #include <memory.h>
ed0a8b #include <time.h>
f8b1cb #include <ctype.h>
d91519 #include "chipio.h"
7baf5a
822d85 #define MAX_CHIPS_PER_BOARD ·64
e191af #define MAX_BOARDS ·········256
59af5a
9e708e static void EXIT_ERR(char *s) { fprintf(stderr, s); exit(1); }
619101 void AutoconfigureScan(FILE *fp, int fullScan, int verbose);
c0e5e4 int QuickCheckRegister(int board, int chip, int register, int value);
cd6c9b void AddSearchUnits(FILE *fp, int board, int chip, int unit, int isGood);
6693c5 long DoFullScan(FILE *fp, int board, int* chips, int verbose);
a7af5a
fcaf5a
ac164b int main(int argc, char **argv) {
413850 ··int testLoops = -1;
1087d8 ··int baseIoPort = 0x210;
2dadb6 ··int i, nextArg, fullScan;
792659 ··int verbose = 0;
51bc33 ··char buffer[200];
4779c7 ··char *fileSpec;
58b166 ··FILE *fp;
9ec1cd ··char *helpMsg = "Usage: autoconf search.cfg [baseIoPort] [-v] [-t#]\n\n"
c24b8d ·················" ·········-v: ·Verbose operation\n"
deec61 ·················" ·search.cfg: ·The output file for the config info.\n"
eccff8 ·················" ·baseIoPort: ·Hex base port of I/O card (default=210 hex)\n"
aa6d8e ·················" ·········-t#: ·Extra testing (see below)\n"
be1228 ·················"\nUse the -t# to do more than a quick test for chips.\n"
25a0c7 ·················" ·········-t0: ·Do full read/write test of chip registers\n"
4e10f3 ·················" ·········-t#: ·Do # iterations of a full system test\n";
16af5a
b0ddd7 ··printf("\nDES Search Engine Configurer (Ver %s, %s). May be export "
84ffaa ·········"controlled.\nWritten 1998 by Cryptography Research "
bc2e08 ·········"(http://www.cryptography.com) for EFF.\n"
75c4fd ·········"This is unsupported "
8b1151 ·········"free software: Use and distribute at your own risk.\n"
```

```
--bbb9 0003461923980020003 Page 2 of autoconf.c
d1805d ·········"---------------------------------------------"
ef04bf ·········"--------------------------------------\n\n\n",
5aa1fb ·········SOFTWARE_VERSION, SOFTWARE_DATE);
6daf5a
aebc9a ··if (argc < 2 || argv[1][0] == '-')
a78298 ····EXIT_ERR(helpMsg);
03e776 ··fileSpec = argv[1];
ba353d ··for (nextArg = 2; nextArg < argc; nextArg++) {
7715da ····if (argv[nextArg][0] == '-' || argv[nextArg][0] == '/') {
83cfff ······if (toupper(argv[nextArg][1]) == 'T') {
1f2647 ········sscanf(argv[nextArg]+2, "%d", &testLoops);
fbac1e ········if (testLoops < 0)
dc4adf ··········testLoops = 0;
4cb396 ······} else if (toupper(argv[nextArg][1]) == 'V')
1e568e ········verbose = 1;
7d3dfa ······else
e18d34 ········EXIT_ERR("Bad parameter (run with no parameters for help)\n");
6d6a79 ····} else {
a869b6 ······sscanf(argv[nextArg], "%x", &baseIoPort);
7c26c3 ······if (baseIoPort <= 0)
1e8d34 ········EXIT_ERR("Bad parameter (run with no parameters for help)\n");
b76fe7 ····}
31df1c ··}
41af5a
aa398a ··if (verbose) printf("Test parameters:\n");
190e23 ··if (verbose) printf(" ··BaseIOPort = %x\n", baseIoPort);
7ae35c ··if (verbose) printf(" ··outfile = \"%s\"\n", fileSpec);
d9d292 ··if (verbose) if (testLoops < 0) printf(" ··Quick scan only\n");
b06835 ··if (verbose) if (testLoops== 0) printf(" ··Full register scan\n");
b9142f ··if (verbose) if (testLoops > 0) printf(" ··%d DES tests\n", testLoops);
d9af5a
64078e ··fp = fopen(fileSpec, "w");
d9b291 ··if (fp == NULL)
a8eee0 ····EXIT_ERR("Error opening output file.\n");
7a575c ··fprintf(fp, "%% Auto-generated search system config file\n");
98932f ··fprintf(fp, "PORT=%x\n", baseIoPort);
baaf5a
253c81 ··SetBaseAddress(baseIoPort);
d96af7 ··fullScan = (testLoops < 0) ? 0 : 1;
91bad4 ··AutoconfigureScan(fp, fullScan, verbose);
aced24 ··fclose(fp);
faaf5a
368f0d ··for (i = 0; i < testLoops; i++) {
b2c130 ····printf("Doing DES test %d of %d.\n", i+1, testLoops);
62bb1a ····fp = fopen(fileSpec, "w+");
a541c7 ····if (fp == NULL)
00495c ······EXIT_ERR("Error reopening output file.\n");
864529 ····fgets(buffer, 190, fp); ·····················/* skip header line */
ef7769 ····fgets(buffer, 190, fp); ·······················/* skip port line */
5d2f5d ····fprintf(stderr, "*** Detailed test not implemented !!!\n");
b0b174 ····fclose(fp);
65df1c ··}
91c86a ··return (0);
57efe6 }
bdaf5a
e4af5a
8daf5a
e238e5 /*
65e484 · * ·Automatically figure out the configuration of the search system.
d66bac · * ·Thus function assumes that SetBaseAddress() has already been called.
dd495d · */
84fb6d void AutoconfigureScan(FILE *fp, int fullScan, int verbose) {
6e4007 ··int board, chip, chipCount, value;
67b920 ··long totalChips = 0;
65021b ··int chips[MAX_CHIPS_PER_BOARD];
2baf5a
dca3b4 ··if (verbose) printf("**** DOING AUTOCONFIGURE SCAN ****\n");
f9378a ··for (board = 0; board < MAX_BOARDS; board++) {
08dfb2 ····printf("CHECKING BOARD 0x%02X: ", board);
06442d ····fflush(stdout);
3680db ····chipCount = 0;
34211c ····for (chip = 0; chip < MAX_CHIPS_PER_BOARD; chip++) {
```

```
--1d3d  0008613f79280020003 Page 3 of autoconf.c

1e563d  ······/* TEST FIRST BYTE OF CIPHERTEXT Ø (REGISTER Øx28) */
79c8a7  ······value = rand() & ØxFF;
527510  ······if (QuickCheckRegister(board, chip, Øx28, value) == Ø ||
5accØc  ··········QuickCheckRegister(board, chip, Øx28, value^255) == Ø) {
78875d  ········chips[chip] = Ø;
8c328b  ········if (verbose) printf("\n ··BOARD Øx%Ø2X CHIP Øx%Ø2X: Not found.",
e9dØØ6  ················board, chip);
bØcfc7  ······} else {
41dd81  ········chips[chip] = 1;
dad3c2  ········chipCount++;
f287c8  ········if (verbose) printf("\n ··BOARD Øx%Ø2X CHIP Øx%Ø2X: FOUND",board,chip);
9Ø3982  ········if (fullScan) {
b2986b  ··········if (verbose) printf("\n ··CHIP Øx%Ø2X: Halting chip for test", chip);
61fde4  ··········SetRegister(board, chip, REG_PTXT_BYTE_MASK, ØxFF);
d17fbØ  ········}
8842cc  ······}
e96fe7  ····}
47f418  ····if (verbose) printf("\n");
347082  ····printf(" ·Found %4d chips total.\n", chipCount);
9Øaf5a
fdcb4a  ····/* DO DETAILED REGISTER SCAN IF REQUESTED */
e9eef1  ····if (fullScan && chipCount) {
45fØb8  ······totalChips = DoFullScan(fp, board, chips, verbose);
e46a79  ····} else {
Ødb79b  ······chipCount = Ø;
e2f9e5  ······for (chip = Ø; chip < MAX_CHIPS_PER_BOARD; chip++) {
77b833  ········if (chips[chip]) {
bØdØ98  ··········chipCount++;
2b3758  ··········totalChips++;
Ø65ead  ··········AddSearchUnits(fp, board, chip, -1, 1);
237fbØ  ········}
cd42cc  ······}
516fe7  ····}
f5df1c  ··}
21397d  ··if (verbose) printf("*** AUTOCONFIGURE SCAN COMPLETE ***\n");
Ø5c77d  ··printf("Found %ld chips total.\n", totalChips);
daefe6  }
f1af5a
c3af5a
66ddaa  int QuickCheckRegister(int board, int chip, int reg, int value) {
ff8Ø85  ··SetRegister(board, chip, reg, value);
953c2d  ··if (GetRegister(board, chip, reg) != value)
25943a  ····return (Ø);
3Ød4d1  ··return (1);
ffefe6  }
a1af5a
dcaf5a
8ccØ43  void AddSearchUnits(FILE *fp, int board, int chip, int unit, int isGood) {
5717eØ  ··int i;
98af5a
e9b3Ø6  ··if (unit < Ø) {
e154bØ  ····for (i = Ø; i < SEARCH_UNITS_PER_CHIP; i++)
265e78  ······AddSearchUnits(fp, board, chip, i, 1);
3349d8  ··} else {
1facØ9  ····fprintf(fp, "%s=Øx%Ø2X Øx%Ø2X Øx%Ø2X\n", isGood ? "UNIT" : "FAIL",
11229d  ············board, chip, unit);
5adf1c  ··}
98efe6  }
feaf5a
Øeaf5a
777b47  long DoFullScan(FILE *fp, int board, int* chips, int verbose) {
8eff49  ··int chip, reg, seed, value, i, j;
33160d  ··int units[24];
Øfb92Ø  ··long totalChips = Ø;
ccaf5a
24d7aØ  ··if (verbose) printf(" ··--- Register scan on board Øx%Ø2X ---\n", board);
deaf5a
623f7a  ··/* PICK A SEED & USE IT TWICE (ONCE WHEN SETTING & ONCE WHEN CHECKING */
a172a5  ··seed = (int)time(NULL);
f4af5a
bb775e  ··/*** SET REGISTERS ***/
86db8d  ··srand(seed);
```

```
--ff7e 00105deab4880020003 Page 4 of autoconf.c

bc3f58 ··for (chip = 0; chip < MAX_CHIPS_PER_BOARD; chip++) {
d05448 ····if (chips[chip] == 0)
325f6a ······continue;
8c9858 ····if (verbose) printf(" ··BOARD 0x%02X CHIP 0x%02X: Setting regs.\n",
d05be4 ············board, chip);
eab177 ····for (reg = 0; reg <= 0xFF; reg++) {
e5beec ······if ((reg >= 0x39 && reg < 0x40) || (reg > 0x40 && (reg & 7) == 7))
7ca511 ········continue;
cec87b ········value = rand() & 255;
9aca50 ········SetRegister(board, chip, reg, value);
7e6fe7 ····}
e2df1c ··}
ebaf5a
60d84d ··/*** CHECK REGISTERS ***/
57db8d ··srand(seed);
843f58 ··for (chip = 0; chip < MAX_CHIPS_PER_BOARD; chip++) {
1a5448 ····if (chips[chip] == 0)
7d5f6a ······continue;
d51775 ····for (i = 0; i < 24; i++)
d30734 ······units[i] = 1;
d4a885 ····if (verbose) printf(" ··BOARD 0x%02X CHIP 0x%02X: Checking...\n",
6c5be4 ············board, chip);
5ab177 ····for (reg = 0; reg <= 0xFF; reg++) {
00beec ······if ((reg >= 0x39 && reg < 0x40) || (reg > 0x40 && (reg & 7) == 7))
17a511 ········continue;
205f9e ······value = rand() & 255;
2da5d1 ······i = GetRegister(board, chip, reg);
3acb31 ······SetRegister(board, chip, reg, value ^ 255);
39b29a ······j = GetRegister(board, chip, reg);
c71a0d ······if (i != value || j != (value ^ 255)) {
cb5495 ········if (chips[chip])
b7125b ··········printf("\n *** BOARD 0x%02X, CHIP 0x%02X FAILED ***\n ·Details: ",
0ba711 ··················board, chip);
6d08d0 ········if (reg < 0x40)
056181 ··········chips[chip] = 0;
a31e5b ········else
d464e9 ··········units[(reg - 0x40)/8] = 0;
0e6b2c ········if (i != value || j != value)
15f088 ··········printf("\n ·Board 0x%02X Chip 0x%02X Reg 0x%02X bad:",
dd88d1 ············board, chip, reg);
6e3a74 ········if (i != value)
1e6ac7 ··········printf(" ·Got 0x%02X, not %02X.", i, value);
c746af ········if (j != (value ^ 255))
1547f8 ··········printf(" ·Got 0x%02X, not %02X.", j, value ^ 255);
d8cfc7 ······} else {
8bef4b ········if (verbose)
dfa942 ··········printf("\n ··Reg 0x%02X good (Read 0x%02X)", reg, value);
8742cc ······}
676fe7 ····}
b15448 ····if (chips[chip] == 0)
e1b2b4 ······printf("\n ·-- CHIP FAILED --\n");
bf83c8 ····else {
2ca741 ······for (i = 0; i < 24; i++)
2e958f ········AddSearchUnits(fp, board, chip, i, units[i]);
3688b7 ······totalChips++;
e46fe7 ····}
ccdf1c ··}
c00cbb ··return (totalChips);
47efe6 }
deaf5a
05af5a
```

```
--4dcb 001b8acf45a80020004 Page 1 of build.bat

eb1685 rem Sample build script (using Microsoft Visual C++)
89af5a
a05793 cl search.c keyblock.c chipio.c des.c
049d12 cl initsrch.c keyblock.c
818947 cl autoconf.c chipio.c
110940 cl testvec.c sim.c des.c
b8af5a
```

```
--27e3  000793f2b7c80020005 Page 1 of chipio.c

8d2d03  /********************************************************************************
a07c89  ·* ·chipio.c ··················································································*
87350a  ·* ············Search Engine Low-Level Hardware Interface Module ············*
be29eb  ·* ·····································································*
3309fc  ·* ···Written 1998 by Cryptography Research (http://www.cryptography.com) ···*
b28aaf  ·* ······and Paul Kocher for the Electronic Frontier Foundation (EFF). ······*
aecaeb  ·* ······Placed in the public domain by Cryptography Research and EFF. ······*
6c4992  ·* ·THIS IS UNSUPPORTED FREE SOFTWARE. USE AND DISTRIBUTE AT YOUR OWN RISK. ·*
6d29eb  ·* ·····································································*
95c755  ·* ·IMPORTANT: U.S. LAW MAY REGULATE THE USE AND/OR EXPORT OF THIS PROGRAM. ·*
f329eb  ·* ·····································································*
12489b  ·********************************************************************************
0e29eb  ·* ·····································································*
596eef  ·* ··REVISION HISTORY: ···························································*
6629eb  ·* ·····································································*
2f28d9  ·* ··Version 1.0: ·Initial release by Cryptography Research to EFF. ·········*
d929eb  ·* ·····································································*
3dd8c3  ·********************************************************************************/
49af5a
c8feb2  #include <stdio.h>
ab1465  #include <conio.h>
efbea3  #include <stdlib.h>
4e1519  #include "chipio.h"
24af5a
fc411c  static int CURRENT_BOARD ····= -1;
0ce1ec  static int CURRENT_CHIP ·····= -1;
b3ed93  static int CURRENT_PORT_CNFG = -1;
766981  static int IO_BASE_ADDRESS = 0x210;
29af5a
ec08d9  #define IO_PORTA_ADDRESS (IO_BASE_ADDRESS+0)
823310  #define IO_PORTB_ADDRESS (IO_BASE_ADDRESS+1)
40fc87  #define IO_PORTC_ADDRESS (IO_BASE_ADDRESS+2)
5f8cee  #define IO_CNFG_ADDRESS ·(IO_BASE_ADDRESS+3)
7d9f2f  #define CNFG_OUTPUT ··0x80
b52497  #define CNFG_INPUT ···0x82
5aaf5a
3c4951  #define CTRL_BASE ········0x1B ·····/* base value onto which others are XORed */
663867  #define CTRL_RST ·········0x20
e7dec1  #define CTRL_RDB ·········0x10
8a8735  #define CTRL_WRB ·········0x08
777b8e  #define CTRL_ALE ·········0x04
dd9757  #define CTRL_ADRSEL2 ····0x02 ······/* in documentation is also called CNTR1 */
e884f1  #define CTRL_ADRSEL1 ····0x01 ······/* in documentation is also called CNTR0 */
49af5a
8738e5  /*
4ce308  ·* ·DELAYS CAN BE ADDED TO DEAL WITH BUS LOADING/CAPACITANCE/ETC.
59495d  ·*/
aee62f  #define DELAY_FACTOR 100L
67ac33  #define DELAY_ADDRESS_SETTLE ··0*DELAY_FACTOR
e5126b  #define DELAY_DATA_SETTLE ·····0*DELAY_FACTOR
b62102  #define DELAY_RST_HOLD ········0*DELAY_FACTOR
3a8807  #define DELAY_RST_RECOVER ·····0*DELAY_FACTOR
c48418  #define DELAY_RDB_HOLD ········0*DELAY_FACTOR
c82d1d  #define DELAY_RDB_RECOVER ·····0*DELAY_FACTOR
439bf5  #define DELAY_WRB_HOLD ········0*DELAY_FACTOR
7532f0  #define DELAY_WRB_RECOVER ·····0*DELAY_FACTOR
97157a  #define DELAY_ALE_SETTLE ······0*DELAY_FACTOR
07d8af  #define DELAY_ADRSEL2_SETTLE ··0*DELAY_FACTOR
b9874e  #define DELAY_ADRSEL1_SETTLE ··0*DELAY_FACTOR
ecaf5a
d72e32  #define ioDelay(delayTime) ····{} ·················/* insert delay if rqd */
d5af5a
08af5a
fcc96f  #ifdef _MSC_VER
f438e5  /*
6a5039  ·* ·Microsoft C++ Direct I/O Functions
b0495d  ·*/
aa4429  static int inportb(int portNum) {
4599d0  ··unsigned char rval;
5a8d6b  ··unsigned short portNumShort = (unsigned short)portNum;
acaf5a
7948ba  ··_asm { mov dx,portNumShort }
```

```
--80c3 000e63846a280020005 Page 2 of chipio.c

05a1b8 ··_asm { in al,dx }
390458 ··_asm { mov rval, al }
5b76c9 ··return (rval);
aeefe6 }
09af5a
0f9285 static void outportb(int portNum, int val) {
3355b6 ··unsigned char valChar = (unsigned char)val;
0b8d6b ··unsigned short portNumShort = (unsigned short)portNum;
64af5a
ac005a ··_asm { mov dx, portNumShort }
6893dc ··_asm { mov al, valChar }
1affc5 ··_asm { out dx, al }
a5efe6 }
987454 #endif
e0af5a
f0af5a
04d629 static void ConfigureIO_Port(int inputOrOutput) {
37d170 ··outportb(IO_CNFG_ADDRESS, inputOrOutput);
a43113 ··CURRENT_PORT_CNFG = inputOrOutput;
7eaf5a
226c42 ··/* ·Warning:
022fbb ···*
38d9be ···* ·Changing the IO port state causes a tiny glitch to go out on the
61e818 ···* ·PC-DIO card. ·This is enough to ocasionally trigger the ALE, which
0f2e99 ···* ·causes read/write errors. ·To avoid this, always explicitly
dcbbe3 ···* ·re-select the chip after switching port directions.
8cf9a6 ···*/
96e4d4 ··CURRENT_CHIP = -1;
71efe6 }
dcaf5a
bbaf5a
334e16 static void SetAddress(int addressValue) {
b354f5 ··outportb(IO_PORTA_ADDRESS, addressValue);
85efe6 }
1caf5a
49af5a
2952e2 static void SetData(int dataValue) {
e81c12 ··outportb(IO_PORTB_ADDRESS, dataValue);
20efe6 }
6aaf5a
08af5a
1db8ab static int GetData(void) {
5899a6 ··return (inportb(IO_PORTB_ADDRESS));
67efe6 }
98af5a
ebaf5a
c6415d static void SetControl(int controlPortValue) {
186000 ··/*
9f0c74 ···* Possible optimization: Don't send value if already correct.
a1f9a6 ···*/
029b83 ··outportb(IO_PORTC_ADDRESS, controlPortValue);
b4efe6 }
83af5a
a8b6a1 static void selectBoard(int board) {
23c7b8 ··SetAddress(board);
92b28f ··SetControl(CTRL_BASE ^ CTRL_ADRSEL1); ···/* put board ID onto address pins */
bcec59 ··ioDelay(max(DELAY_ADDRESS_SETTLE, DELAY_ADRSEL1_SETTLE)); ·········/* wait */
2baf5a
485205 ··SetControl(CTRL_BASE ^ CTRL_ADRSEL1 ^ CTRL_ALE); ·········/* pull ALE high */
d81486 ··ioDelay(DELAY_ALE_SETTLE); ····································/* wait */
14af5a
797450 ··SetControl(CTRL_BASE ^ CTRL_ADRSEL1); ···················/* pull ALE back */
fc1486 ··ioDelay(DELAY_ALE_SETTLE); ····································/* wait */
36af5a
7c9619 ··SetControl(CTRL_BASE); ·······························/* ADRSEL1 done */
b11e79 ··ioDelay(DELAY_ADRSEL1_SETTLE);
39af5a
647dd7 ··CURRENT_BOARD = board;
14d3d3 ··CURRENT_CHIP ·= -1;
c4efe6 }
5baf5a
e6af5a
```

```
--bfd3 000429a03bf80020005 Page 3 of chipio.c

bc4c68 static void selectChip(int chip) {
72cb81 ··SetAddress(chip); ·····································/* select chip */
3ca47d ··ioDelay(DELAY_ADDRESS_SETTLE); ·························/* wait */
caaf5a
1ad034 ··SetControl(CTRL_BASE ^ CTRL_ALE); ····················/* pull ALE high */
fc1486 ··ioDelay(DELAY_ALE_SETTLE); ····························/* wait */
f4af5a
917415 ··SetControl(CTRL_BASE); ································/* pull ALE back */
9b1486 ··ioDelay(DELAY_ALE_SETTLE); ····························/* wait */
85af5a
fb6496 ··CURRENT_CHIP = chip;
4fefe6 }
d6af5a
8baf5a
d13072 void SetBaseAddress(int address) {
eee199 ··IO_BASE_ADDRESS = address;
21efe6 }
34af5a
a7af5a
1a38e5 /*
2c052d ·* ·RESET A SINGLE BOARD
8a775e ·*
810727 ·* ·This function resets an entire board. It is not optimized for speed.
c18338 ·* ·It is necessary to delay after calling this function until the board
30b84c ·* ·reset completes.
11495d ·*/
6aa7b4 int ResetBoard(int board) {
66af5a
65da81 ··/* Configure the IO card (doesn't matter if for data input or output) */
0488b6 ··ConfigureIO_Port(CNFG_INPUT); ····················/* configure the IO port */
3c750b ··ConfigureIO_Port(CNFG_OUTPUT); ···················/* configure the IO port */
0daf5a
23fbb6 ··selectBoard(board); ·····························/* select the board */
3daf5a
350fd9 ··SetControl(CTRL_BASE ^ CTRL_RST); ····················/* RESET THE BOARD */
fd9c65 ··ioDelay(DELAY_RST_HOLD); ··························/* wait */
c33f1e ··SetControl(CTRL_BASE); ·····························/* stop resetting */
63941c ··ioDelay(DELAY_RST_RECOVER); ····························/* wait */
09af5a
274a62 ··CURRENT_BOARD = -1; ·················/* reset this on next IO to be safe */
15e381 ··CURRENT_CHIP ·= -1; ·····························/* reset this to be safe */
56c86a ··return (0);
52efe6 }
65af5a
46af5a
dd070c void SetRegister(int board, int chip, int reg, int value) {
b637bb ··if (CURRENT_PORT_CNFG != CNFG_OUTPUT) ·····/* set IO data lines for output */
a221ba ····ConfigureIO_Port(CNFG_OUTPUT);
5277f8 ··if (CURRENT_BOARD != board) ················/* make sure board is selected */
5e72c3 ····selectBoard(board);
cad37b ··if (CURRENT_CHIP != chip) ···················/* make sure chip is selected */
ae038d ····selectChip(chip);
afaf5a
72a826 ··SetAddress(reg); ·····························/* select the right address */
2e3549 ··SetData(value); ·································/* output the data */
1d964b ··SetControl(CTRL_BASE ^ CTRL_ADRSEL2); ······················/* pull low */
a0fc7b ··ioDelay(max(max(DELAY_ADDRESS_SETTLE,DELAY_DATA_SETTLE), ··········/* wait */
8a43b6 ···········DELAY_ADRSEL2_SETTLE));
bb7938 ··SetControl(CTRL_BASE ^ CTRL_WRB ^ CTRL_ADRSEL2); ···········/* pull WRB low */
72a1d3 ··ioDelay(DELAY_WRB_HOLD); ································/* hold it */
623cfe ··SetControl(CTRL_BASE ^ CTRL_ADRSEL2); ················/* let WRB high again */
060257 ··ioDelay(DELAY_WRB_RECOVER); ····························/* wait */
3ab463 ··SetControl(CTRL_BASE); ·························/* let WRB high again */
ab684d ··ioDelay(DELAY_ADRSEL2_SETTLE); ····························/* wait */
c6efe6 }
dcaf5a
2890e3 int GetRegister(int board, int chip, int reg) {
7a07b4 ··int rval;
c6af5a
0af350 ··if (CURRENT_PORT_CNFG != CNFG_INPUT) ·······/* set IO data lines for input */
f6b51f ····ConfigureIO_Port(CNFG_INPUT);
4277f8 ··if (CURRENT_BOARD != board) ················/* make sure board is selected */
```

```
--7ae2 001a1c4541e80020005 Page 4 of chipio.c
5772c3 ····selectBoard(board);
c0d37b ··if (CURRENT_CHIP != chip) ··················/* make sure chip is selected */
2c038d ····selectChip(chip);
c8af5a
e2a826 ··SetAddress(reg); ································/* select the right address */
8f23d4 ··SetControl(CTRL_BASE ^ CTRL_ADRSEL2); ·················/* pull adrsel2 low */
2275ff ··ioDelay(max(DELAY_ADDRESS_SETTLE, DELAY_ADRSEL2_SETTLE)); ·········/* wait */
6fe7c0 ··SetControl(CTRL_BASE ^ CTRL_RDB ^ CTRL_ADRSEL2); ···········/* pull RDB low */
fa8603 ··ioDelay(DELAY_RDB_HOLD);
5ec058 ··rval = GetData();
bbc573 ··SetControl(CTRL_BASE ^ CTRL_ADRSEL2); ·····················/* let RDB high */
c22935 ··ioDelay(DELAY_RDB_RECOVER);
6dafb3 ··SetControl(CTRL_BASE); ······························/* let ADRSEL2 high */
9ae0ca ··ioDelay(DELAY_ADRSEL2_SETTLE);
25af5a
2b76c9 ··return (rval);
60efe6 }
17af5a
90b207 int CheckRegister(int board, int chip, int reg, int value) {
4717e0 ··int i;
25af5a
9a0cd1 ··i = GetRegister(board, chip, reg);
6a76cd ··if (i != value)
c2400d ····return (-1);
fac86a ··return (0);
15efe6 }
a1af5a
```

```
--5810  001b3720ca780020006 Page 1 of chipio.h

8d2d03  /************************************************************************
1a43fa  ·* chipio.h ··········································· ······················*
7c1e7f  ·* ························Header file for chipio.c ······················*
c629eb  ·* ···················································· ···················*
7709fc  ·* ···Written 1998 by Cryptography Research (http://www.cryptography.com) ···*
218aaf  ·* ······and Paul Kocher for the Electronic Frontier Foundation (EFF). ······*
e6caeb  ·* ······Placed in the public domain by Cryptography Research and EFF. ······*
8b4992  ·* ·THIS IS UNSUPPORTED FREE SOFTWARE. USE AND DISTRIBUTE AT YOUR OWN RISK. ·*
1329eb  ·* ····················································· ···················*
3fc755  ·* ·IMPORTANT: U.S. LAW MAY REGULATE THE USE AND/OR EXPORT OF THIS PROGRAM. ·*
2329eb  ·* ····················································· ···················*
2d489b  ·* ************************************************************************
3229eb  ·* ····················································· ···················*
046eef  ·* ··REVISION HISTORY: ································· ···················*
2b29eb  ·* ····················································· ···················*
ad28d9  ·* ··Version 1.0: ·Initial release by Cryptography Research to EFF. ··········*
ba29eb  ·* ····················································· ···················*
08d8c3  ·* ************************************************************************/
a7af5a
f51920  #ifndef __CHIPIO_H
e6d6b9  #define __CHIPIO_H
d8af5a
a32deb  #define SEARCH_UNITS_PER_CHIP 24
b9af5a
96c928  #define REG_PTXT_VECTOR ·····(0x00)
5821cd  #define REG_PTXT_XOR_MASK ···(0x20)
9db3c1  #define REG_CIPHERTEXT0 ·····(0x28)
211752  #define REG_CIPHERTEXT1 ·····(0x30)
25db81  #define REG_PTXT_BYTE_MASK ··(0x38)
2b107b  #define REG_SEARCHINFO ······(0x3F)
6db9aa  #define REG_SEARCH_KEY(x) ···(0x40 + 8*(x))
c4701d  #define REG_SEARCH_STATUS(x) (0x47+8*(x))
69af5a
4bea1c  void SetBaseAddress(int address);
6bbdbf  int ResetBoard(int board);
b4274a  void SetRegister(int board, int chip, int reg, int value);
ba59e9  int GetRegister(int board, int chip, int reg);
6ea7fa  int CheckRegister(int board, int chip, int reg, int value);
f8af5a
147454  #endif
b3af5a
```

```
--176a 0002909cb8180020007 Page 1 of des.c
8d2d03 /*******************************************************************************
9240d0 * des.c                                                                        *
a8bcaa *                    Software Model of ASIC DES Implementation                 *
9b29eb *                                                                              *
6ed9a2 *  Written 1995-8 by Cryptography Research (http://www.cryptography.com)   *
b2c441 *   Original version by Paul Kocher. Placed in the public domain in 1998.    *
d34992 *  THIS IS UNSUPPORTED FREE SOFTWARE. USE AND DISTRIBUTE AT YOUR OWN RISK.   *
4829eb *                                                                              *
25c755 *  IMPORTANT: U.S. LAW MAY REGULATE THE USE AND/OR EXPORT OF THIS PROGRAM.   *
df29eb *                                                                              *
ce489b *******************************************************************************
8229eb *                                                                              *
6015cb *  IMPLEMENTATION NOTES:                                                        *
2829eb *                                                                              *
217602 *  This DES implementation adheres to the FIPS PUB 46 spec and produces     *
a5ad64 *  standard output. The internal operation of the algorithm is slightly      *
bd2a2b *  different from FIPS 46.  For example, bit orderings are reversed          *
fd1be6 *  (the right-hand bit is now labelled as bit 0), the S tables have         *
bab9c7 *  rearranged to simplify implementation, and several permutations have      *
e3c21e *  been inverted. For simplicity and to assist with testing of hardware     *
c52d8b *  implementations, code size and performance optimizations are omitted.     *
5d29eb *                                                                              *
3c489b *******************************************************************************
1929eb *                                                                              *
e76eef *  REVISION HISTORY:                                                            *
d229eb *                                                                              *
ccc443 *  Version 1.0:  Initial release  -- PCK.                                    *
7bb74c *  Version 1.1:  Altered DecryptDES exchanges to match EncryptDES. -- PCK   *
425c27 *  Version 1.2:  Minor edits and beautifications.  -- PCK                     *
03d930 *  Version 1.3:  Changes and edits for EFF DES Cracker project.             *
ad29eb *                                                                              *
83d8c3 *******************************************************************************/
e8af5a
bffeb2 #include <stdio.h>
45bea3 #include <stdlib.h>
2e324c #include <string.h>
0a2bac #include "des.h"
32af5a
557461 static void ComputeRoundKey(bool roundKey[56], bool key[56]);
2884a3 static void RotateRoundKeyLeft(bool roundKey[56]);
9bccfa static void RotateRoundKeyRight(bool roundKey[56]);
611504 static void ComputeIP(bool L[32], bool R[32], bool inBlk[64]);
3707da static void ComputeFP(bool outBlk[64], bool L[32], bool R[32]);
46017b static void ComputeF(bool fout[32], bool R[32], bool roundKey[56]);
3694fe static void ComputeP(bool output[32], bool input[32]);
ab7fae static void ComputeS_Lookup(int k, bool output[4], bool input[6]);
6aabe7 static void ComputePC2(bool subkey[48], bool roundKey[56]);
a3fd9c static void ComputeExpansionE(bool expandedBlock[48], bool R[32]);
ba2f30 static void DumpBin(char *str, bool *b, int bits);
8c43bc static void Exchange_L_and_R(bool L[32], bool R[32]);
87af5a
27a0e5 static int EnableDumpBin = 0;
02af5a
bdaf5a
ceaf5a
964d6c /*******************************************************************************/
dec68f /*                                                                            */
933c1a /*                               DES TABLES                                   */
46c68f /*                                                                            */
094d6c /*******************************************************************************/
3daf5a
b1af5a
7538e5 /*
f6556a *  IP: Output bit table_DES_IP[i] equals input bit i.
a3495d */
51c166 static int table_DES_IP[64] = {
4f9d69    39,  7, 47, 15, 55, 23, 63, 31,
b9c827    38,  6, 46, 14, 54, 22, 62, 30,
f038ae    37,  5, 45, 13, 53, 21, 61, 29,
5c6de0    36,  4, 44, 12, 52, 20, 60, 28,
86b247    35,  3, 43, 11, 51, 19, 59, 27,
29e709    34,  2, 42, 10, 50, 18, 58, 26,
```

```
--e1e6 00020a1a00d80020007 Page 2 of des.c

a5829e ····33, ·1, 41, ·9, 49, 17, 57, 25,
c511ff ····32, ·0, 40, ·8, 48, 16, 56, 24
b482f7 };
a1af5a
0caf5a
6738e5 /*
b248ca ·* ·FP: Output bit table_DES_FP[i] equals input bit i.
11495d ·*/
eadd2a static int table_DES_FP[64] = {
225b71 ····57, 49, 41, 33, 25, 17, ·9, ·1,
d98cd9 ····59, 51, 43, 35, 27, 19, 11, ·3,
e79996 ····61, 53, 45, 37, 29, 21, 13, ·5,
6eb571 ····63, 55, 47, 39, 31, 23, 15, ·7,
c50e3f ····56, 48, 40, 32, 24, 16, ·8, ·0,
91d997 ····58, 50, 42, 34, 26, 18, 10, ·2,
8dccd8 ····60, 52, 44, 36, 28, 20, 12, ·4,
514da9 ····62, 54, 46, 38, 30, 22, 14, ·6
6f82f7 };
47af5a
20af5a
8038e5 /*
3cda05 ·* ·PC1: Permutation choice 1, used to pre-process the key
d4495d ·*/
c00c38 static int table_DES_PC1[56] = {
8bb89e ····27, 19, 11, 31, 39, 47, 55,
8728e4 ····26, 18, 10, 30, 38, 46, 54,
9c8d2c ····25, 17, ·9, 29, 37, 45, 53,
e21d56 ····24, 16, ·8, 28, 36, 44, 52,
37bf91 ····23, 15, ·7, ·3, 35, 43, 51,
a62feb ····22, 14, ·6, ·2, 34, 42, 50,
5c91e6 ····21, 13, ·5, ·1, 33, 41, 49,
fad02f ····20, 12, ·4, ·0, 32, 40, 48
b082f7 };
55af5a
dfaf5a
8438e5 /*
45f37a ·* ·PC2: Map 56-bit round key to a 48-bit subkey
0a495d ·*/
047fcf static int table_DES_PC2[48] = {
498889 ····24, 27, 20, ·6, 14, 10, ·3, 22,
2e30a5 ·····0, 17, ·7, 12, ·8, 23, 11, ·5,
c23fa5 ····16, 26, ·1, ·9, 19, 25, ·4, 15,
3ce272 ····54, 43, 36, 29, 49, 40, 48, 30,
646356 ····52, 44, 37, 33, 46, 35, 50, 41,
207786 ····28, 53, 51, 55, 32, 45, 39, 42
aa82f7 };
ffaf5a
d1af5a
d838e5 /*
1cdb31 ·* ·E: Expand 32-bit R to 48 bits.
76495d ·*/
ac6a87 static int table_DES_E[48] = {
fae6fb ····31, ·0, ·1, ·2, ·3, ·4, ·3, ·4,
f62634 ·····5, ·6, ·7, ·8, ·7, ·8, ·9, 10,
95d06b ····11, 12, 11, 12, 13, 14, 15, 16,
4b7fa0 ····15, 16, 17, 18, 19, 20, 19, 20,
cf4d0d ····21, 22, 23, 24, 23, 24, 25, 26,
d09708 ····27, 28, 27, 28, 29, 30, 31, ·0
4082f7 };
4faf5a
eeaf5a
ae38e5 /*
bcc34a ·* ·P: Permutation of S table outputs
b7495d ·*/
365137 static int table_DES_P[32] = {
15f612 ····11, 17, ·5, 27, 25, 10, 20, ·0,
d0b9f8 ····13, 21, ·3, 28, 29, ·7, 18, 24,
18cde3 ····31, 22, 12, ·6, 26, ·2, 16, ·8,
9b60a7 ····14, 30, ·4, 19, ·1, ·9, 15, 23
4482f7 };
ceaf5a
20af5a
```

```
--f1a0 000f7378b1880020007 Page 3 of des.c

bc38e5  /*
8e6f34  ·* ·S Tables: Introduce nonlinearity and avalanche
a3495d  ·*/
a11e19  static int table_DES_S[8][64] = {
3cd69a  ····/* table S[0] */
e4846d  ········{ ··13, ·1, ·2, 15, ·8, 13, ·4, ·8, ·6, 10, 15, ·3, 11, ·7, ·1, ·4,
c965af  ··········10, 12, ·9, ·5, ·3, ·6, 14, 11, ·5, ·0, ·0, 14, 12, ·9, ·7, ·2,
95d5b0  ···········7, ·2, 11, ·1, ·4, 14, ·1, ·7, ·9, ·4, 12, 10, 14, ·8, ·2, 13,
8c3ee1  ···········0, 15, ·6, 12, 10, ·9, 13, ·0, 15, ·3, ·3, ·5, ·5, ·6, ·8, 11 ·},
11d2b1  ····/* table S[1] */
d54b6a  ········{ ··4, 13, 11, ·0, ·2, 11, 14, ·7, 15, ·4, ·0, ·9, ·8, ·1, 13, 10,
98df4d  ···········3, 14, 12, ·3, ·9, ·5, ·7, 12, ·5, ·2, 10, 15, ·6, ·8, ·1, ·6,
35f575  ···········1, ·6, ·4, 11, 11, 13, ·8, 12, ·1, ·3, ·4, ·7, 10, 14, ·7,
7b6234  ··········10, ·9, 15, ·5, ·6, ·0, ·8, 15, ·0, 14, ·5, ·2, ·9, ·3, ·2, 12 ·},
d2decc  ····/* table S[2] */
1ef108  ········{ ··12, 10, ·1, 15, 10, ·4, 15, ·2, ·9, ·7, ·2, 12, ·6, ·9, ·8, ·5,
9bd582  ···········0, ·6, 13, ·1, ·3, 13, ·4, 14, 14, ·0, ·7, 11, ·5, ·3, 11, ·8,
7f0bbf  ···········9, ·4, 14, ·3, 15, ·2, ·5, 12, ·2, ·9, ·8, ·5, 12, 15, ·3, 10,
9a7505  ···········7, 11, ·0, 14, ·4, ·1, 10, ·7, ·1, ·6, 13, ·0, 11, ·8, ·6, 13 ·},
68dae7  ····/* table S[3] */
305c4d  ········{ ··2, 14, 12, 11, ·4, ·2, ·1, 12, ·7, ·4, 10, ·7, 11, 13, ·6, ·1,
d80156  ···········8, ·5, ·5, ·0, ·3, 15, 15, 10, 13, ·3, ·0, ·9, 14, ·8, ·9, ·6,
37f5dc  ···········4, 11, ·2, ·8, ·1, 12, 11, ·7, 10, ·1, 13, 14, ·7, ·2, ·8, 13,
ded332  ··········15, ·6, ·9, 15, 12, ·0, ·5, ·9, ·6, 10, ·3, ·4, ·0, ·5, 14, ·3 ·},
5fc636  ····/* table S[4] */
ef4850  ········{ ··7, 13, 13, ·8, 14, 11, ·3, ·5, ·0, ·6, ·6, 15, ·9, ·0, 10, ·3,
14f1a6  ···········1, ·4, ·2, ·7, ·8, ·2, ·5, 12, 11, ·1, 12, 10, ·4, 14, 15, ·9,
45f43f  ··········10, ·3, ·6, 15, ·9, ·0, ·0, ·6, 12, 10, 11, ·1, ·7, 13, 13, ·8,
9ed830  ··········15, ·9, ·1, ·4, ·3, ·5, 14, 11, ·5, 12, ·2, ·7, ·8, ·2, ·4, 14 ·},
49c21d  ····/* table S[5] */
b1ea9b  ········{ ··10, 13, ·0, ·7, ·9, ·0, 14, ·9, ·6, ·3, ·3, ·4, 15, ·6, ·5, 10,
03bd2c  ···········1, ·2, 13, ·8, 12, ·5, ·7, 14, 11, 12, ·4, 11, ·2, 15, ·8, ·1,
bed567  ··········13, ·1, ·6, 10, ·4, 13, ·9, ·0, ·8, ·6, 15, ·9, ·3, ·8, ·0, ·7,
3b8261  ··········11, ·4, ·1, 15, ·2, 14, 12, ·3, ·5, 11, 10, ·5, 14, ·2, ·7, 12 ·},
c3ce60  ····/* table S[6] */
69a636  ········{ ··15, ·3, ·1, 13, ·8, ·4, 14, ·7, ·6, 15, 11, ·2, ·3, ·8, ·4, 14,
38ac1c  ···········9, 12, ·7, ·0, ·2, ·1, 13, 10, 12, ·6, ·0, ·9, ·5, 11, 10, ·5,
6b7311  ···········0, 13, 14, ·8, ·7, 10, 11, ·1, 10, ·3, ·4, 15, 13, ·4, ·1, ·2,
a8b1aa  ···········5, 11, ·8, ·6, 12, ·7, ·6, 12, ·9, ·0, ·3, ·5, ·2, 14, 15, ·9 ·},
ceca4b  ····/* table S[7] */
68cf66  ········{ ··14, ·0, ·4, 15, 13, ·7, ·1, ·4, ·2, 14, 15, ·2, 11, 13, ·8, ·1,
7baacb  ···········3, 10, 10, ·6, ·6, 12, 12, 11, ·5, ·9, ·9, ·5, ·0, ·3, ·7, ·8,
4d2f45  ···········4, 15, ·1, 12, 14, ·8, ·8, ·2, 13, ·4, ·6, ·9, ·2, ·1, 11, ·7,
3f2777  ··········15, ·5, 12, 11, ·9, ·3, ·7, 14, ·3, 10, 10, ·0, ·5, ·6, ·0, 13 ·}
1882f7  };
34af5a
55af5a
e6af5a
fcaf5a
d34d6c  /*****************************************************************/
dec68f  /* ..............................................................*/
fbcabf  /* ...............................DES CODE ......................*/
ffc68f  /* ..............................................................*/
474d6c  /*****************************************************************/
8eaf5a
5baf5a
2a38e5  /*
0fb080  ·* ·EncryptDES: Encrypt a block using DES. Set verbose for debugging info.
4d770b  ·* ·(This loop does both loops on the "DES Encryption" page of the flowchart.)
22495d  ·*/
da5620  void EncryptDES(bool key[56], bool outBlk[64], bool inBlk[64], int verbose) {
062b1c  ··int i,round;
909aa1  ··bool R[32], L[32], fout[32];
6fbfaf  ··bool roundKey[56];
d8af5a
9b1294  ··EnableDumpBin = verbose; ··················/* set debugging on/off flag */
3ccb2a  ··DumpBin("input(left)", inBlk+32, 32);
728fb2  ··DumpBin("input(right)", inBlk, 32);
490a8e  ··DumpBin("raw key(left )", key+28, 28);
d75585  ··DumpBin("raw key(right)", key, 28);
ffaf5a
f7c1be  ··/* Compute the first roundkey by performing PC1 */
```

```
--1527 0005 3c1ed1980020007 Page 4 of des.c
47b264  ··ComputeRoundKey(roundKey, key);
53af5a
0295d4  ··DumpBin("roundKey(L)", roundKey+28, 28);
840a5f  ··DumpBin("roundKey(R)", roundKey, 28);
48af5a
e81340  ··/* Compute the initial permutation and divide the result into L and R */
1ad1a8  ··ComputeIP(L,R,inBlk);
aeaf5a
7777ba  ··DumpBin("after IP(L)", L, 32);
cc7699  ··DumpBin("after IP(R)", R, 32);
baaf5a
1ff437  ··for (round = 0; round < 16; round++) {
4421bf  ····if (verbose)
a491a0  ······printf("------------- BEGIN ENCRYPT ROUND %d ------------\n", round);
838034  ····DumpBin("round start(L)", L, 32);
628117  ····DumpBin("round start(R)", R, 32);
d2af5a
8b7fc3  ····/* Rotate roundKey halves left once or twice (depending on round) */
aec8ba  ····RotateRoundKeyLeft(roundKey);
9b1467  ····if (round != 0 && round != 1 && round != 8 && round != 15)
1950e7  ······RotateRoundKeyLeft(roundKey);
003cd7  ····DumpBin("roundKey(L)", roundKey+28, 28);
bb1bd4  ····DumpBin("roundKey(R)", roundKey, 28);
82af5a
e0033b  ····/* Compute f(R, roundKey) and exclusive-OR onto the value in L */
14d969  ····ComputeF(fout, R, roundKey);
5c54e7  ····DumpBin("f(R,key)", fout, 32);
4a4739  ····for (i = 0; i < 32; i++)
2ba9e6  ······L[i] ^= fout[i];
a5a5ab  ····DumpBin("L^f(R,key)", L, 32);
56af5a
7a68b4  ····Exchange_L_and_R(L,R);
3aaf5a
a3a140  ····DumpBin("round end(L)", L, 32);
fca063  ····DumpBin("round end(R)", R, 32);
4b21bf  ····if (verbose)
a24514  ······printf("-------------- END ROUND %d -------------\n", round);
66df1c  ··}
d9af5a
5e8e68  ··Exchange_L_and_R(L,R);
87af5a
71370b  ··/* Combine L and R then compute the final permutation */
77cf94  ··ComputeFP(outBlk,L,R);
468b91  ··DumpBin("FP out( left)", outBlk+32, 32);
cbf675  ··DumpBin("FP out(right)", outBlk, 32);
b0efe6  }
43af5a
15af5a
01af5a
e038e5  /*
1e9b68  ·* ·DecryptDES: Decrypt a block using DES. Set verbose for debugging info.
6fa5c7  ·* ·(This loop does both loops on the "DES Decryption" page of the flowchart.)
1a495d  ·*/
b66de8  void DecryptDES(bool key[56], bool outBlk[64], bool inBlk[64], int verbose) {
b82b1c  ··int i,round;
299aa1  ··bool R[32], L[32], fout[32];
f9bfaf  ··bool roundKey[56];
24af5a
5a1294  ··EnableDumpBin = verbose; ···················/* set debugging on/off flag */
96cb2a  ··DumpBin("input(left)", inBlk+32, 32);
4b8fb2  ··DumpBin("input(right)", inBlk, 32);
f60a8e  ··DumpBin("raw key(left )", key+28, 28);
395585  ··DumpBin("raw key(right)", key, 28);
82af5a
8cc1be  ··/* Compute the first roundkey by performing PC1 */
a4b264  ··ComputeRoundKey(roundKey, key);
dcaf5a
5f95d4  ··DumpBin("roundKey(L)", roundKey+28, 28);
300a5f  ··DumpBin("roundKey(R)", roundKey, 28);
33af5a
291340  ··/* Compute the initial permutation and divide the result into L and R */
53d1a8  ··ComputeIP(L,R,inBlk);
```

```
--1f01 0005e2de84280020007 Page 5 of des.c

e0af5a
7177ba  ··DumpBin("after IP(L)", L, 32);
3d7699  ··DumpBin("after IP(R)", R, 32);
96af5a
3cf437  ··for (round = 0; round < 16; round++) {
3d21bf  ····if (verbose)
ff2cb4  ······printf("-------------- BEGIN DECRYPT ROUND %d ------------\n", round);
528034  ····DumpBin("round start(L)", L, 32);
e78117  ····DumpBin("round start(R)", R, 32);
22af5a
d3033b  ····/* Compute f(R, roundKey) and exclusive-OR onto the value in L */
06d969  ····ComputeF(fout, R, roundKey);
dc54e7  ····DumpBin("f(R,key)", fout, 32);
b54739  ····for (i = 0; i < 32; i++)
eca9e6  ······L[i] ^= fout[i];
dba5ab  ····DumpBin("L^f(R,key)", L, 32);
50af5a
8e68b4  ····Exchange_L_and_R(L,R);
e9af5a
2dc90d  ····/* Rotate roundKey halves right once or twice (depending on round) */
3210bc  ····DumpBin("roundKey(L)", roundKey+28, 28); ······/* show keys before shift */
be1bd4  ····DumpBin("roundKey(R)", roundKey, 28);
3df5db  ····RotateRoundKeyRight(roundKey);
6711ff  ····if (round != 0 && round != 7 && round != 14 && round != 15)
f97c23  ······RotateRoundKeyRight(roundKey);
02af5a
cea140  ····DumpBin("round end(L)", L, 32);
7ba063  ····DumpBin("round end(R)", R, 32);
4321bf  ····if (verbose)
f04514  ······printf("-------------- END ROUND %d --------------\n", round);
3fdf1c  ··}
61af5a
738e68  ··Exchange_L_and_R(L,R);
71af5a
b9370b  ··/* Combine L and R then compute the final permutation */
b9cf94  ··ComputeFP(outBlk,L,R);
b08b91  ··DumpBin("FP out( left)", outBlk+32, 32);
c1f675  ··DumpBin("FP out(right)", outBlk, 32);
7cefe6  }
59af5a
9aaf5a
1daf5a
a938e5  /*
bd8d8b  ·* ·ComputeRoundKey: Compute PC1 on the key and store the result in roundKey
6c495d  ·*/
94988e  static void ComputeRoundKey(bool roundKey[56], bool key[56]) {
fe17e0  ··int i;
afaf5a
be815b  ··for (i = 0; i < 56; i++)
46d64b  ····roundKey[table_DES_PC1[i]] = key[i];
f3efe6  }
1aaf5a
4caf5a
b3af5a
af38e5  /*
3555cb  ·* ·RotateRoundKeyLeft: Rotate each of the halves of roundKey left one bit
42495d  ·*/
af7d60  static void RotateRoundKeyLeft(bool roundKey[56]) {
e4483e  ··bool temp1, temp2;
c717e0  ··int i;
88af5a
9bf689  ··temp1 = roundKey[27];
3efe1b  ··temp2 = roundKey[55];
bb300b  ··for (i = 27; i >= 1; i--) {
43575a  ····roundKey[i] = roundKey[i-1];
b53242  ····roundKey[i+28] = roundKey[i+28-1];
7adf1c  ··}
4d7b9f  ··roundKey[ 0] = temp1;
e0cf9d  ··roundKey[28] = temp2;
a8efe6  }
f3af5a
5eaf5a
```

```
--1bb7 0002e9cf80d80020007 Page 6 of des.c

e0af5a
d338e5  /*
7dc6ad   * ·RotateRoundKeyRight: Rotate each of the halves of roundKey right one bit
f9495d   */
1ab26c  static void RotateRoundKeyRight(bool roundKey[56]) {
7d483e   ·bool temp1, temp2;
1517e0   ·int i;
c0af5a
7a5025   ·temp1 = roundKey[0];
9c4548   ·temp2 = roundKey[28];
5fe568   ·for (i = 0; i < 27; i++) {
196cc2   ···roundKey[i] = roundKey[i+1];
7809da   ···roundKey[i+28] = roundKey[i+28+1];
ecdf1c   ·}
dfa88d   ·roundKey[27] = temp1;
945d11   ·roundKey[55] = temp2;
e3efe6  }
2caf5a
41af5a
38af5a
7738e5  /*
a32903   * ·ComputeIP: Compute the initial permutation and split into L and R halves.
df495d   */
23ac44  static void ComputeIP(bool L[32], bool R[32], bool inBlk[64]) {
686085   ·bool output[64];
d417e0   ·int i;
a3af5a
77aeaf   ·/* Permute
07f9a6   ··*/
4e6406   ·for (i = 63; i >= 0; i--)
adc750   ···output[table_DES_IP[i]] = inBlk[i];
95af5a
500318   ·/* Split into R and L. ·Bits 63..32 go in L, bits 31..0 go in R.
70f9a6   ··*/
daba85   ·for (i = 63; i >= 0; i--) {
d40368   ···if (i >= 32)
3ef2b8   ·····L[i-32] = output[i];
60842c   ···else
b070b5   ·····R[i] = output[i];
86df1c   ·}
f5efe6  }
4baf5a
70af5a
2aaf5a
3738e5  /*
8e4ffe   * ·ComputeFP: Combine the L and R halves and do the final permutation.
51495d   */
d193a5  static void ComputeFP(bool outBlk[64], bool L[32], bool R[32]) {
f342e9   ·bool input[64];
5c17e0   ·int i;
08af5a
2c6c41   ·/* Combine L and R into input[64]
45f9a6   ··*/
916406   ·for (i = 63; i >= 0; i--)
878397   ···input[i] = (i >= 32) ? L[i - 32] : R[i];
8caf5a
d3aeaf   ·/* Permute
98f9a6   ··*/
1c6406   ·for (i = 63; i >= 0; i--)
85e116   ···outBlk[table_DES_FP[i]] = input[i];
bcefe6  }
18af5a
beaf5a
a8af5a
5e38e5  /*
90810f   * ·ComputeF: Compute the DES f function and store the result in fout.
01495d   */
0c2720  static void ComputeF(bool fout[32], bool R[32], bool roundKey[56]) {
a3f6a2   ·bool expandedBlock[48], subkey[48], sout[32];
adbbe6   ·int i,k;
d9af5a
2e1a04   ·/* Expand R into 48 bits using the E expansion */
```

```
--92d2 000e8f1171f80020007 Page 7 of des.c
fb99d7 ··ComputeExpansionE(expandedBlock, R);
e5f0ba ··DumpBin("expanded E", expandedBlock, 48);
efaf5a
7693ff ··/* Convert the roundKey into the subkey using PC2 */
4a7840 ··ComputePC2(subkey, roundKey);
21d717 ··DumpBin("subkey", subkey, 48);
39af5a
e5154c ··/* XOR the subkey onto the expanded block */
bffcab ··for (i = 0; i < 48; i++)
2d6512 ····expandedBlock[i] ^= subkey[i];
fbaf5a
340740 ··/* Divide expandedBlock into 6-bit chunks and do S table lookups */
0225c6 ··for (k = 0; k < 8; k++)
e985c7 ····ComputeS_Lookup(k, sout+4*k, expandedBlock+6*k);
67af5a
dbfd35 ··/* To complete the f() calculation, do permutation P on the S table output */
6d2d52 ··ComputeP(fout, sout);
b3efe6 }
0caf5a
76af5a
d3af5a
5538e5 /*
eb913f ·* ·ComputeP: Compute the P permutation on the S table outputs.
52495d ·*/
61f410 static void ComputeP(bool output[32], bool input[32]) {
3b17e0 ··int i;
20af5a
b5339a ··for (i = 0; i < 32; i++)
3f7688 ····output[table_DES_P[i]] = input[i];
b1efe6 }
10af5a
94af5a
70af5a
5b38e5 /*
8a859b ·* ·Look up a 6-bit input in S table k and store the result as a 4-bit output.
ad495d ·*/
49a67e static void ComputeS_Lookup(int k, bool output[4], bool input[6]) {
9bf3da ··int inputValue, outputValue;
a5af5a
ad1a9e ··/* Convert the input bits into an integer */
6afccb ··inputValue = input[0] + 2*input[1] + 4*input[2] + 8*input[3] +
f18c1a ··········16*input[4] + 32*input[5];
3faf5a
164a3e ··/* Do the S table lookup */
34b706 ··outputValue = table_DES_S[k][inputValue];
4baf5a
0a8aed ··/* Convert the result into binary form */
0c9a60 ··output[0] = (outputValue & 1) ? 1 : 0;
3a6aec ··output[1] = (outputValue & 2) ? 1 : 0;
d9f487 ··output[2] = (outputValue & 4) ? 1 : 0;
708c7f ··output[3] = (outputValue & 8) ? 1 : 0;
95efe6 }
dfaf5a
78af5a
d2af5a
0338e5 /*
8181cc ·* ·ComputePC2: Map a 56-bit round key onto a 48-bit subkey
2a495d ·*/
22796f static void ComputePC2(bool subkey[48], bool roundKey[56]) {
2817e0 ··int i;
d0af5a
17fcab ··for (i = 0; i < 48; i++)
bec8bc ····subkey[i] = roundKey[table_DES_PC2[i]];
16efe6 }
67af5a
c5af5a
43af5a
2838e5 /*
20459d ·* ·ComputeExpansionE: Compute the E expansion to prepare to use S tables.
b8495d ·*/
4bb46d static void ComputeExpansionE(bool expandedBlock[48], bool R[32]) {
e817e0 ··int i;
```

```
--cf4e 001f263015b80020007 Page 8 of des.c

e0af5a
f3fcab ··for (i = 0; i < 48; i++)
7db971 ····expandedBlock[i] = R[table_DES_E[i]];
0cefe6 }
e0af5a
a1af5a
d8af5a
2e38e5 /*
10f923 ·* ·Exchange_L_and_R: ·Swap L and R
08495d ·*/
c895d1 static void Exchange_L_and_R(bool L[32], bool R[32]) {
5a17e0 ··int i;
aaaf5a
36339a ··for (i = 0; i < 32; i++)
b225db ····L[i] ^= R[i] ^= L[i] ^= R[i]; ················/* exchanges L[i] and R[i] */
f8efe6 }
3eaf5a
84af5a
60af5a
0038e5 /*
489231 ·* ·DumpBin: Display intermediate values if emableDumpBin is set.
41495d ·*/
1ddbd9 static void DumpBin(char *str, bool *b, int bits) {
6e17e0 ··int i;
56af5a
648af7 ··if ((bits % 4)!=0 || bits>48) {
6db2e5 ····printf("Bad call to DumpBin (bits > 48 or bit len not a multiple of 4\n");
5c646c ····exit(1);
42df1c ··}
8eaf5a
413332 ··if (EnableDumpBin) {
3ff079 ····for (i = strlen(str); i < 14; i++)
b7c8c3 ······printf(" ");
655fc3 ····printf("%s: ", str);
98eac8 ····for (i = bits-1; i >= 0; i--)
d2de5b ······printf("%d", b[i]);
8a3177 ····printf(" ");
de821f ····for (i = bits; i < 48; i++)
4ec8c3 ······printf(" ");
6b6b57 ····printf("(");
a705d7 ····for (i = bits-4; i >= 0; i-=4)
0bf78c ······printf("%X", b[i]+2*b[i+1]+4*b[i+2]+8*b[i+3]);
2efa6f ····printf(")\n");
04df1c ··}
01efe6 }
f2af5a
```

```
--5f71 001ba22687980020008 Page 1 of des.h
8d2d03 /*************************************************************************
cb1a06 ·* des.h ···············································*
0f4b62 ·* ························Header file for des.c ·················*
5c29eb ·* ···································································*
57d9a2 ·* ··Written 1995-8 by Cryptography Research (http://www.cryptography.com) ··*
e9c441 ·* ··Original version by Paul Kocher. Placed in the public domain in 1998. ··*
f64992 ·* ·THIS IS UNSUPPORTED FREE SOFTWARE. USE AND DISTRIBUTE AT YOUR OWN RISK. ·*
4329eb ·* ···································································*
ddc755 ·* ·IMPORTANT: U.S. LAW MAY REGULATE THE USE AND/OR EXPORT OF THIS PROGRAM. ·*
3e29eb ·* ···································································*
dd489b ·*************************************************************************
8029eb ·* ···································································*
246eef ·* ··REVISION HISTORY: ···············································*
8b29eb ·* ···································································*
00c443 ·* ··Version 1.0: ·Initial release ·-- PCK. ··························*
87f57b ·* ··Version 1.1: ·Changes and edits for EFF DES Cracker project. ···········*
6029eb ·* ···································································*
ffd8c3 ·**************************************************************************/
45af5a
9da019 #ifndef __DES_H
828311 #define __DES_H
a3af5a
c608c5 typedef char bool;
909629 void EncryptDES(bool key[56], bool outBlk[64], bool inBlk[64], int verbose);
8e8db3 void DecryptDES(bool key[56], bool outBlk[64], bool inBlk[64], int verbose);
bcaf5a
f27454 #endif
baaf5a
```

```
--5736  0007f67bbbf80020009 Page 1 of initsrch.c

8d2d03  /****************************************************************************
2fe318  ·* initsrch.c ·············································································*
fa709c  ·* ················DES Search Engine Search Definition Program ···············*
f829eb  ·* ·······································································································*
5d09fc  ·* ···Written 1998 by Cryptography Research (http://www.cryptography.com) ···*
0b8aaf  ·* ······and Paul Kocher for the Electronic Frontier Foundation (EFF). ······*
bccaeb  ·* ·····Placed in the public domain by Cryptography Research and EFF. ······*
9a4992  ·* ·THIS IS UNSUPPORTED FREE SOFTWARE. USE AND DISTRIBUTE AT YOUR OWN RISK. ·*
8c29eb  ·* ·······································································································*
72c755  ·* ·IMPORTANT: U.S. LAW MAY REGULATE THE USE AND/OR EXPORT OF THIS PROGRAM. ·*
5329eb  ·* ·······································································································*
cf489b  ·* ****************************************************************************
cb29eb  ·* ·······································································································*
3615cb  ·* ··IMPLEMENTATION NOTES: ·················································································*
b629eb  ·* ·······································································································*
c6922a  ·* ··This program is used to define searches that will be run on the DES ····*
b77950  ·* ··search array. ·The program creates a search context file containing ·····*
ec6515  ·* ··the ciphertexts, search parameters, and a list of the key regions ······*
6bec7c  ·* ··to search. ·(A key region is the top 24 bits of a key.) ·················*
5829eb  ·* ·······································································································*
a5489b  ·* ****************************************************************************
4229eb  ·* ·······································································································*
d16eef  ·* ··REVISION HISTORY: ···················································································*
c329eb  ·* ·······································································································*
7828d9  ·* ··Version 1.0: ·Initial release by Cryptography Research to EFF. ··········*
2c29eb  ·* ·······································································································*
aed8c3  ·* ****************************************************************************/
41af5a
6abcd3  #define SOFTWARE_VERSION "1.0"
55a5c9  #define SOFTWARE_DATE ···"04-21-1998"
02af5a
28af5a
c5feb2  #include <stdio.h>
a2bea3  #include <stdlib.h>
9b1465  #include <conio.h>
49324c  #include <string.h>
46c737  #include <memory.h>
2b0a8b  #include <time.h>
93b1cb  #include <ctype.h>
00c94c  #include "search.h"
552ba0  #include "keyblock.h"
ecaf5a
5eb216  #define EXIT_ERR(s) { fprintf(stderr, s); exit(1); }
7146ff  static void dumpBin(char *intro, unsigned char *data, int len);
51ab37  static int unhex(unsigned char *data, char *hex, int byteCount);
66af5a
34af5a
e2164b  int main(int argc, char **argv) {
551309  ··char searchType; ·····················/* valid search types are K,C,E,B,M */
babcdd  ··int nextArg = 1;
7963f8  ··unsigned char plaintext[8];
fa17e0  ··int i;
5fd5d9  ··char *c, buf[100];
8e83f2  ··SEARCH_CTX ctx;
32154a  ··FILE *outfile;
16817e  ··char asciiBytes[] = { ·0, 9, 10, 13,' ','!',·'\"',·'\'',·'(',·')',',','+','-','.',
cbdc95  ···········'0','1','2','3','4','5','6','7','8','9',':',';','?',
90b0c9  ···········'A','B','C','D','E','F','G','H','I','J','K','L','M',
ea6651  ···········'N','O','P','Q','R','S','T','U','V','W','X','Y','Z','^','_','`',
15790e  ···········'a','b','c','d','e','f','g','h','i','j','k','l','m',
78488f  ···········'n','o','p','q','r','s','t','u','v','w','x','y','z' };
c7af5a
53ee0f  ··printf("\nDES Search Definition Util. (Ver %s, %s). May be export "
5bffaa  ·········"controlled.\nWritten 1998 by Cryptography Research "
cf2e08  ·········"(http://www.cryptography.com) for EFF.\n"
c5c4fd  ·········"This is unsupported "
051151  ·········"free software: Use and distribute at your own risk.\n"
50805d  ·········"------------------------------------------"
d504bf  ·········"---------------------------\n\n\n",
8aa1fb  ·········SOFTWARE_VERSION, SOFTWARE_DATE);
d7af5a
7fcf50  ··if (argc == 1) {
```

```
--cfc3 000b6391f9f80020009 Page 2 of initsrch.c
87048b ····printf("Parameters can be entered on the command line or entered "
a20e7c ··········"manually.\n\nUsage modes: ·(ctxt=ciphertext, ptxt=plaintext)\n"
0ea4b3 ··········" ···desbrute search.ctx K (8 bytes ptxt) (8 bytes ctxt)\n"
b34c3c ··········" ···desbrute search.ctx E (8 bytes ctxt0) (8 bytes ctxt1)\n"
192ff0 ··········" ···desbrute search.ctx C (8 bytes IV) (8 bytes ctxt0) "
289890 ················"(8 bytes ctxt1)\n"
ad835b ··········" ···desbrute search.ctx B (1 ctxt byte to repeat)\n"
42dba1 ··········" ···desbrute search.ctx M (ptxtVec) (IV) (ctxt0) (ctxt1)"
171870 ················"(bMask) (schInf)\n\n"
2cf69b ··········"Parameters can also be input from a file (e.g., "
c31498 ··········"\"desbrute < param.in\"\n\n");
36df1c ··}
41af5a
8b3b84 ··/**** OPEN OUTPUT FILE ****/
142284 ··if (argc > nextArg) {
b034d4 ····c = argv[nextArg++];
5449d8 ··} else {
3da6db ····printf("Enter output file for search context [ENTER=\"search.ctx\"]: ");
7e0aa5 ····gets(buf);
7a5331 ····if (*buf == '\0')
6ea68e ······strcpy(buf, "search.ctx");
383b52 ····c = buf;
2bdf1c ··}
e2744c ··outfile = fopen(c, "wb"); ··························/* open output file */
5c046f ··if (outfile == NULL)
b8eee0 ····EXIT_ERR("Error opening output file.\n");
27af5a
28f1d1 ··/**** INITALIZE searchType ****/
e92284 ··if (argc > nextArg) {
0534d4 ····c = argv[nextArg++];
7949d8 ··} else {
1c4645 ····printf("The array supports a variety of search types:\n");
893c39 ····printf(" ··K - Known plaintext (standard brute force).\n");
458386 ····printf(" ··E - ECB ASCII text\n");
ede877 ····printf(" ··C - CBC ASCII text\n");
c042f4 ····printf(" ··B - Blaze challenge\n");
f72546 ····printf(" ··M - Manual parameter specification\n");
457020 ····printf("Enter search type: ");
2e98f5 ····fgets(buf, 99, stdin);
6f3b52 ····c = buf;
16df1c ··}
bde55a ··searchType = (char)toupper(c[0]);
1fb2fb ··if (strchr("KECBM", searchType) == NULL)
d09d35 ····EXIT_ERR("Unknown search type. ·Exiting.\n");
caaf5a
3653c4 ··/**** INITALIZE PARAMETERS FOR KNOWN PLAINTEXT SEARCHES ****/
b606fd ··if (searchType == 'K') {
40af5a
31beaf ····/* Get known plaintext */
b6f875 ····if (argc > nextArg) {
66d208 ······c = argv[nextArg++];
2a6a79 ····} else {
865acf ······printf("Enter known plaintext (16 hex digits): ");
44ec56 ······fgets(buf, 99, stdin);
519eec ······c = buf;
716fe7 ····}
3b2686 ····if (unhex(plaintext, c, 8))
5284f6 ······EXIT_ERR("Invalid plaintext. (Must be 16 hex digits)");
43af5a
d154a2 ····/* Get ciphertext 0 (use same for ciphertext 1) */
99f875 ····if (argc > nextArg) {
b6d208 ······c = argv[nextArg++];
206a79 ····} else {
116433 ······printf("Enter ciphertext (16 hex digits): ");
ebec56 ······fgets(buf, 99, stdin);
d79eec ······c = buf;
306fe7 ····}
a00e9c ····if (unhex(ctx.ciphertext0, c, 8) || unhex(ctx.ciphertext1, c, 8))
ed301c ······EXIT_ERR("Invalid ciphertext. (Must be 16 hex digits.)");
0baf5a
95b74c ····/* Set ctx */
b6b998 ····memset(ctx.plaintextVector, 0, sizeof(ctx.plaintextVector));
```

```
--8f53  000bd86da9880020009 Page 3 of initsrch.c

b10371  ····for (i = 0; i < 8; i++)
0c2965  ······ctx.plaintextVector[plaintext[i]/8] |= (1 << (plaintext[i] % 8));
9d09b5  ····ctx.plaintextByteMask = 0x00;
23175f  ····memset(ctx.plaintextXorMask, 0, sizeof(ctx.plaintextXorMask));
d8f1c6  ····ctx.searchInfo = 16; ···········/* useCBC=0, extraXor=0, boardActiveEn=1 */
73df1c  ··}
10af5a
1a6d39  ··/**** INITALIZE PARAMETERS FOR ASCII SEARCHES ****/
0a4571  ··if (searchType == 'E' || searchType == 'C') {
b1af5a
9d92ba  ····/* Get IV (only if this is ciphertext mode) */
dd5306  ····if (searchType == 'C') {
0ae472  ······if (argc > nextArg) {
eaa6ab  ········c = argv[nextArg++];
dbcfc7  ······} else {
04935c  ········printf("Enter IV (16 hex digits): ");
635c62  ········fgets(buf, 99, stdin);
20cc35  ········c = buf;
8f42cc  ······}
f77471  ······if (unhex(ctx.plaintextXorMask, c, 8))
906bc1  ········EXIT_ERR("Invalid IV. (Must be 16 hex digits.)");
e26fe7  ····}
30af5a
16b543  ····/* Get ciphertext 0 */
8cf875  ····if (argc > nextArg) {
b0d208  ······c = argv[nextArg++];
b86a79  ····} else {
1c0a80  ······printf("Enter ciphertext0 (16 hex digits): ");
c2ec56  ······fgets(buf, 99, stdin);
819eec  ······c = buf;
636fe7  ····}
d0f3c8  ····if (unhex(ctx.ciphertext0, c, 8))
ab36df  ······EXIT_ERR("Invalid ciphertext0. (Must be 16 hex digits.)");
c4af5a
83be07  ····/* Get ciphertext 1 */
2df875  ····if (argc > nextArg) {
7ad208  ······c = argv[nextArg++];
666a79  ····} else {
a98349  ······printf("Enter ciphertext1 (16 hex digits): ");
6cec56  ······fgets(buf, 99, stdin);
e69eec  ······c = buf;
ee6fe7  ····}
54dfef  ····if (unhex(ctx.ciphertext1, c, 8))
8bf3eb  ······EXIT_ERR("Invalid ciphertext1. (Must be 16 hex digits.)");
82af5a
14b74c  ····/* Set ctx */
37b998  ····memset(ctx.plaintextVector, 0, sizeof(ctx.plaintextVector));
6634e6  ····for (i = 0; i < sizeof(asciiBytes); i++)
f7c77d  ······ctx.plaintextVector[asciiBytes[i]/8] |= (1 << (asciiBytes[i] % 8));
7609b5  ····ctx.plaintextByteMask = 0x00;
a84bfc  ····if (searchType == 'E') {
c97dd1  ······memset(ctx.plaintextXorMask, 0, sizeof(ctx.plaintextXorMask));
bc0a6e  ······ctx.searchInfo = 16; ···········/* useCBC=0, extraXor=0, boardActiveEn=1 */
476a79  ····} else {
60ba9b  ······/* already set plaintextXorMask = IV */
6e1c50  ······ctx.searchInfo = 17; ···········/* useCBC=1, extraXor=0, boardActiveEn=1 */
706fe7  ····}
48df1c  ··}
1baf5a
ec0b8e  ··/**** INITALIZE PARAMETERS FOR BLAZE CHALLENGE ****/
9f238e  ··if (searchType == 'B') {
6caf5a
207380  ····/* Get ciphertext byte */
cbf875  ····if (argc > nextArg) {
8fd208  ······c = argv[nextArg++];
266a79  ····} else {
1db847  ······printf("Enter ciphertext byte (2 hex digits): ");
cfec56  ······fgets(buf, 99, stdin);
899eec  ······c = buf;
2c6fe7  ····}
790aab  ····if (unhex(ctx.ciphertext0, c, 1))
bdc25b  ······EXIT_ERR("Invalid ciphertext byte. (Must be 2 hex digits.)");
```

```
--32ca 00084fa6dd680020009 Page 4 of initsrch.c
e0af5a
ce0ca4 ····/* Set all ciphertext0 and ciphertext1 bytes to the input byte */
3f0371 ····for (i = 0; i < 8; i++)
e93cde ······ctx.ciphertext0[i] = ctx.ciphertext1[i] = ctx.ciphertext0[0];
1faf5a
c7b74c ····/* Set ctx */
9fb998 ····memset(ctx.plaintextVector, 0, sizeof(ctx.plaintextVector));
8afeec ····ctx.plaintextVector[0] = 1; ·················/* halt on 00000000???????? */
8805d2 ····ctx.plaintextByteMask = 0x0F; ··············/* halt on 00000000???????? */
ce175f ····memset(ctx.plaintextXorMask, 0, sizeof(ctx.plaintextXorMask));
73be5d ····ctx.searchInfo = 2+16; ·········/* useCBC=0, extraXor=1, boardActiveEn=1 */
91df1c ··}
a2af5a
fd55a2 ··/**** INITALIZE PARAMETERS FOR MANUAL MODE ****/
dc1e07 ··if (searchType == 'M') {
34af5a
cca678 ····/* Get plaintextVector */
21f875 ····if (argc > nextArg) {
edd208 ······c = argv[nextArg++];
9a6a79 ····} else {
ef6b16 ······printf("The plaintextVector specifies which bytes can appear in the\n");
a9a298 ······printf("plaintext. ·The MSB (of the first byte entered) specifies\n");
802647 ······printf("whether 0xFF (255) can appear. The LSB is for 0x00.\n\n");
78b24d ······printf("Enter plaintextVector (64 hex digits): ");
27ec56 ······fgets(buf, 99, stdin);
899eec ······c = buf;
a36fe7 ····}
61e75f ····if (unhex(ctx.plaintextVector, c, 32))
e70a17 ······EXIT_ERR("Invalid plaintextVector. (Must be 64 hex digits.)");
e0af5a
296737 ····/* Get plaintextXorMask */
84f875 ····if (argc > nextArg) {
36d208 ······c = argv[nextArg++];
aa6a79 ····} else {
84b7f3 ······printf("The plaintextXorMask is used for the CBC mode IV.\n");
122794 ······printf("Enter plaintextXorMask (16 hex digits or ENTER=none): ");
98ec56 ······fgets(buf, 99, stdin);
6b6ee8 ······if (buf[0] == '\0');
d39be8 ········strcpy(buf, "0000000000000000");
dc9eec ······c = buf;
e96fe7 ····}
64dd72 ····if (unhex(ctx.plaintextXorMask, c, 8))
9fcece ······EXIT_ERR("Invalid plaintextXorMask. (Must be 16 hex digits.)");
b1af5a
fcb543 ····/* Get ciphertext 0 */
9df875 ····if (argc > nextArg) {
29d208 ······c = argv[nextArg++];
146a79 ····} else {
f00a80 ······printf("Enter ciphertext0 (16 hex digits): ");
efec56 ······fgets(buf, 99, stdin);
ab9eec ······c = buf;
5d6fe7 ····}
19f3c8 ····if (unhex(ctx.ciphertext0, c, 8))
b436df ······EXIT_ERR("Invalid ciphertext0. (Must be 16 hex digits.)");
a7af5a
afbe07 ····/* Get ciphertext 1 */
5ff875 ····if (argc > nextArg) {
cdd208 ······c = argv[nextArg++];
9d6a79 ····} else {
918349 ······printf("Enter ciphertext1 (16 hex digits): ");
adec56 ······fgets(buf, 99, stdin);
799eec ······c = buf;
f26fe7 ····}
cddfef ····if (unhex(ctx.ciphertext1, c, 8))
5ef3eb ······EXIT_ERR("Invalid ciphertext1. (Must be 16 hex digits.)");
d6af5a
67f875 ····if (argc > nextArg) {
b3d208 ······c = argv[nextArg++];
d06a79 ····} else {
ac9ea5 ······printf("The plaintextByteMask specifies which bytes of the plaintext\n");
ea0847 ······printf("are examined in the output. ·Normally this is zero, but if\n");
84a104 ······printf("only partial plaintext is available, the unknown bits can\n");
```

```
--7835 00008e1996880020009 Page 5 of initsrch.c

e2a994 ······printf("be set to 1. For example, if the left-hand plaintext byte\n");
0c1884 ······printf("is unknown, the mask would be 0x80.\n\n");
35f4f5 ······printf("Enter plaintextByteMask (1 byte): ");
9fec56 ······fgets(buf, 99, stdin);
e59eec ······c = buf;
5c6fe7 ····}
11d9bc ····if (unhex(&(ctx.plaintextByteMask), c, 1))
0603d8 ······EXIT_ERR("Invalid plaintextByteMask. (Must be 2 hex digits.)");
d1af5a
9cf875 ····if (argc > nextArg) {
a3d208 ······c = argv[nextArg++];
c46a79 ····} else {
60efb7 ······printf("\n\nThe searchInfo byte has two search parameters:\n");
58f304 ······printf(" ·bit 0x10: boardActiveEnable. ·Set this to one.\n");
6137c1 ······printf(" ·bit 0x02: extraXor. ·If set, after the decryption is done,\n");
6555ba ······printf(" ················the right half is XORed onto the left.\n");
2b6a7f ······printf(" ················This is for Matt Blaze's challenge.\n");
7931e2 ······printf(" ·bit 0x01: useCBC. ·If set, the first ciphertext is XORed\n");
1779e1 ······printf(" ················onto the second plaintext before the second\n");
7a8401 ······printf(" ················plaintext is checked against the ");
c4a056 ······printf(                   "plaintextVector.\n(Higher bits control");
5295d9 ······printf(" searchActive, which is currently unused.)\n");
41f125 ······printf("\nEnter searchInfo (1 byte): ");
6eec56 ······fgets(buf, 99, stdin);
859eec ······c = buf;
a16fe7 ····}
a7ac03 ····if (unhex(&(ctx.searchInfo), c, 1))
196157 ······EXIT_ERR("Invalid searchInfo. (Must be 2 hex digits.)");
a5df1c ··}
42af5a
c7361b ··printf("\n\n\n---------------------------- SEARCH PARAMETERS ");
630dc6 ··printf("-------------------------------\n");
ef6965 ··dumpBin(" ·ptxtVector = ", ctx.plaintextVector, 32);
22cb15 ··dumpBin(" ptxtXorMask = ", ctx.plaintextXorMask, 8);
dcbce6 ··dumpBin(" ciphertext0 = ", ctx.ciphertext0, 8);
51ed2d ··dumpBin(" ciphertext1 = ", ctx.ciphertext1, 8);
48fb0f ··dumpBin("ptxtByteMask = ", &(ctx.plaintextByteMask), 1);
8fe310 ··dumpBin(" ·searchInfo = ", &(ctx.searchInfo), 1);
54a225 ··printf("-----------------------------------------------");
90f41b ··printf("-------------------------------\n");
dfaf5a
022e67 ··/**** WRITE SEARCH PARAMETERS TO OUTPUT FILE ****/
fbeb50 ··printf("\n\nWriting output file...");
14b77b ··fflush(stdout);
1a530e ··WriteSearchContext(outfile, &ctx);
1e55cf ··fclose(outfile);
46b812 ··printf("Done.\n");
2bc86a ··return (0);
faefe6 }
76af5a
03af5a
5e38e5 /*
915ba9 ·* ·Print a descriptive string followed by a binary value (in hex)
4c495d ·*/
15e54b static void dumpBin(char *intro, unsigned char *data, int len) {
1d17e0 ··int i;
313b28 ··printf(intro);
91c199 ··for (i=len-1; i >= 0; i--)
1bcd57 ····printf("%02X", data[i]);
79fee8 ··printf("\n");
c8efe6 }
c5af5a
2daf5a
9f38e5 /*
9cf0ab ·* ·Convert an ASCII digit from hex to an int, or return -1 if not hex.
09495d ·*/
a55514 static int unhexDigit(char c) {
4253c4 ··if (c >= '0' && c <= '9')
cb03d6 ····return (c - '0');
db8db1 ··if (c >= 'a' && c <= 'f')
b20ada ····return (c - 'a' + 10);
0849e3 ··if (c >= 'A' && c <= 'F')
```

```
--2b51 001fdd8d50d80020009 Page 6 of initsrch.c

0da66f ····return (c - 'A' + 10);
59a5eb ··return (-1); ························/* return -1 for error: bad hex digit */
fdefe6 }
1caf5a
5eaf5a
2238e5 /*
1d22f5 ·* ·Convert a string of hex characters into unsigned chars.
a4495d ·*/
62afe2 static int unhex(unsigned char *data, char *hex, int byteCount) {
01e13a ··int i,j;
6aaf5a
e6aea1 ··if (data == NULL ¦¦ hex == NULL)
128f8d ····return(-1);
afaf5a
852a60 ··/* Remove comments and whitespace */
97d4c3 ··for (i=j=0; hex[i] != 0 && hex[i] != '%' && hex[i] != '#'; i++)
f701aa ····if (hex[i] > ' ')
7c72f3 ······hex[j++] = hex[i];
3bf89c ··hex[j] = '\0';
a1af5a
665c18 ··if ((int)strlen(hex) != byteCount*2)
a3400d ····return (-1);
e2ed9d ··memset(data, 0, byteCount);
759629 ··for (i = 0; i < 2*byteCount; i++) {
36eb9c ····j = unhexDigit(hex[i]);
6e001d ····if (j < 0)
47b9b9 ······return (-1);
bc5824 ····data[byteCount - 1 - i/2] |= j << ((i & 1) ? 0 : 4);
66df1c ··}
171eb2 ··for (i = 2*byteCount; i < (int)strlen(hex); i++)
9e21eb ····if (!isspace(hex[i]))
1cb9b9 ······return (-1);
23c86a ··return (0);
f8efe6 }
fcaf5a
baaf5a
fdaf5a
```

```
--c219  0008a71b2228002000a Page 1 of keyblock.c

8d2d03  /****************************************************************************
535ef1  ·* keyblock.c ·················································· ·················*
33ec57  ·* ···············Key Block & Search Context Management Functions ·············*
1c29eb  ·* ·························································· ················ ·····*
bf09fc  ·* ···Written 1998 by Cryptography Research (http://www.cryptography.com) ···*
d58aaf  ·* ········and Paul Kocher for the Electronic Frontier Foundation (EFF). ·······*
36caeb  ·* ·······Placed in the public domain by Cryptography Research and EFF. ·······*
394992  ·* ·THIS IS UNSUPPORTED FREE SOFTWARE. USE AND DISTRIBUTE AT YOUR OWN RISK. ·*
c629eb  ·* ················································································*
11c755  ·* ·IMPORTANT: U.S. LAW MAY REGULATE THE USE AND/OR EXPORT OF THIS PROGRAM. ·*
1b29eb  ·* ················································································*
27489b  ·* ****************************************************************************
ee29eb  ·* ················································································*
a46eef  ·* ··REVISION HISTORY: ············································ ················*
3129eb  ·* ················································································*
0b28d9  ·* ··Version 1.0: ·Initial release by Cryptography Research to EFF. ··········*
4929eb  ·* ················································································*
b5d8c3  ·* ****************************************************************************/
60af5a
56feb2  #include <stdio.h>
a1bea3  #include <stdlib.h>
9b1465  #include <conio.h>
76324c  #include <string.h>
e1c737  #include <memory.h>
0f0a8b  #include <time.h>
88b1cb  #include <ctype.h>
28c94c  #include "search.h"
f92ba0  #include "keyblock.h"
b6af5a
817f4a  static const char fileHeader[] = "This is a binary file containing the "
a9dcbc  ········"parameters for a DES search followed by 2^24 bits "
1a7150  ········"indicating which regions of keyspace are left to search.\n\032";
e8af5a
1d4171  #define CTX_FILE_KEYBLOCKS_OFFSET (sizeof(fileHeader) + 58)
1391d3  #define MAX_KEY_REGION (1L<<24) ·········/* 2^56 keys / 2^32 keys per region */
b8708e  static void EXIT_ERR(char *s) { fprintf(stderr, s); exit(1); }
cfaf5a
839edf  static void WriteParams(FILE *fp, SEARCH_CTX *ctx);
9000a6  static void ReadParams(FILE *fp, SEARCH_CTX *ctx);
2baf5a
82af5a
3938e5  /*
bda837  ·* ·Create a new search context file from a SEARCH_CTX structure
54495d  ·*/
f504e1  void WriteSearchContext(FILE *fp, SEARCH_CTX *ctx) {
91e4cc  ··unsigned char temp[1024/8];
5cac42  ··long i;
7faf5a
d261e8  ··fwrite(fileHeader, 1, sizeof(fileHeader), fp);
0e7f45  ··WriteParams(fp, ctx);
893148  ··memset(temp, 255, 1024/8);
64052f  ··for (i = 0; i < MAX_KEY_REGION/1024; i++)
21d22a  ····fwrite(temp, 1, sizeof(temp), fp);
beefe6  }
73af5a
e0af5a
2c38e5  /*
f292e2  ·* ·Read search params from a FILE_STRUCTURE and get ready for
c0cc06  ·* ···calls to ReserveKeyRegion and FinishKeyRegion.
e0495d  ·*/
4ab92d  void OpenSearchContext(FILE *fp, SEARCH_CTX *ctx) {
70180e  ··long blocksLeft, n;
ca17e0  ··int i;
60649a  ··int c;
fdaf5a
da1d80  ··rewind(fp);
ae0183  ··for (i = 0; i < sizeof(fileHeader); i++)
489aee  ····if (fgetc(fp) != fileHeader[i])
7c9d45  ······EXIT_ERR("Bad file header in search context file.\n");
42af5a
e43738  ··ReadParams(fp, ctx);
8a2eda  ··if (ftell(fp) != CTX_FILE_KEYBLOCKS_OFFSET)
```

```
--e4bf 00087902e818002000a Page 2 of keyblock.c

5346c8 ····EXIT_ERR("Internal error: File length mismatch.");
52af5a
43a1af ··/* INITIALIZE THE SEARCH PROCESS PARAMETERS (except for totalUnits) */
3f0522 ··ctx->nextUnstartedKeyBlock = 0;
30dd9c ··ctx->totalFinishedKeyBlocks = 0;
7b09e5 ··ctx->totalUnstartedKeyBlocks = MAX_KEY_REGION;
36d36a ··ctx->totalPendingKeyBlocks = 0;
c7af5a
9cc760 ··/* FIND OUT HOW MANY KEY BLOCKS ARE LEFT */
e65f7b ··blocksLeft = 0;
0e785b ··for (n = 0; n < MAX_KEY_REGION/8; n++) {
4dee98 ····c = fgetc(fp);
6c373b ····if (c < 0 || c > 255)
0ba78e ······EXIT_ERR("Error or premature EOF reading search context file.\n");
2ab9b9 ····blocksLeft += (c&128)/128 + (c&64)/64 + (c&32)/32 + (c&16)/16 +
e1804b ··········(c&8)/8 + (c&4)/4 + (c&2)/2 + (c&1);
4bdf1c ··}
9f5ea0 ··ctx->totalUnstartedKeyBlocks = blocksLeft;
ad7c26 ··ctx->totalFinishedKeyBlocks = ·MAX_KEY_REGION - blocksLeft;
4defe6 }
76af5a
0aaf5a
f038e5 /*
853511 ·* ·Reserve a key region to search. ·When done searching it, the program
5b54f7 ·* ·should call FinishKeyRegion. ·This function hands out blocks sequentially,
460a86 ·* ·starting with the first unsearched one in the file context file.
6a448b ·* ·If all blocks have been allocated and no free ones are left, the
424769 ·* ·function returns (-1).
9c495d ·*/
f9dcfa long ReserveKeyRegion(FILE *fp, SEARCH_CTX *ctx) {
5c6b50 ··int c,b;
43af5a
8242e7 ··if (ctx->nextUnstartedKeyBlock >= MAX_KEY_REGION)
e48f8d ····return(-1);
d63ef3 ··if (fseek(fp, CTX_FILE_KEYBLOCKS_OFFSET + ctx->nextUnstartedKeyBlock/8,
f96018 ··········SEEK_SET))
276a9d ····EXIT_ERR("Error seeking search context file.\n");
22b482 ··if ((ctx->nextUnstartedKeyBlock & 7) != 0)
1bee98 ····c = fgetc(fp);
a7c101 ··while (ctx->nextUnstartedKeyBlock < MAX_KEY_REGION) {
f208b3 ····b = (int)(ctx->nextUnstartedKeyBlock & 7);
e956ec ····if (b == 0)
40d9d8 ······c = fgetc(fp);
9a373b ····if (c < 0 || c > 255)
df563d ······EXIT_ERR("Error reading from search context file.\n");
d20bfd ····if (b == 0 && c == 0) {
e49e77 ······ctx->nextUnstartedKeyBlock += 8;
d85f6a ······continue;
7e6fe7 ····}
7e9622 ····if ((c << b) & 128)
5d88e1 ······break;
7cac89 ····ctx->nextUnstartedKeyBlock++;
d5df1c ··}
7042e7 ··if (ctx->nextUnstartedKeyBlock >= MAX_KEY_REGION)
2d400d ····return (-1);
204784 ··ctx->totalUnstartedKeyBlocks--;
30b7db ··ctx->totalPendingKeyBlocks++;
e6b95c ··return (ctx->nextUnstartedKeyBlock++);
daefe6 }
caaf5a
adaf5a
1e38e5 /*
450ed1 ·* ·Finish searching a key region by marking it as completed in the contetx
156197 ·* ·file.
33495d ·*/
d1a6a3 void FinishKeyRegion(FILE *fp, SEARCH_CTX *ctx, long keyRegion) {
3e6b50 ··int c,b;
74af5a
04227a ··if (keyRegion < 0 || keyRegion > MAX_KEY_REGION)
859a72 ····EXIT_ERR("Bad key region\n");
4a7978 ··if (fseek(fp, CTX_FILE_KEYBLOCKS_OFFSET + keyRegion/8, SEEK_SET))
8799f2 ····EXIT_ERR("Error seeking in search context file.\n");
```

```
--82de 001f9fbc7698002000a Page 3 of keyblock.c

7d83b3  ··b = (int)(keyRegion & 7);  ·······························/* b = bit in byte */
6a1425  ··c = getc(fp);
94e261  ··if (((c << b) & 128) == 0)
533188  ····printf("WARNING: FinishKeyRegion called, but region already searched!\n");
783a1e  ··else {
961464  ····if (fseek(fp, CTX_FILE_KEYBLOCKS_OFFSET + keyRegion/8, SEEK_SET))
bd410b  ······EXIT_ERR("Error seeking in search context file.\n");
010fe7  ····fputc(c & (255 ^ (128>>b)), fp);
f78f5b  ····fflush(fp);
1af525  ····ctx->totalFinishedKeyBlocks++;
a8f539  ····ctx->totalPendingKeyBlocks--;
ccdf1c  ··}
4fefe6  }
ddaf5a
53af5a
c438e5  /*
bcf380  ·* ·Write a SEARCH_CTX structure to a FILE*
c1495d  ·*/
54c491  static void WriteParams(FILE *fp, SEARCH_CTX *ctx) {
303c52  ··fwrite(ctx->plaintextVector, 1, 32, fp);  ··················/* 32 bytes */
c78ca6  ··fwrite(ctx->plaintextXorMask, 1, 8, fp);  ··················/* ·8 bytes */
f37a57  ··fwrite(ctx->ciphertext0, 1, 8, fp);  ·······················/* ·8 bytes */
473db4  ··fwrite(ctx->ciphertext1, 1, 8, fp);  ·······················/* ·8 bytes */
9945d9  ··fwrite(&(ctx->plaintextByteMask), 1, 1, fp);  ··············/* ·1 byte ·*/
64247e  ··fwrite(&(ctx->searchInfo), 1, 1, fp);  ····················/* ·1 byte ·*/
daefe6  }
60af5a
8038e5  /*
6fc898  ·* ·Read a SEARCH_CTX structure from a FILE*
e7495d  ·*/
782a49  static void ReadParams(FILE *fp, SEARCH_CTX *ctx) {
3f5e7e  ··fread(ctx->plaintextVector, 1, 32, fp);  ···················/* 32 bytes */
868b1a  ··fread(ctx->plaintextXorMask, 1, 8, fp);  ···················/* ·8 bytes */
fb6dea  ··fread(ctx->ciphertext0, 1, 8, fp);  ························/* ·8 bytes */
7fb838  ··fread(ctx->ciphertext1, 1, 8, fp);  ························/* ·8 bytes */
c6f5b4  ··fread(&(ctx->plaintextByteMask), 1, 1, fp);  ···············/* ·1 byte ·*/
942460  ··fread(&(ctx->searchInfo), 1, 1, fp);  ·····················/* ·1 byte ·*/
42efe6  }
f9af5a
```

```
--c618 0012573153180020000b Page 1 of keyblock.h
8d2d03 /**********************************************************************
aea835 ·* keyblock.h ·······················································*
d8ed67 ·* ····················Header file for keyblock.c ····················*
ed29eb ·* ··································································*
0209fc ·* ···Written 1998 by Cryptography Research (http://www.cryptography.com) ···*
4f8aaf ·* ······and Paul Kocher for the Electronic Frontier Foundation (EFF). ······*
abcaeb ·* ······Placed in the public domain by Cryptography Research and EFF. ······*
9f4992 ·* ·THIS IS UNSUPPORTED FREE SOFTWARE. USE AND DISTRIBUTE AT YOUR OWN RISK. ·*
e829eb ·* ··································································*
94c755 ·* ·IMPORTANT: U.S. LAW MAY REGULATE THE USE AND/OR EXPORT OF THIS PROGRAM. ·*
a329eb ·* ··································································*
73489b ·* *********************************************************************
0d29eb ·* ··································································*
866eef ·* ··REVISION HISTORY: ···············································*
bd29eb ·* ··································································*
5128d9 ·* ··Version 1.0: ·Initial release by Cryptography Research to EFF. ·········*
8e29eb ·* ··································································*
93d8c3 ·* *********************************************************************/
44af5a
00c374 #ifndef __KEYBLOCK_H
1f33ca #define __KEYBLOCK_H
0caf5a
334d26 void WriteSearchContext(FILE *fp, SEARCH_CTX *sp);
55d541 void OpenSearchContext(FILE *fp, SEARCH_CTX *ctx);
ae3447 long ReserveKeyRegion(FILE *fp, SEARCH_CTX *ctx);
93a2ae void FinishKeyRegion(FILE *fp, SEARCH_CTX *ctx, long keyRegion);
75af5a
1c7454 #endif
25af5a
```

```
--5629 0005fb2aed48002000c Page 1 of search.c
8d2d03 /*****************************************************************************
e284a4 ·* ·search.c ·········=========Search Engine Controller Program ·············*
8540b6 ·* ·················=========Search Engine Controller Program ·············*
2629eb ·* ·····················································································*
8109fc ·* ···Written 1998 by Cryptography Research (http://www.cryptography.com) ···*
728aaf ·* ······and Paul Kocher for the Electronic Frontier Foundation (EFF). ······*
64caeb ·* ······Placed in the public domain by Cryptography Research and EFF. ······*
204992 ·* ·THIS IS UNSUPPORTED FREE SOFTWARE. USE AND DISTRIBUTE AT YOUR OWN RISK. ·*
9329eb ·* ·····················································································*
b7c755 ·* ·IMPORTANT: U.S. LAW MAY REGULATE THE USE AND/OR EXPORT OF THIS PROGRAM. ·*
a029eb ·* ·····················································································*
5c489b ·* ·····················································································*
5d29eb ·* ·····················································································*
e46eef ·* ·REVISION HISTORY: ····································································*
b629eb ·* ·····················································································*
9028d9 ·* ··Version 1.0: ·Initial release by Cryptography Research to EFF. ·········*
9629eb ·* ·····················································································*
f9d8c3 ·******************************************************************************/
6eaf5a
d4bcd3 #define SOFTWARE_VERSION "1.0"
89a5c9 #define SOFTWARE_DATE ···"04-21-1998"
6baf5a
4baf5a
c9bea3 #include <stdlib.h>
70feb2 #include <stdio.h>
f9bb5f #include <assert.h>
06b1cb #include <ctype.h>
05c737 #include <memory.h>
200a8b #include <time.h>
48324c #include <string.h>
8a1465 #include <conio.h>
c1c94c #include "search.h"
601519 #include "chipio.h"
a12ba0 #include "keyblock.h"
ce2bac #include "des.h"
a1af5a
aaaf5a
3daf5a
a538e5 /*
0e1ae3 ·* ·SEARCH_CHIP STRUCTURE: Contains status information about each chip.
78775e ·*
d2e2cf ·* ···board: ·The board this chip is on (1 byte).
f79e01 ·* ···chip: ·The ID of this chip on the board (1 byte).
057501 ·* ···initialized: ·0=uninitialized, 1=initialized, -1=defective.
d66102 ·* ···region[]: Specifies the top 24 bits of the key being searched by each
3c7c40 ·* ······search unit. A value of -1 means the search unit is idle
195c24 ·* ······(idle), and a value of -2 means the search unit is not used.
ad77ae ·* ···overFlow[]: Specifies the value at which the low 32 bits of the
cd7f25 ·* ······key (the key counter) will have gone through all 2^32
cfc098 ·* ······possibilities. ·Note: this only has the top 24 bits of the
3cb9dd ·* ······counter, which corresponds to key bytes: .. .. .. XX XX XX.. (LSB)
b10b92 ·* ···lastSeen[]: ·The value last seen in the low 32 bits of the key.
5b33e4 ·* ······This has the same encoding as overFlow.
d3495d ·*/
92f9cb typedef struct CHIP_CTX {
7c2fe6 ··unsigned char board, chip;
4d3673 ··int initialized;
f01382 ··long region[SEARCH_UNITS_PER_CHIP];
95dbbf ··long overFlow[SEARCH_UNITS_PER_CHIP];
ceb33b ··long lastDone[SEARCH_UNITS_PER_CHIP];
5861b7 ··struct CHIP_CTX *nextChip;
feb846 } CHIP_CTX;
76af5a
38af5a
1238e5 /*
a225ec ·* ·GLOBAL VARIABLES
17495d ·*/
2329db CHIP_CTX *CHIP_ARRAY = NULL;
f92415 SEARCH_CTX CTX;
4acb69 static int QUIET = 0;
08dcb4 static int VERBOSE = 0;
5f6c5f static FILE *FP_LOG = NULL;
```

```
--2313 0001e8485cc8002000c Page 2 of search.c

e0af5a
1aaf5a
9938e5 /*
aae9fc ·* ·FUNCTION PROTOTYPES & MINI FUNCTIONS & MACROS
2b495d ·*/
54708e static void EXIT_ERR(char *s) { fprintf(stderr, s); exit(1); }
c2f311 long ReadConfig(char *configFilespec);
e0a2be void RunSearch(FILE *ctxFile);
b5e2b2 void InitializeChip(CHIP_CTX *cp, SEARCH_CTX *ctx);
0c49e0 void ServiceChip(CHIP_CTX *cp, SEARCH_CTX *ctx, FILE *ctxFile);
ee873d long GetUnitKeyCounter(int board, int chip, int unit);
ff0862 void CheckAndPrintKey(CHIP_CTX *cp, SEARCH_CTX *ctx, int unit);
5f8767 int ServiceKeyboard(SEARCH_CTX *ctx);
c078a5 int CheckKey(unsigned char key[56], SEARCH_CTX *ctx);
52af5a
64af5a
8538e5 /*
ee2faa ·* ·ReadConfig(): ·Read the search array configuration file. ·This file
9198e6 ·* ····specifies the I/O base port for SetBaseAddress and also the
643bd0 ·* ·····search units. ·It can contain 3 kinds of lines: comments that
a271b3 ·* ·····that with '%', base port with "PORT=210" for port 210 hex, and
a1849f ·* ·····"UNIT= 12 32 8" to add a search unit on board 0x12, chip 0x32,
b97255 ·* ·····and unit 0x08 (all hex). ·The function constructs CHIP_ARRAY
0ac94c ·* ·····as a linked list of chips.
0daf98 ·* ··Returns: Total number of search units.
a0495d ·*/
54eb8e long ReadConfig(char *configFilespec) {
79bc33 ··char buffer[200];
a58685 ··int basePort = -1;
ae08f4 ··int board, chip, unit, i;
31e8aa ··int lastBoard = -1, lastChip = -1;
1ec31e ··long totalUnits = 0;
c344bc ··CHIP_CTX *cp;
07b166 ··FILE *fp;
27af5a
a2d67e ··cp = CHIP_ARRAY;
398d09 ··if (cp != NULL)
6860b7 ····EXIT_ERR("Chip array base isn't NULL. (Internal error.)\n");
7caf5a
c4a9d2 ··fp = fopen(configFilespec, "rb");
d2b291 ··if (fp == NULL)
668f5c ····EXIT_ERR("Error opening configuration filespec.\n");
8caf5a
b994bf ··if (!QUIET) printf("Reading configuration file \"%s\".\n", configFilespec);
5a0a67 ··while (fgets (buffer, 190, fp) != NULL) {
342761 ····if (buffer[0] == '\0' || buffer[0] == '%')
205f6a ······continue;
c04d2e ····if (memcmp(buffer, "PORT=", 5) == 0) {
c1c6f2 ······basePort = 0;
9f6771 ······sscanf(buffer+5, "%x", &basePort);
6ae67c ······if (basePort <= 0)
42a4e2 ········EXIT_ERR("Defective PORT= in configuration file.\n");
b0b41f ······SetBaseAddress(basePort);
50f03a ······if (!QUIET) printf("Set base port to %x\n", basePort);
b4da88 ······if (FP_LOG && VERBOSE) fprintf(FP_LOG, "Set base port=0x%x\n", basePort);
296fe7 ····}
25d89c ····else if (memcmp(buffer, "UNIT=", 5) == 0 ||
1c3b05 ············memcmp(buffer, "FAIL=", 5) == 0) {
3044d4 ······board = chip = unit = -1;
0a1445 ······sscanf(buffer+5, "%x %x %x", &board, &chip, &unit);
ca5e35 ······if (board < 0 || chip < 0 || unit < 0)
f86669 ········EXIT_ERR("Defective UNIT= or FAIL= in configuration file.\n");
8cae4c ······if (board < lastBoard || (board == lastBoard && chip < lastChip))
715fa0 ········EXIT_ERR("Bad UNIT= or FAIL= in config: board & chip must decrease\n");
bf274a ······if (board != lastBoard || chip != lastChip) {
ca772c ········lastBoard = board;
3343e1 ········lastChip = chip;
807e0b ········if (cp == NULL)
629822 ··········cp = CHIP_ARRAY = malloc(sizeof(CHIP_CTX));
7905d7 ········else {
b656fb ··········cp->nextChip = malloc(sizeof(CHIP_CTX));
1e2825 ··········cp = cp->nextChip;
```

```
--4bd2 0003642e9df8002000c Page 3 of search.c
e67fb0 ········}
e237f7 ········cp->board = (unsigned char)board;
927f04 ········cp->chip = (unsigned char)chip;
902174 ········cp->initialized = 0;
b11ffd ········for (i = 0; i < SEARCH_UNITS_PER_CHIP; i++)
2068f5 ········cp->region[i] = -2;
48d968 ········cp->nextChip = NULL;
a342cc ······}
a2fac6 ······if (cp->region[unit] == -2 && memcmp(buffer, "UNIT=", 5) == 0) {
1b9c12 ········totalUnits++;
cf72d7 ········cp->region[unit] = -1; ··················/* mark the unit as extant */
f442cc ······}
936a79 ····} else {
d0f07c ······fprintf(stderr, "IGNORING UNKNOWN CONFIG FILE LINE: \"%s\"\n", buffer);
3c6fe7 ····}
aadf1c ··}
56ed24 ··fclose(fp);
24f7ab ··if (CHIP_ARRAY == NULL)
ca50bd ····EXIT_ERR("Error: Configuration file does not have any valid units.\n");
fbaf5a
ba291a ··if (FP_LOG && VERBOSE) {
0f24bf ····fprintf(FP_LOG, "Configuration summary:\n");
7e5d63 ····for (cp = CHIP_ARRAY; cp != NULL; cp = cp->nextChip) {
4e1222 ······for (i = 0; i < SEARCH_UNITS_PER_CHIP; i++)
f6f2e5 ······if (cp->region[i] != -2)
debb16 ··········fprintf(FP_LOG, "%s=0x%02X 0x%02X 0x%02X\n",
e33ccd ···················(cp->initialized >= 0) ? "UNIT" : "FAIL",
bb9127 ···················cp->board, cp->chip, i);
8d6fe7 ····}
c4df1c ··}
19a980 ··if (!QUIET) printf("Config done: Found %ld search units.\n", totalUnits);
239057 ··if (FP_LOG) fprintf(FP_LOG, "Config found %ld search units.\n", totalUnits);
d43faf ··return (totalUnits);
15efe6 }
0eaf5a
d8af5a
0caf5a
fe79bf void main(int argc, char **argv) {
c1e020 ··FILE *ctxFile;
e417e0 ··int i;
19e624 ··time_t t;
f944bc ··CHIP_CTX *cp;
63af5a
7207b6 ··printf("\nDES Search Engine Controller (Ver %s, %s). May be export "
a2ffaa ·········"controlled.\nWritten 1998 by Cryptography Research "
142e08 ·········"(http://www.cryptography.com) for EFF.\n"
2dc4fd ·········"This is unsupported "
7b1151 ·········"free software: Use and distribute at your own risk.\n"
b0805d ·········"-------------------------------------------"
3b04bf ·········"------------------------------\n\n\n",
44a1fb ·········SOFTWARE_VERSION, SOFTWARE_DATE);
daba53 ··if (argc < 3) {
cfed02 ····fprintf(stderr,
18f2f1 ·········"Usage: ·search configFile contextFile [logfile] [-v] [-q]\n"
da327c ·········" ···configFile: Search array configuration from autoconf\n"
398e60 ·········" ···contextFile: Search context (from init)\n"
ddf370 ·········" ······logfile: Output file with detailed reporting info\n"
fd94cd ·········" ···········-v: verbose output to logfile\n"
578e57 ·········" ···········-q: quiet mode (less output to the screen)\n"
e1a553 ·········" ·(Note: paramaters must be in the order above.)\n");
6b646c ····exit(1);
f5df1c ··}
0a5434 ··for (i = 3; i < argc; i++) {
05d081 ····if (i == 3 && argv[i][0] != '-') {
df3904 ······FP_LOG = fopen(argv[3], "w");
a1dd6b ······if (FP_LOG == NULL)
8bc2fe ········EXIT_ERR("Error opening log file.");
2e14ab ····} else if (stricmp(argv[i], "-v") == 0)
e593ab ······VERBOSE = 1;
fe4009 ····else if (stricmp(argv[i], "-q") == 0)
8b9a4c ······QUIET = 1;
3683c8 ····else {
```

```
--1911 000b393ee878002000c Page 4 of search.c

5e813f ······fprintf(stderr, "Unknown parameter \"%s\"\n", argv[i]);
e6c1d2 ······exit(1);
cc6fe7 ····}
5edf1c ··}
b0af5a
9f305a ··/* READ CONFIGURATION FILE SPECIFYING BASE PORT AND SEARCH UNITS */
5dff7c ··CTX.totalUnits = ReadConfig(argv[1]);
13af5a
76735d ··/* RESET THE SEARCH ARRAY */
861d2e ··if (!QUIET) printf("Resetting the search array.\n");
c4969d ··i = -1;
7e859a ··for (cp = CHIP_ARRAY; cp != NULL; cp = cp->nextChip) {
e607b1 ····if (i != cp->board) {
06ae60 ······i = cp->board;
7b7546 ······ResetBoard(i);
056fe7 ····}
99df1c ··}
71ec6b ··t = time(NULL);
94af5a
3da542 ··/* READ SEARCH FILE SPECIFYING SEARCH INFO & REMAINING KEY BLOCKS */
10ee15 ··ctxFile = fopen(argv[2], "r+b");
20ff66 ··if (ctxFile == NULL) {
c0f8b7 ····fprintf(stderr, "Error opening search context file \"%s\"\n", argv[2]);
4c646c ····exit(1);
10df1c ··}
a9af5a
5d1da1 ··/* MAKE SURE RESET HAD AT LEAST 1 SECOND TO SETTLE. */
7ab357 ··if (!QUIET) printf("Waiting for reset to settle.\n");
445f4 ··while(t + 1 >= time(NULL)) {}
30af5a
b65d7f ··/* RUN THE SEARCH! */
362733 ··RunSearch(ctxFile);
259966 ··fclose(ctxFile);
0f33d0 ··if (!QUIET) printf("Exiting.\n");
86efe6 }
cdaf5a
e1af5a
8538e5 /*
8f13e5 ·* ·Run the search. Uses the search parameters in the
ffec91 ·* ······global linked list CHIP_ARRAY and keeps its context info
c140a5 ·* ·····in the global CTX.
7c495d ·*/
2fb622 void RunSearch(FILE *ctxFile) {
2944bc ··CHIP_CTX *cp;
2d049e ··SEARCH_CTX *ctx = &CTX;
79c4fb ··int halt = 0;
d4ceca ··time_t startTime, lastReportTime, t;
8cd6eb ··long loopCount = 0;
95431e ··char buffer[128];
c3af5a
c9fbd6 ··if (!QUIET) printf("Loading search context file...\n");
578e14 ··OpenSearchContext(ctxFile, ctx);
45af5a
da37ac ··printf("Initialization Successful - Beginning search.\n");
09a530 ··if (QUIET) printf("Quiet mode: Press ? for help during search.\n");
7c2a59 ··if (FP_LOG && VERBOSE) fprintf(FP_LOG, "--- Beginning search ---\n");
46ec5d ··for (cp = CHIP_ARRAY; cp != NULL; cp = cp->nextChip)
e4084a ····InitializeChip(cp, ctx);
9abe63 ··startTime = time(NULL);
155889 ··lastReportTime = 0;
1daf5a
b005cf ··while (halt == 0) {
5ffb77 ····t = time(NULL); ·······························/* report every 5 seconds */
97eba6 ····if (t/5 != lastReportTime/5) {
e24d90 ······sprintf(buffer, "%7ld blocks done, %7ld left, %4ld running (time=%7ld).",
c347d2 ··············ctx->totalFinishedKeyBlocks, ctx->totalUnstartedKeyBlocks +
16efa5 ··············ctx->totalPendingKeyBlocks, ctx->totalPendingKeyBlocks,
db00a9 ··············(long)(t - startTime));
889596 ······if (!QUIET) printf(">%s ('?'=help)\n", buffer);
751c3a ······if (FP_LOG && VERBOSE) fprintf(FP_LOG, "Report: %s\n", buffer);
e61ab3 ······lastReportTime = t;
b36fe7 ····}
```

```
--75c4 000ce8281be8002000c Page 5 of search.c

9d0eaa ····for (cp = CHIP_ARRAY; cp != NULL && halt == 0; cp = cp->nextChip) {
3f8447 ······ServiceChip(cp, ctx, ctxFile);
f591f1 ······if (ServiceKeyboard(ctx) < 0)
e6cd41 ········halt = 1;
4a6fe7 ····}
b2bd80 ····if (ctx->totalFinishedKeyBlocks == (1L<<24))
16865f ······halt = 1;
0b1f76 ····GetRegister(255, 255, 255);
3b5ff2 ····loopCount++;
43df1c ··}
08efe6 }
92af5a
c6af5a
4f38e5 /*
2da22e ·* ·InitializeChip(cp, ctx): ·Initialize a chip whose chip context is
cdf2f7 ·* ·····at cp, using the search parameters at ctx.
cf495d ·*/
087c0e void InitializeChip(CHIP_CTX *cp, SEARCH_CTX *ctx) {
cfe13a ··int i,j;
abaf5a
3c3661 ··if (!QUIET) printf("Initializing board 0x%02X, chip 0x%02X\n",
a40940 ··········cp->board, cp->chip);
faae75 ··if (FP_LOG && VERBOSE) fprintf(FP_LOG,
9c7828 ··········"Initializing board 0x%02X, chip 0x%02X\n", cp->board, cp->chip);
be1207 ··SetRegister(cp->board, cp->chip, REG_PTXT_BYTE_MASK, 0xFF); ··/* halt chip */
0b339a ··for (i = 0; i < 32; i++)
fbd055 ····SetRegister(cp->board, cp->chip, REG_PTXT_VECTOR+i,
cbb8cc ··········ctx->plaintextVector[i]);
131f76 ··for (i = 0; i < 8; i++)
64eca4 ····SetRegister(cp->board, cp->chip,REG_PTXT_XOR_MASK+i,
2689f7 ··········ctx->plaintextXorMask[i]);
001f76 ··for (i = 0; i < 8; i++)
f98081 ····SetRegister(cp->board, cp->chip, REG_CIPHERTEXT0+i, ctx->ciphertext0[i]);
d21f76 ··for (i = 0; i < 8; i++)
174d1c ····SetRegister(cp->board, cp->chip, REG_CIPHERTEXT1+i, ctx->ciphertext1[i]);
ec1eef ··SetRegister(cp->board, cp->chip, REG_PTXT_BYTE_MASK, ctx->plaintextByteMask);
e20a1e ··SetRegister(cp->board, cp->chip, REG_SEARCHINFO, ctx->searchInfo);
0faf5a
70b777 ··/* TO BE SAFE, VERIFY THAT ALL REGISTERS WERE WRITTEN PROPERLY */
20f147 ··/* (Each chip only gets initialized once, so this is quick.) */
060b46 ··j = 0;
e6339a ··for (i = 0; i < 32; i++)
f9b65f ····j += CheckRegister(cp->board, cp->chip, REG_PTXT_VECTOR+i,
beb8cc ············ctx->plaintextVector[i]);
d18715 ··for (i = 0; i < 8; i++)
8fd1da ····j += CheckRegister(cp->board, cp->chip, REG_PTXT_XOR_MASK+i,
9a89f7 ············ctx->plaintextXorMask[i]);
bb5fb5 ····j += CheckRegister(cp->board, cp->chip, REG_CIPHERTEXT0+i,
610e6a ············ctx->ciphertext0[i]);
5854f1 ····j += CheckRegister(cp->board, cp->chip, REG_CIPHERTEXT1+i,
5b91bf ············ctx->ciphertext1[i]);
7bdf1c ··}
1b77a6 ··j += CheckRegister(cp->board, cp->chip, REG_PTXT_BYTE_MASK,
483279 ··········ctx->plaintextByteMask);
e013d5 ··j += CheckRegister(cp->board, cp->chip, REG_SEARCHINFO, ctx->searchInfo);
23fed0 ··if (j != 0) {
c5e719 ····printf("Bad register on board 0x%02X, chip 0x%02X. Chip disabled.\n",
6ad6e1 ··········cp->board, cp->chip);
4e4342 ····if (FP_LOG) fprintf(FP_LOG, "Bad register on board 0x%02X, chip 0x%02X.%s",
8960af ··········cp->board, cp->chip, " Chip disabled.\n");
dadf1c ··}
36af5a
e1791e ··/* UPDATE THE CHIP CONTEXT */
4ff396 ··cp->initialized = (j == 0) ? 1 : -1; ··········/* initialized or defective */
b8efe6 }
79af5a
96af5a
c538e5 /*
a3cc9c ·* ·Service a chip by doing the following:
274c8c ·* ···- Check if it has halted
670a9d ·* ···- Check to see if it has finished its region
ceb01a ·* ···- Restart if it is idle
```

```
--040d 00045bb51768002000c Page 6 of search.c

47495d ·*/
a30d32 void ServiceChip(CHIP_CTX *cp, SEARCH_CTX *ctx, FILE *ctxFile) {
05538a ··int unit;
5019fa ··long k;
2aaf5a
348a5b ··if (cp->initialized < 0)
0f3471 ····return;
25af5a
ec6000 ··/*
b65d45 ···* ·READ KEYS & RESTART ANY HALTED UNITS
adf9a6 ··*/
6700ef ··for (unit = 0; unit < SEARCH_UNITS_PER_CHIP; unit++) {
ea5e8f ····if (cp->region[unit] >= 0) { ·················/* if currently running */
2bca7c ······if (!(GetRegister(cp->board, cp->chip, REG_SEARCH_STATUS(unit)) & 1)) {
29e540 ········CheckAndPrintKey(cp, ctx, unit);
db6490 ········SetRegister(cp->board, cp->chip, REG_SEARCH_STATUS(unit), 1);
1d42cc ······}
cd6fe7 ····}
efdf1c ··}
23af5a
516000 ··/*
ae51e4 ···* ·See if any units have completed their search regions
ba3534 ···* ···Note: If I/O bandwidth was a problem and the clock rate of the
aa4028 ···* ······search system was fixed, we could predict when the keycounter
7c32c2 ···* ······would flip and avoid this check.
9af9a6 ··*/
1600ef ··for (unit = 0; unit < SEARCH_UNITS_PER_CHIP; unit++) {
fda2b3 ····if (cp->region[unit] < 0)
b25f6a ······continue;
fcbaec ····k = GetUnitKeyCounter(cp->board, cp->chip, unit);
637ad2 ····k -= cp->overFlow[unit];
0c9fc8 ····if (k < 0)
db5630 ······k += (1L << 24);
4c9bfb ····if (VERBOSE && FP_LOG) fprintf(FP_LOG,
3d961d ··············"Board 0x%02X chip 0x%02X unit 0x%02X is at 0x%06lX "
91fd7c ··············"(lastDone=0x%06lX, overFlow=%06lX)\n",
a5a2d2 ··············cp->board, cp->chip, unit, k,
02106a ··············cp->lastDone[unit], cp->overFlow[unit]);
9a7e0d ····if (k < cp->lastDone[unit]) {
eb7d4e ······if (!QUIET) printf("Board 0x%02X chip 0x%02X unit 0x%02X finished block "
9e7322 ··············"0x%06lX (lastDone=0x%06lX, got 0x%06lX, overFlow=%06lX)\n",
394e24 ··············cp->board, cp->chip, unit, cp->region[unit],
cc3197 ··············cp->lastDone[unit], k, cp->overFlow[unit]);
64bdf0 ······if (FP_LOG) fprintf(FP_LOG, "Unit 0x%02X 0x%02X 0x%02X finished "
d455fb ··············"0x%06lX (last=%06lX, got %06lX, oFlow=%06lX)\n",
284e24 ··············cp->board, cp->chip, unit, cp->region[unit],
263197 ··············cp->lastDone[unit], k, cp->overFlow[unit]);
c14588 ······FinishKeyRegion(ctxFile, ctx, cp->region[unit]); ····/* region is done */
72c33f ······cp->region[unit] = -1; ························/* unit is now idle */
ba6a79 ····} else {
b01b8b ······cp->lastDone[unit] = k;
de6fe7 ····}
3edf1c ··}
faaf5a
036000 ··/*
beae98 ···* ·Start any units that are currently stalled
38f9a6 ···*/
0000ef ··for (unit = 0; unit < SEARCH_UNITS_PER_CHIP; unit++) {
8faa03 ····if (cp->region[unit] == -1) {
7cb961 ······k = ReserveKeyRegion(ctxFile, ctx);
f9cd11 ······if (k < 0)
b431a8 ········break; ·························/* no more regions... */
35db12 ······if (!QUIET) printf("Starting board 0x%02X, chip 0x%02X, unit 0x%02X... ",
3fe31b ··········cp->board, cp->chip, unit);
bd2b54 ······if (FP_LOG) fprintf(FP_LOG, "Starting unit 0x%02X 0x%02X 0x%02X... ",
e8e31b ··········cp->board, cp->chip, unit);
d148cb ······cp->region[unit] = k;
8faf5a
7523f8 ······/* LOAD UP THE KEY REGION AND LET 'ER RIP... */
49945b ······SetRegister(cp->board, cp->chip, REG_SEARCH_KEY(unit)+6,
6aad2b ············(unsigned char)((k >> 16) & 0xFF));
457b3f ······SetRegister(cp->board, cp->chip, REG_SEARCH_KEY(unit)+5,
```

```
--721d  0002227a35d8002000c Page 7 of search.c
99606b  ··············(unsigned char)((k >> 8) & 0xFF));
4021e3  ······SetRegister(cp->board, cp->chip, REG_SEARCH_KEY(unit)+4,
593bf5  ··············(unsigned char)(k & 0xFF));
d50d06  ······SetRegister(cp->board, cp->chip, REG_SEARCH_KEY(unit)+3, 0);
6a92d3  ······SetRegister(cp->board, cp->chip, REG_SEARCH_KEY(unit)+2, 0);
353abd  ······SetRegister(cp->board, cp->chip, REG_SEARCH_KEY(unit)+1, 0);
37a568  ······SetRegister(cp->board, cp->chip, REG_SEARCH_KEY(unit)+0, 0);
f2af5a
176841  ······SetRegister(cp->board, cp->chip, REG_SEARCH_STATUS(unit), 1); ··/* GO! */
08af5a
d3fd1a  ······/* READ OUT THE KEY COUNTER (3 BYTES) FOR OVERFLOW SENSING */
b20f12  ······k = GetUnitKeyCounter(cp->board, cp->chip, unit);
619957  ······cp->overFlow[unit] = k;
881b8b  ······cp->lastDone[unit] = k;
282f76  ······if (!QUIET) printf("Region=0x%06lX, overFlow=0x%06lX\n",
f3eb34  ··············cp->region[unit], k);
0ac312  ······if (FP_LOG) fprintf(FP_LOG, "Region=0x%06lX, overFlow=0x%06lX\n",
77eb34  ··············cp->region[unit], k);
5a6fe7  ····}
90df1c  ··}
97efe6  }
38af5a
21af5a
e338e5  /*
a964e4  ·* ·Read the value of a rapidly-incrementing key counter register.
58278f  ·* ····The function reads the register twice, finds the most-significant
5e7253  ·* ····bit that changed during the operation, and returns the later
b24a30  ·* ····(higher) value with all bits to the right of the one that changed
224233  ·* ····set to zero.
d494e7  ·* ·The return value is the top 24 bits of the low 32 bits of the
2740a3  ·* ····key counter -- i.e., key bytes (MSB).. .. .. XX XX XX ..(LSB)
57495d  ·*/
5a0094  long GetUnitKeyCounter(int board, int chip, int unit) {
559ab5  ··long v1, v2, m;
31565f  ··do {
76f04f  ····v1 = ((long)GetRegister(board, chip, REG_SEARCH_KEY(unit)+3)) << 16;
0b190c  ····v1 |= ((long)GetRegister(board, chip, REG_SEARCH_KEY(unit)+2)) << 8;
56d778  ····v1 |= ((long)GetRegister(board, chip, REG_SEARCH_KEY(unit)+1));
9bb868  ····v2 = ((long)GetRegister(board, chip, REG_SEARCH_KEY(unit)+3)) << 16;
9a512b  ····v2 |= ((long)GetRegister(board, chip, REG_SEARCH_KEY(unit)+2)) << 8;
996273  ····v2 |= ((long)GetRegister(board, chip, REG_SEARCH_KEY(unit)+1));
184051  ··} while (v1 > v2);
f9fc72  ··for (m = 0x800000L; m != 0; m >>= 1) {
63e73f  ····if ((v1 & m) != (v2 & m)) {
9012d1  ······v2 = (v2 & (0xFFFFFFL - m + 1));
6688e1  ······break;
696fe7  ····}
99df1c  ··}
aa0597  ··return (v2);
2aefe6  }
6daf5a
00af5a
b238e5  /*
8e23dc  ·* ·Get the key out of a halted unit and print it to the screen/logs
d0495d  ·*/
5caa69  void CheckAndPrintKey(CHIP_CTX *cp, SEARCH_CTX *ctx, int unit) {
8a5ec8  ··unsigned char key[7];
4c4fa7  ··unsigned char binKey[56];
bcd5f5  ··char buf[128];
0c193c  ··int i,j, goodKey;
e1af5a
73aec4  ··for (i = 0; i < 7; i++)
615cd8  ····key[i] = (unsigned char)GetRegister(cp->board, cp->chip,
ebd f14  ··········REG_SEARCH_KEY(unit)+i);
1e8cfc  ··if (--(key[0]) == 0xFF) ··························/* Decrement key */
804d72  ····if (--(key[1]) == 0xFF)
bad460  ······if (--(key[2]) == 0xFF)
57a964  ········--key[3];
c8815b  ··for (i = 0; i < 56; i++)
b6f7c3  ····binKey[i] = (key[i/8] >> (i&7)) & 1;
e3b642  ··for (i = 7; i >= 0; i--) {
221e9a  ····j = binKey[i*7]*2 + binKey[i*7+1]*4 + binKey[i*7+2]*8 + binKey[i*7+3]*16 +
```

```
--3b12 000f2b672408002000c Page 8 of search.c

a35717 ········binKey[i*7+4]*32 + binKey[i*7+5]*64 + binKey[i*7+6]*128;
9b3764 ····sprintf(buf+14-2*i, "%02X", j);
5bdf1c ··}
a9af5a
5076d5 ··if (QUIET)
19c6bc ····printf("Halt in %02X.%02X.%02X, K=%s P=", cp->board, cp->chip, unit, buf);
be3a1e ··else {
80b718 ····printf("BOARD 0x%02X, CHIP 0x%02X, UNIT 0x%02X HALTED!\n ···K56 = ",
99c03b ············cp->board, cp->chip, unit);
889ac7 ····for (i = 6; i >= 0; i--) printf("%02X", key[i]);
9d52d1 ····printf("\n ···K64 = %s\n", buf);
8adf1c ··}
5ecce4 ··if (FP_LOG) {
4757b8 ····fprintf(FP_LOG, "Halt@ %02X.%02X.%02X, K=",
82c03b ············cp->board, cp->chip, unit);
2a1890 ····for (i = 6; i >= 0; i--) fprintf(FP_LOG, "%02X", key[i]);
8ba909 ····if (VERBOSE) fprintf(FP_LOG, ", K64=%s", buf);
ccdf1c ··}
31af5a
eedd3c ··goodKey = CheckKey(binKey, ctx); ·····················/* prints plaintexts */
efaf5a
7005cd ··if (QUIET) printf(goodKey ? " (OK!)\n" : " (BAD)\n");
352ace ··else printf(" ···***** KEY IS %s *****\n", goodKey ? " OKAY " : "BAD");
7d1792 ··if (FP_LOG) fprintf(FP_LOG, goodKey ? " (=OK!)\n" : " (=BAD)\n");
24b77b ··fflush(stdout);
8384bd ··if (FP_LOG) fflush(FP_LOG);
35efe6 }
41af5a
2daf5a
d238e5 /*
0b1cdc ·* ·Let the user see what's going on.
f3495d ·*/
6bfd4b int ServiceKeyboard(SEARCH_CTX *ctx) {
c31df9 ··int k, i, board, chip, reg, val;
08431e ··char buffer[128];
e6af5a
57c536 ··while (kbhit()) {
d70480 ····k = toupper(getch());
7d037e ····if (k == '?') {
b83116 ······printf("Keystroke options:\n ···ESC=quit search\n");
2dbdd0 ······printf(" ···R=read a chip\n ···SPACE=status\n ···P=pause\n");
c7e45d ······printf(" ···S=set register\n");
d7aa86 ······printf("Press a command letter, ENTER to continue\n");
fcbc76 ······while (!kbhit()) {}
045f6a ······continue;
4a6fe7 ····}
0eb946 ····if (k == 'P') {
a98ae3 ······fprintf(stderr, " ·--- PAUSED ---\n(Press a command letter, ");
ff44cc ······fprintf(stderr, "ENTER to continue, or ? for help.)\n");
43bc76 ······while (!kbhit()) {}
8a5f6a ······continue;
926fe7 ····}
a30d23 ····if (k == 27) {
70cb2a ······fprintf(stderr, " ·-- ESC PRESSED! HIT 'Y' TO CONFIRM HALT --\n");
8c5d92 ······if (toupper(getch()) == 'Y') {
14ea98 ········fprintf(stderr, "Halting...\n");
f28ef9 ········return (-1);
9e42cc ······}
5e4ac1 ······fprintf(stderr, " ··(Not halting.)\n");
c85f6a ······continue;
d46fe7 ····}
517c47 ····if (k == ' ') {
0a5669 ······fprintf(stderr, "There are %ld search units running\n", ctx->totalUnits);
97531b ······fprintf(stderr, "Of %ld blocks: %ld done, %ld unstarted, %ld pending\n",
a34f0b ············1L<<24, ctx->totalFinishedKeyBlocks, ctx->totalUnstartedKeyBlocks,
99b056 ············ctx->totalPendingKeyBlocks);
cce226 ······fprintf(stderr, "The next key block to start is 0x%06lX.\n",
c1657e ············ctx->nextUnstartedKeyBlock);
afb365 ······fprintf(stderr, "Press a command letter or ENTER to continue\n");
5cbc76 ······while (!kbhit()) {}
256fe7 ····}
f2b110 ····if (k == 'R') {
```

```
--ec05  0009a3bfee08002000c Page 9 of search.c
e2fbb8 ······fprintf(stderr, "Enter board and chip (in hex): ");
e27c75 ······fgets(buffer, 127, stdin);
91f579 ······board = chip = -1;
1aea10 ······sscanf(buffer, "%x %x", &board, &chip);
20e47c ······if (board < 0 || board > 255 || chip < 0 || chip > 255) {
c9e3e0 ········fprintf(stderr, "Bad board (0x%02X) or chip (0x%02X)\n", board, chip);
311474 ········continue;
6042cc ······}
707553 ······for (i = 0; i < 256; i++) {
f98149 ········if ((i & 15) == 0)
85d1e0 ··········printf("\n0x%02X 0x%02X 0x%02X:", board, chip, i);
28fc62 ········printf(" %02X", GetRegister(board, chip, i));
0c42cc ······}
d046a0 ······printf("\n");
41b365 ······fprintf(stderr, "Press a command letter or ENTER to continue\n");
7dbc76 ······while (!kbhit()) {}
555f6a ······continue;
406fe7 ····}
2eb53b ····if (k == 'S') {
a57f96 ······fprintf(stderr, "Enter board chip reg value (all hex): ");
af7c75 ······fgets(buffer, 127, stdin);
d40ef2 ······board = chip = reg = val = -1;
629b24 ······sscanf(buffer, "%x %x %x %x", &board, &chip, &reg, &val);
cffcea ······if (board >= 0 && chip >= 0 && reg >= 0 && val >= 0) {
55a015 ········fprintf(stderr, "Writing 0x%02X to 0x%02X.0x%02X reg 0x%02X\n",
287597 ··········val, board, chip, reg);
0391e8 ········SetRegister(board, chip, reg, val);
b142cc ······}
a69b63 ······fprintf(stderr, "Press a command letter or ENTER to continue.\n");
7cbc76 ······while (!kbhit()) {}
b05f6a ······continue;
dc6fe7 ····}
c5df1c ··}
77c86a ··return (0);
fdefe6 }
02af5a
85af5a
a638e5 /*
554279 ·* ·If needed, this function can be used to decide whether keys are
f53655 ·* ·····actually good or not to reject false positives.
c4ca0f ·* ·Returns 1 if the key is not bad, zero if it is wrong.
80495d ·*/
c318aa int CheckKey(unsigned char key[56], SEARCH_CTX *ctx) {
bb169a ··bool ctxt[64],ptxt0[64],ptxt1[64];
45ac6d ··unsigned char p0[8],p1[8];
937d24 ··int i,c;
7faf5a
5148b0 ··/* Compute the plaintext and try to print it to the screen */
085c33 ··for (i = 0; i < 64; i++)
8e67cf ····ctxt[i] = (ctx->ciphertext0[i/8] >> (i&7)) & 1;
fd0c6e ··DecryptDES((bool*)key, ptxt0, ctxt, 0);
1b8715 ··for (i = 0; i < 8; i++) {
5e24a8 ····p0[i] = (unsigned char)(ptxt0[i*8+0]+ptxt0[i*8+1]*2+ptxt0[i*8+2]*4+
a028a1 ··········ptxt0[i*8+3]*8+ptxt0[i*8+4]*16+ptxt0[i*8+5]*32+ptxt0[i*8+6]*64+
a14997 ··········ptxt0[i*8+7]*128);
9ddf1c ··}
871f76 ··for (i = 0; i < 8; i++)
161698 ····p0[i] ^= ctx->plaintextXorMask[i];
c2eed0 ··if (!QUIET) {
1449b2 ····printf(" ···Plaintext0 =");
216b40 ····for (i = 7; i>=0; i--) printf(" %02X", p0[i]);
2c7bdf ····printf(" ··(\"");
dd9984 ····for (i = 7; i>=0; i--)
ce1bc2 ······printf("%c", (p0[i] < 32) ? '?' : p0[i]);
5bbc64 ····printf("\")\n");
5bdf1c ··}
9ba0a6 ··if (QUIET) for (i = 7; i>=0; i--) printf("%02X", p0[i]);
e4036d ··if (FP_LOG) fprintf(FP_LOG, ", ptxt=");
c74e9a ··if (FP_LOG) for (i = 7; i>=0; i--) fprintf(FP_LOG, "%02X", p0[i]);
60af5a
9a5c33 ··for (i = 0; i < 64; i++)
9ace92 ····ctxt[i] = (ctx->ciphertext1[i/8] >> (i&7)) & 1;
```

```
--fcb9 0011107d9008002000c Page 10 of search.c
3509c3 ··DecryptDES((bool*)key, ptxt1, ctxt, 0);
b18715 ··for (i = 0; i < 8; i++) {
c72b26 ····p1[i] = (unsigned char)(ptxt1[i*8+0]+ptxt1[i*8+1]*2+ptxt1[i*8+2]*4+
9df932 ···········ptxt1[i*8+3]*8+ptxt1[i*8+4]*16+ptxt1[i*8+5]*32+ptxt1[i*8+6]*64+
c301bd ···········ptxt1[i*8+7]*128);
f7df1c ··}
839a9d ··if (ctx->searchInfo & 1) { ················/* if CBC mode, XOR w/ 1st ctxt */
7e0371 ····for (i = 0; i < 8; i++)
d78c4c ······p1[i] ^= ctx->ciphertext0[i];
eedf1c ··}
4bef0f ··if (!QUIET) printf(" ···Plaintext1 =");
b2991b ··if (QUIET) printf("/");
e2a99a ··if (FP_LOG) fprintf(FP_LOG, "/");
615a96 ··if (!QUIET) for (i = 7; i>=0; i--) printf(" %02X", p1[i]);
4c3f73 ··if (QUIET) for (i = 7; i>=0; i--) printf("%02X", p1[i]);
aad14f ··if (FP_LOG) for (i = 7; i>=0; i--) fprintf(FP_LOG, "%02X", p1[i]);
54eed0 ··if (!QUIET) {
867bdf ····printf(" ··(\"");
659984 ····for (i = 7; i>=0; i--)
18d65f ······printf("%c", (p1[i] < 32) ? '?' : p1[i]);
8bbc64 ····printf("\")\n");
1adf1c ··}
edaf5a
70b5e8 ··/* Reject key if doesn't contain good characters */
14ca29 ··for(i = 0; i < 8;i++) {
900762 ····if (((ctx->plaintextByteMask) >> i) & 1)
fb5f6a ······continue;
a14d40 ····c = p0[i];
2e24c1 ····if (((ctx->plaintextVector[c/8] >> (c & 7)) & 1) == 0)
08df24 ······return (0);
2f496b ····c = p1[i];
2624c1 ····if (((ctx->plaintextVector[c/8] >> (c & 7)) & 1) == 0)
d9df24 ······return (0);
29df1c ··}
eaaf5a
9e6000 ··/*
66bb06 ···* ·INSERT ADDITIONAL CODE HERE TO REJECT FALSE POSITIVES
8ef9a6 ···*/
82d4d1 ··return (1);
06efe6 }
11af5a
```

```
--2752 00185ee2d9a8002000d Page 1 of search.h

8d2d03 /**************************************************************************
58bbd7 ·* search.h ·············································*
b0c275 ·* ·······················Header file for search.c ·····················*
a129eb ·* ·····················································*
7d09fc ·* ···Written 1998 by Cryptography Research (http://www.cryptography.com) ···*
b28aaf ·* ······and Paul Kocher for the Electronic Frontier Foundation (EFF). ······*
e4caeb ·* ······Placed in the public domain by Cryptography Research and EFF. ······*
584992 ·* ·THIS IS UNSUPPORTED FREE SOFTWARE. USE AND DISTRIBUTE AT YOUR OWN RISK. ·*
4529eb ·* ·····················································*
a4c755 ·* ·IMPORTANT: U.S. LAW MAY REGULATE THE USE AND/OR EXPORT OF THIS PROGRAM. ·*
a529eb ·* ·····················································*
cd489b ·* **************************************************************************
7b29eb ·* ·····················································*
aa6eef ·* ··REVISION HISTORY: ··········································*
0d29eb ·* ·····················································*
6e28d9 ·* ··Version 1.0: ·Initial release by Cryptography Research to EFF. ··········*
e829eb ·* ·····················································*
fbd8c3 ·* **************************************************************************/
24af5a
01915a #ifndef __SEARCH_H
835ec3 #define __SEARCH_H
32af5a
42f0f7 typedef struct {
28e10b ··/* PARAMETERS DEFINING THE SEARCH (THESE GO IN THE SEARCH CONTEXT FILE) */
613b99 ··unsigned char plaintextVector[256/8];
9b6f32 ··unsigned char plaintextXorMask[8];
69ed17 ··unsigned char ciphertext0[8];
15e93c ··unsigned char ciphertext1[8];
c6b1b4 ··unsigned char plaintextByteMask;
360356 ··unsigned char searchInfo;
83af5a
354b87 ··/* PARAMETERS ABOUT THE SEARCH PROCESS */
d8cecc ··long totalUnits; ··································/* total search units */
2dd51a ··long nextUnstartedKeyBlock; ························/* top 24 bits only */
9a86cd ··long totalFinishedKeyBlocks; ············/* number of completed key blocks */
e769ab ··long totalUnstartedKeyBlocks; ············/* number of blocks left to start */
ae947a ··long totalPendingKeyBlocks; ···············/* number of blocks running */
9a5317 } SEARCH_CTX;
f5af5a
8b7454 #endif
85af5a
```

# 6

# *Chip Source Code*

This chapter contains a complete listing of the chip design language (VHDL) documents that we wrote to show both people and machines how we designed the custom gate array chip in our DES cracker.

Today, it is possible to design a complete chip by writing ordinary documents in text files. They are written in a special hardware programming language, called VHDL. This language is understood by chip simulation software, which works much like an ordinary programming language interpreter. Once the designer is satisfied with their design, this VHDL program text can be fed into a "chip compiler". Instead of producing a binary program as a result, the compiler produces low-level design information for a chip.

The compilation process for a chip needs a lot more attention to detail than the average binary software compilation. For example, in modern computers it doesn't make much difference what exact memory locations your binary program is placed into; the program runs largely the same way. In building a chip, human attention and skill is still needed to "lay out" and "route" the building blocks of the chip so that the result has high performance, low power, low cost, and other desirable attributes. This level of detail is also very dependent on the exact technology and equipment being used to build (fabricate) the chip, though the basic design documents are independent of all that.

Thus, these design files don't tell the whole story. You can't just press a button and out pops a chip. But they are useful for understanding our design, because they specify, in a human readable way, just what the chip will do for any valid combination of inputs.

For details on why these documents are printed this way, and how to scan them into a computer, see Chapter 4, *Scanning the Source Code*.

```
--5db8  0006bbca98980030001 Page 1 of addr_key.vhd

bb997d  --------|---------|---------|---------|---------|---------|---------|---------|
aa533a  -- Author ··········: ·Tom Vu ···································
f06e63  -- Date ·············: ·09/19/97 ·······························
704774  -- Description▷ ····: ·UProcessor interface
b65356  -------------------------------------------------------------------
407faf  library ieee;
6411e9  use IEEE.std_logic_1164.all;
b3da83  use IEEE.std_logic_arith.all;
a0e105  use IEEE.std_logic_unsigned.all;
325356  -------------------------------------------------------------------
426895  entity ADDR_KEY is
9daf5a
5914be  port( ··
c300c5  ·········ADDSEL2 ·········▷: in ····std_logic;
4943c8  ·········CHIP_EN ········▷: in ····std_logic;
53a88e  ·········ADDR ·······▷    : in ····std_logic_vector(7 downto 0);
7faf5a
dae24a  ·········ADDR_KEY0 ······▷: out ···std_logic_vector(6 ·downto 0);
efaf30  ·········ADDR_KEY1 ······▷: out ···std_logic_vector(6 ·downto 0);
cf78be  ·········ADDR_KEY2 ······▷: out ···std_logic_vector(6 ·downto 0);
a835c4  ·········ADDR_KEY3 ······▷: out ···std_logic_vector(6 ·downto 0);
34dfb3  ·········ADDR_KEY4 ······▷: out ···std_logic_vector(6 ·downto 0);
b292c9  ·········ADDR_KEY5 ······▷: out ···std_logic_vector(6 ·downto 0);
e54547  ·········ADDR_KEY6 ······▷: out ···std_logic_vector(6 ·downto 0);
3f083d  ·········ADDR_KEY7 ······▷: out ···std_logic_vector(6 ·downto 0);
8b99b8  ·········ADDR_KEY8 ······▷: out ···std_logic_vector(6 ·downto 0);
46d4c2  ·········ADDR_KEY9 ······▷: out ···std_logic_vector(6 ·downto 0);
0d593c  ·········ADDR_KEY10 ·····▷: out ···std_logic_vector(6 ·downto 0);
a25f83  ·········ADDR_KEY11 ·····▷: out ···std_logic_vector(6 ·downto 0);
6a5442  ·········ADDR_KEY12 ·····▷: out ···std_logic_vector(6 ·downto 0);
fd52fd  ·········ADDR_KEY13 ·····▷: out ···std_logic_vector(6 ·downto 0);
2b43c0  ·········ADDR_KEY14 ·····▷: out ···std_logic_vector(6 ·downto 0);
98457f  ·········ADDR_KEY15 ·····▷: out ···std_logic_vector(6 ·downto 0);
b44ebe  ·········ADDR_KEY16 ·····▷: out ···std_logic_vector(6 ·downto 0);
b94801  ·········ADDR_KEY17 ·····▷: out ···std_logic_vector(6 ·downto 0);
1a6cc4  ·········ADDR_KEY18 ·····▷: out ···std_logic_vector(6 ·downto 0);
d66a7b  ·········ADDR_KEY19 ·····▷: out ···std_logic_vector(6 ·downto 0);
638eb2  ·········ADDR_KEY20 ·····▷: out ···std_logic_vector(6 ·downto 0);
ca880d  ·········ADDR_KEY21 ·····▷: out ···std_logic_vector(6 ·downto 0);
ae83cc  ·········ADDR_KEY22 ·····▷: out ···std_logic_vector(6 ·downto 0);
d58573  ·········ADDR_KEY23 ·····▷: out ···std_logic_vector(6 ·downto 0);
ba19f8  ·········DATAI ·······▷    : in ····std_logic_vector(7 downto 0)
61737c  ····);
56af5a
83af5a
aae532  end ADDR_KEY;
e6af5a
e35356  -------------------------------------------------------------------
337e4e  architecture beh of ADDR_KEY is
455356  -------------------------------------------------------------------
a5af5a
a50f89  begin
fed83c  ·
27337d  ADDR_KEY0(0) <= ·'1' when ((ADDR = ·"01000000") and (CHIP_EN = '1') and (ADDSEL█
128ba3  2 = '0')) else '0';
9b8baa  ADDR_KEY0(1) <= ·'1' when ((ADDR = ·"01000001") and (CHIP_EN = '1') and (ADDSEL█
8d8ba3  2 = '0')) else '0';
209ca5  ADDR_KEY0(2) <= ·'1' when ((ADDR = ·"01000010") and (CHIP_EN = '1') and (ADDSEL█
b28ba3  2 = '0')) else '0';
c72472  ADDR_KEY0(3) <= ·'1' when ((ADDR = ·"01000011") and (CHIP_EN = '1') and (ADDSEL█
a68ba3  2 = '0')) else '0';
3e73b3  ADDR_KEY0(4) <= ·'1' when ((ADDR = ·"01000100") and (CHIP_EN = '1') and (ADDSEL█
258ba3  2 = '0')) else '0';
89cb64  ADDR_KEY0(5) <= ·'1' when ((ADDR = ·"01000101") and (CHIP_EN = '1') and (ADDSEL█
388ba3  2 = '0')) else '0';
74dc6b  ADDR_KEY0(6) <= ·'1' when ((ADDR = ·"01000110") and (CHIP_EN = '1') and (ADDSEL█
fa8ba3  2 = '0')) else '0';
d3af5a
e65c59  ADDR_KEY1(0) <= ·'1' when ((ADDR = ·"01001000") and (CHIP_EN = '1') and (ADDSEL█
fc8ba3  2 = '0')) else '0';
76e48e  ADDR_KEY1(1) <= ·'1' when ((ADDR = ·"01001001") and (CHIP_EN = '1') and (ADDSEL█
6b8ba3  2 = '0')) else '0';
```

```
--35c1 0004198492480030001 Page 2 of addr_key.vhd

bcf381 ADDR_KEY1(2) <= ·'1' when ((ADDR = ·"01001010") and (CHIP_EN = '1') and (ADDSEL█
858ba3 2 = '0')) else '0';
a84b56 ADDR_KEY1(3) <= ·'1' when ((ADDR = ·"01001011") and (CHIP_EN = '1') and (ADDSEL█
de8ba3 2 = '0')) else '0';
6e1c97 ADDR_KEY1(4) <= ·'1' when ((ADDR = ·"01001100") and (CHIP_EN = '1') and (ADDSEL█
0a8ba3 2 = '0')) else '0';
c0a440 ADDR_KEY1(5) <= ·'1' when ((ADDR = ·"01001101") and (CHIP_EN = '1') and (ADDSEL█
0d8ba3 2 = '0')) else '0';
16b34f ADDR_KEY1(6) <= ·'1' when ((ADDR = ·"01001110") and (CHIP_EN = '1') and (ADDSEL█
068ba3 2 = '0')) else '0';
deaf5a
096f96 ADDR_KEY2(0) <= ·'1' when ((ADDR = ·"01010000") and (CHIP_EN = '1') and (ADDSEL█
a18ba3 2 = '0')) else '0';
49d741 ADDR_KEY2(1) <= ·'1' when ((ADDR = ·"01010001") and (CHIP_EN = '1') and (ADDSEL█
c48ba3 2 = '0')) else '0';
5fc04e ADDR_KEY2(2) <= ·'1' when ((ADDR = ·"01010010") and (CHIP_EN = '1') and (ADDSEL█
d08ba3 2 = '0')) else '0';
747899 ADDR_KEY2(3) <= ·'1' when ((ADDR = ·"01010011") and (CHIP_EN = '1') and (ADDSEL█
a38ba3 2 = '0')) else '0';
682f58 ADDR_KEY2(4) <= ·'1' when ((ADDR = ·"01010100") and (CHIP_EN = '1') and (ADDSEL█
ed8ba3 2 = '0')) else '0';
a1978f ADDR_KEY2(5) <= ·'1' when ((ADDR = ·"01010101") and (CHIP_EN = '1') and (ADDSEL█
528ba3 2 = '0')) else '0';
dd8080 ADDR_KEY2(6) <= ·'1' when ((ADDR = ·"01010110") and (CHIP_EN = '1') and (ADDSEL█
538ba3 2 = '0')) else '0';
c5af5a
dd00b2 ADDR_KEY3(0) <= ·'1' when ((ADDR = ·"01011000") and (CHIP_EN = '1') and (ADDSEL█
0f8ba3 2 = '0')) else '0';
bab865 ADDR_KEY3(1) <= ·'1' when ((ADDR = ·"01011001") and (CHIP_EN = '1') and (ADDSEL█
aa8ba3 2 = '0')) else '0';
17af6a ADDR_KEY3(2) <= ·'1' when ((ADDR = ·"01011010") and (CHIP_EN = '1') and (ADDSEL█
318ba3 2 = '0')) else '0';
7d17bd ADDR_KEY3(3) <= ·'1' when ((ADDR = ·"01011011") and (CHIP_EN = '1') and (ADDSEL█
b88ba3 2 = '0')) else '0';
8b407c ADDR_KEY3(4) <= ·'1' when ((ADDR = ·"01011100") and (CHIP_EN = '1') and (ADDSEL█
f68ba3 2 = '0')) else '0';
24f8ab ADDR_KEY3(5) <= ·'1' when ((ADDR = ·"01011101") and (CHIP_EN = '1') and (ADDSEL█
7c8ba3 2 = '0')) else '0';
dfefa4 ADDR_KEY3(6) <= ·'1' when ((ADDR = ·"01011110") and (CHIP_EN = '1') and (ADDSEL█
bb8ba3 2 = '0')) else '0';
46af5a
b81db8 ADDR_KEY4(0) <= ·'1' when ((ADDR = ·"01100000") and (CHIP_EN = '1') and (ADDSEL█
378ba3 2 = '0')) else '0';
12a56f ADDR_KEY4(1) <= ·'1' when ((ADDR = ·"01100001") and (CHIP_EN = '1') and (ADDSEL█
7e8ba3 2 = '0')) else '0';
eeb260 ADDR_KEY4(2) <= ·'1' when ((ADDR = ·"01100010") and (CHIP_EN = '1') and (ADDSEL█
f28ba3 2 = '0')) else '0';
bb0ab7 ADDR_KEY4(3) <= ·'1' when ((ADDR = ·"01100011") and (CHIP_EN = '1') and (ADDSEL█
178ba3 2 = '0')) else '0';
b55d76 ADDR_KEY4(4) <= ·'1' when ((ADDR = ·"01100100") and (CHIP_EN = '1') and (ADDSEL█
118ba3 2 = '0')) else '0';
e4e5a1 ADDR_KEY4(5) <= ·'1' when ((ADDR = ·"01100101") and (CHIP_EN = '1') and (ADDSEL█
4a8ba3 2 = '0')) else '0';
93f2ae ADDR_KEY4(6) <= ·'1' when ((ADDR = ·"01100110") and (CHIP_EN = '1') and (ADDSEL█
a68ba3 2 = '0')) else '0';
5eaf5a
81fd36 ADDR_KEY5(0) <=▷ '1' when ((ADDR = ·"01101000") and (CHIP_EN = '1') and (ADDSEL█
e08ba3 2 = '0')) else '0';
7245e1 ADDR_KEY5(1) <=▷ '1' when ((ADDR = ·"01101001") and (CHIP_EN = '1') and (ADDSEL█
918ba3 2 = '0')) else '0';
cb52ee ADDR_KEY5(2) <=▷ '1' when ((ADDR = ·"01101010") and (CHIP_EN = '1') and (ADDSEL█
398ba3 2 = '0')) else '0';
d7ea39 ADDR_KEY5(3) <=▷ '1' when ((ADDR = ·"01101011") and (CHIP_EN = '1') and (ADDSEL█
d48ba3 2 = '0')) else '0';
dcbdf8 ADDR_KEY5(4) <=▷ '1' when ((ADDR = ·"01101100") and (CHIP_EN = '1') and (ADDSEL█
818ba3 2 = '0')) else '0';
0e052f ADDR_KEY5(5) <=▷ '1' when ((ADDR = ·"01101101") and (CHIP_EN = '1') and (ADDSEL█
f08ba3 2 = '0')) else '0';
e41220 ADDR_KEY5(6) <=▷ '1' when ((ADDR = ·"01101110") and (CHIP_EN = '1') and (ADDSEL█
9e8ba3 2 = '0')) else '0';
61af5a
41cef9 ADDR_KEY6(0) <=▷ '1' when ((ADDR = ·"01110000") and (CHIP_EN = '1') and (ADDSEL█
```

```
--4472 0008b773b2580030001 Page 3 of addr_key.vhd

128ba3 2 = '0')) else '0';
b2762e ADDR_KEY6(1) <=▷ '1' when ((ADDR = ·"01110001") and (CHIP_EN = '1') and (ADDSEL■
378ba3 2 = '0')) else '0';
f56121 ADDR_KEY6(2) <=▷ '1' when ((ADDR = ·"01110010") and (CHIP_EN = '1') and (ADDSEL■
c98ba3 2 = '0')) else '0';
4ed9f6 ADDR_KEY6(3) <=▷ '1' when ((ADDR = ·"01110011") and (CHIP_EN = '1') and (ADDSEL■
8e8ba3 2 = '0')) else '0';
6b8e37 ADDR_KEY6(4) <=▷ '1' when ((ADDR = ·"01110100") and (CHIP_EN = '1') and (ADDSEL■
508ba3 2 = '0')) else '0';
5136e0 ADDR_KEY6(5) <=▷ '1' when ((ADDR = ·"01110101") and (CHIP_EN = '1') and (ADDSEL■
c28ba3 2 = '0')) else '0';
a021ef ADDR_KEY6(6) <=▷ '1' when ((ADDR = ·"01110110") and (CHIP_EN = '1') and (ADDSEL■
748ba3 2 = '0')) else '0';
6faf5a
9ea1dd ADDR_KEY7(0) <=▷ '1' when ((ADDR = ·"01111000") and (CHIP_EN = '1') and (ADDSEL■
1f8ba3 2 = '0')) else '0';
d9190a ADDR_KEY7(1) <=▷ '1' when ((ADDR = ·"01111001") and (CHIP_EN = '1') and (ADDSEL■
cb8ba3 2 = '0')) else '0';
df0e05 ADDR_KEY7(2) <=▷ '1' when ((ADDR = ·"01111010") and (CHIP_EN = '1') and (ADDSEL■
908ba3 2 = '0')) else '0';
fdb6d2 ADDR_KEY7(3) <=▷ '1' when ((ADDR = ·"01111011") and (CHIP_EN = '1') and (ADDSEL■
8d8ba3 2 = '0')) else '0';
4be113 ADDR_KEY7(4) <=▷ '1' when ((ADDR = ·"01111100") and (CHIP_EN = '1') and (ADDSEL■
c98ba3 2 = '0')) else '0';
f859c4 ADDR_KEY7(5) <=▷ '1' when ((ADDR = ·"01111101") and (CHIP_EN = '1') and (ADDSEL■
508ba3 2 = '0')) else '0';
1f4ecb ADDR_KEY7(6) <=▷ '1' when ((ADDR = ·"01111110") and (CHIP_EN = '1') and (ADDSEL■
fe8ba3 2 = '0')) else '0';
86af5a
824397 ADDR_KEY8(0) <=▷ '1' when ((ADDR = ·"10000000") and (CHIP_EN = '1') and (ADDSEL■
178ba3 2 = '0')) else '0';
39fb40 ADDR_KEY8(1) <=▷ '1' when ((ADDR = ·"10000001") and (CHIP_EN = '1') and (ADDSEL■
768ba3 2 = '0')) else '0';
e9ec4f ADDR_KEY8(2) <=▷ '1' when ((ADDR = ·"10000010") and (CHIP_EN = '1') and (ADDSEL■
c18ba3 2 = '0')) else '0';
575498 ADDR_KEY8(3) <=▷ '1' when ((ADDR = ·"10000011") and (CHIP_EN = '1') and (ADDSEL■
ff8ba3 2 = '0')) else '0';
720359 ADDR_KEY8(4) <=▷ '1' when ((ADDR = ·"10000100") and (CHIP_EN = '1') and (ADDSEL■
d58ba3 2 = '0')) else '0';
28bb8e ADDR_KEY8(5) <=▷ '1' when ((ADDR = ·"10000101") and (CHIP_EN = '1') and (ADDSEL■
998ba3 2 = '0')) else '0';
1cac81 ADDR_KEY8(6) <=▷ '1' when ((ADDR = ·"10000110") and (CHIP_EN = '1') and (ADDSEL■
288ba3 2 = '0')) else '0';
6daf5a
af2cb3 ADDR_KEY9(0) <=▷ '1' when ((ADDR = ·"10001000") and (CHIP_EN = '1') and (ADDSEL■
498ba3 2 = '0')) else '0';
389464 ADDR_KEY9(1) <=▷ '1' when ((ADDR = ·"10001001") and (CHIP_EN = '1') and (ADDSEL■
cc8ba3 2 = '0')) else '0';
17836b ADDR_KEY9(2) <=▷ '1' when ((ADDR = ·"10001010") and (CHIP_EN = '1') and (ADDSEL■
7d8ba3 2 = '0')) else '0';
673bbc ADDR_KEY9(3) <=▷ '1' when ((ADDR = ·"10001011") and (CHIP_EN = '1') and (ADDSEL■
f68ba3 2 = '0')) else '0';
1f6c7d ADDR_KEY9(4) <=▷ '1' when ((ADDR = ·"10001100") and (CHIP_EN = '1') and (ADDSEL■
d98ba3 2 = '0')) else '0';
e9d4aa ADDR_KEY9(5) <=▷ '1' when ((ADDR = ·"10001101") and (CHIP_EN = '1') and (ADDSEL■
c58ba3 2 = '0')) else '0';
afc3a5 ADDR_KEY9(6) <=▷ '1' when ((ADDR = ·"10001110") and (CHIP_EN = '1') and (ADDSEL■
558ba3 2 = '0')) else '0';
32af5a
428dee ADDR_KEY10(0) <= '1' when ((ADDR = ·"10010000") and (CHIP_EN = '1') and (ADDSEL■
bd8ba3 2 = '0')) else '0';
feaf93 ADDR_KEY10(1) <= '1' when ((ADDR = ·"10010001") and (CHIP_EN = '1') and (ADDSEL■
c18ba3 2 = '0')) else '0';
4d1f73 ADDR_KEY10(2) <= '1' when ((ADDR = ·"10010010") and (CHIP_EN = '1') and (ADDSEL■
cb8ba3 2 = '0')) else '0';
953d0e ADDR_KEY10(3) <= '1' when ((ADDR = ·"10010011") and (CHIP_EN = '1') and (ADDSEL■
1f8ba3 2 = '0')) else '0';
d7b7aa ADDR_KEY10(4) <= '1' when ((ADDR = ·"10010100") and (CHIP_EN = '1') and (ADDSEL■
458ba3 2 = '0')) else '0';
2a95d7 ADDR_KEY10(5) <= '1' when ((ADDR = ·"10010101") and (CHIP_EN = '1') and (ADDSEL■
198ba3 2 = '0')) else '0';
8b2537 ADDR_KEY10(6) <= '1' when ((ADDR = ·"10010110") and (CHIP_EN = '1') and (ADDSEL■
```

```
--8378 000d61250cd80030001 Page 4 of addr_key.vhd

128ba3 2 = '0')) else '0';
1eaf5a
678b96 ADDR_KEY11(0) <= '1' when ((ADDR = ·"10011000") and (CHIP_EN = '1') and (ADDSEL■
2d8ba3 2 = '0')) else '0';
5da9eb ADDR_KEY11(1) <= '1' when ((ADDR = ·"10011001") and (CHIP_EN = '1') and (ADDSEL■
3d8ba3 2 = '0')) else '0';
71190b ADDR_KEY11(2) <= '1' when ((ADDR = ·"10011010") and (CHIP_EN = '1') and (ADDSEL■
bc8ba3 2 = '0')) else '0';
a93b76 ADDR_KEY11(3) <= '1' when ((ADDR = ·"10011011") and (CHIP_EN = '1') and (ADDSEL■
418ba3 2 = '0')) else '0';
7fb1d2 ADDR_KEY11(4) <= '1' when ((ADDR = ·"10011100") and (CHIP_EN = '1') and (ADDSEL■
828ba3 2 = '0')) else '0';
1893af ADDR_KEY11(5) <= '1' when ((ADDR = ·"10011101") and (CHIP_EN = '1') and (ADDSEL■
868ba3 2 = '0')) else '0';
fc234f ADDR_KEY11(6) <= '1' when ((ADDR = ·"10011110") and (CHIP_EN = '1') and (ADDSEL■
628ba3 2 = '0')) else '0';
e3af5a
5ba111 ADDR_KEY12(0) <= '1' when ((ADDR = ·"10100000") and (CHIP_EN = '1') and (ADDSEL■
2e8ba3 2 = '0')) else '0';
94836c ADDR_KEY12(1) <= '1' when ((ADDR = ·"10100001") and (CHIP_EN = '1') and (ADDSEL■
918ba3 2 = '0')) else '0';
3d338c ADDR_KEY12(2) <= '1' when ((ADDR = ·"10100010") and (CHIP_EN = '1') and (ADDSEL■
da8ba3 2 = '0')) else '0';
f211f1 ADDR_KEY12(3) <= '1' when ((ADDR = ·"10100011") and (CHIP_EN = '1') and (ADDSEL■
328ba3 2 = '0')) else '0';
259b55 ADDR_KEY12(4) <= '1' when ((ADDR = ·"10100100") and (CHIP_EN = '1') and (ADDSEL■
1d8ba3 2 = '0')) else '0';
4fb928 ADDR_KEY12(5) <= '1' when ((ADDR = ·"10100101") and (CHIP_EN = '1') and (ADDSEL■
208ba3 2 = '0')) else '0';
bf09c8 ADDR_KEY12(6) <= '1' when ((ADDR = ·"10100110") and (CHIP_EN = '1') and (ADDSEL■
7f8ba3 2 = '0')) else '0';
beaf5a
f9a769 ADDR_KEY13(0) <= '1' when ((ADDR = ·"10101000") and (CHIP_EN = '1') and (ADDSEL■
298ba3 2 = '0')) else '0';
e48514 ADDR_KEY13(1) <= '1' when ((ADDR = ·"10101001") and (CHIP_EN = '1') and (ADDSEL■
4e8ba3 2 = '0')) else '0';
9c35f4 ADDR_KEY13(2) <= '1' when ((ADDR = ·"10101010") and (CHIP_EN = '1') and (ADDSEL■
b28ba3 2 = '0')) else '0';
411789 ADDR_KEY13(3) <= '1' when ((ADDR = ·"10101011") and (CHIP_EN = '1') and (ADDSEL■
6e8ba3 2 = '0')) else '0';
0e9d2d ADDR_KEY13(4) <= '1' when ((ADDR = ·"10101100") and (CHIP_EN = '1') and (ADDSEL■
bf8ba3 2 = '0')) else '0';
c5bf50 ADDR_KEY13(5) <= '1' when ((ADDR = ·"10101101") and (CHIP_EN = '1') and (ADDSEL■
8c8ba3 2 = '0')) else '0';
7b0fb0 ADDR_KEY13(6) <= '1' when ((ADDR = ·"10101110") and (CHIP_EN = '1') and (ADDSEL■
798ba3 2 = '0')) else '0';
b3af5a
8d0e4a ADDR_KEY14(0) <= '1' when ((ADDR = ·"10110000") and (CHIP_EN = '1') and (ADDSEL■
a98ba3 2 = '0')) else '0';
8d2c37 ADDR_KEY14(1) <= '1' when ((ADDR = ·"10110001") and (CHIP_EN = '1') and (ADDSEL■
608ba3 2 = '0')) else '0';
ac9cd7 ADDR_KEY14(2) <= '1' when ((ADDR = ·"10110010") and (CHIP_EN = '1') and (ADDSEL■
9b8ba3 2 = '0')) else '0';
2abeaa ADDR_KEY14(3) <= '1' when ((ADDR = ·"10110011") and (CHIP_EN = '1') and (ADDSEL■
c08ba3 2 = '0')) else '0';
9b340e ADDR_KEY14(4) <= '1' when ((ADDR = ·"10110100") and (CHIP_EN = '1') and (ADDSEL■
ef8ba3 2 = '0')) else '0';
a51673 ADDR_KEY14(5) <= '1' when ((ADDR = ·"10110101") and (CHIP_EN = '1') and (ADDSEL■
948ba3 2 = '0')) else '0';
eca693 ADDR_KEY14(6) <= '1' when ((ADDR = ·"10110110") and (CHIP_EN = '1') and (ADDSEL■
e08ba3 2 = '0')) else '0';
52af5a
990832 ADDR_KEY15(0) <= '1' when ((ADDR = ·"10111000") and (CHIP_EN = '1') and (ADDSEL■
1c8ba3 2 = '0')) else '0';
702a4f ADDR_KEY15(1) <= '1' when ((ADDR = ·"10111001") and (CHIP_EN = '1') and (ADDSEL■
478ba3 2 = '0')) else '0';
5c9aaf ADDR_KEY15(2) <= '1' when ((ADDR = ·"10111010") and (CHIP_EN = '1') and (ADDSEL■
d78ba3 2 = '0')) else '0';
94b8d2 ADDR_KEY15(3) <= '1' when ((ADDR = ·"10111011") and (CHIP_EN = '1') and (ADDSEL■
4e8ba3 2 = '0')) else '0';
a83276 ADDR_KEY15(4) <= '1' when ((ADDR = ·"10111100") and (CHIP_EN = '1') and (ADDSEL■
d68ba3 2 = '0')) else '0';
```

```
--2e62 000ddaca1ad80030001 Page 5 of addr_key.vhd

24100b  ADDR_KEY15(5) <= '1' when ((ADDR = ·"10111101") and (CHIP_EN = '1') and (ADDSEL■
e98ba3  2 = '0')) else '0';
b0a0eb  ADDR_KEY15(6) <= '1' when ((ADDR = ·"10111110") and (CHIP_EN = '1') and (ADDSEL■
448ba3  2 = '0')) else '0';
e8af5a
e24d71  ADDR_KEY16(0) <= '1' when ((ADDR = ·"11000000") and (CHIP_EN = '1') and (ADDSEL■
a58ba3  2 = '0')) else '0';
486f0c  ADDR_KEY16(1) <= '1' when ((ADDR = ·"11000001") and (CHIP_EN = '1') and (ADDSEL■
888ba3  2 = '0')) else '0';
83dfec  ADDR_KEY16(2) <= '1' when ((ADDR = ·"11000010") and (CHIP_EN = '1') and (ADDSEL■
568ba3  2 = '0')) else '0';
bbfd91  ADDR_KEY16(3) <= '1' when ((ADDR = ·"11000011") and (CHIP_EN = '1') and (ADDSEL■
388ba3  2 = '0')) else '0';
0f7735  ADDR_KEY16(4) <= '1' when ((ADDR = ·"11000100") and (CHIP_EN = '1') and (ADDSEL■
f18ba3  2 = '0')) else '0';
a85548  ADDR_KEY16(5) <= '1' when ((ADDR = ·"11000101") and (CHIP_EN = '1') and (ADDSEL■
578ba3  2 = '0')) else '0';
84e5a8  ADDR_KEY16(6) <= '1' when ((ADDR = ·"11000110") and (CHIP_EN = '1') and (ADDSEL■
038ba3  2 = '0')) else '0';
08af5a
554b09  ADDR_KEY17(0) <= '1' when ((ADDR = ·"11001000") and (CHIP_EN = '1') and (ADDSEL■
9f8ba3  2 = '0')) else '0';
6b6974  ADDR_KEY17(1) <= '1' when ((ADDR = ·"11001001") and (CHIP_EN = '1') and (ADDSEL■
388ba3  2 = '0')) else '0';
40d994  ADDR_KEY17(2) <= '1' when ((ADDR = ·"11001010") and (CHIP_EN = '1') and (ADDSEL■
308ba3  2 = '0')) else '0';
4cfbe9  ADDR_KEY17(3) <= '1' when ((ADDR = ·"11001011") and (CHIP_EN = '1') and (ADDSEL■
4a8ba3  2 = '0')) else '0';
1f714d  ADDR_KEY17(4) <= '1' when ((ADDR = ·"11001100") and (CHIP_EN = '1') and (ADDSEL■
208ba3  2 = '0')) else '0';
4e5330  ADDR_KEY17(5) <= '1' when ((ADDR = ·"11001101") and (CHIP_EN = '1') and (ADDSEL■
138ba3  2 = '0')) else '0';
bbe3d0  ADDR_KEY17(6) <= '1' when ((ADDR = ·"11001110") and (CHIP_EN = '1') and (ADDSEL■
688ba3  2 = '0')) else '0';
32af5a
09a03a  ADDR_KEY18(0) <= '1' when ((ADDR = ·"11010000") and (CHIP_EN = '1') and (ADDSEL■
f58ba3  2 = '0')) else '0';
888247  ADDR_KEY18(1) <= '1' when ((ADDR = ·"11010001") and (CHIP_EN = '1') and (ADDSEL■
e18ba3  2 = '0')) else '0';
da32a7  ADDR_KEY18(2) <= '1' when ((ADDR = ·"11010010") and (CHIP_EN = '1') and (ADDSEL■
3f8ba3  2 = '0')) else '0';
3610da  ADDR_KEY18(3) <= '1' when ((ADDR = ·"11010011") and (CHIP_EN = '1') and (ADDSEL■
648ba3  2 = '0')) else '0';
a99a7e  ADDR_KEY18(4) <= '1' when ((ADDR = ·"11010100") and (CHIP_EN = '1') and (ADDSEL■
ad8ba3  2 = '0')) else '0';
deb803  ADDR_KEY18(5) <= '1' when ((ADDR = ·"11010101") and (CHIP_EN = '1') and (ADDSEL■
c88ba3  2 = '0')) else '0';
1608e3  ADDR_KEY18(6) <= '1' when ((ADDR = ·"11010110") and (CHIP_EN = '1') and (ADDSEL■
c48ba3  2 = '0')) else '0';
b9af5a
66a642  ADDR_KEY19(0) <= '1' when ((ADDR = ·"11011000") and (CHIP_EN = '1') and (ADDSEL■
be8ba3  2 = '0')) else '0';
17843f  ADDR_KEY19(1) <= '1' when ((ADDR = ·"11011001") and (CHIP_EN = '1') and (ADDSEL■
678ba3  2 = '0')) else '0';
7d34df  ADDR_KEY19(2) <= '1' when ((ADDR = ·"11011010") and (CHIP_EN = '1') and (ADDSEL■
8e8ba3  2 = '0')) else '0';
1616a2  ADDR_KEY19(3) <= '1' when ((ADDR = ·"11011011") and (CHIP_EN = '1') and (ADDSEL■
278ba3  2 = '0')) else '0';
089c06  ADDR_KEY19(4) <= '1' when ((ADDR = ·"11011100") and (CHIP_EN = '1') and (ADDSEL■
e48ba3  2 = '0')) else '0';
71be7b  ADDR_KEY19(5) <= '1' when ((ADDR = ·"11011101") and (CHIP_EN = '1') and (ADDSEL■
748ba3  2 = '0')) else '0';
bc0e9b  ADDR_KEY19(6) <= '1' when ((ADDR = ·"11011110") and (CHIP_EN = '1') and (ADDSEL■
6d8ba3  2 = '0')) else '0';
88af5a
7a7d73  ADDR_KEY20(0) <= '1' when ((ADDR = ·"11100000") and (CHIP_EN = '1') and (ADDSEL■
ac8ba3  2 = '0')) else '0';
8f5f0e  ADDR_KEY20(1) <= '1' when ((ADDR = ·"11100001") and (CHIP_EN = '1') and (ADDSEL■
578ba3  2 = '0')) else '0';
64efee  ADDR_KEY20(2) <= '1' when ((ADDR = ·"11100010") and (CHIP_EN = '1') and (ADDSEL■
f48ba3  2 = '0')) else '0';
ddcd93  ADDR_KEY20(3) <= '1' when ((ADDR = ·"11100011") and (CHIP_EN = '1') and (ADDSEL■
```

```
--e4fc 0017e2d76cd80030001 Page 6 of addr_key.vhd
128ba3 2 = '0')) else '0';
fe4737 ADDR_KEY20(4) <= '1' when ((ADDR = ·"11100100") and (CHIP_EN = '1') and (ADDSEL■
e68ba3 2 = '0')) else '0';
6e654a ADDR_KEY20(5) <= '1' when ((ADDR = ·"11100101") and (CHIP_EN = '1') and (ADDSEL■
7e8ba3 2 = '0')) else '0';
52d5aa ADDR_KEY20(6) <= '1' when ((ADDR = ·"11100110") and (CHIP_EN = '1') and (ADDSEL■
878ba3 2 = '0')) else '0';
34af5a
b97b0b ADDR_KEY21(0) <= '1' when ((ADDR = ·"11101000") and (CHIP_EN = '1') and (ADDSEL■
4c8ba3 2 = '0')) else '0';
7a5976 ADDR_KEY21(1) <= '1' when ((ADDR = ·"11101001") and (CHIP_EN = '1') and (ADDSEL■
d88ba3 2 = '0')) else '0';
aae996 ADDR_KEY21(2) <= '1' when ((ADDR = ·"11101010") and (CHIP_EN = '1') and (ADDSEL■
b58ba3 2 = '0')) else '0';
53cbeb ADDR_KEY21(3) <= '1' when ((ADDR = ·"11101011") and (CHIP_EN = '1') and (ADDSEL■
618ba3 2 = '0')) else '0';
9d414f ADDR_KEY21(4) <= '1' when ((ADDR = ·"11101100") and (CHIP_EN = '1') and (ADDSEL■
7d8ba3 2 = '0')) else '0';
fb6332 ADDR_KEY21(5) <= '1' when ((ADDR = ·"11101101") and (CHIP_EN = '1') and (ADDSEL■
918ba3 2 = '0')) else '0';
36d3d2 ADDR_KEY21(6) <= '1' when ((ADDR = ·"11101110") and (CHIP_EN = '1') and (ADDSEL■
2f8ba3 2 = '0')) else '0';
f4af5a
8af320 ADDR_KEY22(0) <= '1' when ((ADDR = ·"11110000") and (CHIP_EN = '1') and (ADDSEL■
5d8ba3 2 = '0')) else '0';
74d15d ADDR_KEY22(1) <= '1' when ((ADDR = ·"11110001") and (CHIP_EN = '1') and (ADDSEL■
b78ba3 2 = '0')) else '0';
db61bd ADDR_KEY22(2) <= '1' when ((ADDR = ·"11110010") and (CHIP_EN = '1') and (ADDSEL■
c88ba3 2 = '0')) else '0';
ef43c0 ADDR_KEY22(3) <= '1' when ((ADDR = ·"11110011") and (CHIP_EN = '1') and (ADDSEL■
c18ba3 2 = '0')) else '0';
19c964 ADDR_KEY22(4) <= '1' when ((ADDR = ·"11110100") and (CHIP_EN = '1') and (ADDSEL■
238ba3 2 = '0')) else '0';
f0eb19 ADDR_KEY22(5) <= '1' when ((ADDR = ·"11110101") and (CHIP_EN = '1') and (ADDSEL■
db8ba3 2 = '0')) else '0';
d05bf9 ADDR_KEY22(6) <= '1' when ((ADDR = ·"11110110") and (CHIP_EN = '1') and (ADDSEL■
038ba3 2 = '0')) else '0';
fcaf5a
91f558 ADDR_KEY23(0) <= '1' when ((ADDR = ·"11111000") and (CHIP_EN = '1') and (ADDSEL■
c18ba3 2 = '0')) else '0';
78d725 ADDR_KEY23(1) <= '1' when ((ADDR = ·"11111001") and (CHIP_EN = '1') and (ADDSEL■
288ba3 2 = '0')) else '0';
6467c5 ADDR_KEY23(2) <= '1' when ((ADDR = ·"11111010") and (CHIP_EN = '1') and (ADDSEL■
178ba3 2 = '0')) else '0';
c345b8 ADDR_KEY23(3) <= '1' when ((ADDR = ·"11111011") and (CHIP_EN = '1') and (ADDSEL■
d48ba3 2 = '0')) else '0';
c5cf1c ADDR_KEY23(4) <= '1' when ((ADDR = ·"11111100") and (CHIP_EN = '1') and (ADDSEL■
bd8ba3 2 = '0')) else '0';
78ed61 ADDR_KEY23(5) <= '1' when ((ADDR = ·"11111101") and (CHIP_EN = '1') and (ADDSEL■
b78ba3 2 = '0')) else '0';
c65d81 ADDR_KEY23(6) <= '1' when ((ADDR = ·"11111110") and (CHIP_EN = '1') and (ADDSEL■
348ba3 2 = '0')) else '0';
7faf5a
605356 -----------------------------------------------------------------------------
c0b08a end beh;
9c5356 -----------------------------------------------------------------------------
7eaf5a
```

```
--f530 0001ae1063b80030002 Page 1 of des.vhd

bb997d ---------¦---------¦---------¦---------¦---------¦---------¦---------¦---------¦
aa533a -- Author ·········: ·Tom Vu ·········································
bf8d0a -- Date ···········: ·09/27/97 ·····································
b4d6cd -- Description▷ ····: ·Left and Right 32-bit registers ·············
a5625a -- ------------------------------------------------------------------
aa7faf library ieee;
5211e9 use IEEE.std_logic_1164.all;
cada83 use IEEE.std_logic_arith.all;
77e105 use IEEE.std_logic_unsigned.all;
df625a -- ------------------------------------------------------------------
4d7373 entity MESG is
a7af5a
e1c57e port( ··CLK ·▷ ···▷      : in ····std_logic;
363f61 ········RST_N ·▷ ··▷     : in ····std_logic;
d21689 ········START▷ ···▷      : in ····std_logic;
fd4f77 ▷       DONE ····▷        : in ····std_logic;
e91049 ▷       MESSAGE ····▷     : in ····std_logic_vector(63 downto 0);
ea38ba ▷       SUBKEY ····▷      : in ····std_logic_vector(47 downto 0);
b1a256 ·······▷RESULT ··▷       : out ···std_logic_vector(63 downto 0)
dd737c ····);
a9af5a
735a26 end MESG;
daaf5a
be625a -- ------------------------------------------------------------------
1e4170 architecture beh of MESG is
c8625a -- ------------------------------------------------------------------
4daf5a
c739ea signal IP_KEY ··▷        : std_logic_vector(63 downto 0);
97e79c signal MESG_LEFT ▷       : std_logic_vector(31 downto 0);
cf7187 signal MESG_RIGHT ▷      : std_logic_vector(31 downto 0);
02342b signal NEW_L ·▷ ▷        : std_logic_vector(31 downto 0);
1ea3a1 signal L ·····▷ ▷        : std_logic_vector(31 downto 0);
814d49 signal R ·····▷ ▷        : std_logic_vector(31 downto 0);
e1d2c1 signal EXPANDED_R▷       : std_logic_vector(47 downto 0);
73178d signal X_KEY▷    ▷       : std_logic_vector(47 downto 0);
b2deb0 signal S_OUT ··▷▷        : std_logic_vector(31 downto 0);
9e1cda signal FP_IN ▷  ▷        : std_logic_vector(63 downto 0);
c90d80 signal FP_OUT ▷ ▷       : std_logic_vector(63 downto 0);
ff907c signal P_IN ▷   ▷        : std_logic_vector(31 downto 0);
b66db2 signal P_OUT ▷  ▷        : std_logic_vector(31 downto 0);
ddaf5a
f02f82 component EX
f214be port( ··
5913ef ········EX_IN ···········: in ···std_logic_vector(31 downto 0);
d5f417 ········EX_OUT ··········: out ···std_logic_vector(47 downto 0));
b1e2c6 end component;
10af5a
cc44e1 component IP
f5cc6d port(
86b12b ········IP_IN ···········: in ····std_logic_vector(63 downto 0);
5e694d ········IP_OUT ··········: out ···std_logic_vector(63 downto 0));
f0e2c6 end component;
44af5a
d00e26 component FP
36cc6d port(
ed41a9 ········FP_IN ···········: in ····std_logic_vector(63 downto 0);
81cea7 ········FP_OUT ··········: out ···std_logic_vector(63 downto 0));
18e2c6 end component;
6caf5a
8d6a7a component P
7ecc6d port(
e4e2cc ········P_IN ···········: in ····std_logic_vector(31 downto 0);
80faaf ········P_OUT ··········: out ···std_logic_vector(31 downto 0));
79e2c6 end component;
21af5a
028893 component S_TABLE
7b96b5 port( ·KEY ·······: in ····std_logic_vector(47 downto 0);
111046 ·······S_OUT ·····: out ···std_logic_vector(31 downto 0));
32e2c6 end component;
87af5a
3b0f89 begin
1aaf5a
```

```
--aaa2 00048aa879b80030002 Page 2 of des.vhd

7d0363 MESSAGE1: EX
8f7097 port map( ·····
e5c895 ▷        EX_IN ···········=> R,
e4f1b2 ·······▷ EX_OUT ········▷=> EXPANDED_R);·
6eaf5a
de647d MESSAGE2: IP
b87097 port map( ·····
f358db ▷        IP_IN ···········=> MESSAGE,
284c3d ·······▷ IP_OUT ········▷=> IP_KEY);·
ceaf5a
0a1b74 MESSAGE3: S_TABLE
dd7097 port map( ·····
06527c ▷        KEY ···········▷ => X_KEY,
0a7ff2 ·······▷ S_OUT ········▷ => S_OUT);·
d6af5a
fdc7d3 MESSAGE4: P
437097 port map( ·····
14299f ▷        P_IN ···········▷=> S_OUT,
5cf3c6 ·······▷ P_OUT ········▷ => P_OUT);·
0faf5a
afaf5a
e8326b MESSAGE5: FP
307097 port map( ·····
b191f5 ▷        FP_IN ···········=> FP_IN,
c8be19 ·······▷ FP_OUT ········▷=> FP_OUT);·
59af5a
b2af5a
cc625a -- ----------------------------------------------------------------------
cf63c2 -- Split_to_LEFT_and_RIGHT: process(IP_KEY)
9b625a -- ----------------------------------------------------------------------
339acc -- ▷    begin
cdd360 -- ▷        for i in 0 to 31 loop
bd964e -- ▷        ····MESG_RIGHT(i) ▷      <= IP_KEY(i);
5ffb1b -- ▷        ····MESG_LEFT(i) ▷       <= IP_KEY(i+32);
913689 -- ▷        end loop;
0d55d2 -- end process Split_to_LEFT_and_RIGHT;
74af5a
191a19 MESG_RIGHT <= IP_KEY(31 downto 0);
7a284c MESG_LEFT ·<= IP_KEY(63 downto 32);
b3625a -- ----------------------------------------------------------------------
726ec6 L_AND_R_REG_PR: process(RST_N,CLK)
74625a -- ----------------------------------------------------------------------
080f89 begin
ac6118 if RST_N = '0' then
8ce37f ▷        L <= (others => '0');
38ab45 ▷        R <= (others => '0');
a684bd elsif CLK'event and CLK = '1' then
560a81 if (START = '1') then
e40d0d ▷        L <= MESG_LEFT;
ff2134 ▷        R <= MESG_RIGHT;
f9def1 else·
f8afcf ▷        L <= R;
0a1c45 ▷        R <= NEW_L;
b4df0b end if;
addf0b end if;
9baf5a
6bb840 end process L_AND_R_REG_PR;
a5af5a
0c625a -- ----------------------------------------------------------------------
1d9726 KEY_XOR_PR: process(SUBKEY,EXPANDED_R)
6e625a -- ----------------------------------------------------------------------
440f89 begin
0b13e9 ▷        for i in 0 to 47 loop
e08bd9 ▷        ····X_KEY(i) ▷    <= SUBKEY(i) xor EXPANDED_R(i);
737aa9 ▷        end loop;
2fa96e end process KEY_XOR_PR;
2eaf5a
a9625a -- ----------------------------------------------------------------------
9f5de9 L_XOR_PR: process(L,P_OUT)
6e625a -- ----------------------------------------------------------------------
db0f89 begin
48d72a ▷        for i in 0 to 31 loop
```

```
--eae4 000c6a93b2480030002 Page 3 of des.vhd
1c3971 ▷        ····NEW_L(i) ▷   <= L(i) xor P_OUT(i);
5a7aa9 ▷        end loop;
40a92f end process L_XOR_PR;
afaf5a
50625a -- -----------------------------------------------------------------
982ac6 -- Combine final L and R to FP
19625a -- -----------------------------------------------------------------
74c45a ▷        FP_IN <= NEW_L(31 downto 0) & R(31 downto 0);
5eaf5a
ad625a -- -----------------------------------------------------------------
76a4c0 RESULT_PR: process(RST_N,CLK)
86625a -- -----------------------------------------------------------------
040f89 begin
e96118 if RST_N = '0' then
beb369 ▷        RESULT <= (others => '0');
b684bd elsif CLK'event and CLK = '1' then
9a4eba if (DONE = '1') then
0e352f ▷        RESULT <= FP_OUT;
ecdf0b end if;
5edf0b end if;
61af5a
d402a3 end process RESULT_PR;
69af5a
05625a -- -----------------------------------------------------------------
d9b08a end beh;
b9625a -- -----------------------------------------------------------------
02af5a
8c7faf library ieee;
1711e9 use IEEE.std_logic_1164.all;
d5da83 use IEEE.std_logic_arith.all;
8ae105 use IEEE.std_logic_unsigned.all;
78625a -- -----------------------------------------------------------------
d86749 entity DES is
36af5a
48c57e port( ··CLK ·▷   ····▷   : in ····std_logic;
223f61 ········RST_N ·▷ ··▷    : in ····std_logic;
1e1689 ········START▷  ····▷   : in ····std_logic;
921049 ▷        MESSAGE ····▷   : in ····std_logic_vector(63 downto 0);
1be2ae ▷        KEY ····▷       : in ····std_logic_vector(55 downto 0);
c319f6 ▷        DONE ····▷      : out ····std_logic;
858cf6 ▷        CNT ····▷       : out ····std_logic_vector(4 downto 0);
65bde3 ········▷DES_OUT ··▷     : out ···std_logic_vector(63 downto 0)
a2737c ····);
2aaf5a
8ccbd8 end DES;
87af5a
fa625a -- -----------------------------------------------------------------
18ff4a architecture beh of DES is
31625a -- -----------------------------------------------------------------
3b4ffd signal SUBKEY▷  ▷       : std_logic_vector(47 downto 0);
6b1864 signal DONE_BAK▷▷       : std_logic;
42af5a
74cf4e component MESG
f9c57e port( ··CLK ·▷   ····▷   : in ····std_logic;
063f61 ········RST_N ·▷ ··▷    : in ····std_logic;
051689 ········START▷  ····▷   : in ····std_logic;
be4f77 ▷        DONE ····▷      : in ····std_logic;
f11049 ▷        MESSAGE ····▷   : in ····std_logic_vector(63 downto 0);
4c38ba ▷        SUBKEY ····▷    : in ····std_logic_vector(47 downto 0);
7ea256 ········▷RESULT ··▷      : out ···std_logic_vector(63 downto 0)
ca737c ····);
77e2c6 end component;
2daf5a
cdddef component KEY_GEN·
15cdc7 port( ··CLK ········: in ····std_logic;
1e320d ········RST_N ······: in ····std_logic;
667f2d ········START ······: in ····std_logic;
46b9ba ········KEY_IN ·····: in ····std_logic_vector(55 downto 0);
cb6da8 ········DONE ·······: out ···std_logic;
19e5f0 ········CNT ········: out ···std_logic_vector(4 downto 0);
bb045e ········KEY_OUT ···: out ···std_logic_vector(47 downto 0));
c6e2c6 end component;
```

```
--381d 00180ac228180030002 Page 4 of des.vhd

e0af5a
4a0f89 begin
e0af5a
554a2f DES1: MESG
2e1940 port map( ··
1392d2 ▷          CLK ·▷ ···▷      => CLK,
49c81c ········RST_N ·▷ ··▷      => RST_N,
223042 ········START▷ ···▷      => START,
feff4b ▷        DONE ····▷       => DONE_BAK,
113f83 ▷        MESSAGE ····▷    => MESSAGE,
f157a1 ▷        SUBKEY ····▷     => SUBKEY,
160e22 ·······▷RESULT ··▷       => DES_OUT
faa415 ····▷   );
b30759 DES2: KEY_GEN
857097 port map( ·····
139892 ········CLK ·······▷     => CLK,
f289c8 ········RST_N ·····▷     => RST_N,
c6ba76 ········START ·····▷     => START,
22bffc ········KEY_IN ····▷     => KEY,
5045c8 ········DONE ······▷     => DONE_BAK,
5b11ad ········CNT ······▷      => CNT,
4ac932 ········KEY_OUT ···▷     => SUBKEY
130886 ▷         );·
15af5a
834dc0 DONE <= DONE_BAK;
60af5a
c9b08a end beh;
80af5a
```

```
--19f8  000b92e30e480030003 Page 1 of des_ctl.vhd

bb997d  --------|---------|---------|---------|---------|---------|---------|---------|
e7625a  --      ---------------------------------------------------------------------
9cde87  -- AUTHOR ·········:  ·TOM VU ···················································--
0773db  -- DATE ···········:  ·10/15/97 ················································--
e54087  -- TITLE ···········:  ·DES ·TEST BENCH ·········································--
8178f4  -- FILE ············:  ·des_ctl.vhd ············································--
1b997d  --------|---------|---------|---------|---------|---------|---------|---------|
8c5356  --      ---------------------------------------------------------------------
9b7faf  library ieee;
c111e9  use IEEE.std_logic_1164.all;
bcda83  use IEEE.std_logic_arith.all;
bde105  use IEEE.std_logic_unsigned.all;
f05c9a  use ieee.std_logic_textio.all;
9faf5a
b03876  entity CTL is
73af5a
47ec7a  port( ··CLK ·············: in ····std_logic;
f42e77  ········RST_N ···········: in ····std_logic;
99d3de  ········START ··········: in ····std_logic;
8abd37  ········DECR ···········: in ····std_logic;
ef5dd7  ········DES_OUT ·········: in ····std_logic_vector(63 downto 0);
d1b4b9  ········DECR_INT ········: out ···std_logic;
8be15e  ········READ_EN ········: out ···std_logic;
d4e72f  ········START_INT ·······: out ···std_logic;
b606d7  ········MESSAGE ·········: out ···std_logic_vector(63 downto 0);
5eb5fb  ········KEY ·········▷  : out ···std_logic_vector(55 downto 0);
b06cd6  ········DATA ·········▷  : inout ·std_logic_vector(31 downto 0)
e2737c  ····);
b1af5a
88eb4c  end CTL;
0daf5a
3e625a  -- ------------------------------------------------------------------------
ee9bda  architecture BEH of CTL is
e3625a  -- ------------------------------------------------------------------------
27af5a
b9c8c3  signal CNT16 ············▷: std_logic_vector(3 downto 0);
446bef  signal MSG0 ············▷ : std_logic_vector(31 downto 0);
716d50  signal MSG1 ············▷ : std_logic_vector(31 downto 0);
905ba6  signal KEY0 ············▷ : std_logic_vector(31 downto 0);
1428a9  signal KEY1 ············▷ : std_logic_vector(23 downto 0);
e7b07c  signal OUT0 ············▷ : std_logic_vector(31 downto 0);
91b6c3  signal OUT1 ············▷ : std_logic_vector(31 downto 0);
b0c721  signal DATA_BAK ········· : std_logic_vector(31 downto 0);
fd3ce5  signal START_INT_D▷    : std_logic;
7caf5a
d50f89  begin
37625a  -- ------------------------------------------------------------------------
88c675  CNT_PR: process(CLK,RST_N)·
3d625a  -- ------------------------------------------------------------------------
230f89  begin
4b1801  ·········if RST_N = '0' then
46c97a  ··················CNT16 <= "0000";
894f5b  ·····▷  ▷          START_INT <= '0';
ed6ab2  ·····▷  ▷          DECR_INT <= '0';
ed9e8f  ········elsif CLK'event and CLK = '1' then
b59193  ·····▷  ▷          START_INT <= START_INT_D;
56b749  ▷    ▷          if CNT16 = 4 then
419236  ·····▷  ▷      ▷      DECR_INT <= DECR;
db124d  ▷        ▷      end if;
863598  ············if START = '1' ·then
ecd5c1  ················CNT16 <= "0001";
e9e93c  ············else
09036d  ················CNT16 <= CNT16 + 1;
8101cd  ············end if;
fcb985  ········end if;
7c5890  end process;
d8af5a
55625a  -- ------------------------------------------------------------------------
542e43  KEY ····<= KEY1 & KEY0;
3998b6  MESSAGE <= MSG1 & MSG0;
8daf5a
b9875a  START_INT_D <= '1' when CNT16 = 4 else '0';
```

```
--5868 000b6ca077a80030003 Page 2 of des_ctl.vhd
3b625a -- ---------------------------------------------------------------------------
f8afe8 REG_IN_PR: process(RST_N,CLK)
f0625a -- ---------------------------------------------------------------------------
bc0f89 begin
636118 if RST_N = '0' then
f8215b ········MSG0 <= (others => '0');
b18806 ········MSG1 <= (others => '0');
83e94c ········KEY0 <= (others => '0');
814011 ········KEY1 <= (others => '0');
b60502 elsif CLK'event and CLK = '0' then
e7f081 ····case CNT16 is
2a0cfb ▷    when ·"0001" =>
973aa4 ········▷      MSG0 <= DATA;
bb9705 ▷    when ·"0010" =>
d56f35 ········▷      MSG1 <= DATA;
a2932e ▷    when ·"0011" =>
b26b0e ········▷      KEY0 <= DATA;
57896f ▷    when ·"0100" =>
e8f94a ········▷      KEY1 <= DATA(23 downto 0);
283cff ▷    when others =>
4634e8 ▷         null;
cf9517 ····end case;
39df0b end if;
c3af5a
2c7f1c end process REG_IN_PR;
638b8d ---------------------------------------------------------------------------------
5d7518 MESSAGE_OUT_P: process (CNT16,DES_OUT)
de0f89 begin
1bf081 ····case CNT16 is
76ac3f ▷    when ·"0110" ¦ "0111" =>
dc5734 ········▷      DATA <= DES_OUT(63 downto 32);
b475bf ▷         ▷   READ_EN <= '1';
9b9950 ▷    when ·"1000" ¦ "1001" =>
e910d3 ········▷      DATA <= DES_OUT(31 downto 0);
5e75bf ▷         ▷   READ_EN <= '1';
3e3cff ▷    when others =>
322d30 ▷         ▷   DATA <= (others => 'Z');
9b6904 ▷         ▷   READ_EN <= '0';
c29517 ····end case;
885890 end process;
28d83c ·
ce6687 --DATA <= DATA_BAK;
645c73 end BEH;
aa625a -- ---------------------------------------------------------------------------
777faf library ieee;
4011e9 use IEEE.std_logic_1164.all;
9dda83 use IEEE.std_logic_arith.all;
47e105 use IEEE.std_logic_unsigned.all;
ab5c9a use ieee.std_logic_textio.all;
d3f403 use std.textio.all;
0daf5a
6faf5a
79bf60 entity DES_CTL is·
d3ec7a port( ··CLK ·············: in ····std_logic;
ef2e77 ········RST_N ···········: in ····std_logic;
e8d3de ········START ···········: in ····std_logic;
67bd37 ········DECR ············: in ····std_logic;
f19930 ········DONE ············: out ····std_logic;
1c714a ········READ_EN ·········: out ····std_logic;
006cd6 ········DATA ·········▷ : inout ·std_logic_vector(31 downto 0)
e3737c ····);
c4af5a
38c0b8 end DES_CTL;
2faf5a
fb5356 ---------------------------------------------------------------------------------
71bf08 architecture beh of DES_CTL is
c7af5a
4ee222 component DES·
15ec7a port( ··CLK ·············: in ····std_logic;
832e77 ········RST_N ···········: in ····std_logic;
d6d3de ········START ···········: in ····std_logic;
b6bd37 ········DECR ············: in ····std_logic;
```

```
--4c0d  001891375c380030003 Page 3 of des_ctl.vhd

e60995  ········MESSAGE ········: in ····std_logic_vector(63 downto 0);
b5604f  ········KEY ···········: in ····std_logic_vector(55 downto 0);
389930  ········DONE ··········: out ····std_logic;
4a3fe1  ········DES_OUT ········: out ···std_logic_vector(63 downto 0)
43737c  ····);
14af5a
cae2c6  end component;
9caf5a
89c2b6  component CTL·
2aec7a  port( ··CLK ···········: in ····std_logic;
322e77  ········RST_N ·········: in ····std_logic;
b4d3de  ········START ·········: in ····std_logic;
19bd37  ········DECR ··········: in ····std_logic;
5f5dd7  ········DES_OUT ········: in ····std_logic_vector(63 downto 0);
c9b4b9  ········DECR_INT ·······: out ···std_logic;
5152ad  ········READ_EN ·······▷: out ···std_logic;
35e72f  ········START_INT ······: out ···std_logic;
4606d7  ········MESSAGE ········: out ···std_logic_vector(63 downto 0);
e2b5fb  ········KEY ··········▷ : out ···std_logic_vector(55 downto 0);
ff6cd6  ········DATA ·········▷ : inout ·std_logic_vector(31 downto 0)
0f737c  ····);
b2e2c6  end component;
6eaf5a
e11578  signal START_INT ····▷ : std_logic;
cc4d61  signal DECR_INT ·······▷: std_logic;
2af53c  signal MESSAGE ········▷: std_logic_vector(63 downto 0);
3c9af4  signal KEY ···········▷: std_logic_vector(55 downto 0);
0e7fd8  signal DES_OUT ········▷: std_logic_vector(63 downto 0);
33af5a
adc009  ------------------------------------------------
800f89  begin
1daf5a
688c8c  DES_CTL1 : DES·
58d9d1  port map(·
01d07d  ········CLK ···········=> CLK,
182dd5  ········RST_N ·········=> RST_N,
d4a453  ········START ·········=> START_INT,
836338  ········DECR ··········=> DECR_INT,
60fb6c  ········MESSAGE ········=> MESSAGE,
dff105  ········KEY ···········=> KEY,
e8de19  ········DONE ··········=> DONE,
9ff5f9  ········DES_OUT ········=> DES_OUT
3e6275  );
8caf5a
0bbe8d  DES_CTL2 : CTL
c215ed  port map( ··CLK ▷        => CLK,
f5a06a  ········RST_N ·▷▷       => RST_N,
2dc2ff  ········START ▷ ▷       => START,
c1276c  ········DECR ▷   ▷      => DECR,
9fd115  ········DES_OUT▷▷       => DES_OUT,
1a0875  ········DECR_INT▷       => DECR_INT,
a721c4  ········READ_EN▷▷       => READ_EN,
7bef90  ········START_INT▷      => START_INT,
cf2a60  ········MESSAGE ▷       => MESSAGE,
2f2a6a  ········KEY▷     ▷      => KEY,
c950dc  ········DATA▷    ▷      => DATA
e5737c  ····);
06af5a
89b08a  end beh;
```

```
--6dad 001b55b5c0880030004 Page 1 of ex.vhd

bb997d ---------:---------:---------:---------:---------:---------:---------:---------:
aa533a -- Author ·········: ·Tom Vu ································
bf8d0a -- Date ···········: ·09/27/97 ································
b4d6cd -- Description▷ ····: ·Left and Right 32-bit registers ··············
a5625a -- ----------------------------------------------------------------------
aa7faf library ieee;
5211e9 use IEEE.std_logic_1164.all;
cada83 use IEEE.std_logic_arith.all;
77e105 use IEEE.std_logic_unsigned.all;
05af5a
59af5a
7b625a -- ----------------------------------------------------------------------
a6c076 entity EX is
59af5a
3714be port( ··
ebba80 ········EX_IN ·▷▷        : in ▷  std_logic_vector(31 downto 0);
be7fd5 ········▷EX_OUT ···▷     : out ···std_logic_vector(47 downto 0)
6c737c ····);
06af5a
6851d9 end EX;
b0af5a
08625a -- ----------------------------------------------------------------------
c32a2a architecture beh of EX is
0e625a -- ----------------------------------------------------------------------
41a039 subtype small_integer is INTEGER range 0 to 31;
ed005c type EX_TYPE is array(0 to 47) of small_integer;
a1af5a
42f2e2 signal EX_TABLE : EX_TYPE;
f7af5a
090f89 begin
e0af5a
1b7095 EX_TABLE <= ▷    (31, 0, 1, 2, 3, 4,
f87e8b ▷          ▷       ··3, 4, 5, 6, 7, 8,
523799 ▷          ▷       ··7, 8, 9,10,11,12,
8d4bab ▷          ▷       ·11,12,13,14,15,16,
d21f04 ▷          ▷       ·15,16,17,18,19,20,
01424a ▷          ▷       ·19,20,21,22,23,24,
275e35 ▷          ▷       ·23,24,25,26,27,28,
392f5c ▷          ▷       ·27,28,29,30,31, 0);▷
dbaf5a
6eaf5a
f7625a -- ----------------------------------------------------------------------
e0c809 EX_PR: process(EX_IN,EX_TABLE)
cd625a -- ----------------------------------------------------------------------
2a0f89 begin
3bf616 ·▷       for i in 0 to 47 loop
af78b9 ·▷          ····EX_OUT(i) <= EX_IN(EX_TABLE(i)) ;
b38a2a ·▷          end loop;
fd2a0c end process EX_PR;
90625a -- ----------------------------------------------------------------------
c1b08a end beh;
b5625a -- ----------------------------------------------------------------------
```

```
--8e68 00126a906e980030005 Page 1 of fp.vhd

bb997d ---------¦---------¦---------¦---------¦---------¦---------¦---------¦---------¦
aa533a -- Author ·········: ·Tom Vu ··································
bf8d0a -- Date ···········: ·09/27/97 ······························
b4d6cd -- Description▷ ···: ·Left and Right 32-bit registers ··············
a5625a -- ---------------------------------------------------------------------
aa7faf library ieee;
5211e9 use IEEE.std_logic_1164.all;
cada83 use IEEE.std_logic_arith.all;
77e105 use IEEE.std_logic_unsigned.all;
05af5a
59af5a
7b625a -- ---------------------------------------------------------------------
98af5a
0b625a -- ---------------------------------------------------------------------
14962b entity FP is
87af5a
b6cc6d port(
9a41a9 ·········FP_IN ···········: in ····std_logic_vector(63 downto 0);
b43f8e ········FP_OUT ··········: out ···std_logic_vector(63 downto 0)
3d737c ····);
31af5a
a7b2d6 end FP;
b2af5a
79625a -- ---------------------------------------------------------------------
8e7c77 architecture beh of FP is
70625a -- ---------------------------------------------------------------------
7f7bd6 subtype small_integer is INTEGER range 0 to 63;
6b698c type FP_TYPE is array(0 to 63) of small_integer;
52af5a
53dabe signal FP_TABLE : FP_TYPE;
62af5a
800f89 begin
21af5a
ed66ec FP_TABLE <= ····(57,49,41,33,25,17, 9, 1,
fa1781 ················59,51,43,35,27,19,11, 3,
7bf5ff ················61,53,45,37,29,21,13, 5,
f2d9a6 ················63,55,47,39,31,23,15, 7,
84783c ················56,48,40,32,24,16, 8, 0,
795d3b ················58,50,42,34,26,18,10, 2,
9abf45 ················60,52,44,36,28,20,12, 4,
36e3e3 ················62,54,46,38,30,22,14, 6);
f0af5a
fdaf5a
71625a -- ---------------------------------------------------------------------
3c3fd4 FP_PR: process(FP_TABLE,FP_IN)
fb625a -- ---------------------------------------------------------------------
dc0f89 begin
623e98 ········for i in 0 to 63 loop
964718 ···········FP_OUT(FP_TABLE(i)) <= FP_IN(i);
9636d5 ·········end loop;
3ea33a end process FP_PR;
61625a -- ---------------------------------------------------------------------
70b08a end beh;
26af5a
```

```
--69ed  0011bd4de4480030006 Page 1 of ip.vhd

bb997d  ---------|---------|---------|---------|---------|---------|---------|---------|
aa533a  -- Author ..........: ·Tom Vu ........................................
bf8d0a  -- Date ...........: ·09/27/97 .......................................
b4d6cd  -- Description▷ ...: ·Left and Right 32-bit registers ...............
a5625a  -- -----------------------------------------------------------------------
aa7faf  library ieee;
5211e9  use IEEE.std_logic_1164.all;
cada83  use IEEE.std_logic_arith.all;
77e105  use IEEE.std_logic_unsigned.all;
05af5a
59af5a
7b625a  -- -----------------------------------------------------------------------
e1aba2  entity IP is
72af5a
c2cc6d  port(
669c71  ▷       IP_IN ····▷        : in ····std_logic_vector(63 downto 0);
02b42e  ·······▷IP_OUT ··▷        : out ···std_logic_vector(63 downto 0)
37737c  ····);
89af5a
2a002f  end IP;
eeaf5a
79625a  -- -----------------------------------------------------------------------
ab41fe  architecture beh of IP is
51625a  -- -----------------------------------------------------------------------
c37bd6  subtype small_integer is INTEGER range 0 to 63;
dfd216  type IP_TYPE is array(0 to 63) of small_integer;
91af5a
a18ac0  signal IP_TABLE : IP_TYPE;
5aaf5a
760f89  begin
a8af5a
8483b9  IP_TABLE <= ▷     (39, 7,47,15,55,23,63,31,
4f63cb  ▷          ▷      ·38, 6,46,14,54,22,62,30,
305108  ▷          ▷      ·37, 5,45,13,53,21,61,29,
401bb2  ▷          ▷      ·36, 4,44,12,52,20,60,28,
2656f9  ▷          ▷      ·35, 3,43,11,51,19,59,27,
601c43  ▷          ▷      ·34, 2,42,10,50,18,58,26,
e53413  ▷          ▷      ·33, 1,41, 9,49,17,57,25,
ce37fe  ▷          ▷      ·32, 0,40, 8,48,16,56,24);▷
8faf5a
16625a  -- -----------------------------------------------------------------------
3f96cf  IP_PR: process(IP_TABLE,IP_IN)
40625a  -- -----------------------------------------------------------------------
310f89  begin
8c77f0  ▷        for i in 0 to 63 loop
5d4d4d  ▷        ····IP_OUT(IP_TABLE(i)) <= IP_IN(i);
6b7aa9  ▷        end loop;
42bace  end process IP_PR;
89625a  -- -----------------------------------------------------------------------
4bb08a  end beh;
1b625a  -- -----------------------------------------------------------------------
```

```
--c4cf 000de4ae31780030007 Page 1 of key_gen.vhd

bb997d ---------¦---------¦---------¦---------¦---------¦---------¦---------¦---------¦
d8b1e9 -- Author ·········: ·Tom Vu
8f8d0a -- Date ···········: ·09/27/97 ····································
e66b31 -- Description▷ ····: ·Generate Schedule Keys to be used by F funtion
da47f7 -- Function▷   ····: ·2 rings of 28 bits each will shift left or right by 1 or
0efb57 --▷         ▷    ·······2 positions depends on ENCR/DECR and counter16
37625a -- -----------------------------------------------------------------------------
ae7faf library ieee;
c111e9 use IEEE.std_logic_1164.all;
d4da83 use IEEE.std_logic_arith.all;
e6e105 use IEEE.std_logic_unsigned.all;
1faf5a
aeaf5a
de625a -- -----------------------------------------------------------------------------
9e1267 entity KEY_GEN is
20af5a
1284ad port( ··CLK ·▷  ····: in ····std_logic;
13ea26 ·········RST_N ·▷ ··: in ····std_logic;
5f772c ·········START▷ ···: in ····std_logic;
5f9a4d --▷     DECR▷   ····: in ····std_logic;
2dba1f ▷       KEY_IN ····: in ····std_logic_vector(55 downto 0);
190f7f ▷       DONE▷  ····: out ····std_logic;
a2970a ·········CNT ·······: out ····std_logic_vector(4 ·downto 0);
1fe70b ·······▷KEY_OUT ····: out ···std_logic_vector(47 downto 0)
6c737c ·····);
ccaf5a
adf875 end KEY_GEN;
20af5a
af625a -- -----------------------------------------------------------------------------
667811 architecture beh of KEY_GEN is
fb625a -- -----------------------------------------------------------------------------
c6af5a
2f801d component PC1·
d114be port( ··
a5ba1f ▷       KEY_IN ····: in ····std_logic_vector(55 downto 0);
33e01d ·······▷KEY_OUT ····: out ···std_logic_vector(55 downto 0)
7d737c ·····);
a6e2c6 end component;
fbaf5a
ac71c8 component PC2
bf14be port( ··
b5ba1f ▷       KEY_IN ····: in ····std_logic_vector(55 downto 0);
b4e70b ·······▷KEY_OUT ····: out ···std_logic_vector(47 downto 0)
b7737c ·····);
20e2c6 end component;
1baf5a
dd4405 signal cnt16 : std_logic_vector(4 downto 0);
66f2bc signal PC1_KEY ··: std_logic_vector(55 downto 0);
9ff549 signal PC1_KEY_C : std_logic_vector(27 downto 0);
07d6e6 signal PC1_KEY_D : std_logic_vector(27 downto 0);
742b5d signal KEY_REG_C : std_logic_vector(27 downto 0);
5e08f2 signal KEY_REG_D : std_logic_vector(27 downto 0);
3c2ca8 signal KEY_REG ··: std_logic_vector(55 downto 0);
a9c0ab signal SHIFT1 ··: std_logic;
27af5a
3baf5a
5d0f89 begin
f3af5a
86625a -- -----------------------------------------------------------------------------
d088e6 -- Permutation Choice #1
16625a -- -----------------------------------------------------------------------------
20af5a
82d755 ▷      PC_1: PC1 port map(KEY_IN => KEY_IN,KEY_OUT => PC1_KEY);
e7af5a
9e625a -- -----------------------------------------------------------------------------
f2d32d Split_to_C_and_D: process(PC1_KEY)
6b625a -- -----------------------------------------------------------------------------
590f89 begin
040e58 ▷      for i in 0 to 27 loop
884cd9 ▷      ·····PC1_KEY_D(i) <= PC1_KEY(i);
571758 ▷      ·····PC1_KEY_C(i) <= PC1_KEY(i+28);
de7aa9 ▷      end loop;
```

--172b 000fd12a9a780030007 Page 2 of key_gen.vhd

```
325890 end process;
bc625a -- -----------------------------------------------------------------------------
f9a60c DONE_P: process(CLK,RST_N)·
50625a -- -----------------------------------------------------------------------------
190f89 begin
614864  ▷        if RST_N = '0' then
6472de  ▷        ····DONE ·<= '0';
e997e5  ▷        ····SHIFT1 ·<= '0';
b2bdcf  ▷        elsif CLK'event and CLK = '1' then
5a0175  ▷        ····if CNT16 = 15 and START = '0' then
9607cc  ▷        ▷        DONE ·<= '1';
46e192  ▷        ····else
f41b77  ▷        ▷        DONE ·<= '0';
36d0c1  ▷        ····end if;
79af5a
617b70  ▷        ····if START = '1' or CNT16 = 7 or CNT16= 14 then
49ed6a  ▷        ▷        SHIFT1 <= '1' ;
c69236  ▷        ····else·
96e62e  ▷        ▷        SHIFT1 <= '0' ;
99d0c1  ▷        ····end if;
ea570d  ▷        end if;
255890 end process;
c1625a -- -----------------------------------------------------------------------------
9bbc40 COUNTER16_P: process(CLK,RST_N)·
0c625a -- -----------------------------------------------------------------------------
140f89 begin
534864  ▷        if RST_N = '0' then
6dc840  ▷        ▷        CNT16 <= (others => '0');
23bdcf  ▷        elsif CLK'event and CLK = '1' then
d76769  ▷        ····if START = '1' ·then
f30000  ▷        ▷        CNT16 <= "00001";
65e192  ▷        ····else
6365a7  ▷        ▷        CNT16 <= CNT16 + 1;
06d0c1  ▷        ····end if;
50570d  ▷        end if;
c15890 end process;
05625a -- -----------------------------------------------------------------------------
442b00 KEY_GEN_REG_P: process(CLK,RST_N)·
85625a -- -----------------------------------------------------------------------------
a60f89 begin
85af5a
b8def7 ····if RST_N = '0' then
bbd4da  ▷        KEY_REG_C <= (others => '0');
ed927a  ▷        KEY_REG_D <= (others => '0');
8fa644 ····elsif CLK'event and CLK = '1' then
4b1780 --▷      if DECR = '0' then ·················
71a735 --▷      ····if START = '1' then -- Load and Shift by 1 from external key
b94049 --▷      ····▷   KEY_REG_C <= PC1_KEY_C(26 downto 0) & PC1_KEY_C(27);
5c49cf --▷      ····▷   KEY_REG_D <= PC1_KEY_D(26 downto 0) & PC1_KEY_D(27);
d55710 --▷      ····elsif SHIFT1 = '1' then -- Shift Left by 1 for 1st key
4d4742 --▷      ····▷   KEY_REG_C <= KEY_REG_C(26 downto 0) & KEY_REG_C(27);
734ec4 --▷      ····▷   KEY_REG_D <= KEY_REG_D(26 downto 0) & KEY_REG_D(27);
6ed797 --▷      ····else
613fd0 --▷      ····▷   KEY_REG_C <= KEY_REG_C(25 downto 0) & KEY_REG_C(27 downto 26);
c747c3 --▷      ····▷   KEY_REG_D <= KEY_REG_D(25 downto 0) & KEY_REG_D(27 downto 26);
9b0b0e --▷      ····end if;
a97edc --▷      else·
df73f5  ▷        ····if START = '1' then
686d58  ▷        ····▷   KEY_REG_C <= PC1_KEY_C; -- Last key was used in Encr
47d271  ▷        ····▷   KEY_REG_D <= PC1_KEY_D;
713c58  ▷        ····elsif SHIFT1 = '1' then
c6e09e  ▷        ▷        -- Shift Right by 1 when cnt16 =1,8,15
a31e3f  ▷        ····▷   KEY_REG_C <= KEY_REG_C(0) & KEY_REG_C(27 downto 1);
a97e34  ▷        ····▷   KEY_REG_D <= KEY_REG_D(0) & KEY_REG_D(27 downto 1);
87e192  ▷        ····else
77ee00  ▷        ▷        -- Shift Right by 2 when cnt16=others
710558  ▷        ····▷   KEY_REG_C <= KEY_REG_C(1 downto 0) & KEY_REG_C(27 downto 2);
72d0b6  ▷        ····▷   KEY_REG_D <= KEY_REG_D(1 downto 0) & KEY_REG_D(27 downto 2);
a1d0c1  ▷        ····end if;
0394c3 ·-- ▷    end if;
705175 ····end if;
fdaf5a
```

```
--2e6c  001be95937580030007 Page 3 of key_gen.vhd

325890  end process;
bc625a  -- ----------------------------------------------------------------------------
44e546  -- Combine final C and D to KEY_REG
cf625a  -- ----------------------------------------------------------------------------
782776  ▷        KEY_REG <= KEY_REG_C(27 downto 0) & KEY_REG_D(27 downto 0);
02625a  -- ----------------------------------------------------------------------------
b8a28e  -- Permutation Choice #2
a2625a  -- ----------------------------------------------------------------------------
e5af5a
d4105b  ▷        PC_2: PC2 port map (KEY_IN => KEY_REG,KEY_OUT => KEY_OUT);
2daf5a
1a625a  -- ----------------------------------------------------------------------------
8dd318  CNT <= CNT16;
10b08a  end beh;
be625a  -- ----------------------------------------------------------------------------
```

```
--a64d 0007ec2795380030008 Page 1 of mux256.vhd

bb997d ---------¦---------¦---------¦---------¦---------¦---------¦---------¦---------¦
aa533a -- Author ·········: ·Tom Vu ·································
3a917e -- Date ···········: ·09/07/97 ···························
36d3c8 -- Description▷ ····: ·Search Unit, 24 search units per ASIC
a35356 ------------------------------------------------------------------------------
657faf library ieee;
f311e9 use IEEE.std_logic_1164.all;
dbda83 use IEEE.std_logic_arith.all;
3ee105 use IEEE.std_logic_unsigned.all;
345356 ------------------------------------------------------------------------------
ae040a entity MUX256 is
29af5a
3314be port( ··
ecaf5a
1ab249 ········SHIFT_OUT ·····▷: in ·▷ ·std_logic_vector(7 downto 0);
5b809f ········PT_VECTOR ·······: in ····std_logic_vector(255 downto 0);
2af4b0 ········BIT_MUX ▷        : out ····std_logic
09737c ····);
96af5a
4eaf5a
645168 end MUX256;
73af5a
335356 ------------------------------------------------------------------------------
323cf3 architecture beh of MUX256 is
dd5356 ------------------------------------------------------------------------------
b0af5a
1faf5a
910f89 begin
0a5356 ------------------------------------------------------------------------------
4f29b4 DECODER_PR: process(SHIFT_OUT,PT_VECTOR)
ff5356 ------------------------------------------------------------------------------
da2daa variable ii ▷   : integer;
650f89 begin
aa688f ii := conv_integer(SHIFT_OUT);
4eff8f case ii is·
bd7180 ▷      when ··0 => BIT_MUX <= PT_VECTOR(0);
ee4dc8 ▷      when ··1 => BIT_MUX <= PT_VECTOR(1);
ec0910 ▷      when ··2 => BIT_MUX <= PT_VECTOR(2);
363558 ▷      when ··3 => BIT_MUX <= PT_VECTOR(3);
2eaf5a
9180a0 ▷      when ··4 => BIT_MUX <= PT_VECTOR(4);
fcbce8 ▷      when ··5 => BIT_MUX <= PT_VECTOR(5);
26f830 ▷      when ··6 => BIT_MUX <= PT_VECTOR(6);
0cc478 ▷      when ··7 => BIT_MUX <= PT_VECTOR(7);
c6af5a
ca9bd1 ▷      when ··8 => BIT_MUX <= PT_VECTOR(8);
16a799 ▷      when ··9 => BIT_MUX <= PT_VECTOR(9);
86dc35 ▷      when ·10 => BIT_MUX <= PT_VECTOR(10);
3205ba ▷      when ·11 => BIT_MUX <= PT_VECTOR(11);
88af5a
62673a ▷      when ·12 => BIT_MUX <= PT_VECTOR(12);
99beb5 ▷      when ·13 => BIT_MUX <= PT_VECTOR(13);
28a23a ▷      when ·14 => BIT_MUX <= PT_VECTOR(14);
887bb5 ▷      when ·15 => BIT_MUX <= PT_VECTOR(15);
daaf5a
411935 ▷      when ·16 => BIT_MUX <= PT_VECTOR(16);
19c0ba ▷      when ·17 => BIT_MUX <= PT_VECTOR(17);
de202b ▷      when ·18 => BIT_MUX <= PT_VECTOR(18);
00f9a4 ▷      when ·19 => BIT_MUX <= PT_VECTOR(19);
5baf5a
5a585f ▷      when ·20 => BIT_MUX <= PT_VECTOR(20);
5d81d0 ▷      when ·21 => BIT_MUX <= PT_VECTOR(21);
a4e350 ▷      when ·22 => BIT_MUX <= PT_VECTOR(22);
b43adf ▷      when ·23 => BIT_MUX <= PT_VECTOR(23);
7baf5a
e02650 ▷      when ·24 => BIT_MUX <= PT_VECTOR(24);
b5ffdf ▷      when ·25 => BIT_MUX <= PT_VECTOR(25);
959d5f ▷      when ·26 => BIT_MUX <= PT_VECTOR(26);
6044d0 ▷      when ·27 => BIT_MUX <= PT_VECTOR(27);
d4af5a
45a441 ▷      when ·28 => BIT_MUX <= PT_VECTOR(28);
7e7dce ▷      when ·29 => BIT_MUX <= PT_VECTOR(29);
```

```
--e5c6  0004c47201180030008 Page 2 of mux256.vhd
292479  ▷        when  ·30 => BIT_MUX <= PT_VECTOR(30);
25fdf6  ▷        when  ·31 => BIT_MUX <= PT_VECTOR(31);
069f76  ▷        when  ·32 => BIT_MUX <= PT_VECTOR(32);
a046f9  ▷        when  ·33 => BIT_MUX <= PT_VECTOR(33);
be5a76  ▷        when  ·34 => BIT_MUX <= PT_VECTOR(34);
5983f9  ▷        when  ·35 => BIT_MUX <= PT_VECTOR(35);
3ee179  ▷        when  ·36 => BIT_MUX <= PT_VECTOR(36);
aa38f6  ▷        when  ·37 => BIT_MUX <= PT_VECTOR(37);
6ad867  ▷        when  ·38 => BIT_MUX <= PT_VECTOR(38);
a101e8  ▷        when  ·39 => BIT_MUX <= PT_VECTOR(39);
1b589a  ▷        when  ·40 => BIT_MUX <= PT_VECTOR(40);
a08115  ▷        when  ·41 => BIT_MUX <= PT_VECTOR(41);
a9e395  ▷        when  ·42 => BIT_MUX <= PT_VECTOR(42);
be3a1a  ▷        when  ·43 => BIT_MUX <= PT_VECTOR(43);
872695  ▷        when  ·44 => BIT_MUX <= PT_VECTOR(44);
d0ff1a  ▷        when  ·45 => BIT_MUX <= PT_VECTOR(45);
569d9a  ▷        when  ·46 => BIT_MUX <= PT_VECTOR(46);
5e4415  ▷        when  ·47 => BIT_MUX <= PT_VECTOR(47);
d5a484  ▷        when  ·48 => BIT_MUX <= PT_VECTOR(48);
ed7d0b  ▷        when  ·49 => BIT_MUX <= PT_VECTOR(49);
4e24bc  ▷        when  ·50 => BIT_MUX <= PT_VECTOR(50);
63fd33  ▷        when  ·51 => BIT_MUX <= PT_VECTOR(51);
3e9fb3  ▷        when  ·52 => BIT_MUX <= PT_VECTOR(52);
da463c  ▷        when  ·53 => BIT_MUX <= PT_VECTOR(53);
cc5ab3  ▷        when  ·54 => BIT_MUX <= PT_VECTOR(54);
8d833c  ▷        when  ·55 => BIT_MUX <= PT_VECTOR(55);
42e1bc  ▷        when  ·56 => BIT_MUX <= PT_VECTOR(56);
193833  ▷        when  ·57 => BIT_MUX <= PT_VECTOR(57);
57d8a2  ▷        when  ·58 => BIT_MUX <= PT_VECTOR(58);
21012d  ▷        when  ·59 => BIT_MUX <= PT_VECTOR(59);
fea0d6  ▷        when  ·60 => BIT_MUX <= PT_VECTOR(60);
727959  ▷        when  ·61 => BIT_MUX <= PT_VECTOR(61);
7e1bd9  ▷        when  ·62 => BIT_MUX <= PT_VECTOR(62);
96c256  ▷        when  ·63 => BIT_MUX <= PT_VECTOR(63);
e7ded9  ▷        when  ·64 => BIT_MUX <= PT_VECTOR(64);
210756  ▷        when  ·65 => BIT_MUX <= PT_VECTOR(65);
0c65d6  ▷        when  ·66 => BIT_MUX <= PT_VECTOR(66);
9fbc59  ▷        when  ·67 => BIT_MUX <= PT_VECTOR(67);
985cc8  ▷        when  ·68 => BIT_MUX <= PT_VECTOR(68);
598547  ▷        when  ·69 => BIT_MUX <= PT_VECTOR(69);
bcdcf0  ▷        when  ·70 => BIT_MUX <= PT_VECTOR(70);
5b057f  ▷        when  ·71 => BIT_MUX <= PT_VECTOR(71);
dd67ff  ▷        when  ·72 => BIT_MUX <= PT_VECTOR(72);
49be70  ▷        when  ·73 => BIT_MUX <= PT_VECTOR(73);
bea2ff  ▷        when  ·74 => BIT_MUX <= PT_VECTOR(74);
b07b70  ▷        when  ·75 => BIT_MUX <= PT_VECTOR(75);
3a19f0  ▷        when  ·76 => BIT_MUX <= PT_VECTOR(76);
62c07f  ▷        when  ·77 => BIT_MUX <= PT_VECTOR(77);
e120ee  ▷        when  ·78 => BIT_MUX <= PT_VECTOR(78);
b2f961  ▷        when  ·79 => BIT_MUX <= PT_VECTOR(79);
b05910  ▷        when  ·80 => BIT_MUX <= PT_VECTOR(80);
56809f  ▷        when  ·81 => BIT_MUX <= PT_VECTOR(81);
95e21f  ▷        when  ·82 => BIT_MUX <= PT_VECTOR(82);
ca3b90  ▷        when  ·83 => BIT_MUX <= PT_VECTOR(83);
a4271f  ▷        when  ·84 => BIT_MUX <= PT_VECTOR(84);
a0fe90  ▷        when  ·85 => BIT_MUX <= PT_VECTOR(85);
ea9c10  ▷        when  ·86 => BIT_MUX <= PT_VECTOR(86);
79459f  ▷        when  ·87 => BIT_MUX <= PT_VECTOR(87);
79a50e  ▷        when  ·88 => BIT_MUX <= PT_VECTOR(88);
207c81  ▷        when  ·89 => BIT_MUX <= PT_VECTOR(89);
b22536  ▷        when  ·90 => BIT_MUX <= PT_VECTOR(90);
c6fcb9  ▷        when  ·91 => BIT_MUX <= PT_VECTOR(91);
929e39  ▷        when  ·92 => BIT_MUX <= PT_VECTOR(92);
a247b6  ▷        when  ·93 => BIT_MUX <= PT_VECTOR(93);
ca5b39  ▷        when  ·94 => BIT_MUX <= PT_VECTOR(94);
9682b6  ▷        when  ·95 => BIT_MUX <= PT_VECTOR(95);
24e036  ▷        when  ·96 => BIT_MUX <= PT_VECTOR(96);
2939b9  ▷        when  ·97 => BIT_MUX <= PT_VECTOR(97);
87d928  ▷        when  ·98 => BIT_MUX <= PT_VECTOR(98);
db00a7  ▷        when  ·99 => BIT_MUX <= PT_VECTOR(99);
70af5a
4c64b8  ▷        when 100 => BIT_MUX <= PT_VECTOR(100);
```

```
--ac24 000bc20cea880030008 Page 3 of mux256.vhd

fb0f61  ▷    when 101 => BIT_MUX <= PT_VECTOR(101);
eab30a  ▷    when 102 => BIT_MUX <= PT_VECTOR(102);
a3d8d3  ▷    when 103 => BIT_MUX <= PT_VECTOR(103);
2ac3cd  ▷    when 104 => BIT_MUX <= PT_VECTOR(104);
c6a814  ▷    when 105 => BIT_MUX <= PT_VECTOR(105);
8b147f  ▷    when 106 => BIT_MUX <= PT_VECTOR(106);
8d7fa6  ▷    when 107 => BIT_MUX <= PT_VECTOR(107);
dd2243  ▷    when 108 => BIT_MUX <= PT_VECTOR(108);
5f499a  ▷    when 109 => BIT_MUX <= PT_VECTOR(109);
8c2f9f  ▷    when 110 => BIT_MUX <= PT_VECTOR(110);
904446  ▷    when 111 => BIT_MUX <= PT_VECTOR(111);
1df82d  ▷    when 112 => BIT_MUX <= PT_VECTOR(112);
5793f4  ▷    when 113 => BIT_MUX <= PT_VECTOR(113);
c088ea  ▷    when 114 => BIT_MUX <= PT_VECTOR(114);
ffe333  ▷    when 115 => BIT_MUX <= PT_VECTOR(115);
305f58  ▷    when 116 => BIT_MUX <= PT_VECTOR(116);
133481  ▷    when 117 => BIT_MUX <= PT_VECTOR(117);
5d6964  ▷    when 118 => BIT_MUX <= PT_VECTOR(118);
7302bd  ▷    when 119 => BIT_MUX <= PT_VECTOR(119);
4cf2f6  ▷    when 120 => BIT_MUX <= PT_VECTOR(120);
5f992f  ▷    when 121 => BIT_MUX <= PT_VECTOR(121);
532544  ▷    when 122 => BIT_MUX <= PT_VECTOR(122);
3c4e9d  ▷    when 123 => BIT_MUX <= PT_VECTOR(123);
8d5583  ▷    when 124 => BIT_MUX <= PT_VECTOR(124);
d83e5a  ▷    when 125 => BIT_MUX <= PT_VECTOR(125);
a78231  ▷    when 126 => BIT_MUX <= PT_VECTOR(126);
6de9e8  ▷    when 127 => BIT_MUX <= PT_VECTOR(127);
46b40d  ▷    when 128 => BIT_MUX <= PT_VECTOR(128);
a5dfd4  ▷    when 129 => BIT_MUX <= PT_VECTOR(129);
d6b9d1  ▷    when 130 => BIT_MUX <= PT_VECTOR(130);
b7d208  ▷    when 131 => BIT_MUX <= PT_VECTOR(131);
d36e63  ▷    when 132 => BIT_MUX <= PT_VECTOR(132);
6505ba  ▷    when 133 => BIT_MUX <= PT_VECTOR(133);
bb1ea4  ▷    when 134 => BIT_MUX <= PT_VECTOR(134);
fa757d  ▷    when 135 => BIT_MUX <= PT_VECTOR(135);
ddc916  ▷    when 136 => BIT_MUX <= PT_VECTOR(136);
02a2cf  ▷    when 137 => BIT_MUX <= PT_VECTOR(137);
d6ff2a  ▷    when 138 => BIT_MUX <= PT_VECTOR(138);
1694f3  ▷    when 139 => BIT_MUX <= PT_VECTOR(139);
cd4035  ▷    when 140 => BIT_MUX <= PT_VECTOR(140);
1e2bec  ▷    when 141 => BIT_MUX <= PT_VECTOR(141);
2a9787  ▷    when 142 => BIT_MUX <= PT_VECTOR(142);
3efc5e  ▷    when 143 => BIT_MUX <= PT_VECTOR(143);
b4e740  ▷    when 144 => BIT_MUX <= PT_VECTOR(144);
138c99  ▷    when 145 => BIT_MUX <= PT_VECTOR(145);
8330f2  ▷    when 146 => BIT_MUX <= PT_VECTOR(146);
815b2b  ▷    when 147 => BIT_MUX <= PT_VECTOR(147);
a106ce  ▷    when 148 => BIT_MUX <= PT_VECTOR(148);
a66d17  ▷    when 149 => BIT_MUX <= PT_VECTOR(149);
f30b12  ▷    when 150 => BIT_MUX <= PT_VECTOR(150);
0160cb  ▷    when 151 => BIT_MUX <= PT_VECTOR(151);
64dca0  ▷    when 152 => BIT_MUX <= PT_VECTOR(152);
1cb779  ▷    when 153 => BIT_MUX <= PT_VECTOR(153);
ebac67  ▷    when 154 => BIT_MUX <= PT_VECTOR(154);
12c7be  ▷    when 155 => BIT_MUX <= PT_VECTOR(155);
f17bd5  ▷    when 156 => BIT_MUX <= PT_VECTOR(156);
13100c  ▷    when 157 => BIT_MUX <= PT_VECTOR(157);
254de9  ▷    when 158 => BIT_MUX <= PT_VECTOR(158);
9b2630  ▷    when 159 => BIT_MUX <= PT_VECTOR(159);
e7d67b  ▷    when 160 => BIT_MUX <= PT_VECTOR(160);
e1bda2  ▷    when 161 => BIT_MUX <= PT_VECTOR(161);
0d01c9  ▷    when 162 => BIT_MUX <= PT_VECTOR(162);
0f6a10  ▷    when 163 => BIT_MUX <= PT_VECTOR(163);
6e710e  ▷    when 164 => BIT_MUX <= PT_VECTOR(164);
431ad7  ▷    when 165 => BIT_MUX <= PT_VECTOR(165);
ffa6bc  ▷    when 166 => BIT_MUX <= PT_VECTOR(166);
85cd65  ▷    when 167 => BIT_MUX <= PT_VECTOR(167);
ba9080  ▷    when 168 => BIT_MUX <= PT_VECTOR(168);
eefb59  ▷    when 169 => BIT_MUX <= PT_VECTOR(169);
539d5c  ▷    when 170 => BIT_MUX <= PT_VECTOR(170);
a3f685  ▷    when 171 => BIT_MUX <= PT_VECTOR(171);
bc4aee  ▷    when 172 => BIT_MUX <= PT_VECTOR(172);
```

--98f5 0005771e94c80030008 Page 4 of mux256.vhd

```
5b2137  ▷        when 173 => BIT_MUX <= PT_VECTOR(173);
fe3a29  ▷        when 174 => BIT_MUX <= PT_VECTOR(174);
9651f0  ▷        when 175 => BIT_MUX <= PT_VECTOR(175);
faed9b  ▷        when 176 => BIT_MUX <= PT_VECTOR(176);
058642  ▷        when 177 => BIT_MUX <= PT_VECTOR(177);
33dba7  ▷        when 178 => BIT_MUX <= PT_VECTOR(178);
3eb07e  ▷        when 179 => BIT_MUX <= PT_VECTOR(179);
152da2  ▷        when 180 => BIT_MUX <= PT_VECTOR(180);
10467b  ▷        when 181 => BIT_MUX <= PT_VECTOR(181);
bdfa10  ▷        when 182 => BIT_MUX <= PT_VECTOR(182);
2191c9  ▷        when 183 => BIT_MUX <= PT_VECTOR(183);
808ad7  ▷        when 184 => BIT_MUX <= PT_VECTOR(184);
64e10e  ▷        when 185 => BIT_MUX <= PT_VECTOR(185);
7c5d65  ▷        when 186 => BIT_MUX <= PT_VECTOR(186);
2f36bc  ▷        when 187 => BIT_MUX <= PT_VECTOR(187);
f06b59  ▷        when 188 => BIT_MUX <= PT_VECTOR(188);
420080  ▷        when 189 => BIT_MUX <= PT_VECTOR(189);
2e6685  ▷        when 190 => BIT_MUX <= PT_VECTOR(190);
330d5c  ▷        when 191 => BIT_MUX <= PT_VECTOR(191);
92b137  ▷        when 192 => BIT_MUX <= PT_VECTOR(192);
4adaee  ▷        when 193 => BIT_MUX <= PT_VECTOR(193);
49c1f0  ▷        when 194 => BIT_MUX <= PT_VECTOR(194);
20aa29  ▷        when 195 => BIT_MUX <= PT_VECTOR(195);
181642  ▷        when 196 => BIT_MUX <= PT_VECTOR(196);
bf7d9b  ▷        when 197 => BIT_MUX <= PT_VECTOR(197);
b5207e  ▷        when 198 => BIT_MUX <= PT_VECTOR(198);
e84ba7  ▷        when 199 => BIT_MUX <= PT_VECTOR(199);
d3af5a
2b9aa2  ▷        when 200 => BIT_MUX <= PT_VECTOR(200);
dcf17b  ▷        when 201 => BIT_MUX <= PT_VECTOR(201);
f94d10  ▷        when 202 => BIT_MUX <= PT_VECTOR(202);
c126c9  ▷        when 203 => BIT_MUX <= PT_VECTOR(203);
bf3dd7  ▷        when 204 => BIT_MUX <= PT_VECTOR(204);
db560e  ▷        when 205 => BIT_MUX <= PT_VECTOR(205);
f4ea65  ▷        when 206 => BIT_MUX <= PT_VECTOR(206);
7381bc  ▷        when 207 => BIT_MUX <= PT_VECTOR(207);
6fdc59  ▷        when 208 => BIT_MUX <= PT_VECTOR(208);
4fb780  ▷        when 209 => BIT_MUX <= PT_VECTOR(209);
0bd185  ▷        when 210 => BIT_MUX <= PT_VECTOR(210);
1eba5c  ▷        when 211 => BIT_MUX <= PT_VECTOR(211);
240637  ▷        when 212 => BIT_MUX <= PT_VECTOR(212);
ed6dee  ▷        when 213 => BIT_MUX <= PT_VECTOR(213);
e276f0  ▷        when 214 => BIT_MUX <= PT_VECTOR(214);
601d29  ▷        when 215 => BIT_MUX <= PT_VECTOR(215);
d7a142  ▷        when 216 => BIT_MUX <= PT_VECTOR(216);
5dca9b  ▷        when 217 => BIT_MUX <= PT_VECTOR(217);
4c977e  ▷        when 218 => BIT_MUX <= PT_VECTOR(218);
e7fca7  ▷        when 219 => BIT_MUX <= PT_VECTOR(219);
350cec  ▷        when 220 => BIT_MUX <= PT_VECTOR(220);
446735  ▷        when 221 => BIT_MUX <= PT_VECTOR(221);
03db5e  ▷        when 222 => BIT_MUX <= PT_VECTOR(222);
48b087  ▷        when 223 => BIT_MUX <= PT_VECTOR(223);
b7ab99  ▷        when 224 => BIT_MUX <= PT_VECTOR(224);
aec040  ▷        when 225 => BIT_MUX <= PT_VECTOR(225);
f27c2b  ▷        when 226 => BIT_MUX <= PT_VECTOR(226);
3317f2  ▷        when 227 => BIT_MUX <= PT_VECTOR(227);
db4a17  ▷        when 228 => BIT_MUX <= PT_VECTOR(228);
9721ce  ▷        when 229 => BIT_MUX <= PT_VECTOR(229);
0947cb  ▷        when 230 => BIT_MUX <= PT_VECTOR(230);
8e2c12  ▷        when 231 => BIT_MUX <= PT_VECTOR(231);
cc9079  ▷        when 232 => BIT_MUX <= PT_VECTOR(232);
68fba0  ▷        when 233 => BIT_MUX <= PT_VECTOR(233);
d0e0be  ▷        when 234 => BIT_MUX <= PT_VECTOR(234);
748b67  ▷        when 235 => BIT_MUX <= PT_VECTOR(235);
7a370c  ▷        when 236 => BIT_MUX <= PT_VECTOR(236);
915cd5  ▷        when 237 => BIT_MUX <= PT_VECTOR(237);
900130  ▷        when 238 => BIT_MUX <= PT_VECTOR(238);
e16ae9  ▷        when 239 => BIT_MUX <= PT_VECTOR(239);
3abe2f  ▷        when 240 => BIT_MUX <= PT_VECTOR(240);
6dd5f6  ▷        when 241 => BIT_MUX <= PT_VECTOR(241);
1d699d  ▷        when 242 => BIT_MUX <= PT_VECTOR(242);
570244  ▷        when 243 => BIT_MUX <= PT_VECTOR(243);
```

```
--e4a5 0015c0b772180030008 Page 5 of mux256.vhd

89195a  ▷        when 244 => BIT_MUX <= PT_VECTOR(244);
d87283  ▷        when 245 => BIT_MUX <= PT_VECTOR(245);
e2cee8  ▷        when 246 => BIT_MUX <= PT_VECTOR(246);
eca531  ▷        when 247 => BIT_MUX <= PT_VECTOR(247);
f8f8d4  ▷        when 248 => BIT_MUX <= PT_VECTOR(248);
8c930d  ▷        when 249 => BIT_MUX <= PT_VECTOR(249);
acf508  ▷        when 250 => BIT_MUX <= PT_VECTOR(250);
4a9ed1  ▷        when 251 => BIT_MUX <= PT_VECTOR(251);
8b22ba  ▷        when 252 => BIT_MUX <= PT_VECTOR(252);
c64963  ▷        when 253 => BIT_MUX <= PT_VECTOR(253);
6c527d  ▷        when 254 => BIT_MUX <= PT_VECTOR(254);
7439a4  ▷        when 255 => BIT_MUX <= PT_VECTOR(255);
8eaf5a
4f4575  ▷        when others => BIT_MUX <= '0';
4f3387  ·end case;
08af5a
9db4f6  end process DECODER_PR;
88af5a
105356  --------------------------------------------------------------------------------
28b08a  end beh;
b85356  --------------------------------------------------------------------------------
5caf5a
```

```
--1b70  0013488c39280030009 Page 1 of p.vhd

bb997d  ---------¦---------¦---------¦---------¦---------¦---------¦---------¦---------¦
aa533a  -- Author ·········: ·Tom Vu ·································
cbb51f  -- Date ···········: ·09/27/98 ····························
ecd6cd  -- Description▷ ····: ·Left and Right 32-bit registers ············
038b7f  -- FILE▷NAME ······: ·p.vhd ···································■
e3cf72  ······
f8625a  -- -----------------------------------------------------------------------------
c57faf  library ieee;
4011e9  use IEEE.std_logic_1164.all;
8eda83  use IEEE.std_logic_arith.all;
b2e105  use IEEE.std_logic_unsigned.all;
b4af5a
beaf5a
2e625a  -- -----------------------------------------------------------------------------
d07bea  entity P is
c1af5a
8cc66d  port(
0cb3bd  ▷         P_IN ····▷         : in ····std_logic_vector(31 downto 0);
a1586a  ········▷P_OUT ··▷           : out ···std_logic_vector(31 downto 0)
fa737c  ····);
c9af5a
b09776  end P;
4daf5a
1b625a  -- -----------------------------------------------------------------------------
d341d7  architecture beh of P is
e3625a  -- -----------------------------------------------------------------------------
60a039  subtype small_integer is INTEGER range 0 to 31;
8aa364  type P_TYPE is array(0 to 31) of small_integer;
b6af5a
d649f0  signal P_TABLE : P_TYPE;
ccaf5a
4c0f89  begin
cfaf5a
1d4bdd  P_TABLE <= ▷    (11,17, 5,27,25,10,20, 0,
436dcf  ▷         ▷      ·13,21, 3,28,29, 7,18,24,
d85d3e  ▷         ▷      ·31,22,12, 6,26, 2,16, 8,
3887c6  ▷         ▷      ·14,30, 4,19, 1, 9,15,23);▷
a5af5a
52625a  -- -----------------------------------------------------------------------------
1e3e5a  P_PR: process(P_TABLE,P_IN)
c8625a  -- -----------------------------------------------------------------------------
3e0f89  begin
0cd72a  ▷         for i in 0 to 31 loop
a6408d  ▷         ····P_OUT(P_TABLE(i)) <= P_IN(i);
a77aa9  ▷         end loop;
c4a57c  end process P_PR;
fb625a  -- -----------------------------------------------------------------------------
40b08a  end beh;
34625a  -- -----------------------------------------------------------------------------
```

```
--344c  001ea7d76d38003000a Page 1 of pc1.vhd
bb997d  ---------|---------|---------|---------|---------|---------|---------|---------|
d8b1e9  -- Author ·········: ·Tom Vu
4a0864  -- Date ············: ·10/02/97 ····························
04f701  -- Description▷ ····: ·Generate Permutation Choice #1
dfc137  -- Function▷     ····: ·Array has the table which tells the mapping
83625a  -- ------------------------------------------------------------------------
0e7faf  library ieee;
e811e9  use IEEE.std_logic_1164.all;
99da83  use IEEE.std_logic_arith.all;
19e105  use IEEE.std_logic_unsigned.all;
00af5a
47af5a
6d625a  -- ------------------------------------------------------------------------
941237  entity PC1 is
33af5a
9514be  port( ··
51ba1f  ▷        KEY_IN ····: in ····std_logic_vector(55 downto 0);
8fe01d  ·······▷KEY_OUT ···: out ···std_logic_vector(55 downto 0)
5a737c  ····);
37a9e7  end PC1;
68625a  -- ------------------------------------------------------------------------
ee8a34  architecture beh of PC1 is
86625a  -- ------------------------------------------------------------------------
1888c2  subtype small_integer is INTEGER range 0 to 55;
f92fa8  type PC1_TYPE is array(0 to 55) of small_integer;
5f77c7  signal PC1_TABLE : PC1_TYPE;
b0af5a
710f89  begin
6aaf5a
d4058b  PC1_TABLE <= ▷   (27,19,11,31,39,47,55,
32b8bd  ▷          ▷      ·26,18,10,30,38,46,54,
c84e55  ▷          ▷      ·25,17, 9,29,37,45,53,
b95fab  ▷          ▷      ·24,16, 8,28,36,44,52,
258218  ▷          ▷      ·23,15, 7, 3,35,43,51,
0f93e6  ▷          ▷      ·22,14, 6, 2,34,42,50,
190a6f  ▷          ▷      ·21,13, 5, 1,33,41,49,
337b37  ▷          ▷      ·20,12, 4, 0,32,40,48);▷
95625a  -- ------------------------------------------------------------------------
94c9d0  Permutation_choice_1: process(KEY_IN,PC1_TABLE)
d8625a  -- ------------------------------------------------------------------------
330f89  begin
a1a5ed  ▷         for i in 0 to 55 loop
5fee97  ▷         ····KEY_OUT(PC1_TABLE(i)) <= KEY_IN(i);
657aa9  ▷         end loop;
fb5890  end process;
c2625a  -- ------------------------------------------------------------------------
2ab08a  end beh;
ea625a  -- ------------------------------------------------------------------------
```

```
--fb57 001701367ee8003000b Page 1 of pc2.vhd

bb997d --------|--------|--------|--------|--------|--------|--------|--------|
025f32 -- Author ········: ·Tom Vu·
d00864 -- Date ···········: ·10/02/97 ···························
85dd69 -- Description▷ ···: ·Generate Permutation Choice #2
69c137 -- Function▷     ···: ·Array has the table which tells the mapping
64625a -- -------------------------------------------------------------------
fb7faf library ieee;
4011e9 use IEEE.std_logic_1164.all;
63da83 use IEEE.std_logic_arith.all;
30e105 use IEEE.std_logic_unsigned.all;
33af5a
78af5a
8f625a -- -------------------------------------------------------------------
cd0ffb entity PC2 is
49af5a
c814be port( ··
bbba1f ▷        KEY_IN ····: in ····std_logic_vector(55 downto 0);
9ae70b ········▷KEY_OUT ···: out ···std_logic_vector(47 downto 0)
ca737c ····);
60af5a
214683 end PC2;
85af5a
59625a -- -------------------------------------------------------------------
3197f8 architecture beh of PC2 is
27625a -- -------------------------------------------------------------------
3888c2 subtype small_integer is INTEGER range 0 to 55;
2c5861 type PC2_TYPE is array(0 to 47) of small_integer;
9494fc signal PC2_TABLE : PC2_TYPE;
a5af5a
620f89 begin
a8af5a
7b87fd PC2_TABLE<= ▷     (24,27,20, 6,14,10, 3,22,
bcb0d3 ▷         ▷      ··0,17, 7,12, 8,23,11, 5,
eda82a ▷         ▷      ·16,26, 1, 9,19,25, 4,15,
60e6d1 ▷         ▷      ·54,43,36,29,40,48,30,
f07eaa ▷         ·▷     ·52,44,37,33,46,35,50,41,
f9c953 ▷         ▷      ·28,53,51,55,32,45,39,42);
44625a -- -------------------------------------------------------------------
9e1c95 Permutation_choice_2: process(KEY_IN,PC2_TABLE)
34625a -- -------------------------------------------------------------------
f30f89 begin
d813e9 ▷       for i in 0 to 47 loop
35f552 ▷       ····KEY_OUT(i) <= KEY_IN(PC2_TABLE(i));
9f7aa9 ▷       end loop;
925890 end process;
a9625a -- -------------------------------------------------------------------
5bb08a end beh;
70625a -- -------------------------------------------------------------------
```

```
--0a1e 000f30f0bc98003000c Page 1 of reg_rdwr.vhd

bb997d ---------!---------!---------!---------!---------!---------!---------!---------!
aa533a -- Author ·········: ·Tom Vu ·······································
f06e63 -- Date ···········: ·09/19/97 ·····································
704774 -- Description▷ ···: ·UProcessor interface
b65356 ------------------------------------------------------------------------------
407faf library ieee;
6411e9 use IEEE.std_logic_1164.all;
b3da83 use IEEE.std_logic_arith.all;
a0e105 use IEEE.std_logic_unsigned.all;
325356 ------------------------------------------------------------------------------
b678aa entity REG_RDWR is
d1af5a
6bcba7 port( ··RST_N ···········: in ····std_logic;
6a2d12 ········BOARD_EN ·······▷: in ····std_logic;
fa7852 ········ALE ···········▷ : in ····std_logic;
dc61d0 ········ADDSEL1 ········▷ : in ····std_logic;
d73455 ········WRB ···········▷ : in ····std_logic;
35c402 ········RDB ···········▷ : in ····std_logic;
3400c5 ········ADDSEL2 ·······▷: in ····std_logic;
90ff5d ········AA_IN ·········▷ : in ····std_logic;
86a88e ········ADDR ········▷ : in ····std_logic_vector(7 downto 0);
ee8827 ········CHIP_ID ······▷ : in ····std_logic_vector(7 downto 0);
dcb08d ········SEARCH_OUT ····▷: in ····std_logic_vector(23 downto 0);
e3f5bb ········SELECT_ONE ·▷ : in ····std_logic_vector(23 downto 0);
d96e10 ········SEARCH_IN ···▷ : in ····std_logic_vector(23 downto 0);
e2af5a
e50f19 ········CHIP_EN ·······▷ : out ···std_logic;
1cb93c ········AA_OUT ·······▷ : out ···std_logic;
5d77f0 ········CHIP_AA_OUT ··▷ : out ···std_logic;
a46aef ········EXTRA_XOR ······: out ···std_logic;
d3a049 ········USE_CBC ·······: out ···std_logic;
2b57ed ········PT_XOR_MASK ···▷: out ···std_logic_vector(63 downto 0);
1346a7 ········PT_BYTE_MASK ·▷ : out ···std_logic_vector(7 downto 0);
787409 ········PT_VECTOR ·····▷: out ···std_logic_vector(255 downto 0);
739c20 ········C0 ·····▷ : out ···std_logic_vector(63 downto 0);
b15335 ········C1 ·····▷ : out ···std_logic_vector(63 downto 0);
8d7bfe ········DATAI ·······▷ : in ····std_logic_vector(7 downto 0);
145cbe ········DATAO ·······▷ : out ···std_logic_vector(7 downto 0)
b9737c ····);
c8af5a
2aaf5a
642639 end REG_RDWR;
73af5a
1d5356 ------------------------------------------------------------------------------
1f6e71 architecture beh of REG_RDWR is
335356 ------------------------------------------------------------------------------
f35b70 type DATA32_ARRAY is array(31 downto 0) of std_logic_vector(7 downto 0);
b9e3bf type DATA8_ARRAY ·is array(7 ·downto 0) of std_logic_vector(7 downto 0);
d1af5a
2d0342 signal PT_VECTOR_REG ········▷ : DATA32_ARRAY;
cdaf5a
1271b6 signal PT_XOR_MASK_REG ·······▷ : DATA8_ARRAY;
f2e6ea signal CIPHER0 ·········▷ ▷ : DATA8_ARRAY;
d2b737 signal CIPHER1 ·········▷ ▷ : DATA8_ARRAY;
f7af5a
8eaf5a
282682 signal SEARCH_INFO_REG ▷: std_logic_vector(7 ·downto 0);
398ba7 signal PT_BYTE_MASK_REG▷: std_logic_vector(7 ·downto 0);
7502ae signal CHIP_REG ▷ : std_logic_vector(7 ·downto 0);
e517a8 signal CHIP_EN_BAK▷ : std_logic;
a1738b signal ALL_ACTIVE ▷ : std_logic;
b32985 signal BAA_EN ▷ : std_logic;
f3ca5d signal AA_OUT_BAK ▷ : std_logic;
7daf5a
090f89 begin
b510c0 CHIP_EN_BAK <= '1' when ((CHIP_ID = CHIP_REG) and BOARD_EN = '1') else '0';
acaf5a
455356 ------------------------------------------------------------------------------
47d4cd CHIP_ID_REG_PR: process(RST_N, ALE)
645356 ------------------------------------------------------------------------------
609ebc begin ··
f33dcd if (RST_N = '0') then
```

```
--9b90 00080b9ffa88003000c Page 2 of reg_rdwr.vhd

a4a147  ▷        CHIP_REG <= (others => '0');
8eb4c0 elsif (ALE'event and ALE= '1') then
63af5a
ff2241 if ((BOARD_EN = '1') and (ADDSEL1 = '1')) then
da905d ········CHIP_REG <= ADDR;
7c62af end if; ·
2962af end if; ·
39d83c ·
10abb9 end process CHIP_ID_REG_PR;
f4af5a
cb5356 --------------------------------------------------------------------------
faceba READ_PR: process(PT_VECTOR_REG, PT_XOR_MASK_REG,
07acbc  ▷        ▷        PT_BYTE_MASK_REG, SEARCH_INFO_REG, CIPHER0, CIPHER1,
8d8679  ▷        ▷        SEARCH_IN, SELECT_ONE, ALL_ACTIVE, AA_OUT_BAK,
70735f  ▷        ▷        CHIP_EN_BAK, ADDSEL2, RDB, ADDR,BAA_EN)
4e5356 --------------------------------------------------------------------------
a49ebc begin ··
64643c if ((CHIP_EN_BAK = '1') and (ADDSEL2 = '0') and (RDB = '0')) then
40bac7  ▷        case ADDR is
98af5a
f95fed  ▷        when "00000000" => DATA0 <= PT_VECTOR_REG(0);
050335  ▷        when "00000001" => DATA0 <= PT_VECTOR_REG(1);
903746  ▷        when "00000010" => DATA0 <= PT_VECTOR_REG(2);
766b9e  ▷        when "00000011" => DATA0 <= PT_VECTOR_REG(3);
9d2038  ▷        when "00000100" => DATA0 <= PT_VECTOR_REG(4);
607ce0  ▷        when "00000101" => DATA0 <= PT_VECTOR_REG(5);
7b4893  ▷        when "00000110" => DATA0 <= PT_VECTOR_REG(6);
93144b  ▷        when "00000111" => DATA0 <= PT_VECTOR_REG(7);
0a167a  ▷        when "00001000" => DATA0 <= PT_VECTOR_REG(8);
7e4aa2  ▷        when "00001001" => DATA0 <= PT_VECTOR_REG(9);
b28a59  ▷        when "00001010" => DATA0 <= PT_VECTOR_REG(10);
aec73f  ▷        when "00001011" => DATA0 <= PT_VECTOR_REG(11);
921259  ▷        when "00001100" => DATA0 <= PT_VECTOR_REG(12);
185f3f  ▷        when "00001101" => DATA0 <= PT_VECTOR_REG(13);
3e54fa  ▷        when "00001110" => DATA0 <= PT_VECTOR_REG(14);
1c199c  ▷        when "00001111" => DATA0 <= PT_VECTOR_REG(15);
2cdc6d  ▷        when "00010000" => DATA0 <= PT_VECTOR_REG(16);
67910b  ▷        when "00010001" => DATA0 <= PT_VECTOR_REG(17);
2d7f16  ▷        when "00010010" => DATA0 <= PT_VECTOR_REG(18);
5c3270  ▷        when "00010011" => DATA0 <= PT_VECTOR_REG(19);
9f2674  ▷        when "00010100" => DATA0 <= PT_VECTOR_REG(20);
ff6b12  ▷        when "00010101" => DATA0 <= PT_VECTOR_REG(21);
1e123b  ▷        when "00010110" => DATA0 <= PT_VECTOR_REG(22);
905f5d  ▷        when "00010111" => DATA0 <= PT_VECTOR_REG(23);
904288  ▷        when "00011000" => DATA0 <= PT_VECTOR_REG(24);
140fee  ▷        when "00011001" => DATA0 <= PT_VECTOR_REG(25);
a876c7  ▷        when "00011010" => DATA0 <= PT_VECTOR_REG(26);
763ba1  ▷        when "00011011" => DATA0 <= PT_VECTOR_REG(27);
9379f3  ▷        when "00011100" => DATA0 <= PT_VECTOR_REG(28);
713495  ▷        when "00011101" => DATA0 <= PT_VECTOR_REG(29);
0c9a56  ▷        when "00011110" => DATA0 <= PT_VECTOR_REG(30);
94d730  ▷        when "00011111" => DATA0 <= PT_VECTOR_REG(31);
64af5a
5c6da3  ▷        when "00100000" => DATA0 <= PT_XOR_MASK_REG(0);
cd7c21  ▷        when "00100001" => DATA0 <= PT_XOR_MASK_REG(1);
78f89a  ▷        when "00100010" => DATA0 <= PT_XOR_MASK_REG(2);
a9e918  ▷        when "00100011" => DATA0 <= PT_XOR_MASK_REG(3);
a4a510  ▷        when "00100100" => DATA0 <= PT_XOR_MASK_REG(4);
6bb492  ▷        when "00100101" => DATA0 <= PT_XOR_MASK_REG(5);
9f3029  ▷        when "00100110" => DATA0 <= PT_XOR_MASK_REG(6);
ae21ab  ▷        when "00100111" => DATA0 <= PT_XOR_MASK_REG(7);
c8af5a
e552d5  ▷        when "00101000" => DATA0 <= CIPHER0(0);
c21c26  ▷        when "00101001" => DATA0 <= CIPHER0(1);
3ca5bd  ▷        when "00101010" => DATA0 <= CIPHER0(2);
85eb4e  ▷        when "00101011" => DATA0 <= CIPHER0(3);
54d908  ▷        when "00101100" => DATA0 <= CIPHER0(4);
0e97fb  ▷        when "00101101" => DATA0 <= CIPHER0(5);
ca2e60  ▷        when "00101110" => DATA0 <= CIPHER0(6);
c86093  ▷        when "00101111" => DATA0 <= CIPHER0(7);
68af5a
80b339  ▷        when "00110000" => DATA0 <= CIPHER1(0);
```

```
--4711 000c5caea668003000c Page 3 of reg_rdwr.vhd
95fdca  ▷        when "00110001" => DATAO <= CIPHER1(1);
e64451  ▷        when "00110010" => DATAO <= CIPHER1(2);
dd0aa2  ▷        when "00110011" => DATAO <= CIPHER1(3);
7038e4  ▷        when "00110100" => DATAO <= CIPHER1(4);
a17617  ▷        when "00110101" => DATAO <= CIPHER1(5);
10cf8c  ▷        when "00110110" => DATAO <= CIPHER1(6);
a2817f  ▷        when "00110111" => DATAO <= CIPHER1(7);
16af5a
b74798  ▷        when "00111000" => DATAO <= PT_BYTE_MASK_REG;
1ba7e9  ▷        when "00111111" => DATAO <= "000" & BAA_EN &·
d268c2  ▷            AA_OUT_BAK & ALL_ACTIVE & SEARCH_INFO_REG(1 downto 0) ;
ffaf5a
06548f  ▷        when "01000111" => DATAO ·<= "000000" & SELECT_ONE(0) ·& SEARCH_IN(0);
63e0de  ▷        when "01001111" => DATAO ·<= "000000" & SELECT_ONE(1) ·& SEARCH_IN(1);
b0a4d4  ▷        when "01010111" => DATAO ·<= "000000" & SELECT_ONE(2) ·& SEARCH_IN(2);
461085  ▷        when "01011111" => DATAO ·<= "000000" & SELECT_ONE(3) ·& SEARCH_IN(3);
2dd7fe  ▷        when "01100111" => DATAO ·<= "000000" & SELECT_ONE(4) ·& SEARCH_IN(4);
3c63af  ▷        when "01101111" => DATAO ·<= "000000" & SELECT_ONE(5) ·& SEARCH_IN(5);
e327a5  ▷        when "01110111" => DATAO ·<= "000000" & SELECT_ONE(6) ·& SEARCH_IN(6);
4493f4  ▷        when "01111111" => DATAO ·<= "000000" & SELECT_ONE(7) ·& SEARCH_IN(7);
9d13d9  ▷        when "10000111" => DATAO ·<= "000000" & SELECT_ONE(8) ·& SEARCH_IN(8);
22a788  ▷        when "10001111" => DATAO ·<= "000000" & SELECT_ONE(9) ·& SEARCH_IN(9);
942170  ▷        when "10010111" => DATAO ·<= "000000" & SELECT_ONE(10) & SEARCH_IN(10);
a89d0d  ▷        when "10011111" => DATAO ·<= "000000" & SELECT_ONE(11) & SEARCH_IN(11);
46a860  ▷        when "10100111" => DATAO ·<= "000000" & SELECT_ONE(12) & SEARCH_IN(12);
13141d  ▷        when "10101111" => DATAO ·<= "000000" & SELECT_ONE(13) & SEARCH_IN(13);
a9a4da  ▷        when "10110111" => DATAO ·<= "000000" & SELECT_ONE(14) & SEARCH_IN(14);
3718a7  ▷        when "10111111" => DATAO ·<= "000000" & SELECT_ONE(15) & SEARCH_IN(15);
35d7bf  ▷        when "11000111" => DATAO ·<= "000000" & SELECT_ONE(16) & SEARCH_IN(16);
4b6bc2  ▷        when "11001111" => DATAO ·<= "000000" & SELECT_ONE(17) & SEARCH_IN(17);
52f40b  ▷        when "11010111" => DATAO ·<= "000000" & SELECT_ONE(18) & SEARCH_IN(18);
b64876  ▷        when "11011111" => DATAO ·<= "000000" & SELECT_ONE(19) & SEARCH_IN(19);
3899a6  ▷        when "11100111" => DATAO ·<= "000000" & SELECT_ONE(20) & SEARCH_IN(20);
8525db  ▷        when "11101111" => DATAO ·<= "000000" & SELECT_ONE(21) & SEARCH_IN(21);
c2829b  ▷        when "11110111" => DATAO ·<= "000000" & SELECT_ONE(22) & SEARCH_IN(22);
023ee6  ▷        when "11111111" => DATAO ·<= "000000" & SELECT_ONE(23) & SEARCH_IN(23);
7f7aab  ▷        when others ····=> DATAO <= (others => 'Z');
07af5a
d492b5  end case;
56523c  else
a35d06  ▷        DATAO <= (others => 'Z');
8adf0b  end if;
6b2c2b  end process READ_PR;
4d5356  --------------------------------------------------------------------------------
f9ab46  PT_VECTOR_PR: process(RST_N, WRB)
795356  --------------------------------------------------------------------------------
c29ebc  begin ··
9f3dcd  if (RST_N = '0') then
9bd72a  ▷        for i in 0 to 31 loop
193d94  ▷        PT_VECTOR_REG(i) <= (others => '0');
4b7aa9  ▷        end loop;
1faf5a
a8df7d  ▷        for i in 0 to 7 loop
bd359a  ▷        PT_XOR_MASK_REG(i) <= (others => '0');
5fdf54  ▷        CIPHER0(i) <= (others => '0');
6adb2f  ▷        CIPHER1(i) <= (others => '0');
a37aa9  ▷        end loop;
3faf5a
40889f  ▷        PT_BYTE_MASK_REG <= (others => '0');
f15de2  ▷        SEARCH_INFO_REG <= (others => '0');
f7af5a
f9ae0d  elsif (WRB'event and WRB= '1') then
6faf5a
32e1c4  if ((CHIP_EN_BAK = '1') and (ADDSEL2 = '0')) then
48bac7  ▷        case ADDR is
51ebd1  ▷        when "00000000" => PT_VECTOR_REG(0) <= DATAI;
94ae1f  ▷        when "00000001" => PT_VECTOR_REG(1) <= DATAI;
69b156  ▷        when "00000010" => PT_VECTOR_REG(2) <= DATAI;
86f498  ▷        when "00000011" => PT_VECTOR_REG(3) <= DATAI;
cef05c  ▷        when "00000100" => PT_VECTOR_REG(4) <= DATAI;
82b592  ▷        when "00000101" => PT_VECTOR_REG(5) <= DATAI;
c5aadb  ▷        when "00000110" => PT_VECTOR_REG(6) <= DATAI;
```

```
--f423 000420fb0478003000c Page 4 of reg_rdwr.vhd
47ef15 ▷        when "00000111" => PT_VECTOR_REG(7)  <= DATAI;
df6af6 ▷        when "00001000" => PT_VECTOR_REG(8)  <= DATAI;
142f38 ▷        when "00001001" => PT_VECTOR_REG(9)  <= DATAI;
409fd3 ▷        when "00001010" => PT_VECTOR_REG(10) <= DATAI;
afcba3 ▷        when "00001011" => PT_VECTOR_REG(11) <= DATAI;
b035ff ▷        when "00001100" => PT_VECTOR_REG(12) <= DATAI;
d3618f ▷        when "00001101" => PT_VECTOR_REG(13) <= DATAI;
512528 ▷        when "00001110" => PT_VECTOR_REG(14) <= DATAI;
8e7158 ▷        when "00001111" => PT_VECTOR_REG(15) <= DATAI;
e39f93 ▷        when "00010000" => PT_VECTOR_REG(16) <= DATAI;
a1cbe3 ▷        when "00010001" => PT_VECTOR_REG(17) <= DATAI;
1fa22c ▷        when "00010010" => PT_VECTOR_REG(18) <= DATAI;
4af65c ▷        when "00010011" => PT_VECTOR_REG(19) <= DATAI;
15ad0c ▷        when "00010100" => PT_VECTOR_REG(20) <= DATAI;
15f97c ▷        when "00010101" => PT_VECTOR_REG(21) <= DATAI;
cbab6f ▷        when "00010110" => PT_VECTOR_REG(22) <= DATAI;
a9ff1f ▷        when "00010111" => PT_VECTOR_REG(23) <= DATAI;
17ada8 ▷        when "00011000" => PT_VECTOR_REG(24) <= DATAI;
28f9d8 ▷        when "00011001" => PT_VECTOR_REG(25) <= DATAI;
a7abcb ▷        when "00011010" => PT_VECTOR_REG(26) <= DATAI;
17ffbb ▷        when "00011011" => PT_VECTOR_REG(27) <= DATAI;
803a3b ▷        when "00011100" => PT_VECTOR_REG(28) <= DATAI;
916e4b ▷        when "00011101" => PT_VECTOR_REG(29) <= DATAI;
fc6480 ▷        when "00011110" => PT_VECTOR_REG(30) <= DATAI;
7d30f0 ▷        when "00011111" => PT_VECTOR_REG(31) <= DATAI;
ceaf5a
bc692a ▷        when "00100000" => PT_XOR_MASK_REG(0) <= DATAI;
6261be ▷        when "00100001" => PT_XOR_MASK_REG(1) <= DATAI;
abce3f ▷        when "00100010" => PT_XOR_MASK_REG(2) <= DATAI;
8dc6ab ▷        when "00100011" => PT_XOR_MASK_REG(3) <= DATAI;
d1c5c1 ▷        when "00100100" => PT_XOR_MASK_REG(4) <= DATAI;
b2cd55 ▷        when "00100101" => PT_XOR_MASK_REG(5) <= DATAI;
4262d4 ▷        when "00100110" => PT_XOR_MASK_REG(6) <= DATAI;
116a40 ▷        when "00100111" => PT_XOR_MASK_REG(7) <= DATAI;
4aaf5a
8bb54a ▷        when "00101000" => CIPHER0(0) <= DATAI;
abe2af ▷        when "00101001" => CIPHER0(1) <= DATAI;
ed700e ▷        when "00101010" => CIPHER0(2) <= DATAI;
2027eb ▷        when "00101011" => CIPHER0(3) <= DATAI;
f65acf ▷        when "00101100" => CIPHER0(4) <= DATAI;
180d2a ▷        when "00101101" => CIPHER0(5) <= DATAI;
379f8b ▷        when "00101110" => CIPHER0(6) <= DATAI;
9ac86e ▷        when "00101111" => CIPHER0(7) <= DATAI;
69af5a
bd18a7 ▷        when "00110000" => CIPHER1(0) <= DATAI;
ea4f42 ▷        when "00110001" => CIPHER1(1) <= DATAI;
58dde3 ▷        when "00110010" => CIPHER1(2) <= DATAI;
f48a06 ▷        when "00110011" => CIPHER1(3) <= DATAI;
0ff722 ▷        when "00110100" => CIPHER1(4) <= DATAI;
86a0c7 ▷        when "00110101" => CIPHER1(5) <= DATAI;
ef3266 ▷        when "00110110" => CIPHER1(6) <= DATAI;
f56583 ▷        when "00110111" => CIPHER1(7) <= DATAI;
1daf5a
7202f9 ▷        when "00111000" => PT_BYTE_MASK_REG <= DATAI;
16af5a
1a1063 ▷        when "00111111" => SEARCH_INFO_REG ·<= DATAI;
70af5a
7aaf5a
27af5a
324c29 ▷        ·when others => null;
a38259 ·········end case;
d262af end if; ·
cf62af end if; ·
3ed83c ·
2f96ba end process PT_VECTOR_PR;
0cd83c ·
5a63e0 PT_VECTOR <= ···PT_VECTOR_REG(31) & PT_VECTOR_REG(30) & PT_VECTOR_REG(29) & PT_■
f70fc6 VECTOR_REG(28) &
2f41de ▷        ▷        PT_VECTOR_REG(27) & PT_VECTOR_REG(26) & PT_VECTOR_REG(25) & PT_■
0878f6 VECTOR_REG(24) &
3433f8 ▷        ▷        PT_VECTOR_REG(23) & PT_VECTOR_REG(22) & PT_VECTOR_REG(21) & PT_■
4255e6 VECTOR_REG(20) &
```

```
--88e5 001f556d3e88003000c Page 5 of reg_rdwr.vhd
048028 ▷        ▷         PT_VECTOR_REG(19) & PT_VECTOR_REG(18) & PT_VECTOR_REG(17) & PT_■
216203 VECTOR_REG(16) &
f87f6b ▷        ▷         PT_VECTOR_REG(15) & PT_VECTOR_REG(14) & PT_VECTOR_REG(13) & PT_■
474f13 VECTOR_REG(12) &
d3dced ▷        ▷         PT_VECTOR_REG(11) & PT_VECTOR_REG(10) & PT_VECTOR_REG(9) ·& PT_■
400ee7 VECTOR_REG(8) &
d19f75 ▷        ▷         PT_VECTOR_REG(7) ·& PT_VECTOR_REG(6) ·& PT_VECTOR_REG(5) ·& PT_■
8679d7 VECTOR_REG(4) &
fadb33 ▷        ▷         PT_VECTOR_REG(3) ·& PT_VECTOR_REG(2) ·& PT_VECTOR_REG(1) ·& PT_■
ab712e VECTOR_REG(0) ;
9daf5a
f79fa6 PT_XOR_MASK ·<= ·PT_XOR_MASK_REG(7) & PT_XOR_MASK_REG(6) & PT_XOR_MASK_REG(5) &■
f47e06 ·PT_XOR_MASK_REG(4) &·
9332e5 ················PT_XOR_MASK_REG(3) & PT_XOR_MASK_REG(2) & PT_XOR_MASK_REG(1) &■
708f30 ·PT_XOR_MASK_REG(0) ;
c6af5a
bce0a8 C1 ·<= ·CIPHER1(7) & CIPHER1(6) & CIPHER1(5) & CIPHER1(4) &·
163040 ········CIPHER1(3) & CIPHER1(2) & CIPHER1(1) & CIPHER1(0) ;
1d1a2d C0 ·<= ·CIPHER0(7) & CIPHER0(6) & CIPHER0(5) & CIPHER0(4) &·
71bfc6 ········CIPHER0(3) & CIPHER0(2) & CIPHER0(1) & CIPHER0(0) ;
58af5a
b05356 --------------------------------------------------------------------------------
aed83c ·
deaf5a
855356 --------------------------------------------------------------------------------
54960e PT_BYTE_MASK ▷    <= PT_BYTE_MASK_REG;
38b8c9 USE_CBC  ▷        <= SEARCH_INFO_REG(0);
a1a0c4 EXTRA_XOR ▷       <= SEARCH_INFO_REG(1);
12bd48 BAA_EN ▷▷         <= SEARCH_INFO_REG(4);
3075ee AA_OUT_BAK▷       <= AA_IN and ALL_ACTIVE when (BAA_EN = '1') else AA_IN;
5d2bdd AA_OUT ▷▷         <= AA_OUT_BAK ;
9aaf5a
be35fc ALL_ACTIVE▷       <= ( SEARCH_OUT(23) and SEARCH_OUT(22) and SEARCH_OUT(21) and S■
9c2c82 EARCH_OUT(20) and
1e4820 ···············SEARCH_OUT(19) and SEARCH_OUT(18) and SEARCH_OUT(17) and S■
cefe9f EARCH_OUT(16) and
ceb3bf ···············SEARCH_OUT(15) and SEARCH_OUT(14) and SEARCH_OUT(13) and S■
4291e9 EARCH_OUT(12) and
d7794d ···············SEARCH_OUT(11) and SEARCH_OUT(10) and SEARCH_OUT(9) ·and ·■
68357c SEARCH_OUT(8) and
8630b9 ···············SEARCH_OUT(7) ·and SEARCH_OUT(6) ·and SEARCH_OUT(5) ·and ·■
3584e6 SEARCH_OUT(4) and
b68753 ···············SEARCH_OUT(3) ·and SEARCH_OUT(2) ·and SEARCH_OUT(1) ·and ·■
0b76b6 SEARCH_OUT(0));
aaf17f CHIP_AA_OUT ▷     <= ·ALL_ACTIVE;
8827f3 CHIP_EN ▷         <= CHIP_EN_BAK;
c45356 --------------------------------------------------------------------------------
32b08a end beh;
595356 --------------------------------------------------------------------------------
f5af5a
```

```
--068f 000b046c2498003000d Page 1 of s_table.vhd
bb997d ---------|---------|---------|---------|---------|---------|---------|---------|
d8b1e9 -- Author ·········: ·Tom Vu
4a0864 -- Date ···········: ·10/02/97 ·······································
dc5b64 -- Description▷ ····: ·Create table for lookup values of S function
415e67 -- Function▷      ····: ·6 inputs are used to lookup in the table and produce·
829e89 --▷         ▷        ·······4 ouputs. ·There are a total of 8 tables
9b625a -- ------------------------------------------------------------------------
3c7faf library ieee;
2011e9 use IEEE.std_logic_1164.all;
95da83 use IEEE.std_logic_arith.all;
b1e105 use IEEE.std_logic_unsigned.all;
ea6414 use ieee.std_logic_arith.conv_std_logic_vector;·
beaf5a
f4af5a
22625a -- ------------------------------------------------------------------------
d8c826 entity S_TABLE is
82af5a
7896b5 port( ·KEY ········: in ····std_logic_vector(47 downto 0);
5c0d73 ·······S_OUT ·····: out ···std_logic_vector(31 downto 0)
00737c ····);
40af5a
56a64c end S_TABLE;
15af5a
95625a -- ------------------------------------------------------------------------
72a250 architecture beh of S_TABLE is
2a625a -- ------------------------------------------------------------------------
09fa2e subtype small_integer is INTEGER range 0 to 15;
cee268 type TABLE_TYPE is array(0 to 63) of small_integer;
35af5a
ac5dd3 signal S1 : TABLE_TYPE;
6dc7f2 signal S2 : TABLE_TYPE;
4e49e2 signal S3 : TABLE_TYPE;
ebfba1 signal S4 : TABLE_TYPE;
4275b1 signal S5 : TABLE_TYPE;
57ef90 signal S6 : TABLE_TYPE;
986180 signal S7 : TABLE_TYPE;
5a8307 signal S8 : TABLE_TYPE;
a5af5a
74625a -- ------------------------------------------------------------------------
1ba248 function lookup(signal table: in TABLE_TYPE;
652795 ▷        ▷        signal key: in std_logic_vector(5 downto 0))·
87af5a
5e4d3e ▷         ·return std_logic_vector is
00af5a
e46717 variable row ···: std_logic_vector(3 downto 0);
c66911 variable col ···: std_logic_vector(1 downto 0);
0f40ce variable addr ··: std_logic_vector(5 downto 0);
324c51 variable index ·: integer;
6166ad variable result : std_logic_vector(3 downto 0);
f6af5a
3f0f89 begin
fdaf5a
dddf25 ····col:= key(5) & key(0);
a6524a ····row:= key(4 downto 1);
af9742 ····addr:= col & row;
9ae23b ····index:= CONV_INTEGER(key);
41af5a
87e25b ····result:= CONV_STD_LOGIC_VECTOR(table(index),4);
39af5a
7214bd ····return result;
e4af5a
980c01 end ·lookup;
36625a -- ------------------------------------------------------------------------
330f89 begin
30625a -- ------------------------------------------------------------------------
f7af5a
0671a2 S1 ▷     <=▷     (13, 1, 2,15, 8,13, 4, 8, 6,10,15, 3,11, 7, 1, 4,
d8e826 ▷        ▷        ·10,12, 9, 5, 3, 6,14,11, 5, 0, 0,14,12, 9, 7, 2,
08aaee ▷        ▷        ··7, 2,11, 1, 4,14, 1, 7, 9, 4,12,10,14, 8, 2,13,
1dac76 ▷        ▷        ··0,15, 6,12,10, 9,13, 0,15, 3, 3, 5, 5, 6, 8,11);
dbaf5a
b0fc37 S2 ▷     <=▷     ( 4,13,11, 0, 2,11,14, 7,15, 4, 0, 9, 8, 1,13,10,
```

```
--1b4d 00142225b498003000d Page 2 of s_table.vhd
68af27  ▷            ▷      ··3,14,12, 3, 9, 5, 7,12, 5, 2,10,15, 6, 8, 1, 6,
dfeb0f  ▷            ▷      ··1, 6, 4,11,11,13,13, 8,12, 1, 3, 4, 7,10,14, 7,
088e69  ▷            ▷      ·10, 9,15, 5, 6, 0, 8,15, 0,14, 5, 2, 9, 3, 2,12);
62af5a
4ad185 S3 ▷         <=▷     (12,10, 1,15,10, 4,15, 2, 9, 7, 2,12, 6, 9, 8, 5,
b53629  ▷            ▷      ··0, 6,13, 1, 3,13, 4,14,14, 0, 7,11, 5, 3,11, 8,
de712b  ▷            ▷      ··9, 4,14, 3,15, 2, 5,12, 2, 9, 8, 5,12,15, 3,10,
37d78f  ▷            ▷      ··7,11, 0,14, 4, 1,10, 7, 1, 6,13, 0,11, 8, 6,13);
27af5a
c63d3c S4 ▷         <=▷     ( 2,14,12,11, 4, 2, 1,12, 7, 4,10, 7,11,13, 6, 1,
d80ade  ▷            ▷      ··8, 5, 5, 0, 3,15,15,10,13, 3, 0, 9,14, 8, 9, 6,
e1d008  ▷            ▷      ··4,11, 2, 8, 1,12,11, 7,10, 1,13,14, 7, 2, 8,13,
84f6fa  ▷            ▷      ·15, 6, 9,15,12, 0, 5, 9, 6,10, 3, 4, 0, 5,14, 3);
aeaf5a
bf6361 S5 ▷         <=▷     ( 7,13,13, 8,14,11, 3, 5, 0, 6, 6,15, 9, 0,10, 3,
f08223  ▷            ▷      ··1, 4, 2, 7, 8, 2, 5,12,11, 1,12,10, 4,14,15, 9,
a72f41  ▷            ▷      ·10, 3, 6,15, 9, 0, 0, 6,12,10,11, 1, 7,13,13, 8,
9492e5  ▷            ▷      ·15, 9, 1, 4, 3, 5,14,11, 5,12, 2, 7, 8, 2, 4,14);
30af5a
e251c8 S6 ▷         <=▷     (10,13, 0, 7, 9, 0,14, 9, 6, 3, 3, 4,15, 6, 5,10,
08bf4f  ▷            ▷      ··1, 2,13, 8,12, 5, 7,14,11,12, 4,11, 2,15, 8, 1,
faa01f  ▷            ▷      ·13, 1, 6,10, 4,13, 9, 0, 8, 6,15, 9, 3, 8, 0, 7,
d2f2c2  ▷            ▷      ·11, 4, 1,15, 2,14,12, 3, 5,11,10, 5,14, 2, 7,12);
49af5a
b6d92c S7 ▷         <=▷     (15, 3, 1,13, 8, 4,14, 7, 6,15,11, 2, 3, 8, 4,14,
b6f59b  ▷            ▷      ··9,12, 7, 0, 2, 1,13,10,12, 6, 0, 9, 5,11,10, 5,
8c0ccc  ▷            ▷      ··0,13,14, 8, 7,10,11, 1,10, 3, 4,15,13, 4, 1, 2,
fa311b  ▷            ▷      ··5,11, 8, 6,12, 7, 6,12, 9, 0, 3, 5, 2,14,15, 9);
d6af5a
b0ba0a S8 ▷         <=▷     (14, 0, 4,15,13, 7, 1, 4, 2,14,15, 2,11,13, 8, 1,
2ac15d  ▷            ▷      ··3,10,10, 6, 6,12,12,11, 5, 9, 9, 5, 0, 3, 7, 8,
54bf1e  ▷            ▷      ··4,15, 1,12,14, 8, 8, 2,13, 4, 6, 9, 2, 1,11, 7,
834ce4  ▷            ▷      ·15, 5,12,11, 9, 3, 7,14, 3,10,10, 0, 5, 6, 0,13);
25af5a
bd8694 S_OUT ▷ <= ▷         lookup(S8,KEY(47 downto 42)) &
553b55 ·········▷           lookup(S7,KEY(41 downto 36)) &
54f229 ·········▷           lookup(S6,KEY(35 downto 30)) &
dd87b3 ·········▷           lookup(S5,KEY(29 downto 24)) &
acd315 ·········▷           lookup(S4,KEY(23 downto 18)) &
9d4724 ·········▷           lookup(S3,KEY(17 downto 12)) &
4a3cc2 ·········▷           lookup(S2,KEY(11 downto ·6)) &
b5a317 ·········▷           lookup(S1,KEY( 5 downto ·0)) ;
daaf5a
95625a -- --------------------------------------------------------------------------
bcb08a end beh;
42625a -- --------------------------------------------------------------------------
```

```
--4fac 00050e451e18003000e Page 1 of search.vhd

bb997d ---------¦---------¦---------¦---------¦---------¦---------¦---------¦---------¦
aa533a -- Author ·········: ·Tom Vu ················································
3a917e -- Date ···········: ·09/07/97 ··············································
857268 -- Description▷ ···: ·Search Unit
2d5356 ------------------------------------------------------------------------------
037faf library ieee;
d811e9 use IEEE.std_logic_1164.all;
e3da83 use IEEE.std_logic_arith.all;
a0e105 use IEEE.std_logic_unsigned.all;
585356 ------------------------------------------------------------------------------
53cbd6 entity SEARCH_UNIT is
72af5a
8dec7a port( ··CLK ·············: in ····std_logic;
ff2e77 ·········RST_N ···········: in ····std_logic;
3d6737 ·········WRB ·············: in ····std_logic;
779760 ·········RDB ·············: in ····std_logic;
f8baaa ·········SEARCH ··········: in ····std_logic;
65a2a9 ·········EXTRA_XOR ·······: in ····std_logic;
39dbdf ·········USE_CBC ·······▷ : in ····std_logic;
dd2913 ·········ADDR_KEY ········: in ····std_logic_vector(6 ·downto 0);
28af5a
4ffddd ·········DATAI ·······▷  : in ·▷ ·std_logic_vector(7 downto 0);
39e965 ·········PT_BYTE_MASK ··▷: in ·▷ ·std_logic_vector(7 downto 0);
07b25c ·········PT_XOR_MASK ··▷ : in ·▷ ·std_logic_vector(63 downto 0);
0d809f ·········PT_VECTOR ·······: in ····std_logic_vector(255 downto 0);
8ff8de ·········C0 ·············: in ····std_logic_vector(63 downto 0);
2c37cb ·········C1 ·············: in ····std_logic_vector(63 downto 0);
ab6756 ·········KEY_OUT ········: out ····std_logic_vector(55 downto 0);
aea74a ·········DES_OUTPUT ·····: out ····std_logic_vector(63 downto 0);
4f7098 -- ······MATCH_OUT ▷ : out ····std_logic;
26fd4f ·········SELECT_ONE ▷ : out ····std_logic;
ce4b50 ·········SEARCH_OUT ▷ : out ····std_logic;
6013c4 ·········CLEAR_SEARCH ▷ : out ····std_logic;
45a552 ·········DATAO ········▷ : out ····std_logic_vector(7 downto 0)
f2737c ····);
31af5a
9faf5a
983e22 end SEARCH_UNIT;
13af5a
195356 ------------------------------------------------------------------------------
8cac3e architecture beh of SEARCH_UNIT is
fc5356 ------------------------------------------------------------------------------
8f0e4c type DATA8_ARRAY is array(7 downto 0) of std_logic_vector(7 downto 0);
50af5a
65a690 signal MESSAGE ··▷        : std_logic_vector(63 downto 0);
fa39ea signal IP_KEY ··▷         : std_logic_vector(63 downto 0);
1d2c74 signal DES_OUT ··▷        : std_logic_vector(63 downto 0);
d77087 signal EXTRA_XOR_OUT ··▷: std_logic_vector(63 downto 0);
ae1589 signal SHIFT_REG ··▷      : DATA8_ARRAY;
227ca3 signal KEY ▷     ▷        : std_logic_vector(55 downto 0);
fb8eac signal D_KEY ▷   ▷        : std_logic_vector(31 downto 0);
d9e79c signal MESG_LEFT ▷        : std_logic_vector(31 downto 0);
660e7b signal CNT▷      ▷        : std_logic_vector(4 downto 0);
6b7f7a signal BIT_SHIFT_REG ▷    : std_logic_vector(7 ·downto 0);
e1b61d signal TEMP_VECTOR ▷      : std_logic_vector(3 ·downto 0);
c07eb2 signal WR1B ▷    ▷        : std_logic;
7a44e0 signal WR_STROBEB▷        : std_logic;
d20d93 signal DONE ▷    ▷        : std_logic;
0e18c7 signal STARTDES ▷         : std_logic;
ae027a signal MATCH ▷   ▷        : std_logic;
ecaec6 signal MATCH_DLY_CYCLE1▷: std_logic;
4676b8 signal MATCH_DLY_CYCLE2▷: std_logic;
73eb38 signal FALSE_MATCH▷       : std_logic;
bc3de8 signal SEARCH_DLY1 ▷      : std_logic;
7c5403 signal SEARCH_DLY2 ▷      : std_logic;
d48b55 signal SEARCH_DLY3 ▷      : std_logic;
7b8fe9 signal SEARCHING ▷        : std_logic;
0d1d38 signal SEARCHING_DLY ▷    : std_logic;
126abc signal LOAD ▷     ▷       : std_logic;
6dc677 signal FIRST_TIME1 ▷      : std_logic;
e0af9c signal FIRST_TIME2 ▷      : std_logic;
50cc54 signal FIRST_LOAD ▷       : std_logic;
```

```
--acØf  ØØØ5aea51108ØØ3ØØØe Page 2 of search.vhd

720e91  signal SELECT1 ▷▷          : std_logic;
c99f2f  signal SELECT1_DLY▷        : std_logic;
339514  signal KEY_ODD_DLY1▷       : std_logic_vector(1 ·downto Ø);
dd4a26  signal KEY_ODD_DLY2▷       : std_logic_vector(1 ·downto Ø);
98ae92  signal CHECK_SAME_KEY▷     : std_logic;
c89aa4  signal KEY_INCR▷▷          : std_logic;
Øc0f34  signal KEY_DECR▷▷          : std_logic;
fa2d2c  signal PRE_DONE▷▷          : std_logic;
48bee1  signal CNT_EQ_1▷▷          : std_logic;
78525d  signal CNT_GT_1Ø▷          : std_logic;
b3d57b  signal CNT_EQ_1Ø▷          : std_logic;
571491  signal CNT_LE_1Ø▷          : std_logic;
6948e5  signal FIRST_DES▷          : std_logic;
91a51e  signal RESET_SEARCHING▷    : std_logic;
f70775  signal CLEAR_SEARCH_BAK ····: std_logic;
d1af5a
60185d  signal EXTRA_SELECT▷       : std_logic_vector(2 downto Ø);
ebaf5a
bebef1  signal BIT_MUX▷ ▷          : std_logic;
23af5a
326ad1  component DES
baec7a  port( ··CLK ···········: in ····std_logic;
792e77  ·········RST_N ········: in ····std_logic;
61d3de  ·········START ········: in ····std_logic;
370995  ·········MESSAGE ········: in ····std_logic_vector(63 downto Ø);
2b6Ø4f  ·········KEY ············: in ····std_logic_vector(55 downto Ø);
91993Ø  ·········DONE ···········: out ····std_logic;
effe96  ·········CNT ········▷  : out ····std_logic_vector(4 downto Ø);
b93Ø5Ø  ·········DES_OUT ········: out ····std_logic_vector(63 downto Ø)
3c737c  ····);
cde2c6  end component;
77af5a
bbaf5a
925282  component MUX256
b314be  port( ··
e5af5a
6cc584  ·········SHIFT_OUT ·······: in ····std_logic_vector(7 downto Ø);
61809f  ·········PT_VECTOR ·······: in ····std_logic_vector(255 downto Ø);
dØa4d5  ·········BIT_MUX ········: out ····std_logic
5e737c  ····);
13e2c6  end component;
ffaf5a
270f89  begin
dd2Øf2  M256: MUX256
da241Ø  port map( ··▷     SHIFT_OUT ··▷    => SHIFT_REG(7),
9e877a  ▷        ·········PT_VECTOR ··▷    => PT_VECTOR,
78715f  ·······▷ ·▷       BIT_MUX ·▷      => BIT_MUX
96737c  ····);
a7af5a
c9Øb4Ø  DES1: DES
9bc589  port map( ··▷     CLK ···········=> CLK,
4c283b  ·········▷       RST_N ··········=> RST_N,
ee5acf  ▷        ·········START ·········=> STARTDES,
833479  ·······▷ ·▷      MESSAGE ········=> MESSAGE,
87bbda  ·······▷ ▷       KEY ············=> KEY,
56184c  ········▷        DONE ···········=> DONE,
4e32Ø3  ·········▷       CNT ········▷    => CNT,
a4fb8c  ·········▷       DES_OUT ········=> DES_OUT
cb737c  ····);
ae432Ø  MESSAGE ▷        <= CØ when (SELECT1 = 'Ø') else C1;
5b5356  ---------------------------------------------------------------
1ec753  PCSETSEARCH_PR: process(RST_N,CLK)
f85356  ---------------------------------------------------------------
8a9ebc  begin ··
cd6118  if RST_N = 'Ø' then
481a15  ········FIRST_TIME1 <= 'Ø';
Ø66e7c  ········FIRST_TIME2 <= 'Ø';
ce38Øc  ········SEARCH_DLY1 <= 'Ø';
4e4c65  ········SEARCH_DLY2 <= 'Ø';
556Ø42  ········SEARCH_DLY3 <= 'Ø';
addf7d  ▷        for i in Ø to 7 loop
5a3d5f  ········SHIFT_REG(i) <= (others => 'Ø');
```

```
--d38f 000147baec08003000e Page 3 of search.vhd
1e7aa9  ▷       end loop;
5484bd  elsif CLK'event and CLK = '1' then
c4af5a
8b67c5  ▷
ddf62d  ········FIRST_TIME2 <= FIRST_TIME1;
90f778  ▷       if (DONE = '1') then
e7af5a
469339  ▷       ▷       if (SEARCH = '1') then
ff379e  ·······▷ ▷      FIRST_TIME1 <= '1';
e3124d  ▷       ▷       end if;
caaf5a
1c1f25  ········SEARCH_DLY1 <= SEARCH;
59cf68  ········SEARCH_DLY2 <= SEARCH_DLY1 ;
9579ec  ········SEARCH_DLY3 <= SEARCH_DLY2 ;
78570d  ▷       end if;
1f3044  ▷       if (CNT_EQ_1 = '1') then
283e1b  ▷       ▷       SHIFT_REG(7) <= EXTRA_XOR_OUT(63 downto 56);
4e4037  ▷       ▷       SHIFT_REG(6) <= EXTRA_XOR_OUT(55 downto 48);
2f075a  ▷       ▷       SHIFT_REG(5) <= EXTRA_XOR_OUT(47 downto 40);
931200  ▷       ▷       SHIFT_REG(4) <= EXTRA_XOR_OUT(39 downto 32);
7b9e12  ▷       ▷       SHIFT_REG(3) <= EXTRA_XOR_OUT(31 downto 24);
81026f  ▷       ▷       SHIFT_REG(2) <= EXTRA_XOR_OUT(23 downto 16);
f4dcb8  ▷       ▷       SHIFT_REG(1) <= EXTRA_XOR_OUT(15 downto ·8);
ff2343  ▷       ▷       SHIFT_REG(0) <= EXTRA_XOR_OUT( 7 downto ·0);
75f52f  ▷       else
0ff4ba  ▷       ▷       for i in 0 to 6 loop
e566d9  ▷       ▷       SHIFT_REG(i+1) <= SHIFT_REG(i);▷▷
b12966  ▷       ▷       end loop;
a0570d  ▷       end if;
0262af  end if; ·
35d83c  ·
951258  end process PCSETSEARCH_PR;
30af5a
43af5a
635356  --------------------------------------------------------------------------
b24d11  ---- Use to clear away invalid matches before PC loads ··-----------------
c17216  FIRST_LOAD <= FIRST_TIME1 and not(FIRST_TIME2);
7a5356  --------------------------------------------------------------------------
6aaf5a
d8af5a
517400  BIT_SHIFT_PR: process(RST_N,CLK)
da5356  --------------------------------------------------------------------------
d00f89  begin
2b6118  if RST_N = '0' then
0e33cd  ▷       BIT_SHIFT_REG <= (others => '1');
a284bd  elsif CLK'event and CLK = '1' then
14af5a
21f6a6  -------▷ SHIFT -------------------------
564a26  ▷       if (CNT_LE_10 = '1') then
dff4ba  ▷       ▷       for i in 0 to 6 loop
62bed3  ▷       ▷       BIT_SHIFT_REG(i+1) <= BIT_SHIFT_REG(i);▷▷
7a2966  ▷       ▷       end loop;
7611d6  ▷       ▷       BIT_SHIFT_REG(0) <= BIT_MUX;
70570d  ▷       end if;
44880d  -------▷
61df0b  end if;
5b960a  end process BIT_SHIFT_PR;
1daf5a
415356  --------------------------------------------------------------------------
556d3a  MATCH_PR: process(RST_N,CLK)
725356  --------------------------------------------------------------------------
960f89  begin
356118  if RST_N = '0' then
679fc5  ········MATCH <= '0';
0ac778  ·▷      MATCH_DLY_CYCLE1 <= '0';
ecb311  ·▷      MATCH_DLY_CYCLE2 <= '0';
b6f02a  ·▷      KEY_ODD_DLY1 ····<= "00";
332854  ·▷      KEY_ODD_DLY2 ····<= "00";
9484bd  elsif CLK'event and CLK = '1' then
6472b3  ▷       if (CNT = 10) then
3253c1  ▷       ▷       if ((BIT_SHIFT_REG(0) = '1' or (PT_BYTE_MASK(0) = '1')) and
149f48  ▷       ▷       ····(BIT_SHIFT_REG(1) = '1' or (PT_BYTE_MASK(1) = '1')) and
```

```
--9c5f 00039b83bb58003000e Page 4 of search.vhd
7aec5e ▷          ▷           ····(BIT_SHIFT_REG(2) = '1' or (PT_BYTE_MASK(2) = '1')) and
053aa3 ▷          ▷           ····(BIT_SHIFT_REG(3) = '1' or (PT_BYTE_MASK(3) = '1')) and
ac0a72 ▷          ▷           ····(BIT_SHIFT_REG(4) = '1' or (PT_BYTE_MASK(4) = '1')) and
fddc8f ▷          ▷           ····(BIT_SHIFT_REG(5) = '1' or (PT_BYTE_MASK(5) = '1')) and
08af99 ▷          ▷           ····(BIT_SHIFT_REG(6) = '1' or (PT_BYTE_MASK(6) = '1')) and
49dbf9 ▷          ▷           ····(BIT_SHIFT_REG(7) = '1' or (PT_BYTE_MASK(7) = '1'))) then
44af5a
94087d ▷          ▷           MATCH <= '1';
9d0601 ▷          ▷           else
5914c6 ▷          ▷           MATCH <= '0';
f4124d ▷          ▷           end if;
2e570d ▷          end if;
289cfc ----------------------
75406a ▷          if (FIRST_LOAD = '1') then
2e14c6 ▷          ▷           MATCH <= '0';
a4570d ▷          end if;
029cfc --------------------
ee72b3 ▷          if (CNT = 10) then
34c66f ▷          ▷           MATCH_DLY_CYCLE2 <= MATCH_DLY_CYCLE1;
814dc2 ▷          ▷           MATCH_DLY_CYCLE1 <= MATCH ;
8f570d ▷          end if;
d39cfc --------------------
9c2e23 ▷          if (PRE_DONE = '1') then
b6b05a ▷        ·▷           KEY_ODD_DLY2 ····<= KEY_ODD_DLY1;
dd4a58 ·▷         ▷           KEY_ODD_DLY1 ····<= KEY(1 downto 0);
9c570d ▷          end if;
79df0b end if;
cb400f end process MATCH_PR;
e6af5a
2e5356 ------------------------------------------------------------------------------
4c503c WRITE_STROBE_PR: process(RST_N,CLK)
645356 ------------------------------------------------------------------------------
890f89 begin
df6118 if RST_N = '0' then
a6b9e5 ········WR1B <= '1';
e68ae4 ········WR_STROBEB <= '1';
e084bd elsif CLK'event and CLK = '1' then
ad4c03 ········WR_STROBEB <= WR1B;
362ccf ········WR1B <= WRB;
2bdf0b end if;
74a3db end process WRITE_STROBE_PR;
4daf5a
525356 ------------------------------------------------------------------------------
c33157 KEY_PR: process(RST_N,CLK)
775356 ------------------------------------------------------------------------------
930f89 begin
391ce4 if (RST_N = '0')then
c56889 ········KEY <= (others => '0');
6684bd elsif CLK'event and CLK = '1' then
c66a63 ········if (WR1B = '0'and ADDR_KEY(0) = '1') then
9591ac ············KEY(7 ·downto ·0) <= DATAI;
baca4b ········elsif (PRE_DONE = '1') then
c4ca28 ············KEY(7 ·downto 0) <= D_KEY(7 ·downto 0);
a3b985 ········end if;
c368d3 -----
fb2249 ········if (WR1B = '0'and ADDR_KEY(1) = '1') then
af95f6 ············KEY(15 downto ·8) <= DATAI;
b2ca4b ········elsif (PRE_DONE = '1') then
5718d4 ············KEY(15 downto ·8) <= D_KEY(15 downto ·8);
3fb985 ········end if;
3868d3 -----
0efa37 ········if (WR1B = '0'and ADDR_KEY(2) = '1') then
8cec8a ············KEY(23 downto 16) <= DATAI;
24ca4b ········elsif (PRE_DONE = '1') then
e55971 ············KEY(23 downto 16) <= D_KEY(23 downto 16);
49b985 ········end if;
6668d3 -----
76b21d ········if (WR1B = '0'and ADDR_KEY(3) = '1') then
b82429 ············KEY(31 downto 24) <= DATAI;
e4ca4b ········elsif (PRE_DONE = '1') then
a6e0f1 ············KEY(31 downto 24) <= D_KEY(31 downto 24);
39b985 ········end if;
```

```
--a17f  00076022f608003000e  Page 5 of search.vhd

2068d3  -----
e442da  ········if (WR1B = '0'and ADDR_KEY(4) = '1') then
072921  ················KEY(39 downto 32) <= DATAI;
59b985  ········end if;
ba68d3  -----
c40af0  ········if (WR1B = '0'and ADDR_KEY(5) = '1') then
7598b8  ················KEY(47 downto 40) <= DATAI;
4db985  ········end if;
9868d3  -----
5fd28e  ········if (WR1B = '0'and ADDR_KEY(6) = '1') then
78f517  ················KEY(55 downto 48) <= DATAI;
b2b985  ········end if;
1faf5a
1baf5a
f6af5a
26df0b  end if;
b7b3ce  end process KEY_PR;
3eaf5a
a65356  -----------------------------------------------------------------------------
f46a76  READ_KEY_PR: process(ADDR_KEY, RDB, KEY)
fd5356  -----------------------------------------------------------------------------
de0f89  begin
da4f55  if (RDB = '0') then
18af5a
677d5c  ▷       if (ADDR_KEY(0) = '1') then
85bd50  ▷       DATAO <= KEY(7 ·downto ·0) ;
57df62  ▷       elsif (ADDR_KEY(1) = '1') then
c639da  ▷       DATAO <= KEY(15 downto ·8) ;
46071c  ▷       elsif (ADDR_KEY(2) = '1') then
9e67f6  ▷       DATAO <= KEY(23 downto 16) ;
634f36  ▷       elsif (ADDR_KEY(3) = '1') then
a66347  ▷       DATAO <= KEY(31 downto 24) ;
5fbff1  ▷       elsif (ADDR_KEY(4) = '1') then
830d86  ▷       DATAO <= KEY(39 downto 32) ;
03f7db  ▷       elsif (ADDR_KEY(5) = '1') then
185c03  ▷       DATAO <= KEY(47 downto 40) ;
8c2fa5  ▷       elsif (ADDR_KEY(6) = '1') then
7c1867  ▷       DATAO <= KEY(55 downto 48) ;
44f52f  ▷       else
3e8b86  ▷       DATAO <= (others ·=> 'Z');
0b570d  ▷       end if;
b4523c  else
968b86  ▷       DATAO <= (others ·=> 'Z');
1bdf0b  end if;
c5a5d7  end process READ_KEY_PR;
5caf5a
36af5a
925356  -----------------------------------------------------------------------------
6ada3c  KEY_ALU_PR: process(KEY_DECR,KEY_INCR,KEY)
ad5356  -----------------------------------------------------------------------------
8c0f89  begin
fbaf5a
70af5a
96fbc9  if (KEY_INCR = '1') and (KEY_DECR = '0')then
ef0742  ▷       D_KEY <= KEY(31 downto 0) + 1;
af672e  elsif (KEY_DECR = '1') ·and (KEY_INCR = '0') then
df3cda  ▷       D_KEY <= KEY(31 downto 0) - 1;
a3523c  else
2da1d0  ▷       D_KEY <= KEY(31 downto 0);
a1df0b  end if;
5aaf5a
95eaaa  end process KEY_ALU_PR;
e8af5a
f45356  -----------------------------------------------------------------------------
1ba4fa  EXTRA_XOR_PR: process(PT_XOR_MASK,EXTRA_SELECT, DES_OUT, C0)
0e5356  -----------------------------------------------------------------------------
680f89  begin
dd0898  case EXTRA_SELECT is
1e78af  when "000" =>·
58585d  ········EXTRA_XOR_OUT <= DES_OUT xor PT_XOR_MASK;
17e77a  when "001" =>·
76585d  ········EXTRA_XOR_OUT <= DES_OUT xor PT_XOR_MASK;
```

```
--de52 000e582fcfc8003000e Page 6 of search.vhd

1ef910 when "010" =>·
db72de ········EXTRA_XOR_OUT <= ((DES_OUT(63 downto 56) ·xor DES_OUT(31 downto 24)) &
ddf11d  ▷         ▷         ▷        ··(DES_OUT(55 downto 48) ·xor DES_OUT(23 downto 16)) &
6356d8  ▷         ▷         ▷        ··(DES_OUT(47 downto 40) ·xor DES_OUT(15 downto ·8)) &
a0d1e7  ▷         ▷         ▷        ··(DES_OUT(39 downto 32) ·xor DES_OUT( 7 downto ·0)) &
bd7630  ▷         ▷         ▷        ···DES_OUT(31 downto ·0)) xor PT_XOR_MASK;·
fbcd5e -------------------------
e4aa87 when "101" =>·
b8c89f ········EXTRA_XOR_OUT <= DES_OUT xor C0;
71b4ed when "110" =>·
561724 ········EXTRA_XOR_OUT <= (DES_OUT(63 downto 56) xor DES_OUT(31 downto 24)) &
01c057  ▷         ▷         ▷       ·(DES_OUT(55 downto 48) xor DES_OUT(23 downto 16)) &
5eaac9  ▷         ▷         ▷       ·(DES_OUT(47 downto 40) xor DES_OUT(15 downto ·8)) &
444d11  ▷         ▷         ▷       ·(DES_OUT(39 downto 32) xor DES_OUT( 7 downto ·0)) &
7c4bb5  ▷         ▷         ▷       ·DES_OUT(31 downto ·0) ;·
5caf5a
dfaf5a
cc6f48 when others =>·
0aabcd  ▷      EXTRA_XOR_OUT <= DES_OUT;
7caf5a
7b92b5 end case;
bc11f0 end process EXTRA_XOR_PR;
c96a82 EXTRA_SELECT <= SELECT1_DLY & EXTRA_XOR & USE_CBC;
f3309b --EXTRA_SELECT <= SELECT1 & EXTRA_XOR & USE_CBC;
555356 -------------------------------------------------------------------
7f774c STARTDES_PR: process(RST_N,CLK)
ca5356 -------------------------------------------------------------------
610f89 begin
ec6118 if RST_N = '0' then
bf83ec  ▷        STARTDES <= '0';
8084bd elsif CLK'event and CLK = '1' then
a25435 --▷      STARTDES <= DONE or LOAD; ·-- ·17 clocks
fabe3f  ▷       STARTDES <= PRE_DONE or LOAD; ·--- ·16 clocks
6baf5a
f2df0b end if;
7d3b06 end process STARTDES_PR;
f3af5a
905356 -------------------------------------------------------------------
14d499 KEY_INCR_DECR_PR: process(RST_N,CLK)
a15356 -------------------------------------------------------------------
750f89 begin
236118 if RST_N = '0' then
e500ed  ▷        KEY_INCR <= '0';
28b39e  ▷        KEY_DECR <= '0';
b784bd elsif CLK'event and CLK = '1' then
c7c055 --
472b5c KEY_INCR ·<= ·(CNT_GT_10 and not(DONE) and SEARCHING_DLY) and (
935a62  ▷       not(MATCH) ·or ·--- normal case
6f7d3b  ▷       SELECT1 or ·▷    --- false match
7dc579  ▷       FIRST_DES);
db4587 KEY_DECR <= ▷   (CNT_GT_10 and not(DONE) and SEARCHING_DLY) and ·--timing
73bc59  ▷        ▷        (MATCH and not(SELECT1)) ·-- only backup if match on C0
55d0e4  ▷        ▷        and not(FIRST_DES); ·
69af5a
86df0b end if;
0a0e68 end process KEY_INCR_DECR_PR;
acaf5a
589268 FALSE_MATCH ·<= '1' when (MATCH_DLY_CYCLE2 = '1') and (MATCH = '0') and (SEARCH■
94bed5 ING_DLY = '1')
e14761  ▷         ▷         ▷            else '0';
942b60 ------------------------------------------------
fc4e98 ---- timing block, sensitive to START ·----------
bf2b60 ------------------------------------------------
22f539 PRE_DONE <= '1' when (CNT = "01111") else '0';
e07bdd RESET_SEARCHING <= '1' when (CNT = "01100") else '0';
fbaf5a
7b9367 CNT_EQ_1 ·<= '1' when (CNT = 1 ) else '0';
684cb0 CNT_LE_10 <= '1' when (CNT > 1 and CNT < 10) else '0';
563699 CNT_EQ_10 <= '1' when (CNT = 10) else '0';
9328ae CNT_GT_10 <= '1' when (CNT > 10) else '0';
a85356 -------------------------------------------------------------------
e5c874 SEARCHING_PR: process(RST_N,CLK)
```

```
--9006  0016131d0b28003000e Page 7 of search.vhd
b65356  ------------------------------------------------------------------------------------
bf0f89  begin
286118  if RST_N = '0' then
5a14d7  ········SEARCHING <= '0';
4e3178  ········SEARCHING_DLY <= '0';
289c7f  ········CLEAR_SEARCH ·······<= '0';
3b84bd  elsif CLK'event and CLK = '1' then
d5b815  ········SEARCHING_DLY <= SEARCHING;
c8af5a
61fa1b  --------------- search active -------------------
42dc18  ▷        if ((LOAD = '1') or (SEARCHING = '1')) then
1d15d2  ▷        ▷        SEARCHING ·<= '1';
82570d  ▷        end if;
19af5a
09b5fd  --------------- found C1 ----------------------
561061  ▷        if (CLEAR_SEARCH_BAK = '1') then
e00969  ▷        ▷        SEARCHING ·<= '0';
b9570d  ▷        end if;
feaf5a
80f3b4  ---------------
f52661  ▷        CLEAR_SEARCH ·······<= CLEAR_SEARCH_BAK;
c0df0b  end if;
69d83c  ·
b2650d  end process SEARCHING_PR;
5a053c  ▷        CHECK_SAME_KEY <= '1' when (KEY(1 downto 0) = KEY_ODD_DLY2) else '0';
74af5a
b85356  ------------------------------------------------------------------------------------
5c5406  SELECT1_PR: process(RST_N,CLK)
b45356  ------------------------------------------------------------------------------------
db0f89  begin
b76118  if RST_N = '0' then
633057  ········SELECT1 <= '1';
4384bd  elsif CLK'event and CLK = '1' then
79af5a
1358c1  --------------- found C0, look for C1 ·----------
3654be  ▷        if ((MATCH = '1') and (SELECT1 = '0') and (PRE_DONE = '1')) ·then
50ed0d  ▷        ▷        SELECT1 ·<= '1';
16570d  ▷        end if;
78af5a
365ec8  --------------- Restart by PC or C1 is not a match ----------
e56df5  ▷        if ·-- (LOAD = '1') ·or ·
5861ba  ▷        ((SELECT1 = '1') and (PRE_DONE = '1') and (SEARCHING_DLY = '1')) then
9df1b6  ▷        ▷        SELECT1 ·<= '0';
3a570d  ▷        end if;
f5f3b4  ---------------
7e2e23  ▷        if (PRE_DONE = '1') then
410eef  ▷        ▷        SELECT1_DLY <= SELECT1 ;
bf570d  ▷        end if;
7fdf0b  end if;
7dd83c  ·
355784  end process SELECT1_PR;
ff5356  ------------------------------------------------------------------------------------
559ec2  SEARCH_OUT ▷      <= SEARCHING;
9acfcc  LOAD ▷    ▷       <= SEARCH_DLY1 and PRE_DONE and not(SEARCH_DLY2); -- 17 clocks
18880e  FIRST_DES ▷       <= SEARCH_DLY2 and not(SEARCH_DLY3);·
a1188e  CLEAR_SEARCH_BAK ▷       <=·
070e22  ▷        ▷        '1' when ((MATCH = '1') and (SELECT1 = '0')·
ad8de4  ··············and (SELECT1_DLY = '1') and (RESET_SEARCHING = '1')·
5ebdd4  ▷             ▷     and (SEARCHING = '1')) else '0';
9aaf5a
a358fe  SELECT_ONE▷       <= SELECT1;
dadf11  ·KEY_OUT ▷        <= KEY;
545ff8  ·DES_OUTPUT▷      <= DES_OUT;
0f628a  -- MATCH_OUT▷     <= MATCH;
925356  ------------------------------------------------------------------------------------
3fb08a  end beh;
5a5356  ------------------------------------------------------------------------------------
61af5a
```

```
--ed38 000a88fc9858003000f Page 1 of start_re.vhd
bb997d --------|---------|---------|---------|---------|---------|---------|---------|
aa533a -- Author ·········: ·Tom Vu ···································
f06e63 -- Date ·············: ·09/19/97 ·······························
704774 -- Description▷ ····: ·UProcessor interface
b65356 ----------------------------------------------------------------------
407faf library ieee;
6411e9 use IEEE.std_logic_1164.all;
b3da83 use IEEE.std_logic_arith.all;
a0e105 use IEEE.std_logic_unsigned.all;
325356 ----------------------------------------------------------------------
ba69f6 entity START_REG is
c2af5a
69cba7 port( ··RST_N ···········: in ····std_logic;
83c75f ········CHIP_EN ······▷ : in ····std_logic;
2c3455 ········WRB ··········▷  : in ····std_logic;
ae00c5 ········ADDSEL2 ·······▷: in ····std_logic;
27a88e ·······ADDR ·······▷   : in ····std_logic_vector(7 downto 0);
d381d2 ·······CLEAR_SEARCH ···: in ····std_logic_vector(23 downto 0);
b2af5a
a71892 ········SEARCH_IN ···▷  : OUT ····std_logic_vector(23 downto 0);
7419f8 ·······DATAI ·······▷   : in ····std_logic_vector(7 downto 0)
c4737c ····);
a7af5a
9aaf5a
77b995 end START_REG;
43af5a
ff5356 ----------------------------------------------------------------------
c401be architecture beh of START_REG is
ca5356 ----------------------------------------------------------------------
2caf5a
d6af5a
4be6ee signal SEARCH_IN_REG ▷ : std_logic_vector(23 ·downto 0);
bc4c76 signal SEARCH_RST_N_0 ▷ : std_logic;
6c5c79 signal SEARCH_RST_N_1 ▷ : std_logic;
386c68 signal SEARCH_RST_N_2 ▷ : std_logic;
7a7c67 signal SEARCH_RST_N_3 ▷ : std_logic;
c40c4a signal SEARCH_RST_N_4 ▷ : std_logic;
7d1c45 signal SEARCH_RST_N_5 ▷ : std_logic;
a42c54 signal SEARCH_RST_N_6 ▷ : std_logic;
6a3c5b signal SEARCH_RST_N_7 ▷ : std_logic;
e8cc0e signal SEARCH_RST_N_8 ▷ : std_logic;
01dc01 signal SEARCH_RST_N_9 ▷ : std_logic;
6b9f5a signal SEARCH_RST_N_10 ▷: std_logic;
2e114a signal SEARCH_RST_N_11 ▷: std_logic;
ad8b6b signal SEARCH_RST_N_12 ▷: std_logic;
4c057b signal SEARCH_RST_N_13 ▷: std_logic;
69b738 signal SEARCH_RST_N_14 ▷: std_logic;
913928 signal SEARCH_RST_N_15 ▷: std_logic;
66a309 signal SEARCH_RST_N_16 ▷: std_logic;
322d19 signal SEARCH_RST_N_17 ▷: std_logic;
cfcf9e signal SEARCH_RST_N_18 ▷: std_logic;
f0418e signal SEARCH_RST_N_19 ▷: std_logic;
26af4b signal SEARCH_RST_N_20 ▷: std_logic;
4b215b signal SEARCH_RST_N_21 ▷: std_logic;
ccbb7a signal SEARCH_RST_N_22 ▷: std_logic;
d1356a signal SEARCH_RST_N_23 ▷: std_logic;
deaf5a
b10f89 begin
aeaf5a
df5356 ----------------------------------------------------------------------
09905b SEARCH_IN0_PR: process(SEARCH_RST_N_0, WRB)
5b5356 ----------------------------------------------------------------------
e09ebc begin ··
a1a8c8 ----------------------------------------------------------
c0fed4 if (SEARCH_RST_N_0 = '0') then
1d5a3e ▷       SEARCH_IN_REG(0) <= '0';
d9ae0d elsif (WRB'event and WRB= '1') then
07e982 if ((CHIP_EN = '1') and (ADDSEL2 = '0') and (ADDR = "01000111")) then
a6766d ▷       SEARCH_IN_REG(0) <= DATAI(0);
5f523c else
cedec9 ▷       SEARCH_IN_REG(0) <= SEARCH_IN_REG(0);
a862af end if; ·
```

```
--7851 000ad1683558003000f Page 2 of start_re.vhd
5562af end if; ·
7da8c8 ---------------------------------------------------------------
eb2dfd end process SEARCH_IN0_PR;
295356 -------------------------------------------------------------------
af1cdd SEARCH_IN1_PR: process(SEARCH_RST_N_1, WRB)
a45356 -------------------------------------------------------------------
e89ebc begin ··
26803e if (SEARCH_RST_N_1 = '0') then
890faf ▷         SEARCH_IN_REG(1) <= '0';
aeae0d elsif (WRB'event and WRB= '1') then
8eec2f if ((CHIP_EN = '1') and (ADDSEL2 = '0') and (ADDR = "01001111")) then
34f87d ▷         SEARCH_IN_REG(1) <= DATAI(0);
5462af end if; ·
6462af end if; ·
91a8c8 ---------------------------------------------------------------
ee29d6 end process SEARCH_IN1_PR;
fc5356 -------------------------------------------------------------------
a58146 SEARCH_IN2_PR: process(SEARCH_RST_N_2, WRB)
795356 -------------------------------------------------------------------
b59ebc begin ··
a40300 if (SEARCH_RST_N_2 = '0') then
ccf11c ▷         SEARCH_IN_REG(2) <= '0';
17ae0d elsif (WRB'event and WRB= '1') then
119768 if ((CHIP_EN = '1') and (ADDSEL2 = '0') and (ADDR = "01010111")) then
76625c ▷         SEARCH_IN_REG(2) <= DATAI(0);
2d62af end if; ·
8c62af end if; ·
daa8c8 ---------------------------------------------------------------
0725ab end process SEARCH_IN2_PR;
9f5356 -------------------------------------------------------------------
fc0dc0 SEARCH_IN3_PR: process(SEARCH_RST_N_3, WRB)
6b5356 -------------------------------------------------------------------
2d9ebc begin ··
f47dea if (SEARCH_RST_N_3 = '0') then
aea48d ▷         SEARCH_IN_REG(3) <= '0';
21ae0d elsif (WRB'event and WRB= '1') then
5092c5 if ((CHIP_EN = '1') and (ADDSEL2 = '0') and (ADDR = "01011111")) then
7cec4c ▷         SEARCH_IN_REG(3) <= DATAI(0);
b462af end if; ·
4362af end if; ·
2ba8c8 ---------------------------------------------------------------
1e2180 end process SEARCH_IN3_PR;
c35356 -------------------------------------------------------------------
7eb261 SEARCH_IN4_PR: process(SEARCH_RST_N_4, WRB)
b25356 -------------------------------------------------------------------
af9ebc begin ··
750d6d if (SEARCH_RST_N_4 = '0') then
dc046b ▷         SEARCH_IN_REG(4) <= '0';
2dae0d elsif (WRB'event and WRB= '1') then
2fa1a8 if ((CHIP_EN = '1') and (ADDSEL2 = '0') and (ADDR = "01100111")) then
cb5e0f ▷         SEARCH_IN_REG(4) <= DATAI(0);
e162af end if; ·
5462af end if; ·
99a8c8 ---------------------------------------------------------------
133d51 end process SEARCH_IN4_PR;
595356 -------------------------------------------------------------------
123ee7 SEARCH_IN5_PR: process(SEARCH_RST_N_5, WRB)
0d5356 -------------------------------------------------------------------
e19ebc begin ··
0a7387 if (SEARCH_RST_N_5 = '0') then
6051fa ▷         SEARCH_IN_REG(5) <= '0';
96ae0d elsif (WRB'event and WRB= '1') then
7da405 if ((CHIP_EN = '1') and (ADDSEL2 = '0') and (ADDR = "01101111")) then
a2d01f ▷         SEARCH_IN_REG(5) <= DATAI(0);
1362af end if; ·
ab62af end if; ·
3ea8c8 ---------------------------------------------------------------
1d397a end process SEARCH_IN5_PR;
a45356 -------------------------------------------------------------------
53a37c SEARCH_IN6_PR: process(SEARCH_RST_N_6, WRB)
845356 -------------------------------------------------------------------
ad9ebc begin ··
```

```
--a70b  000bb004fd08003000f Page 3 of start_re.vhd

84f0b9  if (SEARCH_RST_N_6 = '0') then
5eaf49  ▷         SEARCH_IN_REG(6) <= '0';
4aae0d  elsif (WRB'event and WRB= '1') then
a0df42  if ((CHIP_EN = '1') and (ADDSEL2 = '0') and (ADDR = "01110111")) then
084a3e  ▷         SEARCH_IN_REG(6) <= DATAI(0);
9562af  end if;  ·
b362af  end if;  ·
15a8c8  -------------------------------------------------------------------
ef3507  end process SEARCH_IN6_PR;
de5356  ---------------------------------------------------------------------------
082ffa  SEARCH_IN7_PR: process(SEARCH_RST_N_7, WRB)
655356  ---------------------------------------------------------------------------
2a9ebc  begin  ··
fa8e53  if (SEARCH_RST_N_7 = '0') then
d0fad8  ▷         SEARCH_IN_REG(7) <= '0';
e3ae0d  elsif (WRB'event and WRB= '1') then
b5daef  if ((CHIP_EN = '1') and (ADDSEL2 = '0') and (ADDR = "01111111")) then
7bc42e  ▷         SEARCH_IN_REG(7) <= DATAI(0);
4562af  end if;  ·
9a62af  end if;  ·
cba8c8  -------------------------------------------------------------------
eb312c  end process SEARCH_IN7_PR;
845356  ---------------------------------------------------------------------------
68d42f  SEARCH_IN8_PR: process(SEARCH_RST_N_8, WRB)
f75356  ---------------------------------------------------------------------------
829ebc  begin  ··
f811b7  if (SEARCH_RST_N_8 = '0') then
9ee694  ▷         SEARCH_IN_REG(8) <= '0';
0dae0d  elsif (WRB'event and WRB= '1') then
ef779d  if ((CHIP_EN = '1') and (ADDSEL2 = '0') and (ADDR = "10000111")) then
bc26a9  ▷         SEARCH_IN_REG(8) <= DATAI(0);
e962af  end if;  ·
d562af  end if;  ·
3ca8c8  -------------------------------------------------------------------
920ca5  end process SEARCH_IN8_PR;
765356  ---------------------------------------------------------------------------
0b58a9  SEARCH_IN9_PR: process(SEARCH_RST_N_9, WRB)
275356  ---------------------------------------------------------------------------
8a9ebc  begin  ··
016f5d  if (SEARCH_RST_N_9 = '0') then
d0b305  ▷         SEARCH_IN_REG(9) <= '0';
58ae0d  elsif (WRB'event and WRB= '1') then
057230  if ((CHIP_EN = '1') and (ADDSEL2 = '0') and (ADDR = "10001111")) then
44a8b9  ▷         SEARCH_IN_REG(9) <= DATAI(0);
e062af  end if;  ·
ae62af  end if;  ·
36a8c8  -------------------------------------------------------------------
7a088e  end process SEARCH_IN9_PR;
0f5356  ---------------------------------------------------------------------------
dabff6  SEARCH_IN10_PR: process(SEARCH_RST_N_10, WRB)
9b5356  ---------------------------------------------------------------------------
e89ebc  begin  ··
c5b8e4  if (SEARCH_RST_N_10 = '0') then
e109db  ▷         SEARCH_IN_REG(10) <= '0';
7bae0d  elsif (WRB'event and WRB= '1') then
350977  if ((CHIP_EN = '1') and (ADDSEL2 = '0') and (ADDR = "10010111")) then
fe8b04  ▷         SEARCH_IN_REG(10) <= DATAI(0);
5962af  end if;  ·
da62af  end if;  ·
f6a8c8  -----------------------------------------------------------------
b6c353  end process SEARCH_IN10_PR;
fe5356  ---------------------------------------------------------------------------
c59206  SEARCH_IN11_PR: process(SEARCH_RST_N_11, WRB)
525356  ---------------------------------------------------------------------------
3a9ebc  begin  ··
28c60e  if (SEARCH_RST_N_11 = '0') then
e15c4a  ▷         SEARCH_IN_REG(11) <= '0';
5bae0d  elsif (WRB'event and WRB= '1') then
350cda  if ((CHIP_EN = '1') and (ADDSEL2 = '0') and (ADDR = "10011111")) then
410514  ▷         SEARCH_IN_REG(11) <= DATAI(0);
0c62af  end if;  ·
bb62af  end if;  ·
```

```
--6b0b 000e1be5cae8003000f Page 4 of start_re.vhd

80a8c8  -------------------------------------------------------------
8bc778  end process SEARCH_IN11_PR;
355356  -------------------------------------------------------------
8fe416  SEARCH_IN12_PR: process(SEARCH_RST_N_12, WRB)
fb5356  -------------------------------------------------------------
119ebc  begin ··
754530  if (SEARCH_RST_N_12 = '0') then
46a2f9  ▷         SEARCH_IN_REG(12) <= '0';
f1ae0d  elsif (WRB'event and WRB= '1') then
373fb7  if ((CHIP_EN = '1') and (ADDSEL2 = '0') and (ADDR = "10100111")) then
759f35  ▷         SEARCH_IN_REG(12) <= DATAI(0);
4262af  end if; ·
8e62af  end if; ·
92a8c8  -------------------------------------------------------------
80cb05  end process SEARCH_IN12_PR;
1d5356  -------------------------------------------------------------
05c9e6  SEARCH_IN13_PR: process(SEARCH_RST_N_13, WRB)
915356  -------------------------------------------------------------
a89ebc  begin ··
d73bda  if (SEARCH_RST_N_13 = '0') then
ccf768  ▷         SEARCH_IN_REG(13) <= '0';
aeae0d  elsif (WRB'event and WRB = '1') then
943a1a  if ((CHIP_EN = '1') and (ADDSEL2 = '0') and (ADDR = "10101111")) then
321125  ▷         SEARCH_IN_REG(13) <= DATAI(0);
ba62af  end if; ·
2a62af  end if; ·
8ca8c8  -------------------------------------------------------------
c3cf2e  end process SEARCH_IN13_PR;
145356  -------------------------------------------------------------
c00836  SEARCH_IN14_PR: process(SEARCH_RST_N_14, WRB)
9a5356  -------------------------------------------------------------
cb9ebc  begin ··
af4b5d  if (SEARCH_RST_N_14 = '0') then
31578e  ▷         SEARCH_IN_REG(14) <= '0';
fbae0d  elsif (WRB'event and WRB = '1') then
17415d  if ((CHIP_EN = '1') and (ADDSEL2 = '0') and (ADDR = "10110111")) then
c2a366  ▷         SEARCH_IN_REG(14) <= DATAI(0);
4862af  end if; ·
f462af  end if; ·
30a8c8  -------------------------------------------------------------
78d3ff  end process SEARCH_IN14_PR;
d85356  -------------------------------------------------------------
a225c6  SEARCH_IN15_PR: process(SEARCH_RST_N_15, WRB)
815356  -------------------------------------------------------------
699ebc  begin ··
a735b7  if (SEARCH_RST_N_15 = '0') then
5e021f  ▷         SEARCH_IN_REG(15) <= '0';
e0ae0d  elsif (WRB'event and WRB = '1') then
8444f0  if ((CHIP_EN = '1') and (ADDSEL2 = '0') and (ADDR = "10111111")) then
492d76  ▷         SEARCH_IN_REG(15) <= DATAI(0);
db62af  end if; ·
0d62af  end if; ·
f7a8c8  -------------------------------------------------------------
9ad7d4  end process SEARCH_IN15_PR;
195356  -------------------------------------------------------------
5753d6  SEARCH_IN16_PR: process(SEARCH_RST_N_16, WRB)
d25356  -------------------------------------------------------------
f19ebc  begin ··
5db689  if (SEARCH_RST_N_16 = '0') then
10fcac  ▷         SEARCH_IN_REG(16) <= '0';
69ae0d  elsif (WRB'event and WRB = '1') then
9bf98d  if ((CHIP_EN = '1') and (ADDSEL2 = '0') and (ADDR = "11000111")) then
5fb757  ▷         SEARCH_IN_REG(16) <= DATAI(0);
dd62af  end if; ·
a262af  end if; ·
d2a8c8  -------------------------------------------------------------
8bdba9  end process SEARCH_IN16_PR;
375356  -------------------------------------------------------------
c77e26  SEARCH_IN17_PR: process(SEARCH_RST_N_17, WRB)
325356  -------------------------------------------------------------
e39ebc  begin ··
e1c863  if (SEARCH_RST_N_17 = '0') then
```

```
--8e92 00090f533fa8003000f Page 5 of start_re.vhd

7da93d  ▷        SEARCH_IN_REG(17) <= '0';
a4ae0d elsif (WRB'event and WRB= '1') then
01fc20 if ((CHIP_EN = '1') and (ADDSEL2 = '0') and (ADDR = "11001111")) then
6b3947  ▷        SEARCH_IN_REG(17) <= DATAI(0);
8e62af end if; ·
9b62af end if; ·
60a8c8 ----------------------------------------------------------------
8adf82 end process SEARCH_IN17_PR;
7d5356 ------------------------------------------------------------------------------
1fd867 SEARCH_IN18_PR: process(SEARCH_RST_N_18, WRB)
6d5356 ------------------------------------------------------------------------------
919ebc begin ··
335787 if (SEARCH_RST_N_18 = '0') then
bcb571  ▷        SEARCH_IN_REG(18) <= '0';
aeae0d elsif (WRB'event and WRB= '1') then
ac8767 if ((CHIP_EN = '1') and (ADDSEL2 = '0') and (ADDR = "11010111")) then
8adbc0  ▷        SEARCH_IN_REG(18) <= DATAI(0);
2962af end if; ·
7962af end if; ·
01a8c8 ----------------------------------------------------------------
83e20b end process SEARCH_IN18_PR;
fc5356 ------------------------------------------------------------------------------
7df597 SEARCH_IN19_PR: process(SEARCH_RST_N_19, WRB)
3e5356 ------------------------------------------------------------------------------
cc9ebc begin ··
87296d if (SEARCH_RST_N_19 = '0') then
3fe0e0  ▷        SEARCH_IN_REG(19) <= '0';
35ae0d elsif (WRB'event and WRB= '1') then
1b82ca if ((CHIP_EN = '1') and (ADDSEL2 = '0') and (ADDR = "11011111")) then
3655d0  ▷        SEARCH_IN_REG(19) <= DATAI(0);
ff62af end if; ·
8862af end if; ·
efa8c8 ----------------------------------------------------------------
54e620 end process SEARCH_IN19_PR;
f65356 ------------------------------------------------------------------------------
a5af01 SEARCH_IN20_PR: process(SEARCH_RST_N_20, WRB)
865356 ------------------------------------------------------------------------------
6c9ebc begin ··
af609a if (SEARCH_RST_N_20 = '0') then
248e35  ▷        SEARCH_IN_REG(20) <= '0';
c4ae0d elsif (WRB'event and WRB= '1') then
98b1a7 if ((CHIP_EN = '1') and (ADDSEL2 = '0') and (ADDR = "11100111")) then
aebb15  ▷        SEARCH_IN_REG(20) <= DATAI(0);
5062af end if; ·
0762af end if; ·
fca8c8 ----------------------------------------------------------------
1a6b3d end process SEARCH_IN20_PR;
bc5356 ------------------------------------------------------------------------------
ef82f1 SEARCH_IN21_PR: process(SEARCH_RST_N_21, WRB)
065356 ------------------------------------------------------------------------------
ff9ebc begin ··
b21e70 if (SEARCH_RST_N_21 = '0') then
80dba4  ▷        SEARCH_IN_REG(21) <= '0';
c0ae0d elsif (WRB'event and WRB= '1') then
c2b40a if ((CHIP_EN = '1') and (ADDSEL2 = '0') and (ADDR = "11101111")) then
4e3505  ▷        SEARCH_IN_REG(21) <= DATAI(0);
9d62af end if; ·
b262af end if; ·
04a8c8 ----------------------------------------------------------------
126f16 end process SEARCH_IN21_PR;
4c5356 ------------------------------------------------------------------------------
5ef4e1 SEARCH_IN22_PR: process(SEARCH_RST_N_22, WRB)
bc5356 ------------------------------------------------------------------------------
9e9ebc begin ··
2c9d4e if (SEARCH_RST_N_22 = '0') then
012517  ▷        SEARCH_IN_REG(22) <= '0';
9fae0d elsif (WRB'event and WRB= '1') then
52cf4d if ((CHIP_EN = '1') and (ADDSEL2 = '0') and (ADDR = "11110111")) then
38af24  ▷        SEARCH_IN_REG(22) <= DATAI(0);
9362af end if; ·
5d62af end if; ·
90a8c8 ----------------------------------------------------------------
```

```
--f11c  001f74fa4a58003000f Page 6 of start_re.vhd
c1636b  end process SEARCH_IN22_PR;
ec5356  ----------------------------------------------------------------------------
81d911  SEARCH_IN23_PR: process(SEARCH_RST_N_23, WRB)
245356  ----------------------------------------------------------------------------
519ebc  begin ··
54e3a4  if (SEARCH_RST_N_23 = '0') then
127086  ▷        SEARCH_IN_REG(23) <= '0';
ccae0d  elsif (WRB'event and WRB= '1') then
61cae0  if ((CHIP_EN = '1') and (ADDSEL2 = '0') and (ADDR = "11111111")) then
bb2134  ▷        SEARCH_IN_REG(23) <= DATAI(0);
4962af  end if; ·
8262af  end if; ·
f8a8c8  ----------------------------------------------------------------------------
586740  end process SEARCH_IN23_PR;
8ca8c8  ----------------------------------------------------------------------------
c4af5a
b435b2  SEARCH_RST_N_0  ·<= RST_N and not(CLEAR_SEARCH(0));
0a943e  SEARCH_RST_N_1  ·<= RST_N and not(CLEAR_SEARCH(1));
0b7ebb  SEARCH_RST_N_2  ·<= RST_N and not(CLEAR_SEARCH(2));
4adf37  SEARCH_RST_N_3  ·<= RST_N and not(CLEAR_SEARCH(3));
bfa3a0  SEARCH_RST_N_4  ·<= RST_N and not(CLEAR_SEARCH(4));
fc022c  SEARCH_RST_N_5  ·<= RST_N and not(CLEAR_SEARCH(5));
34e8a9  SEARCH_RST_N_6  ·<= RST_N and not(CLEAR_SEARCH(6));
d34925  SEARCH_RST_N_7  ·<= RST_N and not(CLEAR_SEARCH(7));
011187  SEARCH_RST_N_8  ·<= RST_N and not(CLEAR_SEARCH(8));
a1b00b  SEARCH_RST_N_9  ·<= RST_N and not(CLEAR_SEARCH(9));
b5e1a0  SEARCH_RST_N_10 <= RST_N and not(CLEAR_SEARCH(10));
83402c  SEARCH_RST_N_11 <= RST_N and not(CLEAR_SEARCH(11));
1faaa9  SEARCH_RST_N_12 <= RST_N and not(CLEAR_SEARCH(12));
940b25  SEARCH_RST_N_13 <= RST_N and not(CLEAR_SEARCH(13));
0e77b2  SEARCH_RST_N_14 <= RST_N and not(CLEAR_SEARCH(14));
06d63e  SEARCH_RST_N_15 <= RST_N and not(CLEAR_SEARCH(15));
e33cbb  SEARCH_RST_N_16 <= RST_N and not(CLEAR_SEARCH(16));
4a9d37  SEARCH_RST_N_17 <= RST_N and not(CLEAR_SEARCH(17));
0ec595  SEARCH_RST_N_18 <= RST_N and not(CLEAR_SEARCH(18));
fb6419  SEARCH_RST_N_19 <= RST_N and not(CLEAR_SEARCH(19));
f332ef  SEARCH_RST_N_20 <= RST_N and not(CLEAR_SEARCH(20));
ae9363  SEARCH_RST_N_21 <= RST_N and not(CLEAR_SEARCH(21));
8c79e6  SEARCH_RST_N_22 <= RST_N and not(CLEAR_SEARCH(22));
bed86a  SEARCH_RST_N_23 <= RST_N and not(CLEAR_SEARCH(23));
0ad83c  ·
b47227  SEARCH_IN ▷      <= SEARCH_IN_REG;
bbaf5a
875356  ----------------------------------------------------------------------------
19b08a  end beh;
2d5356  ----------------------------------------------------------------------------
f7af5a
```

```
--205d 00068e4609b80030010 Page 1 of top.vhd

bb997d ---------¦---------¦---------¦---------¦---------¦---------¦---------¦---------¦
aa533a -- Author ·········: ·Tom Vu ······································
3a917e -- Date ···········: ·09/07/97 ···································
5eeff0 -- Description▷ ····: ·TOP level for DES KEY Search array
845356 --------------------------------------------------------------------
737faf library ieee;
7511e9 use IEEE.std_logic_1164.all;
4cda83 use IEEE.std_logic_arith.all;
b0e105 use IEEE.std_logic_unsigned.all;
cb5356 --------------------------------------------------------------------
ffe642 entity TOP is
84af5a
c0ec7a port( ··CLK ·············: in ····std_logic;
712e77 ········RST_N ···········: in ····std_logic;
c71a55 ········BOARD_EN ········: in ····std_logic;
d52b30 ········ALE ············: in ····std_logic;
375697 ········ADDSEL1 ·········: in ····std_logic;
476737 ········WRB ············: in ····std_logic;
939760 ········RDB ············: in ····std_logic;
f93782 ········ADDSEL2 ·········: in ····std_logic;
9b4c8d ········AA_IN ···········: in ····std_logic;
35b47e ········ADDR ············: in ····std_logic_vector(7 downto 0);
696ad7 ········CHIP_ID ·········: in ····std_logic_vector(7 downto 0);
08ea5e ········AA_OUT ··········: out ···std_logic;
0ff367 ········CHIP_AA_OUT ····▷: out ···std_logic;
4ee24e ········DATA ······▷    : inout▷ std_logic_vector(7 downto 0)
ac737c ····);
1faf5a
abaf5a
d24c52 end TOP;
2baf5a
d05356 --------------------------------------------------------------------
657e41 architecture beh of TOP is
bd5356 --------------------------------------------------------------------
240e4c type DATA8_ARRAY is array(7 downto 0) of std_logic_vector(7 downto 0);
9cda9c type DATA7_ARRAY is array(23 downto 0) of std_logic_vector(6 downto 0);
27af5a
501589 signal SHIFT_REG ··▷    : DATA8_ARRAY;
5d81c4 signal SELECT_ONE ▷    ▷       : std_logic_vector(23 downto 0);
787bfe signal SEARCH_IN ▷     : std_logic_vector(23 downto 0);
66da4d signal SEARCH_OUT ▷    : std_logic_vector(23 downto 0);
a918df signal CLEAR_SEARCH ▷  : std_logic_vector(23 downto 0);
f7e4a1 signal PT_XOR_MASK ·······: std_logic_vector(63 downto 0);
d936e3 signal PT_BYTE_MASK ·····: std_logic_vector(7 downto 0);
ac9da4 signal PT_VECTOR ········: std_logic_vector(255 downto 0);
675681 signal C0 ··············: std_logic_vector(63 downto 0);
f78a11 signal C1 ··············: std_logic_vector(63 downto 0);
44af5a
aca105 signal USE_CBC ▷▷      : std_logic;
21672b signal EXTRA_XOR▷      : std_logic;
ac8b87 signal TEMPS ▷    ▷    : std_logic;
a27ca3 signal KEY ▷     ▷    : std_logic_vector(55 downto 0);
677a3e ·signal DATAO▷    ▷    : std_logic_vector(7 downto 0);
ad639f ·signal DATAI▷    ▷    : std_logic_vector(7 downto 0);
304718 signal ADDR_KEY▷▷     : DATA7_ARRAY;
e3af5a
0da322 component SEARCH_UNIT
8cec7a port( ··CLK ·············: in ····std_logic;
272e77 ········RST_N ···········: in ····std_logic;
a16737 ········WRB ············: in ····std_logic;
349760 ········RDB ············: in ····std_logic;
02baaa ········SEARCH ·········: in ····std_logic;
d19ea8 ········PT_BYTE_MASK ····: in ····std_logic_vector(7 downto 0);
cc58af ········PT_XOR_MASK ····▷: in ····std_logic_vector(63 downto 0);
012913 ········ADDR_KEY ········: in ····std_logic_vector(6 ·downto 0);
830925 ········EXTRA_XOR ·······: in ····std_logic;
92c9d3 ········USE_CBC ·········: in ····std_logic;
d4af5a
afaf5a
ab4d79 ········DATAI ··········: in ····std_logic_vector(7 downto 0);
ed809f ········PT_VECTOR ······: in ····std_logic_vector(255 downto 0);
68f8de ········C0 ·············: in ····std_logic_vector(63 downto 0);
```

```
--acfd 0006a1a758a80030010 Page 2 of top.vhd

e637cb ········C1 ············: in ····std_logic_vector(63 downto 0);
cc33a4 ········SEARCH_OUT ·····: out ····std_logic;
706b53 ········CLEAR_SEARCH ····▷    : out ····std_logic;
cfc5fc ········SELECT_ONE ··▷ : out ····std_logic;
1e60f9 ········DATAO ···········: out ···std_logic_vector(7 downto 0)
47737c ····);
6daf5a
cfe2c6 end component;
8daf5a
62af5a
b76102 component UPI
3ccba7 port( ··RST_N ············: in ····std_logic;
e51a55 ········BOARD_EN ········: in ····std_logic;
3a2b30 ········ALE ·············: in ····std_logic;
485697 ········ADDSEL1 ·········: in ····std_logic;
a26737 ········WRB ·············: in ····std_logic;
d09760 ········RDB ·············: in ····std_logic;
c13782 ········ADDSEL2 ·········: in ····std_logic;
e64c8d ········AA_IN ···········: in ····std_logic;
c3b47e ········ADDR ············: in ····std_logic_vector(7 downto 0);
976ad7 ········CHIP_ID ·········: in ····std_logic_vector(7 downto 0);
3d053a ········SELECT_ONE ······: in ····std_logic_vector(23 downto 0);
118f32 ········SEARCH_IN ·······: OUT ····std_logic_vector(23 downto 0);
42be0c ········SEARCH_OUT ······: in ····std_logic_vector(23 downto 0);
7a8f53 ········CLEAR_SEARCH ··▷: in ····std_logic_vector(23 downto 0);
9e6aef ········EXTRA_XOR ·······: out ····std_logic;
96a049 ········USE_CBC ·········: out ····std_logic;
b5f367 ········CHIP_AA_OUT ···▷: out ····std_logic;
4bea5e ········AA_OUT ··········: out ····std_logic;
2aaf5a
03af5a
60596c ········PT_XOR_MASK ·····: out ····std_logic_vector(63 downto 0);
84a457 ········PT_BYTE_MASK ····: out ····std_logic_vector(7 downto 0);
46e186 ········PT_VECTOR ·······: out ····std_logic_vector(255 downto 0);
d4f79c ········C0 ·············: out ····std_logic_vector(63 downto 0);
dc3889 ········C1 ·············: out ····std_logic_vector(63 downto 0);
63eccb ········ADDR_KEY0 ·······: out ····std_logic_vector(6 ·downto 0);
6da1b1 ········ADDR_KEY1 ·······: out ····std_logic_vector(6 ·downto 0);
f7763f ········ADDR_KEY2 ·······: out ····std_logic_vector(6 ·downto 0);
d03b45 ········ADDR_KEY3 ·······: out ····std_logic_vector(6 ·downto 0);
9bd132 ········ADDR_KEY4 ·······: out ····std_logic_vector(6 ·downto 0);
2b9c48 ········ADDR_KEY5 ·······: out ····std_logic_vector(6 ·downto 0);
b94bc6 ········ADDR_KEY6 ·······: out ····std_logic_vector(6 ·downto 0);
8f06bc ········ADDR_KEY7 ·······: out ····std_logic_vector(6 ·downto 0);
e59739 ········ADDR_KEY8 ·······: out ····std_logic_vector(6 ·downto 0);
0dda43 ········ADDR_KEY9 ·······: out ····std_logic_vector(6 ·downto 0);
1057bd ········ADDR_KEY10 ······: out ····std_logic_vector(6 ·downto 0);
765102 ········ADDR_KEY11 ······: out ····std_logic_vector(6 ·downto 0);
555ac3 ········ADDR_KEY12 ······: out ····std_logic_vector(6 ·downto 0);
3d5c7c ········ADDR_KEY13 ······: out ····std_logic_vector(6 ·downto 0);
874d41 ········ADDR_KEY14 ······: out ····std_logic_vector(6 ·downto 0);
7b4bfe ········ADDR_KEY15 ······: out ····std_logic_vector(6 ·downto 0);
b0403f ········ADDR_KEY16 ······: out ····std_logic_vector(6 ·downto 0);
4d4680 ········ADDR_KEY17 ······: out ····std_logic_vector(6 ·downto 0);
986245 ········ADDR_KEY18 ······: out ····std_logic_vector(6 ·downto 0);
4664fa ········ADDR_KEY19 ······: out ····std_logic_vector(6 ·downto 0);
438033 ········ADDR_KEY20 ······: out ····std_logic_vector(6 ·downto 0);
89868c ········ADDR_KEY21 ······: out ····std_logic_vector(6 ·downto 0);
1f8d4d ········ADDR_KEY22 ······: out ····std_logic_vector(6 ·downto 0);
f08bf2 ········ADDR_KEY23 ······: out ····std_logic_vector(6 ·downto 0);
81ac07 ········DATAI ···········: in ·std_logic_vector(7 downto 0);
88a365 ········DATAO ···········: out ·std_logic_vector(7 downto 0)
61737c ····);
0aaf5a
bee2c6 end component;
79af5a
aa0f89 begin
b29114 UPI0: UPI
f34a4b port map(
432dd5 ········RST_N ············=> RST_N,
33c652 ········BOARD_EN ········=> BOARD_EN,
6aed26 ········ALE ·············=> ALE,
```

```
--45ab 0005d8a996b80030010 Page 3 of top.vhd

a9d50f ········ADDSEL1 ········=> ADDSEL1,
1b14b5 ········WRB ··········=> WRB,
b07402 ········RDB ··········=> RDB,
0aa93e ········ADDSEL2 ···········=> ADDSEL2,
2e9c40 ········ADDR ·········=> ADDR,
a39156 ········CHIP_ID ·······=> CHIP_ID,
a3b23e ········SEARCH_IN ····▷ => SEARCH_IN,
ed0bbe ·······SELECT_ONE ·▷   => SELECT_ONE,
32c3de ·······SEARCH_OUT ···▷=> SEARCH_OUT,
657dc4 ·······EXTRA_XOR ····▷ => EXTRA_XOR,
2d4a03 ·······USE_CBC ····▷   => USE_CBC,
a80130 ·······CLEAR_SEARCH ···=> CLEAR_SEARCH,
244f03 ········AA_IN ····▷    => AA_IN,
772945 ········AA_OUT ····▷   => AA_OUT,
014dfc ·······CHIP_AA_OUT ···▷=> CHIP_AA_OUT,
59af5a
0a0949 ·······PT_XOR_MASK ····=> PT_XOR_MASK,
ea084d ·······PT_BYTE_MASK ···=> PT_BYTE_MASK,
1e415b ·······PT_VECTOR ······=> PT_VECTOR,
15cc6e ·······C0 ···········=> C0,
463fef ·······C1 ···········=> C1,
f36a1c ·······ADDR_KEY0 ······=> ADDR_KEY(0) ,
9b6523 ·······ADDR_KEY1 ······=> ADDR_KEY(1) ,
d67462 ·······ADDR_KEY2 ······=> ADDR_KEY(2) ,
437b5d ·······ADDR_KEY3 ······=> ADDR_KEY(3) ,
e356e0 ·······ADDR_KEY4 ······=> ADDR_KEY(4) ,
f259df ·······ADDR_KEY5 ······=> ADDR_KEY(5) ,
a6489e ·······ADDR_KEY6 ······=> ADDR_KEY(6) ,
9947a1 ·······ADDR_KEY7 ······=> ADDR_KEY(7) ,
1013e4 ·······ADDR_KEY8 ······=> ADDR_KEY(8) ,
1b1cdb ·······ADDR_KEY9 ······=> ADDR_KEY(9) ,
d0f618 ·······ADDR_KEY10 ·····=> ADDR_KEY(10),
bab1e7 ·······ADDR_KEY11 ·····=> ADDR_KEY(11),
f979e6 ·······ADDR_KEY12 ·····=> ADDR_KEY(12),
aa3e19 ·······ADDR_KEY13 ·····=> ADDR_KEY(13),
dce1f5 ·······ADDR_KEY14 ·····=> ADDR_KEY(14),
a8a60a ·······ADDR_KEY15 ·····=> ADDR_KEY(15),
d06e0b ·······ADDR_KEY16 ·····=> ADDR_KEY(16),
8e29f4 ·······ADDR_KEY17 ·····=> ADDR_KEY(17),
e6d9c2 ·······ADDR_KEY18 ·····=> ADDR_KEY(18),
8b9e3d ·······ADDR_KEY19 ·····=> ADDR_KEY(19),
96e759 ·······ADDR_KEY20 ·····=> ADDR_KEY(20),
bfa0a6 ·······ADDR_KEY21 ·····=> ADDR_KEY(21),
4168a7 ·······ADDR_KEY22 ·····=> ADDR_KEY(22),
e12f58 ·······ADDR_KEY23 ·····=> ADDR_KEY(23),
a70cc1 ········DATAI ·········=> DATAI,
e15edf ········DATAO ·········=> DATAO
0f737c ····);
a3af5a
2b5356 --------------------------------------------------------------------------------
fa1c46 gen0: for i in 0 to 23 generate
3601bf SEARCH_UNITX: SEARCH_UNIT
c72b2b port map(CLK ···········=> CLK,
57a41e ········RST_N ·········=> RST_N,
528a27 ········WRB ··········=> WRB,
b87e43 ········RDB ··········=> RDB,
0aba0c ·······PT_BYTE_MASK ····=> PT_BYTE_MASK,
ecda55 ·······PT_XOR_MASK ····=> PT_XOR_MASK,
17b2a2 ········SEARCH ········=> SEARCH_IN(i),
a8e424 ·······SELECT_ONE ······=> SELECT_ONE(i),
c964e3 ·······ADDR_KEY ·······=> ADDR_KEY(i),
2ff394 ·······EXTRA_XOR ····▷ => EXTRA_XOR,
7b93d0 ········USE_CBC ····▷   => USE_CBC,
62d83c ·
4b0cc1 ········DATAI ·········=> DATAI,
6bc7fa ·······PT_VECTOR ·······=> PT_VECTOR,
408f81 ········C0 ···········=> C0,
eb5c94 ········C1 ···········=> C1,
fd082a ········SEARCH_OUT ······=> SEARCH_OUT(i),
d7b652 ·······CLEAR_SEARCH ····=> CLEAR_SEARCH(i),
2e5edf ········DATAO ·········=> DATAO
5d737c ····);
```

--6a27 0012f356e1f80030010 Page 4 of top.vhd

```
fc7522 end generate;
755356 --------------------------------------------------------------------------------
722595 ·DATAI <= DATA;
6b598a ·DATA <= DATAO when (RDB = '0' and ADDSEL2 = '0') else (others => 'Z');
92b08a end beh;
f05356 --------------------------------------------------------------------------------
17af5a
5aaf5a
2faf5a
```

```
--f1c1 00070fef0c680030011 Page 1 of upi.vhd

bb997d ---------|---------|---------|---------|---------|---------|---------|---------|
aa533a -- Author .........: ·Tom Vu ...........................................
f06e63 -- Date ...........: ·09/19/97 .......................................
704774 -- Description▷ ....: ·UProcessor interface
b65356 --------------------------------------------------------------------------
407faf library ieee;
6411e9 use IEEE.std_logic_1164.all;
b3da83 use IEEE.std_logic_arith.all;
a0e105 use IEEE.std_logic_unsigned.all;
325356 --------------------------------------------------------------------------
4be38a entity UPI is
0eaf5a
31cba7 port( ··RST_N ...........: in ....std_logic;
392d12 .........BOARD_EN ......▷: in ....std_logic;
227852 .........ALE .........▷ : in ....std_logic;
3a61d0 .........ADDSEL1 .......▷: in ....std_logic;
3a3455 .........WRB .........▷ : in ....std_logic;
44c402 .........RDB .........▷ : in ....std_logic;
f200c5 .........ADDSEL2 ......▷: in ....std_logic;
69ff5d .........AA_IN ........▷ : in ....std_logic;
37a88e .........ADDR ......▷ : in ....std_logic_vector(7 downto 0);
ec8827 .........CHIP_ID ......▷ : in ....std_logic_vector(7 downto 0);
70b08d .........SEARCH_OUT ....▷: in ....std_logic_vector(23 downto 0);
30c3c4 .........CLEAR_SEARCH ....▷ : in ....std_logic_vector(23 downto 0);
5bf5bb .........SELECT_ONE ·▷ : in ....std_logic_vector(23 downto 0);
c9af5a
68b93c .........AA_OUT ......▷ : out ...std_logic;
6977f0 .........CHIP_AA_OUT ..▷ : out ...std_logic;
896aef .........EXTRA_XOR ......: out ...std_logic;
09a049 .........USE_CBC .......: out ...std_logic;
121892 .........SEARCH_IN ..▷ : OUT ....std_logic_vector(23 downto 0);
dd57ed .........PT_XOR_MASK ..▷: out ....std_logic_vector(63 downto 0);
c346a7 .........PT_BYTE_MASK ·▷ : out ....std_logic_vector(7 downto 0);
077409 .........PT_VECTOR ....▷: out ....std_logic_vector(255 downto 0);
ca9c20 .........C0 ....▷ : out ....std_logic_vector(63 downto 0);
a15335 .........C1 ....▷ : out ....std_logic_vector(63 downto 0);
0ae24a .........ADDR_KEY0 ....▷: out ....std_logic_vector(6 ·downto 0);
78af30 .........ADDR_KEY1 ....▷: out ....std_logic_vector(6 ·downto 0);
ef78be .........ADDR_KEY2 ....▷: out ....std_logic_vector(6 ·downto 0);
4935c4 .........ADDR_KEY3 ....▷: out ....std_logic_vector(6 ·downto 0);
b9dfb3 .........ADDR_KEY4 ....▷: out ....std_logic_vector(6 ·downto 0);
f692c9 .........ADDR_KEY5 ....▷: out ....std_logic_vector(6 ·downto 0);
164547 .........ADDR_KEY6 ....▷: out ....std_logic_vector(6 ·downto 0);
e9083d .........ADDR_KEY7 ....▷: out ....std_logic_vector(6 ·downto 0);
4299b8 .........ADDR_KEY8 ....▷: out ....std_logic_vector(6 ·downto 0);
dad4c2 .........ADDR_KEY9 ....▷: out ....std_logic_vector(6 ·downto 0);
b9593c .........ADDR_KEY10 ...▷: out ....std_logic_vector(6 ·downto 0);
7e5f83 .........ADDR_KEY11 ...▷: out ....std_logic_vector(6 ·downto 0);
5b5442 .........ADDR_KEY12 ...▷: out ....std_logic_vector(6 ·downto 0);
3252fd .........ADDR_KEY13 ...▷: out ....std_logic_vector(6 ·downto 0);
9343c0 .........ADDR_KEY14 ...▷: out ....std_logic_vector(6 ·downto 0);
b2457f .........ADDR_KEY15 ...▷: out ....std_logic_vector(6 ·downto 0);
934ebe .........ADDR_KEY16 ...▷: out ....std_logic_vector(6 ·downto 0);
344801 .........ADDR_KEY17 ...▷: out ....std_logic_vector(6 ·downto 0);
1c6cc4 .........ADDR_KEY18 ...▷: out ....std_logic_vector(6 ·downto 0);
956a7b .........ADDR_KEY19 ...▷: out ....std_logic_vector(6 ·downto 0);
ab8eb2 .........ADDR_KEY20 ...▷: out ....std_logic_vector(6 ·downto 0);
3c880d .........ADDR_KEY21 ...▷: out ....std_logic_vector(6 ·downto 0);
2c83cc .........ADDR_KEY22 ...▷: out ....std_logic_vector(6 ·downto 0);
218573 .........ADDR_KEY23 ...▷: out ....std_logic_vector(6 ·downto 0);
477bfe .........DATAI ......▷ : in ....std_logic_vector(7 downto 0);
555cbe .........DATAO ......▷ : out ....std_logic_vector(7 downto 0)
c3737c ....);
4faf5a
a0af5a
782fc5 end UPI;
08af5a
f35356 --------------------------------------------------------------------------
d17b89 architecture beh of UPI is
605356 --------------------------------------------------------------------------
94af5a
70af5a
```

```
--9953 00085f7c1db80030011 Page 2 of upi.vhd
b11f14 signal SEARCH_IN_BAK ▷     : std_logic_vector(23 ·downto 0);
cf1b46 signal CHIP_EN ▷▷          : std_logic;
a9af5a
c00c34 component ADDR_KEY
2b14be port( ··
943782 ········ADDSEL2 ·········: in ····std_logic;
d5748f ········CHIP_EN ·········: in ····std_logic;
3eb47e ········ADDR ···········: in ····std_logic_vector(7 downto 0);
c8af5a
83eccb ········ADDR_KEY0 ·······: out ···std_logic_vector(6 ·downto 0);
c9a1b1 ········ADDR_KEY1 ·······: out ···std_logic_vector(6 ·downto 0);
59763f ········ADDR_KEY2 ·······: out ···std_logic_vector(6 ·downto 0);
903b45 ········ADDR_KEY3 ·······: out ···std_logic_vector(6 ·downto 0);
7bd132 ········ADDR_KEY4 ·······: out ···std_logic_vector(6 ·downto 0);
449c48 ········ADDR_KEY5 ·······: out ···std_logic_vector(6 ·downto 0);
684bc6 ········ADDR_KEY6 ·······: out ···std_logic_vector(6 ·downto 0);
9506bc ········ADDR_KEY7 ·······: out ···std_logic_vector(6 ·downto 0);
2c9739 ········ADDR_KEY8 ·······: out ···std_logic_vector(6 ·downto 0);
58da43 ········ADDR_KEY9 ·······: out ···std_logic_vector(6 ·downto 0);
b157bd ········ADDR_KEY10 ······: out ···std_logic_vector(6 ·downto 0);
0a5102 ········ADDR_KEY11 ······: out ···std_logic_vector(6 ·downto 0);
645ac3 ········ADDR_KEY12 ······: out ···std_logic_vector(6 ·downto 0);
785c7c ········ADDR_KEY13 ······: out ···std_logic_vector(6 ·downto 0);
844d41 ········ADDR_KEY14 ······: out ···std_logic_vector(6 ·downto 0);
a34bfe ········ADDR_KEY15 ······: out ···std_logic_vector(6 ·downto 0);
ab403f ········ADDR_KEY16 ······: out ···std_logic_vector(6 ·downto 0);
2b4680 ········ADDR_KEY17 ······: out ···std_logic_vector(6 ·downto 0);
446245 ········ADDR_KEY18 ······: out ···std_logic_vector(6 ·downto 0);
5164fa ········ADDR_KEY19 ······: out ···std_logic_vector(6 ·downto 0);
378033 ········ADDR_KEY20 ······: out ···std_logic_vector(6 ·downto 0);
02868c ········ADDR_KEY21 ······: out ···std_logic_vector(6 ·downto 0);
128d4d ········ADDR_KEY22 ······: out ···std_logic_vector(6 ·downto 0);
08a27f ········ADDR_KEY23 ······: out ···std_logic_vector(6 ·downto 0)
85737c ····);
3ae2c6 end component;
a4d83c ·
94af5a
5323a1 component REG_RDWR
3dcba7 port( ··RST_N ··········: in ····std_logic;
be1a55 ········BOARD_EN ·······: in ····std_logic;
502b30 ········ALE ···········: in ····std_logic;
d55697 ········ADDSEL1 ········: in ····std_logic;
0d6737 ········WRB ···········: in ····std_logic;
f19760 ········RDB ···········: in ····std_logic;
213782 ········ADDSEL2 ········: in ····std_logic;
d14c8d ········AA_IN ·········: in ····std_logic;
d5b47e ········ADDR ··········: in ····std_logic_vector(7 downto 0);
8b6ad7 ········CHIP_ID ········: in ····std_logic_vector(7 downto 0);
9bbe0c ········SEARCH_OUT ·····: in ····std_logic_vector(23 downto 0);
f3053a ········SELECT_ONE ·····: in ····std_logic_vector(23 downto 0);
bdfc73 ········SEARCH_IN ······: in ····std_logic_vector(23 downto 0);
9faf5a
25bcc9 ········CHIP_EN ········: out ···std_logic;
b9ea5e ········AA_OUT ·········: out ···std_logic;
dec420 ········CHIP_AA_OUT ····: out ···std_logic;
606aef ········EXTRA_XOR ······: out ···std_logic;
43a049 ········USE_CBC ········: out ···std_logic;
b3596c ········PT_XOR_MASK ····: out ···std_logic_vector(63 downto 0);
a1a457 ········PT_BYTE_MASK ···: out ···std_logic_vector(7 downto 0);
a8e186 ········PT_VECTOR ······: out ···std_logic_vector(255 downto 0);
37f79c ········C0 ············: out ···std_logic_vector(63 downto 0);
2d3889 ········C1 ············: out ···std_logic_vector(63 downto 0);
774d79 ········DATAI ·········: in ····std_logic_vector(7 downto 0);
8660f9 ········DATAO ·········: out ···std_logic_vector(7 downto 0)
5c737c ····);
15e2c6 end component;
35af5a
23d83c ·
b4af5a
6d9b9d component ·START_REG
becba7 port( ··RST_N ··········: in ····std_logic;
85748f ········CHIP_EN ········: in ····std_logic;
```

```
--5396 0005b52193180030011 Page 3 of upi.vhd

5d6737 ········WRB ············: in ····std_logic;
dd3782 ········ADDSEL2 ·········: in ····std_logic;
5cb47e ········ADDR ············: in ····std_logic_vector(7 downto 0);
5981d2 ········CLEAR_SEARCH ···: in ····std_logic_vector(23 downto 0);
baaf5a
b58af1 ········SEARCH_IN ·······: OUT ····std_logic_vector(23 downto 0);
1b25bf ········DATAI ···········: in ····std_logic_vector(7 downto 0)
ca737c ····);
01e2c6 end component;
89af5a
3b0f89 begin
375356 ------------------------------------------------------------------------
81e5b8 ADDR_KEYX : ADDR_KEY
104a4b port map(
4dc99d ········ADDSEL2 ·········=> ADDSEL2,
341404 ········CHIP_EN ·········=> CHIP_EN,
639c40 ········ADDR ············=> ADDR,
88af5a
e7bffa ········ADDR_KEY0 ·······=> ADDR_KEY0,
2b4c7b ········ADDR_KEY1 ·······=> ADDR_KEY1,
8650e9 ········ADDR_KEY2 ·······=> ADDR_KEY2,
bda368 ········ADDR_KEY3 ·······=> ADDR_KEY3,
1d69cd ········ADDR_KEY4 ·······=> ADDR_KEY4,
cf9a4c ········ADDR_KEY5 ·······=> ADDR_KEY5,
f386de ········ADDR_KEY6 ·······=> ADDR_KEY6,
b3755f ········ADDR_KEY7 ·······=> ADDR_KEY7,
c01b85 ········ADDR_KEY8 ·······=> ADDR_KEY8,
94e804 ········ADDR_KEY9 ·······=> ADDR_KEY9,
db75b1 ········ADDR_KEY10 ······=> ADDR_KEY10,
028630 ········ADDR_KEY11 ······=> ADDR_KEY11,
239aa2 ········ADDR_KEY12 ······=> ADDR_KEY12,
c76923 ········ADDR_KEY13 ······=> ADDR_KEY13,
f1a386 ········ADDR_KEY14 ······=> ADDR_KEY14,
125007 ········ADDR_KEY15 ······=> ADDR_KEY15,
0a4c95 ········ADDR_KEY16 ······=> ADDR_KEY16,
bbbf14 ········ADDR_KEY17 ······=> ADDR_KEY17,
a3d1ce ········ADDR_KEY18 ······=> ADDR_KEY18,
de224f ········ADDR_KEY19 ······=> ADDR_KEY19,
12c236 ········ADDR_KEY20 ······=> ADDR_KEY20,
6b31b7 ········ADDR_KEY21 ······=> ADDR_KEY21,
e42d25 ········ADDR_KEY22 ······=> ADDR_KEY22,
792d66 ········ADDR_KEY23 ······=> ADDR_KEY23
30a8ec ▷      );
41af5a
130fd0 REG_RDWRX : REG_RDWR
c3b1c0 port map(RST_N ··········=> RST_N,
c4c652 ········BOARD_EN ········=> BOARD_EN,
8fed26 ········ALE ·············=> ALE,
53d50f ········ADDSEL1 ·········=> ADDSEL1,
bb14b5 ········WRB ·············=> WRB,
0c7402 ········RDB ·············=> RDB,
79c99d ········ADDSEL2 ·········=> ADDSEL2,
98c77b ········AA_IN ···········=> AA_IN,
479c40 ········ADDR ············=> ADDR,
639156 ········CHIP_ID ·········=> CHIP_ID,
59f877 ········SEARCH_OUT ······=> SEARCH_OUT,
5e4270 ········SELECT_ONE ······=> SELECT_ONE,
381fc9 ········SEARCH_IN ·······=> SEARCH_IN_BAK,
19af5a
a01404 ········CHIP_EN ·········=> CHIP_EN,
f3e285 ········AA_OUT ··········=> AA_OUT,
11750c ········CHIP_AA_OUT ····=> CHIP_AA_OUT,
272b3b ········EXTRA_XOR ·······=> EXTRA_XOR,
89b843 ········USE_CBC ·········=> USE_CBC,
320949 ········PT_XOR_MASK ····=> PT_XOR_MASK,
25084d ········PT_BYTE_MASK ···=> PT_BYTE_MASK,
f4415b ········PT_VECTOR ·······=> PT_VECTOR,
accc6e ········C0 ·············=> C0,
313fef ········C1 ·············=> C1,
7ef6a8 ········DATAI ···········=> DATAI,
6a8c67 ········DATAO ···········=> DATAO
5b737c ····);
```

```
--25a4 0013211398f80030011 Page 4 of upi.vhd

789938 START_REGX : ·START_REG
6cb1c0 port map(RST_N ··········=> RST_N,
7d1404 ········CHIP_EN ·········=> CHIP_EN,
0414b5 ········WRB ············=> WRB,
f1c99d ········ADDSEL2 ·········=> ADDSEL2,
bd9c40 ········ADDR ···········=> ADDR,
600130 ········CLEAR_SEARCH ···=> CLEAR_SEARCH,
38af5a
b71fc9 ········SEARCH_IN ······=> SEARCH_IN_BAK,
2a6bdf ········DATAI ··········=> DATAI
d7737c ····);
e689ea SEARCH_IN <= SEARCH_IN_BAK;
ecb08a end beh;
c95356 --------------------------------------------------------------------------------
32af5a
```

# 7

# *Chip Simulator Source Code*

This chapter contains C-language software that simulates the operation of the custom DES Cracker chip. This software is useful for showing people how the chip works, and to make test-vectors to let machines determine whether chips are properly fabricated.

We wrote this simulator before the chip was designed, to explore different design ideas. It should produce results identical to the final chips. We designed it for clarity of description, and flexibility in trying out new ideas, rather than speed. If you don't understand how the chip works, you can try some experiments by building this software on an ordinary PC or Unix machine with an ordinary C compiler, such as Borland C++ 3.1.

Building physical chips is an error-prone process. Each chip might be contaminated by dust or flaws in the silicon materials. There's no way to tell whether a given chip will work or not, without trying it out. So chip-building companies require that when you design a chip, you also provide test vectors. These list the voltages to put on each input pin on the chip, and how the chip-testing machine should vary them over time. The vectors also specify exactly what output signals the chip-tester should be able to measure on the chip's output pins. If the chip tester feeds all the input signals to the chip, step by step, and sees all the corresponding output signals, the chip "passes" the test. If any output signals differ from the specification, the chip "fails" the test and is discarded.

Passing such a test doesn't prove that a chip has been fabricated correctly. It only proves that the chip can run the small set of tests that the designer provided. Creating test vectors which verify all parts of a chip is an art. The expense of testing a chip is proportional to the size of the tests, so they are usually short and direct. Thus, they also act as small examples that you can use to explore your understanding of how the chip works.

Chapter 4, *Scanning the Source Code*, explains how to read or scan in these documents.

```
--9a44 0014b4364e180040001 Page 1 of MANIFEST

7bf681  1  MANIFEST
63b635  2  README
476ecc  3  blaze.scr
8a49aa  4  cbc1.scr
581046  5  cbc2.scr
1feade  6  cbc3.scr
868e30  7  des.c
f3db2a  8  des.h
bbf31a  9  ecb.scr
039f0d  10 mini.scr
02ce39  11 misc.c
60fc96  12 misc.h
b51b5d  13 random.scr
cfb60c  14 ref.c
aa84bd  15 sim.c
0beac5  16 sim.h
4b2104  17 testvec.c
```

```
--926a 0011c402f8d80040002 Page 1 of README

e0af5a
3f1c37 testvec.c (compile with sim.c and des.c): ·Generates and runs test
9a0001 vectors. ·This program will both run existing input vectors, or·
08239f generate new ones (either randomly or from a script). ·When compiled
c43481 under DOS, it can either produce Unix (LF only) or DOS (CR/LF)
37d2c3 output files (select with the RAW parameter)
a1af5a
26a7b8 To run the ecb.scr sample script and:
473eef ··Store test vectors which go to the chip in TOCHIP.EXT
5b66ea ··Store test vectors received from the chip in FROMCHIP.EXT,
0763b5 ··Produce Unix-style output (LF only)
9e1741 ··Store debugging output in debug.out.
10af5a
f46e57 ····rm *.EXT
a1f54e ····testvec TOCHIP.EXT FROMCHIP.EXT RAW < ecb.scr > debug.out
c7ed9a ··································
1ff74b If TOCHIP.EXE already exists when the program is run, it will
917018 read it (instead of expecting a script from stdin).
60af5a
b4a916 Use the script random.scr to produce a random test vector, e.g.:
b7bdcd ····testvec TOCHIP.EXT FROMCHIP.EXT RAW < random.scr > debug.out
52af5a
d7ecf1 -----------------------------------------------------------------------
b3af5a
4eaf5a
b0a8a2 ref.c (compile with des.c misc.c): ·Runs test scripts (.scr files)
0b7e68 and prints any keys that match. ·This is basically a stripped-down
abd9fb test vector generator for debugging purposes. ·(It doesn't make any
9749f1 attempt to match timings.)
2caf5a
1caf5a
```

```
--a854 001ab3b125780040003 Page 1 of blaze.scr

95a107 00 01 02 03 04 05 06 07 10 11 12 13 14 15 16 1720 21 22 23 24 25 26 2730 31 32 ∎
2e79b3 33 34 35 36 3740 41 42 43 44 45 46 4750 51 52 53 54 55 56 57
159ec4 0000000000000000 ···' XOR MASK
7e10d0 123456789ABCDEF0 ···' Ciphertext 0
690908 123456789ABCDEF0 ···' Ciphertext 1
9cb374 0F ················' Plaintext byte mask
ebed5e 0 ·················' use CBC
72af2d 1 ·················' extra XOR
a25b0d 1 ·················' don't seed PRNG (use this input file)
fa2fcc 01020304050607 ······' starting key
2b6f6b 8000 ···············' number of clocks
f8af5a
49af5a
29c4d8 d6 e9 89 fa ·'DES_DECRYPT(k=0D020304050612, c=123456789ABCDEF0)=B8 C0 1B 3E 35 ∎
84c98d DB 2F DE ·······00 01 02 03 04 05 06 07 08 09 0A 0B 0C 0D 0E 0F 10 11 12 13 14 ∎
b1422d 15 16 17 18 19 1A 1B 1C 1D 1E 1F 20 21 22 23 24 25 26 27 28 29 2A 2B 2C 2D 2E 2∎
89c4e2 F30 31 32 33 34 35 36 37 38 39 3A 3B 3C 3D 3E 3F 40 41 42 43 44 45 46 47 48 49 ∎
f7e1db 4A 4B 4C 4D 4E 4F50 51 52 53 54 55 56 57 58 59 5A 5B 5C 5D 5E 5F 60 61 62 63 64∎
58e46f ·65 66 67 68 69 6A 6B 6C 6D 6E 6F70 71 72 73 74 75 76 77 78 79 7A 7B 7C 7D 7E 7∎
ff0795 F 80 81 82 83 84 85 86 87 88 89 8A 8B 8C 8D 8E 8F90 91 92 93 94 95 96 97 98 99 ∎
505b42 9A 9B 9C 9D 9E 9F ·A0 A1 A2 A3 A4 A5 A6 A7 A8 A9 AA AB AC AD AE AFB0 B1 B2 B3 B∎
7fa3b9 4 B5 B6 B7 B8 B9 BA BB BC BD BE BF C0 C1 C2 C3 C4 C5 C6 C7 C8 C9 CA CB CC CD CE∎
f6f44d ·CFD0 D1 D2 D3 D4 D5 D6 D7 D8 D9 DA DB DC DD DE DF E0 E1 E2 E3 E4 E5 E6 E7 E8 E∎
ea8b9b 9 EA EB EC ED EE EFF0 F1 F2 F3 F4 F5 F6 F7 F8 F9 FA FB FC FD FE·
abaf5a
```

```
--a728 0015c860f9980040004 Page 1 of cbc1.scr

f64ce1 00 01 02 03 04 05 06 07 08 09 0A 0B 0C 0D 0E 0F 10 11 12 13 14 15 16 17 18 19 1■
b53734 A 1B 1C 1D 1E 1F 20 21 22 23 24 25 26 27 28 29 2A 2B 2C 2D 2E 2F 30 31 32 33 34■
5f0653 ·35 36 37 38 39 3A 3B 3C 3D 3E 3F 40 41 42 43 44 45 46 47 48 49 4A 4B 4C 4D 4E■
bc6d97 4F 50 51 52 53 54 55 56 57 58 59 5A 5B 5C 5D 5E 5F 60 61 62 63 64 65 66 67 68 6■
a1cb67 9 6A 6B 6C 6D 6E 6F 70 71 72 73 74 75 76 77 78 79 7A 7B 7C 7D 7E 7F 80 81 82 83■
b32164 ·84 85 86 87 88 89 8A 8B 8C 8D 8E 8F 90 91 92 93 94 95 96 97 98 99 9A 9B #9C 9D■
d8a908 ·9E 9F A0 A1 A2 A3 A4 A5 A6 A7 A8 A9 AA AB AC AD AE AF B0 B1 B2 B3 B4 B5 B6 B7 ■
babb7d B8 B9 BA BB BC BD BE BF C0 C1 C2 C3 C4 C5 C6 C7 C8 C9 CA CB CC CD CE CF D0 D1 D■
54b467 2 D3 D4 D5 D6 D7 D8 D9 DA DB DC DD DE DF E0 E1 E2 E3 E4 E5 E6 E7 E8 E9 EA EB EC■
c890fe ·ED EE EF F0 F1 F2 F3 F4 F5 F6 F7 F8 F9 FA FB FC FD FE FF
2f281f 37393b51def84190 ···' XOR MASK
1810d0 123456789ABCDEF0 ···' Ciphertext 0
596a3f 0102030405060708 ···' Ciphertext 1
b98c19 00 ················' Plaintext byte mask
56cdad 1 ················' use CBC
b0d84f 0 ················' extra XOR
095b0d 1 ················' don't seed PRNG (use this input file)
322fcc 0102030405060708 ······' starting key
359df9 10000 ·············' number of clocks
5caf5a
```

```
--a112 00101ebc6db80040005 Page 1 of cbc2.scr
f64ce1 00 01 02 03 04 05 06 07 08 09 0A 0B 0C 0D 0E 0F 10 11 12 13 14 15 16 17 18 19 1■
b53734 A 1B 1C 1D 1E 1F 20 21 22 23 24 25 26 27 28 29 2A 2B 2C 2D 2E 2F 30 31 32 33 34■
5f0653 ·35 36 37 38 39 3A 3B 3C 3D 3E 3F 40 41 42 43 44 45 46 47 48 49 4A 4B 4C 4D 4E ■
bc6d97 4F 50 51 52 53 54 55 56 57 58 59 5A 5B 5C 5D 5E 5F 60 61 62 63 64 65 66 67 68 6■
a1cb67 9 6A 6B 6C 6D 6E 6F 70 71 72 73 74 75 76 77 78 79 7A 7B 7C 7D 7E 7F 80 81 82 83■
237dda ·84 85 86 87 88 89 8A 8B 8C 8D 8E 8F 90 91 92 93 94 95 96 97 98 99 9A 9B 9C 9D ■
23435f 9E 9F A0 A1 A2 A3 A4 A5 A6 A7 A8 A9 AA AB AC AD AE AF B0 B1 B2 B3 B4 B5 B6 B7 B■
1ce1f9 8 B9 BA # BB BC BD BE BF C0 C1 C2 C3 C4 C5 C6 C7 C8 C9 CA CB CC CD CE CF D0 D1 ■
80796d D2 D3 D4 D5 D6 D7 D8 D9 DA DB DC DD DE DF E0 E1 E2 E3 E4 E5 E6 E7 E8 E9 EA EB E■
0b8b2a C ED EE EF F0 F1 F2 F3 F4 F5 F6 F7 F8 F9 FA FB FC FD FE FF
56ac5f 423412341234123F ···' XOR MASK
0b327c 0000000000000000 ···' Ciphertext 0
ee53f1 1578345691832465 ···' Ciphertext 1
23e767 04 ················' Plaintext byte mask
20cdad 1 ·················' use CBC
00d84f 0 ·················' extra XOR
795b0d 1 ·················' don't seed PRNG (use this input file)
12de95 FFFFFFFFFFFFFFF0 ······' starting key
309df9 10000 ··············' number of clocks
01af5a
```

```
--3fb8 001348ab9e680040006 Page 1 of cbc3.scr

2c9f3b 00 01 02 03 04 05 07 08 09 0D 0E 0F 10 11 12 14 15 17 1A 1B 1C 1D 1F 20 21 24 2■
bd57bd 5 28 29 2A 2B 2C 2E 30 31 32 35 36 37 39 3A 3C 3D 3E 40 42 43 44 45 48 49 4A 4B■
1b6fb2 ·4C 4F 50 51 53 54 56 57 58 59 5C 5D 5F 61 62 63 64 66 67 69 6B 6C 6D 6F 70 71 ■
6e57e8 72 73 77 78 7A 7B 7D 7E 7F 80 82 86 87 89 8A 8B 8C 8D 8E 90 92 93 94 95 97 98 9■
753dfa 9 9A 9B 9E 9F A0 A2 A3 A4 A5 A6 A8 AA AC AD AE AF B0 B1 B3 B4 B7 B8 B9 F8 F9 FA■
958c0a ·FB FC FD FF BB BC BD BE C0 C1 C3 C5 C6 C7 C8 C9 CA CB CC CD CE CF D0 D1 D2 D3 ■
09fa11 D4 D5 D6 D7 D8 D9 DA DB DC DD DE DF E0 E1 E2 E3 E4 # E5 E6 E7 E8 E9 EA EB EC ED■
473f52 ·EE EF F0 F1 F2 F3 F4 F5 F6 F7 F8 F9 FA FB FC FD FE FF
638b27 0124801248012480 ···'  XOR MASK
3745a7 FFFFFFFFFFFFFFFF ···'  Ciphertext 0
1d2ba4 0000000000000000 ···'  Ciphertext 1
d6b12c 80 ················'  Plaintext byte mask
72cdad 1 ·················'  use CBC
37d84f 0 ·················'  extra XOR
e85b0d 1 ·················'  don't seed PRNG (use this input file)
afa481 0000000000000000 ······'  starting key
e49df9 10000 ··············'  number of clocks
34af5a
```

```
--b787 000d22ad6f780040007 Page 1 of des.c

8d2d03 /************************************************************************
d729eb  * .............................................................................*
b2074d  * ..................Software Model of ASIC DES Implementation. ................*
4a29eb  * .............................................................................*
9f9048  * .Written by Paul Kocher, Tel: 415-397-0111, Email: paul@cryptography.com .*
ce29eb  * .............................................................................*
e7489b  ************************************************************************
de29eb  * .............................................................................*
c515cb  * ..IMPLEMENTATION NOTES: .....................................................*
3429eb  * .............................................................................*
987602  * ..This DES implementation adheres to the FIPS PUB 46 spec and produces ...*
a90da9  * ..standard output. .The internal operation of the algorithm is quite .....*
9a876e  * ..different from the FIPS. .For example, bit orderings are reversed .......*
a41be6  * ..(the right-hand bit is now labelled as bit 0), the S tables have ........*
06b9c7  * ..rearranged to simplify implementation, and several permutations have ...*
44966d  * ..been inverted. .No performance optimizations were attempted. ............*
1829eb  * .............................................................................*
3e489b  ************************************************************************
aa29eb  * .............................................................................*
496eef  * ..REVISION HISTORY: .........................................................*
ba29eb  * .............................................................................*
0bc443  * ..Version 1.0: .Initial release .-- PCK. ....................................*
d7b74c  * ..Version 1.1: .Altered DecryptDES exchanges to match EncryptDES. -- PCK .*
fa5c27  * ..Version 1.2: .Minor edits and beautifications. .-- PCK ....................*
e0d8c3  ************************************************************************/
9aaf5a
a8af5a
00feb2 #include <stdio.h>
a3bea3 #include <stdlib.h>
94324c #include <string.h>
e92bac #include "des.h"
fbaf5a
f77461 static void ComputeRoundKey(bool roundKey[56], bool key[56]);
6d84a3 static void RotateRoundKeyLeft(bool roundKey[56]);
57ccfa static void RotateRoundKeyRight(bool roundKey[56]);
741504 static void ComputeIP(bool L[32], bool R[32], bool inBlk[64]);
1c07da static void ComputeFP(bool outBlk[64], bool L[32], bool R[32]);
fe017b static void ComputeF(bool fout[32], bool R[32], bool roundKey[56]);
ef94fe static void ComputeP(bool output[32], bool input[32]);
7f7fae static void ComputeS_Lookup(int k, bool output[4], bool input[6]);
25abe7 static void ComputePC2(bool subkey[48], bool roundKey[56]);
fdfd9c static void ComputeExpansionE(bool expandedBlock[48], bool R[32]);
662f30 static void DumpBin(char *str, bool *b, int bits);
ad43bc static void Exchange_L_and_R(bool L[32], bool R[32]);
39af5a
efc223 int EnableDumpBin = 0;
f5af5a
7caf5a
84af5a
d84d6c /************************************************************************/
a5c68f /* .........................................................................*/
033c1a /* ..................DES TABLES ............................................*/
14c68f /* .........................................................................*/
264d6c /************************************************************************/
6faf5a
76af5a
8838e5 /*
aa556a  * .IP: Output bit table_DES_IP[i] equals input bit i.
30495d  */
09c166 static int table_DES_IP[64] = {
829d69 ....39, .7, 47, 15, 55, 23, 63, 31,
10c827 ....38, .6, 46, 14, 54, 22, 62, 30,
4b38ae ....37, .5, 45, 13, 53, 21, 61, 29,
2b6de0 ....36, .4, 44, 12, 52, 20, 60, 28,
f5b247 ....35, .3, 43, 11, 51, 19, 59, 27,
c7e709 ....34, .2, 42, 10, 50, 18, 58, 26,
28829e ....33, .1, 41, .9, 49, 17, 57, 25,
4811ff ....32, .0, 40, .8, 48, 16, 56, 24
2882f7 };
39af5a
95af5a
d238e5 /*
```

```
--43e9 000e122426b80040007 Page 2 of des.c

ac48ca  · * ·FP: Output bit table_DES_FP[i] equals input bit i.
c0495d  ·*/
2ddd2a  static int table_DES_FP[64] = {
675b71  ····57, 49, 41, 33, 25, 17, ·9, ·1,
768cd9  ····59, 51, 43, 35, 27, 19, 11, ·3,
b79996  ····61, 53, 45, 37, 29, 21, 13, ·5,
93b571  ····63, 55, 47, 39, 31, 23, 15, ·7,
040e3f  ····56, 48, 40, 32, 24, 16, ·8, ·0,
62d997  ····58, 50, 42, 34, 26, 18, 10, ·2,
f5ccd8  ····60, 52, 44, 36, 28, 20, 12, ·4,
664da9  ····62, 54, 46, 38, 30, 22, 14, ·6
2d82f7  };
7baf5a
b0af5a
0f38e5  /*
85da05  · * ·PC1: Permutation choice 1, used to pre-process the key
da495d  ·*/
a40c38  static int table_DES_PC1[56] = {
0db89e  ····27, 19, 11, 31, 39, 47, 55,
bb28e4  ····26, 18, 10, 30, 38, 46, 54,
cf8d2c  ····25, 17, ·9, 29, 37, 45, 53,
ce1d56  ····24, 16, ·8, 28, 36, 44, 52,
62bf91  ····23, 15, ·7, ·3, 35, 43, 51,
d72feb  ····22, 14, ·6, ·2, 34, 42, 50,
b491e6  ····21, 13, ·5, ·1, 33, 41, 49,
b0d02f  ····20, 12, ·4, ·0, 32, 40, 48
1782f7  };
67af5a
16af5a
b638e5  /*
2af37a  · * ·PC2: Map 56-bit round key to a 48-bit subkey
89495d  ·*/
097fcf  static int table_DES_PC2[48] = {
e98889  ····24, 27, 20, ·6, 14, 10, ·3, 22,
1b30a5  ·····0, 17, ·7, 12, ·8, 23, 11, ·5,
893fa5  ····16, 26, ·1, ·9, 19, 25, ·4, 15,
dee272  ····54, 43, 36, 29, 49, 40, 48, 30,
566356  ····52, 44, 37, 33, 46, 35, 50, 41,
ab7786  ····28, 53, 51, 55, 32, 45, 39, 42
2a82f7  };
11af5a
c0af5a
2238e5  /*
9adb31  · * ·E: Expand 32-bit R to 48 bits.
35495d  ·*/
846a87  static int table_DES_E[48] = {
78e6fb  ····31, ·0, ·1, ·2, ·3, ·4, ·3, ·4,
fa2634  ·····5, ·6, ·7, ·8, ·7, ·8, ·9, 10,
16d06b  ····11, 12, 11, 12, 13, 14, 15, 16,
117fa0  ····15, 16, 17, 18, 19, 20, 19, 20,
184d0d  ····21, 22, 23, 24, 23, 24, 25, 26,
139708  ····27, 28, 27, 28, 29, 30, 31, ·0
8a82f7  };
79af5a
cdaf5a
a738e5  /*
69c34a  · * ·P: Permutation of S table outputs
ea495d  ·*/
745137  static int table_DES_P[32] = {
aaf612  ····11, 17, ·5, 27, 25, 10, 20, ·0,
3fb9f8  ····13, 21, ·3, 28, 29, ·7, 18, 24,
8fcde3  ····31, 22, 12, ·6, 26, ·2, 16, ·8,
d560a7  ····14, 30, ·4, 19, ·1, ·9, 15, 23
8482f7  };
79af5a
8eaf5a
d038e5  /*
2b6f34  · * ·S Tables: Introduce nonlinearity and avalanche
d2495d  ·*/
b71e19  static int table_DES_S[8][64] = {
8bd69a  ····/* table S[0] */
e1846d  ········{ ··13, ·1, ·2, 15, ·8, 13, ·4, ·8, ·6, 10, 15, ·3, 11, ·7, ·1, ·4,
```

```
--1f22 000be80f13a80040007 Page 3 of des.c

f065af ·············10, 12, ·9, ·5, ·3, ·6, 14, 11, ·5, ·0, ·0, 14, 12, ·9, ·7, ·2,
12d5b0 ·············7, ·2, 11, ·1, ·4, 14, ·1, ·7, ·9, ·4, 12, 10, 14, ·8, ·2, 13,
5a3ee1 ·············0, 15, ·6, 12, 10, ·9, 13, ·0, 15, ·3, ·3, ·5, ·5, ·6, ·8, 11 ·},
d0d2b1 ····/* table S[1] */
8b4b6a ········{ ··4, 13, 11, ·0, ·2, 11, 14, ·7, 15, ·4, ·0, ·9, ·8, ·1, 13, 10,
0cdf4d ·············3, 14, 12, ·3, ·9, ·5, ·7, 12, ·5, ·2, 10, 15, ·6, ·8, ·1, ·6,
8bf575 ·············1, ·6, ·4, 11, 11, 13, 13, ·8, 12, ·1, ·3, ·4, ·7, 10, 14, ·7,
cf6234 ·············10, ·9, 15, ·5, ·6, ·0, ·8, 15, ·0, 14, ·5, ·2, ·9, ·3, ·2, 12 ·},
38decc ····/* table S[2] */
7df108 ········{ ··12, 10, ·1, 15, 10, ·4, 15, ·2, ·9, ·7, ·2, 12, ·6, ·9, ·8, ·5,
a3d582 ·············0, ·6, 13, ·1, ·3, 13, ·4, 14, 14, ·0, ·7, 11, ·5, ·3, 11, ·8,
fd0bbf ·············9, ·4, 14, ·3, 15, ·2, ·5, 12, ·2, ·9, ·8, ·5, 12, 15, ·3, 10,
137505 ·············7, 11, ·0, 14, ·4, ·1, 10, ·7, ·1, ·6, 13, ·0, 11, ·8, ·6, 13 ·},
9fdae7 ····/* table S[3] */
f35c4d ········{ ··2, 14, 12, 11, ·4, ·2, ·1, 12, ·7, ·4, 10, ·7, 11, 13, ·6, ·1,
2c0156 ·············8, ·5, ·5, ·0, ·3, 15, 15, 10, 13, ·3, ·0, ·9, 14, ·8, ·9, ·6,
def5dc ·············4, 11, ·2, ·8, ·1, 12, 11, ·7, 10, ·1, 13, 14, ·7, ·2, ·8, 13,
62d332 ·············15, ·6, ·9, 15, 12, ·0, ·5, ·9, ·6, 10, ·3, ·4, ·0, ·5, 14, ·3 ·},
97c636 ····/* table S[4] */
d74850 ········{ ··7, 13, 13, ·8, 14, 11, ·3, ·5, ·0, ·6, ·6, 15, ·9, ·0, 10, ·3,
aef1a6 ·············1, ·4, ·2, ·7, ·8, ·2, ·5, 12, 11, ·1, 12, 10, ·4, 14, 15, ·9,
5af43f ·············10, ·3, ·6, 15, ·9, ·0, ·0, ·6, 12, 10, 11, ·1, ·7, 13, 13, ·8,
87d830 ·············15, ·9, ·1, ·4, ·3, ·5, 14, 11, ·5, 12, ·2, ·7, ·8, ·2, ·4, 14 ·},
fbc21d ····/* table S[5] */
e2ea9b ········{ ··10, 13, ·0, ·7, ·9, ·0, 14, ·9, ·6, ·3, ·3, ·4, 15, ·6, ·5, 10,
35bd2c ·············1, ·2, 13, ·8, 12, ·5, ·7, 14, 11, 12, ·4, 11, ·2, 15, ·8, ·1,
55d567 ·············13, ·1, ·6, 10, ·4, 13, ·9, ·0, ·8, ·6, 15, ·9, ·3, ·8, ·0, ·7,
9b8261 ·············11, ·4, ·1, 15, ·2, 14, 12, ·3, ·5, 11, 10, ·5, 14, ·2, ·7, 12 ·},
09ce60 ····/* table S[6] */
fea636 ········{ ··15, ·3, ·1, 13, ·8, ·4, 14, ·7, ·6, 15, 11, ·2, ·3, ·8, ·4, 14,
baac1c ·············9, 12, ·7, ·0, ·2, ·1, 13, 10, 12, ·6, ·0, ·9, ·5, 11, 10, ·5,
677311 ·············0, 13, 14, ·8, ·7, 10, 11, ·1, 10, ·3, ·4, 15, 13, ·4, ·1, ·2,
f8b1aa ·············11, ·1, ·8, ·6, 12, ·7, ·6, 12, ·9, ·0, ·3, ·5, ·2, 14, 15, ·9 ·},
c1ca4b ····/* table S[7] */
e8cf66 ········{ ··14, ·0, ·4, 15, 13, ·7, ·1, ·4, ·2, 14, 15, ·2, 11, 13, ·8, ·1,
e3aacb ·············3, 10, 10, ·6, ·6, 12, 12, 11, ·5, ·9, ·9, ·5, ·0, ·3, ·7, ·8,
fa2f45 ·············4, 15, ·1, 12, 14, ·8, ·8, ·2, 13, ·4, ·6, ·9, ·2, ·1, 11, ·7,
252777 ·············15, ·5, 12, 11, ·9, ·3, ·7, 14, ·3, 10, 10, ·0, ·5, ·6, ·0, 13 ·}
0d82f7 };
44af5a
88af5a
1eaf5a
51af5a
be4d6c /*********************************************************************/
25c68f /* ················································· ···················*/
4ecabf /* ····························DES CODE ···························*/
77c68f /* ·················································· ··················*/
494d6c /*********************************************************************/
e8af5a
8aaf5a
9138e5 /*
11b080 ·* ·EncryptDES: Encrypt a block using DES. Set verbose for debugging info.
65770b ·* ·(This loop does both loops on the "DES Encryption" page of the flowchart.)
1e495d ·*/
5a5620 void EncryptDES(bool key[56], bool outBlk[64], bool inBlk[64], int verbose) {
d72b1c ··int i,round;
3a9aa1 ··bool R[32], L[32], fout[32];
1cbfaf ··bool roundKey[56];
24af5a
eb94e2 ··EnableDumpBin = verbose; ··················/* set debugging on/off flag */
ebcb2a ··DumpBin("input(left)", inBlk+32, 32);
558fb2 ··DumpBin("input(right)", inBlk, 32);
bc0a8e ··DumpBin("raw key(left )", key+28, 28);
8a5585 ··DumpBin("raw key(right)", key, 28);
eeaf5a
f4c1be ··/* Compute the first roundkey by performing PC1 */
53b264 ··ComputeRoundKey(roundKey, key);
86af5a
6795d4 ··DumpBin("roundKey(L)", roundKey+28, 28);
070a5f ··DumpBin("roundKey(R)", roundKey, 28);
09af5a
be1340 ··/* Compute the initial permutation and divide the result into L and R */
```

```
--e2ca 0004f895fba80040007 Page 4 of des.c
d8d1a8 ··ComputeIP(L,R,inBlk);
c8af5a
b277ba ··DumpBin("after IP(L)", L, 32);
4b7699 ··DumpBin("after IP(R)", R, 32);
56af5a
44f437 ··for (round = 0; round < 16; round++) {
d221bf ····if (verbose)
5f91a0 ······printf("-------------- BEGIN ENCRYPT ROUND %d -------------\n", round);
aa8034 ····DumpBin("round start(L)", L, 32);
ec8117 ····DumpBin("round start(R)", R, 32);
d8af5a
f27fc3 ····/* Rotate roundKey halves left once or twice (depending on round) */
3ec8ba ····RotateRoundKeyLeft(roundKey);
031467 ····if (round != 0 && round != 1 && round != 8 && round != 15)
9650e7 ······RotateRoundKeyLeft(roundKey);
dd3cd7 ····DumpBin("roundKey(L)", roundKey+28, 28);
3f1bd4 ····DumpBin("roundKey(R)", roundKey, 28);
8baf5a
2a033b ····/* Compute f(R, roundKey) and exclusive-OR onto the value in L */
73d969 ····ComputeF(fout, R, roundKey);
1054e7 ····DumpBin("f(R,key)", fout, 32);
834739 ····for (i = 0; i < 32; i++)
eaa9e6 ······L[i] ^= fout[i];
aca5ab ····DumpBin("L^f(R,key)", L, 32);
92af5a
8f68b4 ····Exchange_L_and_R(L,R);
c2af5a
a5a140 ····DumpBin("round end(L)", L, 32);
9da063 ····DumpBin("round end(R)", R, 32);
0c21bf ····if (verbose)
ee4514 ······printf("-------------- END ROUND %d -------------\n", round);
bedf1c ··}
39af5a
f08e68 ··Exchange_L_and_R(L,R);
7baf5a
a7370b ··/* Combine L and R then compute the final permutation */
e3cf94 ··ComputeFP(outBlk,L,R);
668b91 ··DumpBin("FP out( left)", outBlk+32, 32);
a4f675 ··DumpBin("FP out(right)", outBlk, 32);
ffefe6 }
bbaf5a
64af5a
1faf5a
2638e5 /*
c19b68 ·* ·DecryptDES: Decrypt a block using DES. Set verbose for debugging info.
83a5c7 ·* ·(This loop does both loops on the "DES Decryption" page of the flowchart.)
7e495d ·*/
c36de8 void DecryptDES(bool key[56], bool outBlk[64], bool inBlk[64], int verbose) {
c02b1c ··int i,round;
a89aa1 ··bool R[32], L[32], fout[32];
52bfaf ··bool roundKey[56];
87af5a
6e94e2 ··EnableDumpBin = verbose; ··················/* set debugging on/off flag */
e2cb2a ··DumpBin("input(left)", inBlk+32, 32);
ef8fb2 ··DumpBin("input(right)", inBlk, 32);
340a8e ··DumpBin("raw key(left)", key+28, 28);
ed5585 ··DumpBin("raw key(right)", key, 28);
9faf5a
3ac1be ··/* Compute the first roundkey by performing PC1 */
20b264 ··ComputeRoundKey(roundKey, key);
afaf5a
c595d4 ··DumpBin("roundKey(L)", roundKey+28, 28);
c90a5f ··DumpBin("roundKey(R)", roundKey, 28);
f4af5a
311340 ··/* Compute the initial permutation and divide the result into L and R */
03d1a8 ··ComputeIP(L,R,inBlk);
a8af5a
c277ba ··DumpBin("after IP(L)", L, 32);
2f7699 ··DumpBin("after IP(R)", R, 32);
a6af5a
1bf437 ··for (round = 0; round < 16; round++) {
4f21bf ····if (verbose)
```

```
--4cd6 000642b0cd180040007 Page 5 of des.c

db2cb4 ········printf("-------------- BEGIN DECRYPT ROUND %d -------------\n", round);
908034 ····DumpBin("round start(L)", L, 32);
a48117 ····DumpBin("round start(R)", R, 32);
c5af5a
3d033b ····/* Compute f(R, roundKey) and exclusive-OR onto the value in L */
b5d969 ····ComputeF(fout, R, roundKey);
5d54e7 ····DumpBin("f(R,key)", fout, 32);
c84739 ····for (i = 0; i < 32; i++)
d5a9e6 ······L[i] ^= fout[i];
5ba5ab ····DumpBin("L^f(R,key)", L, 32);
b2af5a
fa68b4 ····Exchange_L_and_R(L,R);
18af5a
f3c90d ····/* Rotate roundKey halves right once or twice (depending on round) */
6e48f3 ····DumpBin("roundKey(L)", roundKey+28, 28); ·/* show keys before shift */
7f1bd4 ····DumpBin("roundKey(R)", roundKey, 28);
90f5db ····RotateRoundKeyRight(roundKey);
8711ff ····if (round != 0 && round != 7 && round != 14 && round != 15)
ba7c23 ······RotateRoundKeyRight(roundKey);
5baf5a
69a140 ····DumpBin("round end(L)", L, 32);
c6a063 ····DumpBin("round end(R)", R, 32);
f621bf ····if (verbose)
784514 ······printf("-------------- END ROUND %d -------------\n", round);
23df1c ··}
30af5a
ec8e68 ··Exchange_L_and_R(L,R);
f5af5a
f5370b ··/* Combine L and R then compute the final permutation */
f5cf94 ··ComputeFP(outBlk,L,R);
8d8b91 ··DumpBin("FP out( left)", outBlk+32, 32);
94f675 ··DumpBin("FP out(right)", outBlk, 32);
efefe6 }
3daf5a
deaf5a
41af5a
fc38e5 /*
4b8d8b ·* ·ComputeRoundKey: Compute PC1 on the key and store the result in roundKey
c1495d ·*/
3e988e static void ComputeRoundKey(bool roundKey[56], bool key[56]) {
9e17e0 ··int i;
60af5a
f9815b ··for (i = 0; i < 56; i++)
70d64b ····roundKey[table_DES_PC1[i]] = key[i];
54efe6 }
24af5a
8caf5a
daaf5a
1b38e5 /*
8155cb ·* ·RotateRoundKeyLeft: Rotate each of the halves of roundKey left one bit
44495d ·*/
737d60 static void RotateRoundKeyLeft(bool roundKey[56]) {
cf483e ··bool temp1, temp2;
7217e0 ··int i;
c7af5a
0ff689 ··temp1 = roundKey[27];
83fe1b ··temp2 = roundKey[55];
9c300b ··for (i = 27; i >= 1; i--) {
95575a ····roundKey[i] = roundKey[i-1];
0b3242 ····roundKey[i+28] = roundKey[i+28-1];
aadf1c ··}
bc7b9f ··roundKey[ 0] = temp1;
b3cf9d ··roundKey[28] = temp2;
51efe6 }
fbaf5a
5caf5a
51af5a
0c38e5 /*
3bc6ad ·* ·RotateRoundKeyRight: Rotate each of the halves of roundKey right one bit
87495d ·*/
57b26c static void RotateRoundKeyRight(bool roundKey[56]) {
64483e ··bool temp1, temp2;
```

```
--20a0 000e89a59d480040007 Page 6 of des.c

eb17e0  ··int i;
71af5a
085025  ··temp1 = roundKey[0];
754548  ··temp2 = roundKey[28];
78e568  ··for (i = 0; i < 27; i++) {
806cc2  ····roundKey[i] = roundKey[i+1];
fd09da  ····roundKey[i+28] = roundKey[i+28+1];
c1df1c  ··}
d5a88d  ··roundKey[27] = temp1;
365d11  ··roundKey[55] = temp2;
29efe6  }
5daf5a
45af5a
d8af5a
2f38e5  /*
022903  ·* ·ComputeIP: Compute the initial permutation and split into L and R halves.
fb495d  ·*/
fcac44  static void ComputeIP(bool L[32], bool R[32], bool inBlk[64]) {
826085  ··bool output[64];
f917e0  ··int i;
bdaf5a
81aeaf  ··/* Permute
71f9a6  ···*/
466406  ··for (i = 63; i >= 0; i--)
a8c750  ····output[table_DES_IP[i]] = inBlk[i];
0aaf5a
af0318  ··/* Split into R and L. ·Bits 63..32 go in L, bits 31..0 go in R.
54f9a6  ···*/
b8ba85  ··for (i = 63; i >= 0; i--) {
5b0368  ····if (i >= 32)
67f2b8  ······L[i-32] = output[i];
50842c  ····else
7970b5  ······R[i] = output[i];
22df1c  ··}
04efe6  }
46af5a
c0af5a
96af5a
6a38e5  /*
d84ffe  ·* ·ComputeFP: Combine the L and R halves and do the final permutation.
65495d  ·*/
9893a5  static void ComputeFP(bool outBlk[64], bool L[32], bool R[32]) {
ee42e9  ··bool input[64];
0b17e0  ··int i;
0faf5a
056c41  ··/* Combine L and R into input[64]
30f9a6  ···*/
836406  ··for (i = 63; i >= 0; i--)
5a8397  ····input[i] = (i >= 32) ? L[i - 32] : R[i];
4caf5a
97aeaf  ··/* Permute
1cf9a6  ···*/
e16406  ··for (i = 63; i >= 0; i--)
fbe116  ····outBlk[table_DES_FP[i]] = input[i];
c4efe6  }
3baf5a
13af5a
b9af5a
a438e5  /*
33810f  ·* ·ComputeF: Compute the DES f function and store the result in fout.
14495d  ·*/
af2720  static void ComputeF(bool fout[32], bool R[32], bool roundKey[56]) {
a9f6a2  ··bool expandedBlock[48], subkey[48], sout[32];
51bbe6  ··int i,k;
23af5a
291a04  ··/* Expand R into 48 bits using the E expansion */
a599d7  ··ComputeExpansionE(expandedBlock, R);
f1f0ba  ··DumpBin("expanded E", expandedBlock, 48);
81af5a
7c93ff  ··/* Convert the roundKey into the subkey using PC2 */
f17840  ··ComputePC2(subkey, roundKey);
e8d717  ··DumpBin("subkey", subkey, 48);
```

```
--4509 0001cf13c2680040007 Page 7 of des.c

e0af5a
c3154c  ··/* XOR the subkey onto the expanded block */
adfcab  ··for (i = 0; i < 48; i++)
4f6512  ····expandedBlock[i] ^= subkey[i];
c0af5a
870740  ··/* Divide expandedBlock into 6-bit chunks and do S table lookups */
1d25c6  ··for (k = 0; k < 8; k++)
6585c7  ····ComputeS_Lookup(k, sout+4*k, expandedBlock+6*k);
f8af5a
b3fd35  ··/* To complete the f() calculation, do permutation P on the S table output */
e92d52  ··ComputeP(fout, sout);
deefe6  }
3baf5a
25af5a
0faf5a
8438e5  /*
00913f  ·* ·ComputeP: Compute the P permutation on the S table outputs.
25495d  ·*/
0bf410  static void ComputeP(bool output[32], bool input[32]) {
5a17e0  ··int i;
b6af5a
95339a  ··for (i = 0; i < 32; i++)
347688  ····output[table_DES_P[i]] = input[i];
57efe6  }
80af5a
67af5a
75af5a
e638e5  /*
2a859b  ·* ·Look up a 6-bit input in S table k and store the result as a 4-bit output.
2e495d  ·*/
59a67e  static void ComputeS_Lookup(int k, bool output[4], bool input[6]) {
d0f3da  ··int inputValue, outputValue;
3daf5a
261a9e  ··/* Convert the input bits into an integer */
e2fccb  ··inputValue = input[0] + 2*input[1] + 4*input[2] + 8*input[3] +
468c1a  ··········16*input[4] + 32*input[5];
1caf5a
a64a3e  ··/* Do the S table lookup */
a2b706  ··outputValue = table_DES_S[k][inputValue];
eeaf5a
df8aed  ··/* Convert the result into binary form */
529a60  ··output[0] = (outputValue & 1) ? 1 : 0;
2c6aec  ··output[1] = (outputValue & 2) ? 1 : 0;
a4f487  ··output[2] = (outputValue & 4) ? 1 : 0;
208c7f  ··output[3] = (outputValue & 8) ? 1 : 0;
27efe6  }
dcaf5a
d8af5a
f4af5a
5938e5  /*
9781cc  ·* ·ComputePC2: Map a 56-bit round key onto a 48-bit subkey
a8495d  ·*/
07796f  static void ComputePC2(bool subkey[48], bool roundKey[56]) {
ea17e0  ··int i;
2faf5a
64fcab  ··for (i = 0; i < 48; i++)
c3c8bc  ····subkey[i] = roundKey[table_DES_PC2[i]];
f8efe6  }
89af5a
4eaf5a
8eaf5a
3b38e5  /*
7a459d  ·* ·ComputeExpansionE: Compute the E expansion to prepare to use S tables.
89495d  ·*/
89b46d  static void ComputeExpansionE(bool expandedBlock[48], bool R[32]) {
bf17e0  ··int i;
94af5a
79fcab  ··for (i = 0; i < 48; i++)
d9b971  ····expandedBlock[i] = R[table_DES_E[i]];
8fefe6  }
9daf5a
1caf5a
```

```
--bb13 0016ae66eb080040007 Page 8 of des.c

e0af5a
d338e5 /*
4cf923 ·* ·Exchange_L_and_R: ·Swap L and R
ba495d ·*/
f195d1 static void Exchange_L_and_R(bool L[32], bool R[32]) {
3f17e0 ··int i;
c2af5a
74339a ··for (i = 0; i < 32; i++)
19fe8b ····L[i] ^= R[i] ^= L[i] ^= R[i];  ····/* exchanges L[i] and R[i] */
3cefe6 }
4faf5a
72af5a
feaf5a
a438e5 /*
439231 ·* ·DumpBin: Display intermediate values if emableDumpBin is set.
52495d ·*/
9cdbd9 static void DumpBin(char *str, bool *b, int bits) {
0217e0 ··int i;
80af5a
c98af7 ··if ((bits % 4)!=0 || bits>48) {
17b2e5 ····printf("Bad call to DumpBin (bits > 48 or bit len not a multiple of 4\n");
4b646c ····exit(1);
a6df1c ··}
adaf5a
783332 ··if (EnableDumpBin) {
35f079 ····for (i = strlen(str); i < 14; i++)
1ac8c3 ······printf(" ");
1c5fc3 ····printf("%s: ", str);
56eac8 ····for (i = bits-1; i >= 0; i--)
22de5b ······printf("%d", b[i]);
123177 ····printf(" ");
9c821f ····for (i = bits; i < 48; i++)
72c8c3 ······printf(" ");
d86b57 ····printf("(");
9105d7 ····for (i = bits-4; i >= 0; i-=4)
c6f78c ······printf("%X", b[i]+2*b[i+1]+4*b[i+2]+8*b[i+3]);
89fa6f ····printf(")\n");
e4df1c ··}
56efe6 }
6aaf5a
```

```
--e8aa 0017f449fe180040008 Page 1 of des.h

3008c5 typedef char bool;
d29629 void EncryptDES(bool key[56], bool outBlk[64], bool inBlk[64], int verbose);
2e8db3 void DecryptDES(bool key[56], bool outBlk[64], bool inBlk[64], int verbose);
7faf5a
```

```
--842b 001c97afa9d80040009 Page 1 of ecb.scr

f64ce1 00 01 02 03 04 05 06 07 08 09 0A 0B 0C 0D 0E 0F 10 11 12 13 14 15 16 17 18 19 1█
fdb9bc A 1B 1C 1D 1E 1F 20 21 22 23 24 25 26 27 28 29 2A 2B 2C 2D 2E 2F30 31 32 33 34 █
b5f9a7 35 36 37 38 39 3A 3B 3C 3D 3E 3F 40 41 42 43 44 45 46 47 48 49 4A 4B 4C 4D 4E 4█
4c9b42 F50 51 52 53 54 55 56 57 58 59 5A 5B 5C 5D 5E 5F 60 61 62 63 64 65 66 67 68 69 █
57b101 6A 6B 6C 6D 6E 6F70 71 72 73 74 75 76 77 78 79 7A 7B 7C 7D 7E 7F 80 81 82 83 84█
5c2c39 ·85 86 87 88 89 8A 8B 8C 8D 8E 8F90 91 92 93 94 95 96 97 98 99 9A 9B 9C 9D 9E 9█
4a1c73 F # A0 A1 A2 A3 A4 A5 A6 A7 A8 A9 AA AB AC AD AE AFB0 B1 B2 B3 B4 B5 B6 B7 B8 B█
36fc0a 9 BA BB BC BD BE BF C0 C1 C2 C3 C4 C5 C6 C7 C8 C9 CA CB CC CD CE CFD0 D1 D2 D3 █
5b5b61 D4 D5 D6 D7 D8 D9 DA DB DC DD DE DF E0 E1 E2 E3 E4 E5 E6 E7 E8 E9 EA EB EC ED E█
ea9439 E EFF0 F1 F2 F3 F4 F5 F6 F7 F8 F9 FA FB FC FD FE FF
829ec4 0000000000000000 ···' XOR MASK
b745a7 FFFFFFFFFFFFFFFF ···' Ciphertext 0
642ba4 0000000000000000 ···' Ciphertext 1
658c19 00 ················' Plaintext byte mask
aacdad 1 ·················' use CBC
ffd84f 0 ·················' extra XOR
fb5b0d 1 ·················' don't seed PRNG (use this input file)
332fcc 01020304050607 ······' starting key
769df9 10000 ··············' number of clocks
c9af5a
```

```
--cc30  001d5e0f0268004000a Page 1 of mini.scr

d6f4f1  5C416114B9D1D2D9B2550DF690FA75E798CC26203B1D79EB346229EDADE314B483321AA44BA4233■
8ec7a2  8899568FDF85C1A9DEF1DE864EB2EAB4E52D7E075ADAA992D85DBAC85DD3A9A32
f39ec4  0000000000000000 ···'  XOR MASK
fc10d0  123456789ABCDEF0 ···'  Ciphertext 0
2e6a3f  0102030405060708 ···'  Ciphertext 1
8b8c19  00 ················'  Plaintext byte mask
a1ed5e  0 ·················'  use CBC
89d84f  0 ·················'  extra XOR
ad5b0d  1 ·················'  don't seed PRNG (use this input file)
6eabc7  010203040505D5 ······'  starting key
80d03f  2000 ··············'  number of clocks
d5af5a
```

```
--1b19 000748214c28004000b Page 1 of misc.c

56feb2 #include <stdio.h>
a1bea3 #include <stdlib.h>
a9c737 #include <memory.h>
79324c #include <string.h>
242bac #include "des.h"
3da50a #include "misc.h"
feaf5a
985854 #define VERBOSE
69af5a
1ac502 void GetUserInfo(unsigned char plaintextVector[32],·
d257e7 ········unsigned char plaintextXorMask[8],·
13910f ········unsigned char ciphertext0[8], unsigned char ciphertext[8],
5e446e ········unsigned char *plaintextByteMask, int *useCBC, int *extraXor,
0ee00d ········int *quickStart, unsigned char startKey[7], long *numClocks);
2b0986 void increment32(unsigned char *v);
5fb70b void decrement32(unsigned char *v);
61f314 void desDecrypt(unsigned char m[8], unsigned char c[8], unsigned char k[7]);
f5a5c5 void printHexString(char *tag, unsigned char *data, int len);
29708e static void EXIT_ERR(char *s) { fprintf(stderr, s); exit(1); }
f1560a int hex2bin(char *hex, unsigned char *bin);
87af5a
f3af5a
56c502 void GetUserInfo(unsigned char plaintextVector[32],·
6e57e7 ········unsigned char plaintextXorMask[8],·
d31fa8 ········unsigned char ciphertext0[8], unsigned char ciphertext1[8],
ad446e ········unsigned char *plaintextByteMask, int *useCBC, int *extraXor,
7c3170 ········int *quickStart, unsigned char startKey[7], long *numClocks) {
970e71 ··char buffer[1024];
8cc6d6 ··unsigned char tmp[512];
ea17e0 ··int i;
b8af5a
ff4264 #ifdef VERBOSE
18659f ··printf("Enter plaintextVector values: ");
657454 #endif
89766e ··gets(buffer);
30b72a ··i = hex2bin(buffer, tmp);
b053dd ··if (i <= 0 || i >= 256)
bc112c ····EXIT_ERR("Must have at least 1 plaintextVector entry and at most 255.\n");
141bcb ··memset(plaintextVector, 0, 32);
55f545 ··while (i--)
4a0422 ····plaintextVector[tmp[i]/8] |= (128 >> (tmp[i] % 8));
46af5a
f74264 #ifdef VERBOSE
92ee8b ··printf(" ···Enter plaintext xor mask: ");
267454 #endif
7d766e ··gets(buffer);
ecb72a ··i = hex2bin(buffer, tmp);
a11856 ··if (i != 8)
9ea670 ····EXIT_ERR("Must have 8 plaintext xor mask bytes.");
11b657 ··memcpy(plaintextXorMask, tmp, 8);
8caf5a
0d4264 #ifdef VERBOSE
3c3a0c ··printf(" ········Enter ciphertext 0: ");
9c7454 #endif
91766e ··gets(buffer);
34b72a ··i = hex2bin(buffer, tmp);
211856 ··if (i != 8)
adcf62 ····EXIT_ERR("Must have 8 bytes in ciphertext 0.");
6398f3 ··memcpy(ciphertext0, tmp, 8);
2baf5a
cd4264 #ifdef VERBOSE
31a5d9 ··printf(" ········Enter ciphertext 1: ");
797454 #endif
a6766e ··gets(buffer);
52b72a ··i = hex2bin(buffer, tmp);
a01856 ··if (i != 8)
eccb49 ····EXIT_ERR("Must have 8 bytes in ciphertext 1.");
b11da6 ··memcpy(ciphertext1, tmp, 8);
05af5a
184264 #ifdef VERBOSE
f5d221 ··printf(" ··Enter plaintext byte mask: ");
747454 #endif
```

```
--9cbe 0004b9f4b098004000b Page 2 of misc.c
74766e ··gets(buffer);
82b72a ··i = hex2bin(buffer, tmp);
8a8448 ··if (i != 1)
b7f706 ····EXIT_ERR("Plaintext byte mask is 1 byte long.");
6bc2b5 ··*plaintextByteMask = tmp[0];
7aaf5a
9d4264 #ifdef VERBOSE
7d1b21 ··printf(" ······Enter useCBC (0 or 1): ");
f57454 #endif
56766e ··gets(buffer);
eab72a ··i = hex2bin(buffer, tmp);
e515b9 ··if (i != 1 || tmp[0] > 1)
b819c6 ····EXIT_ERR("Must enter 0 or 1 for useCBC.");
68e2c1 ··*useCBC = tmp[0];
37af5a
264264 #ifdef VERBOSE
7bf965 ··printf(" ····Enter extraXor (0 or 1): ");
887454 #endif
4e766e ··gets(buffer);
61b72a ··i = hex2bin(buffer, tmp);
7e15b9 ··if (i != 1 || tmp[0] > 1)
776c75 ····EXIT_ERR("Must enter 0 or 1 for extraXor.");
522353 ··*extraXor = tmp[0];
29af5a
a04264 #ifdef VERBOSE
a7e0e1 ··printf(" ··Enter quickStart (0 or 1): ");
757454 #endif
ce766e ··gets(buffer);
19b72a ··i = hex2bin(buffer, tmp);
a015b9 ··if (i != 1 || tmp[0] > 1)
b12f69 ····EXIT_ERR("Must enter 0 or 1 for quickStart\n");
83bd7b ··*quickStart = tmp[0];
91af5a
0eaf5a
514264 #ifdef VERBOSE
02c8bf ··printf(" ··········Enter starting key: ");
187454 #endif
d3766e ··gets(buffer);
08e684 ··if (hex2bin(buffer, tmp) != 7)
f6a5e4 ····EXIT_ERR("Must enter 7 hex bytes as the key.\n");
130ed3 ··memcpy(startKey, tmp, 7);
86af5a
5f4264 #ifdef VERBOSE
43f4f6 ··printf(" ·····Enter number of clocks: ");
1c7454 #endif
6f766e ··gets(buffer);
c677e8 ··sscanf(buffer, "%ld", numClocks);
4b8b81 ··if (*numClocks < 1 || *numClocks > 1000000000L)
d6b093 ····EXIT_ERR("Must have between 1 and 1 billion clocks.\n");
6daf5a
134264 #ifdef VERBOSE
db186d ··printHexString("\n ·PtxtVector = ", plaintextVector, 32);
a4a738 ··printHexString(" PtxtXorMask = ", plaintextXorMask, 8);
5dffc6 ··printHexString("Ciphertext 0 = ", ciphertext0, 8);
b93b57 ··printHexString("Ciphertext 1 = ", ciphertext1, 8);
99dd31 ··printHexString("PtxtByteMask = ", plaintextByteMask, 1);
72e15b ··printf( ······" ·····useCBC = %d\n", *useCBC);
2b2f30 ··printf( ······" ···extraXor = %d\n", *extraXor);
6817dc ··printf( ······" ·quickStart = %d\n", *quickStart);
5f1535 ··printHexString("Starting key = ", startKey, 7);
157214 ··printf( ······"Total clocks = %ld\n\n", *numClocks);
517454 #endif
ebefe6 }
7caf5a
25af5a
020b42 void increment32(unsigned char *v) {
fae2f8 ··if ((++(v[3])) == 0)
c7ab75 ····if ((++(v[2])) == 0)
74b31a ······if ((++(v[1])) == 0)
584058 ········++v[0];
9befe6 }
4baf5a
```

```
--0a18 0005d5aab618004000b Page 3 of misc.c

e45411 void decrement32(unsigned char *v) {
0dc266 ··if (((v[3])--) == 0)
b2dbd7 ····if (((v[2])--) == 0)
f033fc ······if (((v[1])--) == 0)
2a3c05 ········v[0]--;
d8efe6 }
adaf5a
e6bc23 void desDecrypt(unsigned char m[8], unsigned char c[8], unsigned char k[7]) {
15f65b ··bool key[56], message[64];
fd17e0 ··int i;
68af5a
54ec0c // ·printf("DES_DECRYPT(k="); for (i=0; i<7;i++) printf("%02X",k[i]); ·//!!!
4cf514 // ·printf(", c="); for (i=0; i<8;i++) printf("%02X",c[i]); ············//!!!
f8af5a
13815b ··for (i = 0; i < 56; i++)
ae9345 ····key[55-i] = ((k[i/8] << (i & 7)) & 128) ? 1 : 0;
f35c33 ··for (i = 0; i < 64; i++)
10e5ed ····message[63-i] = ((c[i/8] << (i & 7)) & 128) ? 1 : 0;
eac59d ··DecryptDES(key, message, message, 0);
5b1f76 ··for (i = 0; i < 8; i++)
6f452e ····m[i] = 0;
f55c33 ··for (i = 0; i < 64; i++)
fa7511 ····if (message[63-i])
59fe29 ······m[i/8] |= 128 >> (i%8);
f2af5a
04641f // ·printf(")="); for (i=0; i<8;i++) printf("%02X",m[i]); printf("\n"); //!!!
b8af5a
43efe6 }
17af5a
e5af5a
30c2bf int unhex(char c) {
bc53c4 ··if (c >= '0' && c <= '9')
1603d6 ····return (c - '0');
8d8db1 ··if (c >= 'a' && c <= 'f')
480ada ····return (c - 'a' + 10);
3449e3 ··if (c >= 'A' && c <= 'F')
28a66f ····return (c - 'A' + 10);
c712d4 ··return (-1);
2eefe6 }
85af5a
46af5a
ed4579 int hex2bin(char *hex, unsigned char *bin) {
53c22f ··int i = 0;
876a41 ··int j = 0;
efaf5a
598ef6 ··/* Trim string if comments present */
b08b28 ··if (strchr(hex, '#') != NULL)
c252e6 ····*strchr(hex, '#') = 0;
1ba3ed ··if (strchr(hex, '*') != NULL)
7760d1 ····*strchr(hex, '*') = 0;
e7a6e5 ··if (strchr(hex, '\'') != NULL)
7c2462 ····*strchr(hex, '\'') = 0;
abaf5a
5a1f4a ··for (i = 0; i < strlen(hex); i++) {
6a8e69 ····if (hex[i] >= '0' && unhex(hex[i]) < 0)
fed278 ······EXIT_ERR("Bad hex digit encountered.\n");
09df1c ··}
4baf5a
4f1f4a ··for (i = 0; i < strlen(hex); i++) {
c1f5b0 ····if (hex[i] < '0')
2f5f6a ······continue;
26643e ····if (hex[i] >= '0' && hex[i+1] >= '0') {
567935 ······bin[j++] = unhex(hex[i])*16+unhex(hex[i+1]);
dbc028 ······i++; ···// skip one
195f6a ······continue;
8b6fe7 ····}
3fe16f ····if (hex[i] >= '0') {
a78539 ······bin[j++] = unhex(hex[i]);
ea6fe7 ····}
efdf1c ··}
68c1d2 ··return (j);
5defe6 }
```

```
e0af5a
1aaf5a
027b71 void printHexString(char *tag, unsigned char *data, int len) {
aa17e0 ··int i;
20af5a
469650 ··printf("%s", tag);
526c12 ··for (i = 0; i < len; i++)
21cd57 ····printf("%02X", data[i]);
bafee8 ··printf("\n");
b6efe6 }
48af5a
```

```
--77c4 001029468fd8004000c Page 1 of misc.h

e0af5a
32c502 void GetUserInfo(unsigned char plaintextVector[32],·
6657e7 ········unsigned char plaintextXorMask[8],·
e5910f ········unsigned char ciphertext0[8], unsigned char ciphertext[8],
4c446e ········unsigned char *plaintextByteMask, int *useCBC, int *extraXor,
25e00d ········int *quickStart, unsigned char startKey[7], long *numClocks);
560986 void increment32(unsigned char *v);
edb70b void decrement32(unsigned char *v);
4cf314 void desDecrypt(unsigned char m[8], unsigned char c[8], unsigned char k[7]);
fea5c5 void printHexString(char *tag, unsigned char *data, int len);
f9560a int hex2bin(char *hex, unsigned char *bin);
02af5a
```

```
--91c4 001d95d620a8004000d Page 1 of random.scr

1b9f56 00
4e9ec4 0000000000000000 ···'  XOR MASK
c4327c 0000000000000000 ···'  Ciphertext 0
892ba4 0000000000000000 ···'  Ciphertext 1
918c19 00 ················'  Plaintext byte mask
05ed5e 0 ·················'  use CBC
37d84f 0 ·················'  extra XOR
260627 0 ·················'  random vector (0=seed with timer, 1=use input, >1=seed)
63a481 00000000000000 ·····'  starting key
8bd03f 2000 ··············'  number of clocks
d9af5a
```

```
--0289 000317f111e8004000e Page 1 of ref.c

56feb2 #include <stdio.h>
a1bea3 #include <stdlib.h>
a9c737 #include <memory.h>
79324c #include <string.h>
242bac #include "des.h"
3da50a #include "misc.h"
feaf5a
e7f8b5 #define CLOCKS_PER_DES 18
d8af5a
7a4525 int plaintextMatch(unsigned char plaintextVector[32], unsigned char m[8],
c46e85 ········unsigned char plaintextByteMask, int ciphertext, unsigned char key[7]);
8787d4 void checkKey(unsigned char key[7], unsigned char plaintextVector[32],·
4357e7 ········unsigned char plaintextXorMask[8],·
d31fa8 ········unsigned char ciphertext0[8], unsigned char ciphertext1[8],
7d5e1b ········unsigned char plaintextByteMask, int useCBC, int extraXor);
64af5a
57a2c4 void main(void) {
2b7ab8 ··unsigned char startKey[7], plaintextVector[32];
776f32 ··unsigned char plaintextXorMask[8];
01ed17 ··unsigned char ciphertext0[8];
52e93c ··unsigned char ciphertext1[8];
37b1b4 ··unsigned char plaintextByteMask;
36c9d8 ··int useCBC, extraXor, quickStart;
38e13a ··int i,j;
948520 ··long numClocks;
ac5ec8 ··unsigned char key[7];
d7af5a
8a50e3 ··GetUserInfo(plaintextVector, plaintextXorMask, ciphertext0, ciphertext1,·
8fd756 ··········&plaintextByteMask, &useCBC, &extraXor, &quickStart, startKey,
47ab3c ··········&numClocks);
2aaf5a
7fee44 ··for (i = 0; i < numClocks; i += CLOCKS_PER_DES) {
dea2d3 ····for (j = 0; j < 24; j++) {
22beb4 ······memcpy(key, startKey, 8);
08c578 ······key[0] += j;
ab91ec ······checkKey(key, plaintextVector, plaintextXorMask, ciphertext0,·
5320a7 ··········ciphertext1, plaintextByteMask, useCBC, extraXor);
3e6fe7 ····}
71ddad ····increment32(startKey+3);
96df1c ··}
aeefe6 }
8caf5a
00af5a
d287d4 void checkKey(unsigned char key[7], unsigned char plaintextVector[32],·
5c57e7 ········unsigned char plaintextXorMask[8],·
381fa8 ········unsigned char ciphertext0[8], unsigned char ciphertext1[8],
5f4479 ········unsigned char plaintextByteMask, int useCBC, int extraXor) {
3c0a0b ··unsigned char m[8];
1417e0 ··int i;
d4af5a
a4f09d ··desDecrypt(m, ciphertext0, key);
26835d ··printf("DES_decrypt(K="); for (i = 0; i < 7; i++) printf("%02X", key[i]);·
188cf0 ··printf(", C0="); for (i = 0; i < 8; i++) printf("%02X", ciphertext0[i]);
d849c7 ··printf(") -> "); for (i = 0; i < 8; i++) printf("%02X", m[i]); printf("\n");
24667c ··if (extraXor) {
0bd985 ····m[0] ^= m[4];
db406b ····m[1] ^= m[5];
f2e248 ····m[2] ^= m[6];
607ba6 ····m[3] ^= m[7];
7cdf1c ··}
bb1f76 ··for (i = 0; i < 8; i++)
45e88c ····m[i] ^= plaintextXorMask[i];
17af5a
c64534 ··if (plaintextMatch(plaintextVector, m, plaintextByteMask, 0, key)) {
b53498 ····desDecrypt(m, ciphertext1, key);
96553a ····printf("DES_decrypt(K="); for (i = 0; i < 7; i++) printf("%02X", key[i]);·
6dda88 ····printf(", C1="); for (i = 0; i < 8; i++) printf("%02X", ciphertext1[i]);
ead221 ····printf(") -> "); for (i = 0; i < 8; i++) printf("%02X", m[i]); printf("\n");
37952a ····if (extraXor) {
af2ad3 ······m[0] ^= m[4];
b6b33d ······m[1] ^= m[5];
31111e ······m[2] ^= m[6];
```

```
--62a0 0018ac4c1498004000e Page 2 of ref.c

4c88f0 ·······m[3] ^= m[7];
5b6fe7 ····}
5b662a ····if (useCBC) {
429494 ······for (i = 0; i < 8; i++)
e1f3f9 ········m[i] ^= ciphertext0[i];
2b6fe7 ····}
10e5be ····if (plaintextMatch(plaintextVector, m, plaintextByteMask, 1, key)) {
5246ff ······printf("------- VALID MATCH-------\n");
059a8a ······fprintf(stderr, "Match found at key =");
c22526 ······for (i = 0; i < 7; i++)
3f44d0 ········fprintf(stderr, "%02X", key[i]);
0f5501 ······fprintf(stderr, "\n");
736fe7 ····}
6adf1c ··}
19efe6 }
81af5a
01af5a
004525 int plaintextMatch(unsigned char plaintextVector[32], unsigned char m[8],
8aa762 ········unsigned char plaintextByteMask, int ciphertext, unsigned char key[7]) {
b817e0 ··int i;
f0af5a
068715 ··for (i = 0; i < 8; i++) {
c585ef ····if ((plaintextByteMask & (128>>i)) == 1)
388e03 ······continue; ··/* this byte is skipped */
b98ec8 ····if (plaintextVector[m[i]/8] & (128 >> (m[i]%8)))
d65f6a ······continue;
854210 ····return (0); ··········/* no match */
13df1c ··}
ceaf5a
957381 ··printf("Match of C%d with key ", ciphertext);
2daec4 ··for (i = 0; i < 7; i++)
80dac3 ····printf("%02X", key[i]);
b461e2 ··printf(" = ");
021f76 ··for (i = 0; i < 8; i++)
6511eb ····printf("%02X", m[i]);
b7fee8 ··printf("\n");
93af5a
35ec77 ··fprintf(stderr, "Match of C%d with key ", ciphertext);
bdaec4 ··for (i = 0; i < 7; i++)
5fedd0 ····fprintf(stderr, "%02X", key[i]);
d29064 ··fprintf(stderr, " = ");
371f76 ··for (i = 0; i < 8; i++)
d7651e ····fprintf(stderr, "%02X", m[i]);
96c77e ··fprintf(stderr, "\n");
10af5a
e0d4d1 ··return (1);
d9efe6 }
a1af5a
8aaf5a
```

```
--c93c  000f4b51cf08004000f Page 1 of sim.c

8d2d03  /*****************************************************************************
0833b1  ·* ·sim.c ···································································*
b33dcc  ·* ·················Software Simulator for DES keysearch ASIC ·············*
6a29eb  ·* ·····································································*
4509fc  ·* ···Written 1998 by Cryptography Research (http://www.cryptography.com) ···*
5f8aaf  ·* ······and Paul Kocher for the Electronic Frontier Foundation (EFF). ·····*
38caeb  ·* ······Placed in the public domain by Cryptography Research and EFF. ······*
f74992  ·* ·THIS IS UNSUPPORTED FREE SOFTWARE. USE AND DISTRIBUTE AT YOUR OWN RISK. ·*
c129eb  ·* ·····································································*
66c755  ·* ·IMPORTANT: U.S. LAW MAY REGULATE THE USE AND/OR EXPORT OF THIS PROGRAM. ·*
8129eb  ·* ·····································································*
fb489b  ·* ·······························································************
a729eb  ·* ·····································································*
126eef  ·* ··REVISION HISTORY: ················································*
e329eb  ·* ·····································································*
d97744  ·* ··Version 1.0: ·Initial version. ··································*
4fbaf4  ·* ··Version 1.1: ·Initial release by Cryptography Research to EFF. ·········*
6ce429  ·* ·················(Fixed byte/bit ordering notation to match VHDL.) ·········*
3a29eb  ·* ·····································································*
74d8c3  ·*****************************************************************************/
9daf5a
33feb2  #include <stdio.h>
b5bea3  #include <stdlib.h>
b8c737  #include <memory.h>
80324c  #include <string.h>
e72bac  #include "des.h"
2fbd71  #include "sim.h"
0aaf5a
b051c3  #define DEBUG
d6af5a
67a99d  long getClockCounter(void);
54b42e  int peekState(int addr);
1d7608  int RunChip(char *input, FILE *outfile, int useRaw);
2aaf5a
28708e  static void EXIT_ERR(char *s) { fprintf(stderr, s); exit(1); }
62725e  static void parseInput(char *input, int *reset, int *boardEn, int *ale,
7f8541  ········int *adrsel1, int *web, int *rdb, int *adrsel2, int *allactIn,
a060c4  ········int *addr, int *chipId, int *data);
bb79bd  static int unhex(char c);
9bf453  static void RunClock(void);
f9d39e  static void desDecrypt(unsigned char m[8], unsigned char c[8],
753286  ········unsigned char k[7]);
a2acca  static void increment32(unsigned char *num);
91cc8b  static void decrement32(unsigned char *num);
b8b1ae  static void printKeyInfo(FILE *outDev, char *preamble, int searchUnit);
31af5a
34ec7c  static unsigned char ALLACTIVE_IN = 1; ············/* not held between calls */
0dfec4  unsigned char ALLACTIVE_OUT ·····= 0;
40af5a
6ee4e3  unsigned char STATE[256];
41e3e4  unsigned char SELECTED_CHIP;
710ab3  ·········long CLOCK_COUNTER = 1;
cc8af3  ·········int DES_POSITION;
0c913b  unsigned char WORKING_CTXT[24*8]; ·········/* last DES input ·················*/
538181  unsigned char WORKING_PTXT[24*8]; ·········/* last DES out (for ptxt check) ·*/
c053df  unsigned char RAW_DES_OUT[24*8]; ·········/* raw DES outputs ················*/
daa765  int ········WORKING_KDELTA[24]; ·········/* key delta (-1, 0, or +1) ········*/
533efd  unsigned char WORKING_LAST_SELECTOR[24]; ··/* last ciphertext selector ········*/
4ce4be  unsigned char WORKING_NEXT_SELECTOR[24]; ··/* next ciphertext selector ·······*/
689e18  ·········int STARTUP_DELAY[24]; ·········/* startup delay ···················*/
24f67e  unsigned char THIS_KEY[24*7]; ············/* current DES key ················*/
d35f18  unsigned char NEXT_KEY[24*7]; ············/* next DES key ···················*/
1c11b6  ·········int ·PENDING_UPDATE_ADDR1 = -1, PENDING_UPDATE_DATA1 = -1;
cb8c2d  ·········int ·PENDING_UPDATE_ADDR2 = -1, PENDING_UPDATE_DATA2 = -1;
3300ab  ·········int ·PENDING_UPDATE_ADDR3 = -1, PENDING_UPDATE_DATA3 = -1;
17c6c2  unsigned char MATCH[24];
23af5a
11af5a
d1af5a
b1a885  static void resetChip(void) {
1aab8b  ··memset(STATE, 0, sizeof(STATE)); ·····························/* RESET */
f46530  ··SELECTED_CHIP = 0;
```

```
--ba12 0009cc27d6a8004000f Page 2 of sim.c
417126 ··DES_POSITION = 13;
9fa8d9 ··memset(WORKING_CTXT, 0, sizeof(WORKING_CTXT));
e2ae80 ··memset(WORKING_PTXT, 0, sizeof(WORKING_PTXT));
b5afb1 ··memset(RAW_DES_OUT, 0, sizeof(RAW_DES_OUT));
677ba0 ··memset(WORKING_KDELTA, 0, sizeof(WORKING_KDELTA));
c1e6c6 ··memset(WORKING_LAST_SELECTOR, 1, sizeof(WORKING_LAST_SELECTOR));
c48102 ··memset(WORKING_NEXT_SELECTOR, 1, sizeof(WORKING_NEXT_SELECTOR));
699bcb ··memset(STARTUP_DELAY, 0, sizeof(STARTUP_DELAY));
8f3fe2 ··memset(THIS_KEY, 0, sizeof(THIS_KEY));
849161 ··memset(NEXT_KEY, 0, sizeof(NEXT_KEY));
850ce5 ··PENDING_UPDATE_ADDR1 = -1;
c98635 ··PENDING_UPDATE_ADDR2 = -1;
28078a ··PENDING_UPDATE_ADDR3 = -1;
4f19ae ··memset(MATCH, 0, sizeof(MATCH));
49efe6 }
52af5a
04af5a
51a5b0 long getClockCounter(void) {
8eb11d ··return (CLOCK_COUNTER);
7eefe6 }
85af5a
98af5a
5f22bd int peekState(int addr) {
c69e96 ··return (STATE[addr]);
78efe6 }
c0af5a
7caf5a
66664b int RunChip(char *input, FILE *outfile, int useRaw) {
686c17 ··int reset,boardEn,ale,adrsel1,web,rdb,adrsel2,allactiveIn,addr,chipId,data;
ef86d5 ··int dataOut;
41e13a ··int i,j;
6eaf5a
75261a ··parseInput(input, &reset, &boardEn, &ale, &adrsel1, &web, &rdb, &adrsel2,
29b7df ··········&allactiveIn, &addr, &chipId, &data);
4e7493 ··ALLACTIVE_IN = (unsigned char)allactiveIn;
30af5a
183f21 ··dataOut = data; ·······················································/* default */
9d58d6 ··if (reset == 0) { ·····················································/* reset? */
54b64f ····resetChip();
a281d3 ····RunClock();
129dff ··} else if (boardEn == 0) { ·····························/* board disabled? */
5581d3 ····RunClock();
3cbc66 ··} else if (ale == 1) { ·······························/* select chip/board */
0081d3 ····RunClock();
fa6af8 ····if (adrsel1 == 1)
bb80de ······SELECTED_CHIP = (unsigned char)addr;
90842c ····else
21294b ······{ /* board select done off-chip */ }
7302c3 ··} else if (chipId != SELECTED_CHIP) { ·················/* chipId not ours? */
8781d3 ····RunClock();
66d581 ··} else if (web == 0) { ·······························/* writing register? */
df81d3 ····RunClock();
ebb10b ····if (addr >= REG_SEARCH_KEY(0)) {
7b50c6 ······PENDING_UPDATE_ADDR2 = addr; ······································/* key */
3bda60 ······PENDING_UPDATE_DATA2 = data;
b64b08 ······if (((addr & 7) == 7) && (data & 1) && ((STATE[addr] & 1) == 0)) {
2b22fc ········if (CLOCK_COUNTER < 750)
33d675 ··········STARTUP_DELAY[(addr - 0x47) / 8] = 21; ·················/* adjust? */
f805d7 ········else {
c78561 ··········STARTUP_DELAY[(addr - 0x47) / 8] = 2*CLOCKS_PER_DES - DES_POSITION;
44c934 ··········if (DES_POSITION >= 15)
b2a6a3 ············STARTUP_DELAY[(addr - 0x47) / 8] += CLOCKS_PER_DES;
59e0f6 #if 0 ····························/* uncomment for debugging message on halts */
143237 ··········fprintf(stderr,"Startup with DES_POSITION=%d in unit %d, delay=%d\n",
545d8e ···············DES_POSITION, (addr-0x47)/8, STARTUP_DELAY[(addr - 0x47) / 8]);
977454 #endif
be7fb0 ········}
7342cc ······}
056a79 ····} else {
a6b05a ······PENDING_UPDATE_ADDR2 = addr; ····························/* other reg */
f5da60 ······PENDING_UPDATE_DATA2 = data;
9c6fe7 ····}
```

```
--eb12 000b9c238be8004000f Page 3 of sim.c
5be4b8 ··} else if (rdb == 0) { ·································/* read a register */
e34a99 ····dataOut = STATE[addr];
2e81d3 ····RunClock();
1249d8 ··} else {
8981d3 ····RunClock();
fadf1c ··}
eaaf5a
671c5c ··if (CLOCK_COUNTER >= 2) {
123cea ····if (useRaw) {
e1a3f4 ······fprintf(outfile, "%02X %d\n", dataOut, ALLACTIVE_OUT);
9c6a79 ····} else {
fe2044 ······fprintf(outfile, " (Addr: %02X) ·(Exp: 00) (Get: %02X) at Cycle:%ld\n",
e9f86f ············addr, dataOut, CLOCK_COUNTER);
01457c ······for (i = 0; i < 24; i++) {
31e69a ········for (j = 6; j >= 0; j--)
ff590a ··········fprintf(outfile, "%02X", STATE[REG_SEARCH_KEY(i)+j]);
91798f ········fprintf(outfile, " ");
35555b ········if (CLOCK_COUNTER < 22)
78dc93 ··········fprintf(outfile, "0000000000000000");
fe00e6 ········else if (CLOCK_COUNTER <= 37)
3054ea ··········fprintf(outfile, "094CCE83D677160F");
8305d7 ········else {
a8dcd6 ··········for (j = 7; j >= 0; j--)
5cad27 ············fprintf(outfile, "%02X", RAW_DES_OUT[8*i+j]);
387fb0 ········}
9978b2 #if 0 ·····················/* uncomment to print information about the MATCH */
c42b60 ··········{
451685 ············static int latch[24]={0,0,0,0,0,0,0,0,0,0,0,0,0,0,
4515b3 ············································0,0,0,0,0,0,0,0,0,0};
c2132c ············if (DES_POSITION==10) latch[i] = MATCH[i];
a6ab83 ············fprintf(outfile, " %d", latch[i]);
ad7fb0 ········}
b67454 #endif
2ca770 #if 0 ·····················/* uncomment to print information about NEXT_SELECTOR */
a32b60 ········{
c51fc2 ············static int latch[24]={1,1,1,1,1,1,1,1,1,1,1,1,1,1,
2c5bf8 ············································1,1,1,1,1,1,1,1,1,1};
298e7e ············if (DES_POSITION==15) latch[i] = WORKING_NEXT_SELECTOR[i];
1a4ad8 ············fprintf(outfile, "%d", latch[i]);
8f7fb0 ········}
017454 #endif
3767a5 ········fprintf(outfile, " : Unit%d\n", i);
6a42cc ······}
22b96e ······fprintf(outfile, "\n");
e86fe7 ····}
23df1c ··}
a3755d ··CLOCK_COUNTER++;
f75593 ··return (dataOut);
0cefe6 }
d7af5a
e7af5a
d4725e static void parseInput(char *input, int *reset, int *boardEn, int *ale,
ce8541 ········int *adrsel1, int *web, int *rdb, int *adrsel2, int *allactIn,
746a3d ········int *addr, int *chipId, int *data) {
a117e0 ··int i;
47af5a
c69eb9 ··if (strlen(input) < 17 || input[8]!=' ' || input[11]!=' ' || input[14]!=' ')
ccda15 ····EXIT_ERR("Bad input.\n");
558715 ··for (i = 0; i < 8; i++) {
c1c3f7 ····if (input[i] != '0' && input[i] != '1')
93b045 ······EXIT_ERR("Bad input (first 8 digits must be binary.)\n");
c1df1c ··}
38b959 ··if (unhex(input[9]) < 0 || unhex(input[10]) < 0 ||
70bbf9 ······unhex(input[12]) < 0 || unhex(input[13]) < 0 ||
6401b9 ······unhex(input[15]) < 0 || unhex(input[16]) < 0) {
78422f ····EXIT_ERR("Bad input (addr, chipId, data must be hex)");
fddf1c ··}
d4af5a
958f00 ··*reset ··· = input[0]-'0';
4a25a2 ··*boardEn ·= input[1]-'0';
7c660a ··*ale ····· = input[2]-'0';
b92dfa ··*adrsel1 ·= input[3]-'0';
```

```
48111b  ··*web ·····= input[4]-'0';
71de77  ··*rdb ·····= input[5]-'0';
060751  ··*adrsel2 ·= input[6]-'0';
c1d2b3  ··*allactIn = input[7]-'0';
449a0b  ··*addr ····= 16*unhex(input[9]) + unhex(input[10]);
3842c3  ··*chipId ··= 16*unhex(input[12]) + unhex(input[13]);
2d9e2a  ··*data ····= 16*unhex(input[15]) + unhex(input[16]);
0fefe6  }
c0af5a
0caf5a
62d93f  /* Decodes a hex char or returns -1 if bad. */
8d8462  static int unhex(char c) {
6b53c4  ··if (c >= '0' && c <= '9')
f203d6  ····return (c - '0');
2f8db1  ··if (c >= 'a' && c <= 'f')
3f0ada  ····return (c - 'a' + 10);
a149e3  ··if (c >= 'A' && c <= 'F')
86a66f  ····return (c - 'A' + 10);
0f12d4  ··return (-1);
95efe6  }
f4af5a
7baf5a
1baf5a
4f38e5  /*
dea850  ·* ··Run the system for one clock cycle and update the state.
89495d  ·*/
4442ee  void RunClock(void) {
5c6275  ··int i,j,k,b;
dd470b  ··unsigned char key[7], m[8], c[8];
77af5a
9c9101  ··for (i = 0; i < 24; i++) {
84543c  ····if (STARTUP_DELAY[i] > 0) {
604f54  ······STARTUP_DELAY[i]--;
3a4600  ······if (STARTUP_DELAY[i] == 0)
340ea6  ········STARTUP_DELAY[i] = -1; ···············/* prevent stop if 1st C0=match */
8e6fe7  ····}
76df1c  ··}
14af5a
586df4  ··/* DES CLOCK 5: Plaintext vector result from last DES is ready. */
e94ae1  ··if (DES_POSITION == 5) {
8e23cf  ····for (i = 0; i < 24; i++) { ················/* i = search engine ···········*/
c6d1c1  ······k = 0; ·····························/* k = result of byte lookups ··*/
bd642b  ······for (j = 0; j < 8; j++) { ···········/* j = byte idx ················*/
a0178a  ········b = WORKING_PTXT[8*i+j]; ···········/* b = byte value ··············*/
c9fb5d  ········if (STATE[b/8] & (1 << (b%8))) ·····/* check plaintext vector ······*/
ce346c  ··········k = (k >> 1) | 128; ·············/* ··match = load 1 in k msb ···*/
1e359e  ········else ··························/* ···························*/
f40eb7  ··········k = (k >> 1) | 0; ··············/* ··no match = load 0 into k ··*/
a042cc  ······}
f83f33  ······k |= STATE[REG_PTXT_BYTE_MASK]; ······/* set bits where bytemask=1 ···*/
b11a90  ······MATCH[i] = (unsigned char)((k == 255) ? 1 : 0);
f1af5a
dd663d  ······if ((STATE[REG_SEARCH_STATUS(i)] & 1) == 0 || STARTUP_DELAY[i] > 0) {
b9b83a  ········/* If search not active, key delta = 0 and do C0 next */
e3472c  ········WORKING_KDELTA[i] = 0;
dfe9d7  ········WORKING_NEXT_SELECTOR[i] = 1;
0f373c  ······} else if (k != 0xFF || (STATE[REG_SEARCH_STATUS(i)] & 2) ||
4b09fe  ············STARTUP_DELAY[i] < 0) {
28e722  ········/* If no match or CURRENTLY doing C1 or first DES result,
3da57c  ········* ···key delta = 1 and do C0 next.
a05af3  ········*/
701df0  ········WORKING_KDELTA[i] = 1;
8bb30b  ········WORKING_NEXT_SELECTOR[i] = 0;
cad29b  ········if (k==0xFF)
de670b  ··········printKeyInfo(stderr, "ALERT: Skip match while doing C1 ", i);
ee2e47  ········if (k == 0xFF && STARTUP_DELAY[i] < 0)
9b3369  ··········printKeyInfo(stderr, "ALERT: ···(C1 above is startup phantom.)", i);
2869ea  ······} else if (WORKING_LAST_SELECTOR[i] == 0) {
d2b8e7  ········/* If doing C0 and got a match from C0, back up and do C1 */
ced05d  ········WORKING_KDELTA[i] = -1;
4ae9d7  ········WORKING_NEXT_SELECTOR[i] = 1;
648f35  ········printKeyInfo(stderr, "ALERT: Match C0; will backup for C1 ", i);
```

```
--0c27 000479329b38004000f Page 5 of sim.c

6ccfc7 ·······} else {
8a2ce9 ········/* If doing C0 and got a match from C1, halt */
b22aaa ·······STATE[REG_SEARCH_STATUS(i)] &= (255-1);
62472c ·······WORKING_KDELTA[i] = 0;
1be9d7 ·······WORKING_NEXT_SELECTOR[i] = 1;
dd98d4 ·······printKeyInfo(stderr, "ALERT: Matched C1; halting ", i);
ea42cc ······}
8eb3e1 ······if (STARTUP_DELAY[i] < 0)
5ece10 ·······STARTUP_DELAY[i]++;
326fe7 ····}
cedf1c ··}
aeaf5a
c03071 ··if (DES_POSITION == 15) {
fa2135 ····for (i = 0; i < 24; i++) {
ccc53f ······memcpy(THIS_KEY+i*7, NEXT_KEY+i*7, 7);
ef7e92 ······memcpy(NEXT_KEY+i*7, STATE+REG_SEARCH_KEY(i), 7);
136fe7 ····}
8adf1c ··}
d0af5a
018fcd ··/* END OF DES CYCLE: Extract results */
77ea42 ··if (DES_POSITION == CLOCKS_PER_DES-1) {
6b2135 ····for (i = 0; i < 24; i++) {
7aaf5a
d9c284 ······/* Do the DES decryption */
8502ce ······for (j = 0; j < 7; j++)
9e22c0 ········key[j] = THIS_KEY[i*7+(6-j)];
77b37c ······for (j = 0; j < 8; j++)
a3ccfb ········c[j] = WORKING_CTXT[8*i+7-j];
0d481f ······desDecrypt(m, c, key);
481503 ······for (j = 0; j < 8; j++) {
7d3bd1 ········WORKING_PTXT[8*i+7-j] = m[j];
a60d03 ········RAW_DES_OUT[8*i+7-j] = m[j];
b042cc ······}
20af5a
84b9ef ······if (STATE[REG_SEARCHINFO] & 2) { ················/* if extraXOR ···*/
025020 ········WORKING_PTXT[8*i+4] ^= WORKING_PTXT[8*i+0]; ···/* ···L = L xor R */
fe6d21 ········WORKING_PTXT[8*i+5] ^= WORKING_PTXT[8*i+1]; ···/* ······" ······*/
ceada9 ········WORKING_PTXT[8*i+6] ^= WORKING_PTXT[8*i+2]; ···/* ······" ······*/
6615de ········WORKING_PTXT[8*i+7] ^= WORKING_PTXT[8*i+3]; ···/* ······" ······*/
1542cc ······}
ea89a7 ······if ((STATE[REG_SEARCH_STATUS(i)] & 2) == 0) { ·······/* if c0, ·······*/
cd6b8a ········WORKING_PTXT[8*i+0] ^= STATE[REG_PTXT_XOR_MASK+0]; ·/* do ptxtXorMsk */
265511 ········WORKING_PTXT[8*i+1] ^= STATE[REG_PTXT_XOR_MASK+1]; ·/* ······" ······*/
6800b2 ········WORKING_PTXT[8*i+2] ^= STATE[REG_PTXT_XOR_MASK+2]; ·/* ······" ······*/
78cbdc ········WORKING_PTXT[8*i+3] ^= STATE[REG_PTXT_XOR_MASK+3]; ·/* ······" ······*/
3aabf4 ········WORKING_PTXT[8*i+4] ^= STATE[REG_PTXT_XOR_MASK+4]; ·/* ······" ······*/
36609a ········WORKING_PTXT[8*i+5] ^= STATE[REG_PTXT_XOR_MASK+5]; ·/* ······" ······*/
353539 ········WORKING_PTXT[8*i+6] ^= STATE[REG_PTXT_XOR_MASK+6]; ·/* ······" ······*/
5f3c97 ········WORKING_PTXT[8*i+7] ^= STATE[REG_PTXT_XOR_MASK+7]; ·/* ······" ······*/
4d5d4c ······} else {                                          ·/* if c1 ·······*/
9afc9c ········if (STATE[REG_SEARCHINFO] & 1) {                ·/* if useCBC ····*/
b784fd ··········WORKING_PTXT[8*i+0] ^= STATE[REG_CIPHERTEXT0+0]; ·/* xor with c0 ··*/
8c4de8 ··········WORKING_PTXT[8*i+1] ^= STATE[REG_CIPHERTEXT0+1]; ·/* ······" ······*/
3605d1 ··········WORKING_PTXT[8*i+2] ^= STATE[REG_CIPHERTEXT0+2]; ·/* ······" ······*/
dcc5c9 ··········WORKING_PTXT[8*i+3] ^= STATE[REG_CIPHERTEXT0+3]; ·/* ······" ······*/
8995a3 ··········WORKING_PTXT[8*i+4] ^= STATE[REG_CIPHERTEXT0+4]; ·/* ······" ······*/
6c55bb ··········WORKING_PTXT[8*i+5] ^= STATE[REG_CIPHERTEXT0+5]; ·/* ······" ······*/
811d82 ··········WORKING_PTXT[8*i+6] ^= STATE[REG_CIPHERTEXT0+6]; ·/* ······" ······*/
33dd9a ··········WORKING_PTXT[8*i+7] ^= STATE[REG_CIPHERTEXT0+7]; ·/* ······" ······*/
637fb0 ········}
e942cc ······}
1aaf5a
e370b8 ······/* Update ciphertext selector (state & last) */
569701 ······WORKING_LAST_SELECTOR[i] = (STATE[0x47+8*i] & 2) ? 1 : 0;
5ad73b ······STATE[0x47+8*i] &= 0xFD; ·····················/* select ciphertext 0 ··*/
25abd6 ······if (WORKING_NEXT_SELECTOR[i]) ················/* ... unless we want c1 */
8e98a9 ········STATE[0x47+8*i] |= 2; ·····················/* ... then select c1 ···*/
206fe7 ····}
1ddf1c ··}
a1af5a
80cda8 ··/* LAST DES CLOCK: Load in the updated key */
473b35 ··if (DES_POSITION == 14) {
```

```
--4c9a  0007dd476568004000f Page 6 of sim.c

e02135  ····for (i = 0; i < 24; i++) {
b45d9d  ······if (WORKING_KDELTA[i] == 1) { ·····················/* ··if key delta = 1 */
635981  ········increment32(STATE+REG_SEARCH_KEY(i));
4242cc  ······}
a6f8e9  ······if (WORKING_KDELTA[i] == -1) { ·················/* ··if key delta = -1 */
e80a03  ········decrement32(STATE+REG_SEARCH_KEY(i));
0a42cc  ······}
406fe7  ····}
dedf1c  ··}
d1af5a
a964de  ··/* DES CLOCK 0: Latch in new working keys and working ciphertexts */
5c6cb5  ··if (DES_POSITION == 0) {
f70d66  ····for (i = 0; i < 24; i++) { ·····················/* i = search engine */
34dbbd  ······/* pick between ctxt 0 and ctxt 1? */
d38aeb  ······if ((STATE[REG_SEARCH_STATUS(i)] & 2) == 0 && STARTUP_DELAY[i] == 0)
b7afe2  ········memcpy(WORKING_CTXT+8*i, STATE+REG_CIPHERTEXT0, 8); ·······/* copy c0 */
f13dfa  ······else
4ff6ee  ········memcpy(WORKING_CTXT+8*i, STATE+REG_CIPHERTEXT1, 8); ·······/* copy c1 */
1a6fe7  ····}
eedf1c  ··}
0faf5a
c82d95  ··/* Update ChipAllActive, board all active */
57519a  ··j = 1;
a763d6  ··for (i = 0; i < 24; i++)
bd9656  ····j &= STATE[0x47+i*8];
455974  ··j = (j & 1) ? 1 : 0;
fefe54  ··STATE[REG_SEARCHINFO] &= (255-4); ········/* set ChipAllActive ·············*/
e632f7  ··STATE[REG_SEARCHINFO] |= (4*j); ··········/* ···" ························*/
95fdfb  ··if ((STATE[REG_SEARCHINFO] & 16) == 0) ··/* If board all active enable = 0 */
3b3c9d  ····ALLACTIVE_OUT = ALLACTIVE_IN;
051bd0  ··else
b33a4d  ····ALLACTIVE_OUT = ALLACTIVE_IN & j;
045e2a  ··STATE[REG_SEARCHINFO] &= (255-8); ··················/* set board all active */
5c7b9a  ··STATE[REG_SEARCHINFO] |= (8*ALLACTIVE_OUT); ·······/* set board all active */
71af5a
b34cd8  ··/* Do any pending updates and update DES cycle position */
52cfb8  ··if (PENDING_UPDATE_ADDR1 >= 0)
f286c6  ····STATE[PENDING_UPDATE_ADDR1] = PENDING_UPDATE_DATA1;
023f74  ··PENDING_UPDATE_ADDR1 = PENDING_UPDATE_ADDR2;
c854a4  ··PENDING_UPDATE_DATA1 = PENDING_UPDATE_DATA2;
9e3a49  ··PENDING_UPDATE_ADDR2 = PENDING_UPDATE_ADDR3;
6a5199  ··PENDING_UPDATE_DATA2 = PENDING_UPDATE_DATA3;
9f078a  ··PENDING_UPDATE_ADDR3 = -1;
6cc7f8  ··DES_POSITION = (DES_POSITION + 1) % CLOCKS_PER_DES;
8eefe6  }
c9af5a
a4af5a
34d39e  static void desDecrypt(unsigned char m[8], unsigned char c[8],
cc0b79  ········unsigned char k[7]) {
77f65b  ··bool key[56], message[64];
5717e0  ··int i;
16af5a
2dd545  #ifdef DEBUG
e060e0  ··printf("DES_DECRYPT(k="); for (i=0; i<7;i++) printf("%02X",k[i]);
75e4d8  ··printf(", c="); for (i=0; i<8;i++) printf("%02X",c[i]);
ad7454  #endif
20af5a
9f815b  ··for (i = 0; i < 56; i++)
6e9345  ····key[55-i] = ((k[i/8] << (i & 7)) & 128) ? 1 : 0;
8f5c33  ··for (i = 0; i < 64; i++)
0de5ed  ····message[63-i] = ((c[i/8] << (i & 7)) & 128) ? 1 : 0;
c3c59d  ··DecryptDES(key, message, message, 0);
be1f76  ··for (i = 0; i < 8; i++)
4d452e  ····m[i] = 0;
c35c33  ··for (i = 0; i < 64; i++)
9d7511  ····if (message[63-i])
42fe29  ······m[i/8] |= 128 >> (i%8);
45af5a
72d545  #ifdef DEBUG
ea47c0  ··printf(")=");
3d17d3  ··for (i=0; i<8;i++)
7dcdbd  ····printf("%02X",m[i]);
```

```
--a790 001522c46c68004000f Page 7 of sim.c

3bfeb7 ··printf(", clk=%ld\n",CLOCK_COUNTER);
b87454 #endif
1eaf5a
87efe6 }
97af5a
26af5a
e3af5a
2eaf5a
dba6b0 static void printKeyInfo(FILE *outDev, char *preamble, int searchUnit) {
eac359 ··fprintf(outDev, preamble);
b97d84 ··fprintf(outDev, "(K=%02X%02X%02X%02X%02X%02X%02X, clk=%ld, searchUnit=%d)\n",
d06867 ···················STATE[0x40+8*searchUnit+6],STATE[0x40+8*searchUnit+5],
9fa184 ···················STATE[0x40+8*searchUnit+4],STATE[0x40+8*searchUnit+3],
3b1668 ···················STATE[0x40+8*searchUnit+2],STATE[0x40+8*searchUnit+1],
10ceed ···················STATE[0x40+8*searchUnit+0], CLOCK_COUNTER, searchUnit);
b3af5a
607332 ··printf(preamble);
b7f622 ··printf("(K=%02X%02X%02X%02X%02X%02X%02X, clk=%ld, searchUnit=%d)\n",
e66867 ···················STATE[0x40+8*searchUnit+6],STATE[0x40+8*searchUnit+5],
f6a184 ···················STATE[0x40+8*searchUnit+4],STATE[0x40+8*searchUnit+3],
ba1668 ···················STATE[0x40+8*searchUnit+2],STATE[0x40+8*searchUnit+1],
abceed ···················STATE[0x40+8*searchUnit+0], CLOCK_COUNTER, searchUnit);
adaf5a
58efe6 }
c0af5a
e6af5a
67838f static void increment32(unsigned char *num) {
68708d ··if ((++(num[0])) == 0)
f2c3c0 ····if ((++(num[1])) == 0)
0949d0 ······if ((++(num[2])) == 0)
7754ed ········++(num[3]);
e7efe6 }
b8af5a
f5af5a
1fd062 static void decrement32(unsigned char *num) {
ded7cb ··if (((num[0])--) == 0)
8334ba ····if (((num[1])--) == 0)
654eee ······if (((num[2])--) == 0)
251e5b ········(num[3])--;
a0efe6 }
44af5a
52af5a
```

```
--6ca6 001193e4aa680040010 Page 1 of sim.h
8d2d03 /**********************************************************************************
516967 .* sim.h ........................................................................*
8c93bc .* ...................................Header file for sim.c ......................*
d629eb .* ............................................................................*
dd09fc .* ...Written 1998 by Cryptography Research (http://www.cryptography.com) ...*
708aaf .* ......and Paul Kocher for the Electronic Frontier Foundation (EFF). ......*
20caeb .* ......Placed in the public domain by Cryptography Research and EFF. ......*
784992 .* .THIS IS UNSUPPORTED FREE SOFTWARE. USE AND DISTRIBUTE AT YOUR OWN RISK. .*
c329eb .* ............................................................................*
afc755 .* .IMPORTANT: U.S. LAW MAY REGULATE THE USE AND/OR EXPORT OF THIS PROGRAM. .*
0629eb .* ............................................................................*
eb489b .* **********************************************************************************
4629eb .* ............................................................................*
726eef .* .REVISION HISTORY: ..........................................................*
6829eb .* ............................................................................*
8628d9 .* .Version 1.0: .Initial release by Cryptography Research to EFF. .........*
6129eb .* ............................................................................*
75d8c3 .* **********************************************************************************/
a1af5a
2aaf5a
1ac928 #define REG_PTXT_VECTOR .....(0x00)
f821cd #define REG_PTXT_XOR_MASK ...(0x20)
75b3c1 #define REG_CIPHERTEXT0 .....(0x28)
5a1752 #define REG_CIPHERTEXT1 .....(0x30)
74db81 #define REG_PTXT_BYTE_MASK ..(0x38)
39107b #define REG_SEARCHINFO ......(0x3F)
b2b9aa #define REG_SEARCH_KEY(x) ...(0x40 + 8*(x))
86701d #define REG_SEARCH_STATUS(x) (0x47+8*(x))
1d60ef #define CLOCKS_PER_DES ......16
ebaf5a
bd7608 int RunChip(char *input, FILE *outfile, int useRaw);
7da99d long getClockCounter(void);
5273d4 int peekState(int reg); ...................../* runs chip & returns DATA value */
19af5a
```

```
--dfa5 000a2c967de80040011 Page 1 of testvec.c
8d2d03  /***********************************************************************
a1132a  ·* ·testvec.c ···········································································*
8bd58f  ·* ···········DES ASIC Simlator, Test Vector Generation Program ············*
9429eb  ·* ·····································································*
5409fc  ·* ···Written 1998 by Cryptography Research (http://www.cryptography.com) ···*
058aaf  ·* ······and Paul Kocher for the Electronic Frontier Foundation (EFF). ······*
71caeb  ·* ······Placed in the public domain by Cryptography Research and EFF. ······*
5e4992  ·* ·THIS IS UNSUPPORTED FREE SOFTWARE. USE AND DISTRIBUTE AT YOUR OWN RISK. ·*
9529eb  ·* ·····································································*
15c755  ·* ·IMPORTANT: U.S. LAW MAY REGULATE THE USE AND/OR EXPORT OF THIS PROGRAM. ·*
5a29eb  ·* ·····································································*
65489b  ·* ·····································································*
b629eb  ·* ·····································································*
d815cb  ·* ··IMPLEMENTATION NOTES: ·············································*
8829eb  ·* ·····································································*
53a8b8  ·* ··This program automatically determines the configuration of a search ····*
521db9  ·* ··array. ·Additional diagnostic code should be added to detect common ····*
9a87f9  ·* ··chip failures (once these are known). ·······························*
e029eb  ·* ·····································································*
76489b  ·* ·····································································*
6329eb  ·* ·····································································*
566eef  ·* ··REVISION HISTORY: ·················································*
ba29eb  ·* ·····································································*
a028d9  ·* ·Version 1.0: ·Initial release by Cryptography Research to EFF. ·········*
5b29eb  ·* ·····································································*
aad8c3  ·***********************************************************************/
a8af5a
d6feb2  #include <stdio.h>
63bea3  #include <stdlib.h>
9fc737  #include <memory.h>
93324c  #include <string.h>
1a0a8b  #include <time.h>
11bd71  #include "sim.h"
9aaf5a
31decb  int USE_RAW_IO = 0;
b0a91d  FILE *FILE_TOCHIP, *FILE_FROMCHIP; ········/* TOCHIP can be input *or* output */
4fca8d  int ·CREATING_VECTOR; ·····················/* reading vs writing TOCHIP file */
3e98dc  unsigned char HARDWIRED_CHIP_ID ·= 0x3A;
e0af5a
7f583a  int ALLACTIVE_IN = 1; ···························/* gets toggled randomly */
2ce03a  int BOARD_EN_IN ·= 1; ·····················/* input value for run_set/check */
13b9cd  int ADRSEL1_IN ··= 1;
36af5a
60af5a
e17897  void GetUserInfo(unsigned char plaintextVector[32],
302461  ········unsigned char plaintextXorMask[8],
90910f  ········unsigned char ciphertext0[8], unsigned char ciphertext[8],
b5446e  ········unsigned char *plaintextByteMask, int *useCBC, int *extraXor,
7bc016  ········int *randomVector, unsigned char startKey[7], long *totalClocks);
cd1884  void LoadState(unsigned char plaintextVector[32],
fb2461  ········unsigned char plaintextXorMask[8],
481fa8  ········unsigned char ciphertext0[8], unsigned char ciphertext1[8],
d0a024  ········unsigned char plaintextByteMask, int useCBC, int extraXor,
c80ccc  ········unsigned char startKey[7]);
511a5e  void RunSimulator_SetRegister(int addr, int data);
8b5fd9  unsigned char RunSimulator_CheckRegister(int addr);
80703f  void RunSimulator_DummyIO(void);
94708e  static void EXIT_ERR(char *s) { fprintf(stderr, s); exit(1); }
ebaf5a
d6f314  void desDecrypt(unsigned char m[8], unsigned char c[8], unsigned char k[7]);
6eabe4  void increment32(unsigned char *num);
42cba5  void decrement32(unsigned char *num);
2d560a  int hex2bin(char *hex, unsigned char *bin);
77a5c5  void printHexString(char *tag, unsigned char *data, int len);
33f163  void OpenFiles(char *toChipFilename, char *fromChipFilename, int useRaw);
b2bd55  void printKeyInfo(FILE *outDev, char *preamble, int searchUnit);
65a99d  long getClockCounter(void);
8b3363  void proceedNormal(long totalClocks);
c7a6a5  void proceedRandom(void);
caaf5a
11af5a
a238e5  /*
```

```
--8051 0009399d7c480040011 Page 2 of testvec.c
4f775e  ·*
ac775e  ·*
0ff92c  ·* ··THESE FUNCTIONS CREATE AND MANAGE THE TEST VECTORS.
5b775e  ·*
9a775e  ·*
81775e  ·*
2d495d  ·*/
b6af5a
6daf5a
b179bf  void main(int argc, char **argv) {
5a7ab8  ··unsigned char startKey[7], plaintextVector[32];
736f32  ··unsigned char plaintextXorMask[8];
aded17  ··unsigned char ciphertext0[8];
fce93c  ··unsigned char ciphertext1[8];
81b1b4  ··unsigned char plaintextByteMask;
5bcc34  ··int useCBC, extraXor, randomVector;
b9f974  ··long totalClocks;
ac92d0  ··char buffer[512];
1aaf5a
0796ed  ··if (argc != 3 && argc != 4) {
c0795d  ····fprintf(stderr,"Command line: TO_CHIP.OUT FROM_CHIP.OUT [RAW]\n");
5626d6  ····fprintf(stderr," ·TO_CHIP.OUT ····File for data going to chip\n");
8134ad  ····fprintf(stderr," ········(If this file exists, it will be simulated.\n");
114f39  ····fprintf(stderr," ········Otherwise, a new file will be created.)\n");
67803c  ····fprintf(stderr," ·FROM_CHIP.OUT ···File for chip's output\n");
703172  ····fprintf(stderr," ·RAW ············Gives unix CRLFs & no header.\n");
8b646c  ····exit(1);
37df1c  ··}
16af5a
026000  ··/*
802ba4  ···* Open files and set CREATING_VECTOR to:
3369bb  ···* ····0=reading TOCHIP file,
cfdf37  ···* ····1=create TOCHIP from user input,
7fbbb4  ···* ····2=create random vector
def9a6  ···*/
18bbf9  ··OpenFiles(argv[1], argv[2], (argc == 4) ? 1 : 0);
a3af5a
97ee0b  ··if (CREATING_VECTOR == 0) {
ac50a4  ····fprintf(stderr, "Using input vector from file.\n");
e6eb83  ····while (1) {
66b843  ······if (fgets(buffer, 500, FILE_TOCHIP) == NULL)
a52d5f  ········break;
01563f  ······if (strlen(buffer) < 10)
1a2d5f  ········break;
97f0ee  ······RunChip(buffer, FILE_FROMCHIP, USE_RAW_IO);
b86fe7  ····}
4a49d8  ··} else {
89ae2b  ····GetUserInfo(plaintextVector, plaintextXorMask, ciphertext0, ciphertext1,
08828a  ············&plaintextByteMask, &useCBC, &extraXor, &randomVector, startKey,
f497e4  ············&totalClocks);
ac3a38  ····if (randomVector == 0) {
f635be  ······fprintf(stderr, "Seed=random (time-based)\n");
b694d0  ······srand((unsigned) time(NULL));
95c26c  ······HARDWIRED_CHIP_ID = (unsigned char)(rand() & 255);
717a5a  ····} else if (randomVector == 1) {
a1a0a2  ······fprintf(stderr, "Using user params.\n");
e16a79  ····} else {
5ac986  ······fprintf(stderr, "Seed=%d\n", randomVector);
cfccdd  ······srand(randomVector);
91c26c  ······HARDWIRED_CHIP_ID = (unsigned char)(rand() & 255);
456fe7  ····}
33af5a
21f70d  ····/* Reset chip and set the chip ID */
a00659  ····sprintf(buffer, "01011111 00 %02X 00\n", HARDWIRED_CHIP_ID);
5c55a3  ····RunChip(buffer, FILE_FROMCHIP, USE_RAW_IO); fputs(buffer, FILE_TOCHIP);
3d55a3  ····RunChip(buffer, FILE_FROMCHIP, USE_RAW_IO); fputs(buffer, FILE_TOCHIP);
cd55a3  ····RunChip(buffer, FILE_FROMCHIP, USE_RAW_IO); fputs(buffer, FILE_TOCHIP);
7655a3  ····RunChip(buffer, FILE_FROMCHIP, USE_RAW_IO); fputs(buffer, FILE_TOCHIP);
62a71b  ····sprintf(buffer, "11011111 %02X %02X 00\n", HARDWIRED_CHIP_ID,
9ff16b  ············HARDWIRED_CHIP_ID);
1eb67c  ····RunChip(buffer, FILE_FROMCHIP, USE_RAW_IO);
93084e  ····fputs(buffer, FILE_TOCHIP);
```

```
--02cc 00029e33ba580040011 Page 3 of testvec.c

ba5b1f  ····buffer[2] = '1';
34b67c  ····RunChip(buffer, FILE_FROMCHIP, USE_RAW_IO);
7a084e  ····fputs(buffer, FILE_TOCHIP);
ce47a4  ····buffer[2] = '0';
e3b67c  ····RunChip(buffer, FILE_FROMCHIP, USE_RAW_IO);
80084e  ····fputs(buffer, FILE_TOCHIP);
b0af5a
fd317c  ····if (randomVector == 1) {
971b90  ······LoadState(plaintextVector, plaintextXorMask, ciphertext0, ciphertext1,
4b91ef  ················plaintextByteMask, useCBC, extraXor, startKey);
6d3cb4  ······proceedNormal(totalClocks);
916a79  ····} else {
92057c  ······proceedRandom();
7f6fe7  ····}
4bdf1c  ··}
a7af5a
a46b7f  ··/* Clean up a bit (doesn't really matter -- this is test code :-) */
fd9918  ··fclose(FILE_FROMCHIP);
a9650b  ··fclose(FILE_TOCHIP);
0defe6  }
b7af5a
b4af5a
b3bbdb  void proceedNormal(long totalClocks) {
3be2b8  ··long numClocks = getClockCounter();
341614  ··unsigned char goodKey[8];
0b929f  ··int i,j,r;
80af5a
27a415  ··while (++numClocks < totalClocks) {
a40a43  ····r = RunSimulator_CheckRegister(REG_SEARCHINFO);
021f4e  ····if (r & 4) {
e8b4b9  ······fprintf(stderr, "------- Idle --------\n");
318957  ······RunSimulator_DummyIO();
325f6a  ······continue;
9b6fe7  ····}
442135  ····for (i = 0; i < 24; i++) {
9ab4ea  ······/* If we're going to see a stall, give some settling time */
d7bdac  ······if ((peekState(REG_SEARCH_STATUS(i)) & 1) == 0) { ··········/* stalled? */
3ca6ab  ········RunSimulator_DummyIO(); ·······················/* wait before read */
b9fe40  ········RunSimulator_DummyIO();
d4fe40  ········RunSimulator_DummyIO();
ff42cc  ······}
c7d86b  ······r = RunSimulator_CheckRegister(REG_SEARCH_STATUS(i));
7e760d  ······if ((r & 1) == 0) { ·································/* stalled? */
598b76  ········goodKey[6] = RunSimulator_CheckRegister(REG_SEARCH_KEY(i)+0);
4c6426  ········goodKey[5] = RunSimulator_CheckRegister(REG_SEARCH_KEY(i)+1);
c910b2  ········goodKey[4] = RunSimulator_CheckRegister(REG_SEARCH_KEY(i)+2);
2cb297  ········goodKey[3] = RunSimulator_CheckRegister(REG_SEARCH_KEY(i)+3);
91b4ef  ········goodKey[2] = RunSimulator_CheckRegister(REG_SEARCH_KEY(i)+4);
1b5bbf  ········goodKey[1] = RunSimulator_CheckRegister(REG_SEARCH_KEY(i)+5);
1a2f2b  ········goodKey[0] = RunSimulator_CheckRegister(REG_SEARCH_KEY(i)+6);
fbaf5a
abf636  ········fprintf(stderr, "ALERT: Full match in unit %d; extracted k = ", i);
b15425  ········printf("ALERT: Full match in unit %d; extracted k = ", i);
64677e  ········for (j = 0; j < 7; j++) {
652f98  ··········fprintf(stderr, "%02X", goodKey[j]);
1d7e87  ··········printf("%02X", goodKey[j]);
9e7fb0  ········}
0de535  ········fprintf(stderr, "\n");
e10493  ········printf("\n");
db75ed  ········RunSimulator_DummyIO(); ·······················/* Settling time */
6afe40  ········RunSimulator_DummyIO();
e336ec  ········RunSimulator_SetRegister(REG_SEARCH_STATUS(i), 1); ········/* restart */
4242cc  ······}
dd6fe7  ····}
06df1c  ··}
f1efe6  }
adaf5a
0baf5a
d31874  void proceedRandom(void) {
840515  ··unsigned char readout[256];
74a4ed  ··unsigned char goodKey[7];
29e13a  ··int i,j;
```

```
--a796 0002667342680040011 Page 4 of testvec.c
4afe41  ··unsigned char plaintextVector[32];
14d1fd  ··char buffer[256];
23af5a
6c852a  ··/* chip has already been set and the chip ID has been loaded */
73af5a
42c34a  ··/* Create plaintext vector with 181 bits set */
ae477e  ··memset(plaintextVector, 0, sizeof(plaintextVector));
70a328  ··i = 0;
0d13b4  ··while (i < 181) {
926486  ····j = rand() & 255;
21e479  ····if ((plaintextVector[j/8] & (1 << (j % 8))) == 0) {
54e749  ······plaintextVector[j/8] |= (1 << (j % 8));
52079a  ······i++;
2f6fe7  ····}
dcdf1c  ··}
84af5a
68fd4c  ··/* Load state */
03339a  ··for (i = 0; i < 32; i++)
579479  ····RunSimulator_SetRegister(REG_PTXT_VECTOR + i, plaintextVector[i]);
c61f76  ··for (i = 0; i < 8; i++)
d332be  ····RunSimulator_SetRegister(REG_PTXT_XOR_MASK + i, rand() & 255);
671f76  ··for (i = 0; i < 8; i++)
cce0be  ····RunSimulator_SetRegister(REG_CIPHERTEXT0 + i, rand() & 255);
631f76  ··for (i = 0; i < 8; i++)
7849e3  ····RunSimulator_SetRegister(REG_CIPHERTEXT1 + i, rand() & 255);
e1c5ca  ··RunSimulator_SetRegister(REG_PTXT_BYTE_MASK, 1 << (rand() & 7));
c99aac  ··i = (rand() % 3) + (rand() & 16); ·/* 0/1/2 for CBC & extraXor. 16=activOn */
0bf2a6  ····fprintf(stderr, "Using mode %d with ActiveOn=%d.\n", (i&3), i/16);
02b125  ····RunSimulator_SetRegister(REG_SEARCHINFO, i);
040688  ··for (i = 0; i < 24; i++) ·························/* for each engine */
891cca  ····for (j = 0; j < 7; j++) ·························/* set random start key */
0b98b9  ······RunSimulator_SetRegister(REG_SEARCH_KEY(i)+j, rand() & 255);
ecfdd9  ····RunSimulator_SetRegister(REG_SEARCH_STATUS(i), 1);
98df1c  ··}
daaf5a
8ea083  ··/* Read out all registers (real and not) except for ptxt vector */
df1999  ··for (i = 255; i >= 32; i--)
6b1901  ····readout[i] = RunSimulator_CheckRegister(i);
d59097  ··/* Change the key in any stopped units */
219101  ··for (i = 0; i < 24; i++) {
385173  ····if ((readout[REG_SEARCH_STATUS(i)] & 1) == 0) ···············/* stalled? */
3d6ca2  ······RunSimulator_SetRegister(REG_SEARCH_KEY(i),
65571a  ········readout[REG_SEARCH_KEY(i)] ^ 0x08); ···············/* fix key */
51df1c  ··}
b31dc8  ··/* Read out ptxt vector */
632004  ··for (i = 31; i >= 0; i--)
151901  ····readout[i] = RunSimulator_CheckRegister(i);
8c809e  ··/* scan stopped units */
539101  ··for (i = 0; i < 24; i++) {
f12abb  ····if ((readout[REG_SEARCH_STATUS(i)] & 1) == 0) { ···········/* stalled? */
97e66a  ······goodKey[6] = RunSimulator_CheckRegister(REG_SEARCH_KEY(i)+0);
b1093a  ······goodKey[5] = RunSimulator_CheckRegister(REG_SEARCH_KEY(i)+1);
217dae  ······goodKey[4] = RunSimulator_CheckRegister(REG_SEARCH_KEY(i)+2);
d2df8b  ······goodKey[3] = RunSimulator_CheckRegister(REG_SEARCH_KEY(i)+3);
cfd9f3  ······goodKey[2] = RunSimulator_CheckRegister(REG_SEARCH_KEY(i)+4);
1536a3  ······goodKey[1] = RunSimulator_CheckRegister(REG_SEARCH_KEY(i)+5);
3b4237  ······goodKey[0] = RunSimulator_CheckRegister(REG_SEARCH_KEY(i)+6);
1d0767  ······if (rand() % 8)
8436ec  ········RunSimulator_SetRegister(REG_SEARCH_STATUS(i), 1); ········/* restart */
53ca8d  ······fprintf(stderr, "****** Full match in unit %d; extracted k = ", i);
02b8df  ······for (j = 0; j < 7; j++) {
8a3d3b  ········fprintf(stderr, "%02X", goodKey[j]);
b905c9  ········printf("%02X", goodKey[j]);
8642cc  ······}
c65501  ······fprintf(stderr, "\n");
de6fe7  ····}
cbdf1c  ··}
fbaf5a
ab917c  ··/* pick a different chip, read/write some registers, and reset chip id */
3fef47  ··do { i = rand() & 255; } while (i == HARDWIRED_CHIP_ID);
308260  ··sprintf(buffer, "11011111 %02X %02X 00\n", i, HARDWIRED_CHIP_ID);
2621ff  ··RunChip(buffer, FILE_FROMCHIP, USE_RAW_IO);
```

```
--5543 0004f88973480040011 Page 5 of testvec.c

477f59 ··fputs(buffer, FILE_TOCHIP);
146c5f ··buffer[2] = '1';
8921ff ··RunChip(buffer, FILE_FROMCHIP, USE_RAW_IO);
527f59 ··fputs(buffer, FILE_TOCHIP);
0f70e4 ··buffer[2] = '0';
a421ff ··RunChip(buffer, FILE_FROMCHIP, USE_RAW_IO);
b07f59 ··fputs(buffer, FILE_TOCHIP);
6b1f76 ··for (i = 0; i < 8; i++)
feca76 ····RunSimulator_SetRegister(rand() & 255, rand() & 255);
161f76 ··for (i = 0; i < 8; i++)
46b8cf ····RunSimulator_CheckRegister(rand() & 255);
6615e8 ·sprintf(buffer, "11011111 %02X %02X 00\n", HARDWIRED_CHIP_ID,
04867c ··········HARDWIRED_CHIP_ID);
5b21ff ··RunChip(buffer, FILE_FROMCHIP, USE_RAW_IO);
a57f59 ··fputs(buffer, FILE_TOCHIP);
836c5f ··buffer[2] = '1';
ed21ff ··RunChip(buffer, FILE_FROMCHIP, USE_RAW_IO);
1f7f59 ··fputs(buffer, FILE_TOCHIP);
cc70e4 ··buffer[2] = '0';
7b21ff ··RunChip(buffer, FILE_FROMCHIP, USE_RAW_IO);
1c7f59 ··fputs(buffer, FILE_TOCHIP);
9daf5a
3074d9 ··/* Test board enable and ADRSEL1 */
234255 ··BOARD_EN_IN = 0;
71cb06 ··ADRSEL1_IN = 0;
732414 ··for (i = 0; i < 4; i++)
42ca76 ····RunSimulator_SetRegister(rand() & 255, rand() & 255);
0e2414 ··for (i = 0; i < 4; i++)
0fb8cf ····RunSimulator_CheckRegister(rand() & 255);
594255 ··BOARD_EN_IN = 0;
9891da ··ADRSEL1_IN = 1;
241f76 ··for (i = 0; i < 8; i++)
71ca76 ····RunSimulator_SetRegister(rand() & 255, rand() & 255);
7b1f76 ··for (i = 0; i < 8; i++)
54b8cf ····RunSimulator_CheckRegister(rand() & 255);
2c1889 ··BOARD_EN_IN = 1;
fbcb06 ··ADRSEL1_IN = 0;
da1f76 ··for (i = 0; i < 8; i++)
aeca76 ····RunSimulator_SetRegister(rand() & 255, rand() & 255);
e41f76 ··for (i = 0; i < 8; i++)
b8b8cf ····RunSimulator_CheckRegister(rand() & 255);
f81889 ··BOARD_EN_IN = 1;
1491da ··ADRSEL1_IN = 1;
4caf5a
8ce7e0 ··/* Make a final pass reading all the registers */
99741b ··for (i = 255; i >= 0; i--)
771901 ····readout[i] = RunSimulator_CheckRegister(i);
7e809e ··/* scan stopped units */
199101 ··for (i = 0; i < 24; i++) {
b02abb ····if ((readout[REG_SEARCH_STATUS(i)] & 1) == 0) { ·············/* stalled? */
76e66a ······goodKey[6] = RunSimulator_CheckRegister(REG_SEARCH_KEY(i)+0);
c2093a ······goodKey[5] = RunSimulator_CheckRegister(REG_SEARCH_KEY(i)+1);
287dae ······goodKey[4] = RunSimulator_CheckRegister(REG_SEARCH_KEY(i)+2);
96df8b ······goodKey[3] = RunSimulator_CheckRegister(REG_SEARCH_KEY(i)+3);
43d9f3 ······goodKey[2] = RunSimulator_CheckRegister(REG_SEARCH_KEY(i)+4);
eb36a3 ······goodKey[1] = RunSimulator_CheckRegister(REG_SEARCH_KEY(i)+5);
c34237 ······goodKey[0] = RunSimulator_CheckRegister(REG_SEARCH_KEY(i)+6);
9bc697 ······RunSimulator_SetRegister(REG_SEARCH_STATUS(i), 1); ·········/* restart */
5aca8d ······fprintf(stderr, "****** Full match in unit %d; extracted k = ", i);
34b8df ······for (j = 0; j < 7; j++) {
883d3b ········fprintf(stderr, "%02X", goodKey[j]);
fc05c9 ········printf("%02X", goodKey[j]);
f742cc ······}
d85501 ······fprintf(stderr, "\n");
a56fe7 ····}
04df1c ··}
81efe6 }
b2af5a
8baf5a
dbaf5a
be7897 void GetUserInfo(unsigned char plaintextVector[32],
4f2461 ········unsigned char plaintextXorMask[8],
```

```
--53eb 000af645a6880040011 Page 6 of testvec.c

261fa8 ········unsigned char ciphertext0[8], unsigned char ciphertext1[8],
49446e ········unsigned char *plaintextByteMask, int *useCBC, int *extraXor,
8b9f02 ········int *randomVector, unsigned char startKey[7], long *totalClocks) {
ef0e71 ··char buffer[1024];
98c6d6 ··unsigned char tmp[512];
fe17e0 ··int i;
b5af5a
77659f ··printf("Enter plaintextVector values: ");
10766e ··gets(buffer);
13b72a ··i = hex2bin(buffer, tmp);
4953dd ··if (i <= 0 || i >= 256)
b0112c ···EXIT_ERR("Must have at least 1 plaintextVector entry and at most 255.\n");
481bcb ··memset(plaintextVector, 0, 32);
83f545 ··while (i--)
24f3bf ···plaintextVector[tmp[i]/8] |= (1 << (tmp[i] % 8));
9aaf5a
51ee8b ··printf(" ···Enter plaintext xor mask: ");
14766e ··gets(buffer);
2db72a ··i = hex2bin(buffer, tmp);
aa1856 ··if (i != 8)
fba670 ···EXIT_ERR("Must have 8 plaintext xor mask bytes.");
91b657 ··memcpy(plaintextXorMask, tmp, 8);
b9af5a
b83a0c ··printf(" ·········Enter ciphertext 0: ");
b6766e ··gets(buffer);
67b72a ··i = hex2bin(buffer, tmp);
a21856 ··if (i != 8)
c0cf62 ···EXIT_ERR("Must have 8 bytes in ciphertext 0.");
2998f3 ··memcpy(ciphertext0, tmp, 8);
16af5a
e9a5d9 ··printf(" ·········Enter ciphertext 1: ");
eb766e ··gets(buffer);
26b72a ··i = hex2bin(buffer, tmp);
c41856 ··if (i != 8)
21cb49 ···EXIT_ERR("Must have 8 bytes in ciphertext 1.");
1e1da6 ··memcpy(ciphertext1, tmp, 8);
51af5a
fed221 ··printf(" ··Enter plaintext byte mask: ");
9f766e ··gets(buffer);
b5b72a ··i = hex2bin(buffer, tmp);
968448 ··if (i != 1)
69f706 ···EXIT_ERR("Plaintext byte mask is 1 byte long.");
1dc2b5 ··*plaintextByteMask = tmp[0];
93af5a
a51b21 ··printf(" ······Enter useCBC (0 or 1): ");
72766e ··gets(buffer);
1bb72a ··i = hex2bin(buffer, tmp);
a415b9 ··if (i != 1 || tmp[0] > 1)
1519c6 ···EXIT_ERR("Must enter 0 or 1 for useCBC.");
cde2c1 ··*useCBC = tmp[0];
7caf5a
bdf965 ··printf(" ····Enter extraXor (0 or 1): ");
28766e ··gets(buffer);
3ab72a ··i = hex2bin(buffer, tmp);
e915b9 ··if (i != 1 || tmp[0] > 1)
7a6c75 ···EXIT_ERR("Must enter 0 or 1 for extraXor.");
8e2353 ··*extraXor = tmp[0];
92af5a
2e04d5 ··printf(" Enter randomVector (0=randomize, 1=user input, >1=seed): ");
35766e ··gets(buffer);
3eb72a ··i = hex2bin(buffer, tmp);
a68448 ··if (i != 1)
6fbb66 ···EXIT_ERR("Must enter 0=randomize 1=use input, >1=value for prng seed).");
9db530 ··*randomVector = tmp[0];
d4af5a
40c8bf ··printf(" ·········Enter starting key: ");
a2766e ··gets(buffer);
07e684 ··if (hex2bin(buffer, tmp) != 7)
c3a5e4 ···EXIT_ERR("Must enter 7 hex bytes as the key.\n");
f30ed3 ··memcpy(startKey, tmp, 7);
6caf5a
aff4f6 ··printf(" ·····Enter number of clocks: ");
```

```
--5aef 000e933bd7d80040011 Page 7 of testvec.c
74766e ··gets(buffer);
775582 ··sscanf(buffer, "%ld", totalClocks);
0f9780 ··if (*totalClocks < 1 || *totalClocks > 1000000000L)
e4b093 ····EXIT_ERR("Must have between 1 and 1 billion clocks.\n");
33af5a
62186d ··printHexString("\n ·PtxtVector = ", plaintextVector, 32);
5aa738 ··printHexString(" PtxtXorMask = ", plaintextXorMask, 8);
44ffc6 ··printHexString("Ciphertext 0 = ", ciphertext0, 8);
913b57 ··printHexString("Ciphertext 1 = ", ciphertext1, 8);
83dd31 ··printHexString("PtxtByteMask = ", plaintextByteMask, 1);
37e15b ··printf( ·······" ·····useCBC = %d\n", *useCBC);
012f30 ··printf( ·······" ···extraXor = %d\n", *extraXor);
bbe751 ··printf( ·······"randomVector = %x\n", *randomVector);
b81535 ··printHexString("Starting key = ", startKey, 7);
bed787 ··printf( ·······"Total clocks = %ld\n\n", *totalClocks);
e2efe6 }
e0af5a
daaf5a
711884 void LoadState(unsigned char plaintextVector[32],
182461 ········unsigned char plaintextXorMask[8],
541fa8 ········unsigned char ciphertext0[8], unsigned char ciphertext1[8],
e3a024 ········unsigned char plaintextByteMask, int useCBC, int extraXor,
40e619 ········unsigned char startKey[7]) {
c917e0 ··int i;
0baf5a
af339a ··for (i = 0; i < 32; i++)
a19479 ····RunSimulator_SetRegister(REG_PTXT_VECTOR + i, plaintextVector[i]);
371f76 ··for (i = 0; i < 8; i++)
c0a554 ····RunSimulator_SetRegister(REG_PTXT_XOR_MASK + i, plaintextXorMask[7-i]);
131f76 ··for (i = 0; i < 8; i++)
6d2b06 ····RunSimulator_SetRegister(REG_CIPHERTEXT0 + i, ciphertext0[7-i]);
031f76 ··for (i = 0; i < 8; i++)
02abab ····RunSimulator_SetRegister(REG_CIPHERTEXT1 + i, ciphertext1[7-i]);
05ea2e ··RunSimulator_SetRegister(REG_PTXT_BYTE_MASK, plaintextByteMask);
5b35f1 ··RunSimulator_SetRegister(REG_SEARCHINFO, (useCBC?1:0) |
7e824a ········(extraXor?2:0) | 16); ···················/* enable board active */
9d0688 ··for (i = 0; i < 24; i++) { ················/* for each engine */
c40441 ····RunSimulator_SetRegister(REG_SEARCH_KEY(i)+0, startKey[6]);
da0982 ····RunSimulator_SetRegister(REG_SEARCH_KEY(i)+1, startKey[5]);
d432d7 ····RunSimulator_SetRegister(REG_SEARCH_KEY(i)+2, startKey[4]);
751204 ····RunSimulator_SetRegister(REG_SEARCH_KEY(i)+3, startKey[3]);
a3696d ····RunSimulator_SetRegister(REG_SEARCH_KEY(i)+4, startKey[2]);
b864ae ····RunSimulator_SetRegister(REG_SEARCH_KEY(i)+5, startKey[1]);
4d13e5 ····RunSimulator_SetRegister(REG_SEARCH_KEY(i)+6, (startKey[0] + i) & 255);
e7fdd9 ····RunSimulator_SetRegister(REG_SEARCH_STATUS(i), 1);
8adf1c ··}
54efe6 }
15af5a
5daf5a
adaf5a
8b5194 void RunSimulator_SetRegister(int addr, int data) {
abd1fd ··char buffer[256];
f8af5a
3c9186 ··/* RESET,BOARD_EN,ALE,ADRSEL1,WRB,RDB,ADRSEL2,ALLACT_IN,ADDR,CHIP_ID,DATA */
d25f05 ··sprintf(buffer, "1%d0%d110%d %02x %02x %02x\n", BOARD_EN_IN, ADRSEL1_IN,
afa8dd ········ALLACTIVE_IN, addr, HARDWIRED_CHIP_ID, data);
7721ff ··RunChip(buffer, FILE_FROMCHIP, USE_RAW_IO);
047f59 ··fputs(buffer, FILE_TOCHIP);
d1af5a
6ecb50 ··sprintf(buffer, "1%d0%d010%d %02x %02x %02x\n", BOARD_EN_IN, ADRSEL1_IN,
93a8dd ········ALLACTIVE_IN, addr, HARDWIRED_CHIP_ID, data);
c621ff ··RunChip(buffer, FILE_FROMCHIP, USE_RAW_IO);
3d7f59 ··fputs(buffer, FILE_TOCHIP);
44af5a
bb5f05 ··sprintf(buffer, "1%d0%d110%d %02x %02x %02x\n", BOARD_EN_IN, ADRSEL1_IN,
cda8dd ········ALLACTIVE_IN, addr, HARDWIRED_CHIP_ID, data);
8821ff ··RunChip(buffer, FILE_FROMCHIP, USE_RAW_IO);
b57f59 ··fputs(buffer, FILE_TOCHIP);
6faf5a
073db7 ··if ((rand() & 31) == 0)
1debd9 ····ALLACTIVE_IN = 1-ALLACTIVE_IN;
e9efe6 }
```

```
--0bd8 000b2bfff2680040011 Page 8 of testvec.c

e0af5a
1aaf5a
562371 void RunSimulator_DummyIO(void) {
5fd1fd ··char buffer[256];
dd5ffc ··int i,b,addr,chip;
f0af5a
bbb5a8 ··if ((rand() & 3) > 0) {
6df7c5 ····addr = rand() & 255;
7c7b22 ····chip = (rand() & 7) ? HARDWIRED_CHIP_ID : (rand() & 255);
b40f2c ····b = (rand() & 7) ? 1 : 0;
116e4c ····/*RESET,BOARD_EN,ALE,ADRSEL1,WRB,RDB,ADRSEL2,ALLACT_IN,ADDR,CHIP_ID,DATA*/
58d814 ····sprintf(buffer, "1%d01110%d %02x %02x 00\n", b, ALLACTIVE_IN, addr, chip);
34b67c ····RunChip(buffer, FILE_FROMCHIP, USE_RAW_IO);
e1084e ····fputs(buffer, FILE_TOCHIP);
b7b67c ····RunChip(buffer, FILE_FROMCHIP, USE_RAW_IO);
4a084e ····fputs(buffer, FILE_TOCHIP);
dea7f6 ····sprintf(buffer, "1%d01100%d %02x %02x 00\n", b, ALLACTIVE_IN, addr, chip);
26b67c ····RunChip(buffer, FILE_FROMCHIP, USE_RAW_IO);
7d084e ····fputs(buffer, FILE_TOCHIP);
e2b67c ····RunChip(buffer, FILE_FROMCHIP, USE_RAW_IO);
b2084e ····fputs(buffer, FILE_TOCHIP);
0cdda8 ····sprintf(buffer, "1%d01111%d %02x %02x 00\n", b, ALLACTIVE_IN, addr, chip);
d9b67c ····RunChip(buffer, FILE_FROMCHIP, USE_RAW_IO);
a3084e ····fputs(buffer, FILE_TOCHIP);
dbb67c ····RunChip(buffer, FILE_FROMCHIP, USE_RAW_IO);
d1084e ····RunChip(buffer, FILE_FROMCHIP, USE_RAW_IO);
64b67c ····RunChip(buffer, FILE_FROMCHIP, USE_RAW_IO);
53084e ····fputs(buffer, FILE_TOCHIP);
1149d8 ··} else {
1ad2a6 ····sprintf(buffer, "1101111%d FF %02x FF\n", ALLACTIVE_IN, HARDWIRED_CHIP_ID);
6cd137 ····for (i = rand() & 7; i > 0; i--) {
73f0ee ······RunChip(buffer, FILE_FROMCHIP, USE_RAW_IO);
3ad7ef ······fputs(buffer, FILE_TOCHIP);
0e6fe7 ····}
98df1c ··}
f8efe6 }
50af5a
55af5a
4caf5a
aba166 unsigned char RunSimulator_CheckRegister(int addr) {
9299d0 ··unsigned char rval;
d7d1fd ··char buffer[256];
72af5a
229186 ··/* RESET,BOARD_EN,ALE,ADRSEL1,WRB,RDB,ADRSEL2,ALLACT_IN,ADDR,CHIP_ID,DATA */
fbac2d ··sprintf(buffer, "1%d0%d0110%d %02x %02x 00\n", BOARD_EN_IN, ADRSEL1_IN,
e0278e ··········ALLACTIVE_IN, addr, HARDWIRED_CHIP_ID /*no data*/);
4121ff ··RunChip(buffer, FILE_FROMCHIP, USE_RAW_IO);
317f59 ··fputs(buffer, FILE_TOCHIP);
09af5a
0faa92 ··sprintf(buffer, "1%d0%d100%d %02x %02x 00\n", BOARD_EN_IN, ADRSEL1_IN,
35278e ··········ALLACTIVE_IN, addr, HARDWIRED_CHIP_ID /*no data*/);
cf49fa ··rval=(unsigned char)RunChip(buffer, FILE_FROMCHIP, USE_RAW_IO);
dc7f59 ··fputs(buffer, FILE_TOCHIP);
deaf5a
a2234b ··sprintf(buffer, "1%d0%d111%d %02x %02x 00\n", BOARD_EN_IN, ADRSEL1_IN,
ac278e ··········ALLACTIVE_IN, addr, HARDWIRED_CHIP_ID /*no data*/);
0321ff ··RunChip(buffer, FILE_FROMCHIP, USE_RAW_IO);
b77f59 ··fputs(buffer, FILE_TOCHIP);
cbaf5a
2076c9 ··return (rval);
c6efe6 }
36af5a
adaf5a
4bc2bf int unhex(char c) {
af53c4 ··if (c >= '0' && c <= '9')
f203d6 ····return (c - '0');
618db1 ··if (c >= 'a' && c <= 'f')
180ada ····return (c - 'a' + 10);
e449e3 ··if (c >= 'A' && c <= 'F')
d7a66f ····return (c - 'A' + 10);
9912d4 ··return (-1);
b2efe6 }
```

```
--3d19 000c2e4763180040011 Page 9 of testvec.c

e0af5a
1aaf5a
4c4579 int hex2bin(char *hex, unsigned char *bin) {
dcc22f ··int i = 0;
a66a41 ··int j = 0;
66af5a
688ef6 ··/* Trim string if comments present */
078b28 ··if (strchr(hex, '#') != NULL)
a052e6 ····*strchr(hex, '#') = 0;
d8a3ed ··if (strchr(hex, '*') != NULL)
2560d1 ····*strchr(hex, '*') = 0;
d8a6e5 ··if (strchr(hex, '\'') != NULL)
762462 ····*strchr(hex, '\'') = 0;
6caf5a
9447de ··for (i = 0; i < (int)strlen(hex); i++) {
d28e69 ····if (hex[i] >= '0' && unhex(hex[i]) < 0)
d3d278 ······EXIT_ERR("Bad hex digit encountered.\n");
81df1c ··}
27af5a
1b47de ··for (i = 0; i < (int)strlen(hex); i++) {
34f5b0 ····if (hex[i] < '0')
875f6a ······continue;
51643e ····if (hex[i] >= '0' && hex[i+1] >= '0') {
57f2a4 ······bin[j++] = (unsigned char)(unhex(hex[i])*16+unhex(hex[i+1]));
0039d3 ······i++; ·····························································/* skip one */
245f6a ······continue;
ab6fe7 ····}
a3e16f ····if (hex[i] >= '0') {
339eae ······bin[j++] = (unsigned char)(unhex(hex[i]));
3d6fe7 ····}
5fdf1c ··}
ebc1d2 ··return (j);
8cefe6 }
c2af5a
f2af5a
847b71 void printHexString(char *tag, unsigned char *data, int len) {
3d17e0 ··int i;
dbaf5a
449650 ··printf("%s", tag);
fc6c12 ··for (i = 0; i < len; i++)
20cd57 ····printf("%02X", data[i]);
8afee8 ··printf("\n");
eaefe6 }
8aaf5a
24af5a
18bb19 void OpenFiles(char *toChipFilename, char *fromChipFilename, int useRaw) {
e27959 ··FILE_TOCHIP = fopen(toChipFilename, useRaw ? "rb" : "r");
c0f096 ··if (FILE_TOCHIP != NULL) {
9d1260 ····CREATING_VECTOR = 0;
6449d8 ··} else {
335eff ····FILE_TOCHIP = fopen(toChipFilename, useRaw ? "wb" : "w");
c5d318 ····if (FILE_TOCHIP == NULL) {
445716 ······fprintf(stderr, "Can't open \"s\" for toChip file\n", toChipFilename);
e4c1d2 ······exit(1);
d56fe7 ····}
0c48bc ····CREATING_VECTOR = 1;
69df1c ··}
ebaf5a
7da670 ··FILE_FROMCHIP = fopen(fromChipFilename, useRaw ? "wb" : "w");
8d870f ··if (FILE_FROMCHIP == NULL) {
9842e1 ····fprintf(stderr, "Can't open \"s\" for fromChip file\n", fromChipFilename);
25646c ····exit(1);
fddf1c ··}
7baf5a
d359dc ··USE_RAW_IO = useRaw;
7dc563 #if 0 ·············/* Activate this to add column descriptors in the output */
4e14fa ··if (!useRaw){
e382e3 ····fprintf(FILE_TOCHIP, "RESET\n");
4d7cf5 ····fprintf(FILE_TOCHIP, "|BOARD_EN\n");
d6f02c ····fprintf(FILE_TOCHIP, "||ALE\n");
da1111 ····fprintf(FILE_TOCHIP, "|||ADRSEL1\n");
c287b0 ····fprintf(FILE_TOCHIP, "||||WRB\n");
```

```
--c2ba 001857ff29a80040011 Page 10 of testvec.c
93a32c ····fprintf(FILE_TOCHIP, "|||||RDB\n");
71b3bd ····fprintf(FILE_TOCHIP, "||||||ADRSEL2\n");
d017df ····fprintf(FILE_TOCHIP, "|||||||ALLACTIVE_IN\n");
6bed08 ····fprintf(FILE_TOCHIP, "||||||||| ADDR\n");
173c97 ····fprintf(FILE_TOCHIP, "||||||||| /\\ CHIP_ID\n");
f1102a ····fprintf(FILE_TOCHIP, "||||||||| || /\\ DATA\n");
4aea2f ····fprintf(FILE_TOCHIP, "||||||||| || || /\\ ALLACTIVE_OUT\n");
e1e4e9 ····fprintf(FILE_FROMCHIP, "DATA\n");
541499 ····fprintf(FILE_FROMCHIP, "/\\ ALLACTIVE_OUT\n");
4dc3ec ····fprintf(FILE_FROMCHIP, "|| | /-- IsActive [0..23] --\\\n");
a6df1c ··}
187454 #endif
217c65 ··fprintf(FILE_FROMCHIP, "KEY ···········DES_OUT ········MATCH & SELECT1:\n");
1aefe6 }
85af5a
```

*In This chapter:*
- *Board Schematics*
- *Sun-4/470 backplane modifications*
- *PC Interfaces*
- *Errata*

# 8

# *Hardware Board Schematics*

This chapter contains schematic diagrams of the printed-circuit boards that we designed and built for the DES Cracker. It also includes a few other details about the hardware.

Each hardware board holds 64 DES Cracker chips. In this schematic, we only show how 8 of the chips are wired. The rest are wired almost identically. Each "All Active Out" pin is daisy-chained to the next "All Active In" pin. The "Chip ID" pins on each chip are connected directly to either ground or power, to tell the chip its binary chip number among all the chips on the board. If you examine these pins for the eight chips shown, you'll see how they change.

The boards fit into card-cages which are connected to each other and to the host computer by a 50-pin ribbon cable. The card-cages are modified Sun-4/470 server card cages. The modifications we made to their backplanes are detailed toward the end of the chapter.

## *Board Schematics*

The schematics begin on the next page.

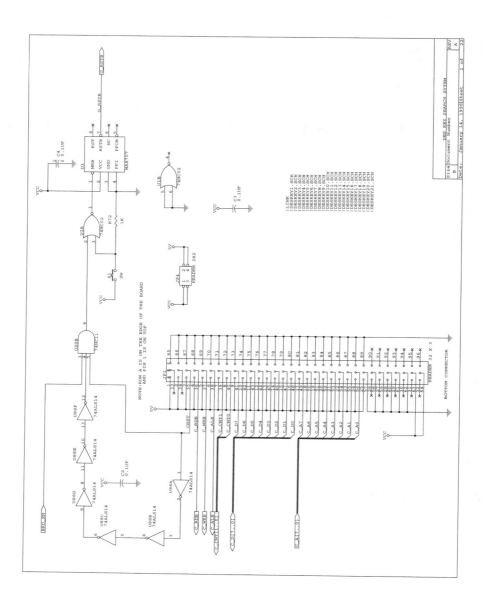

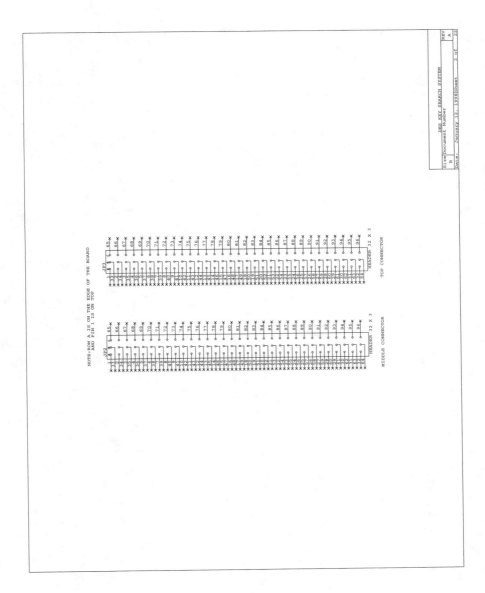

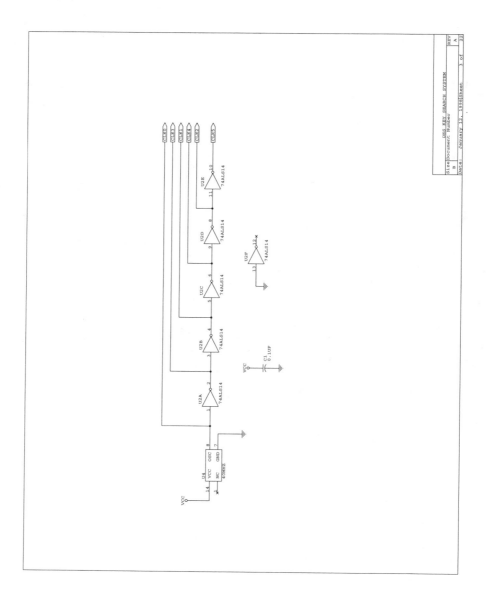

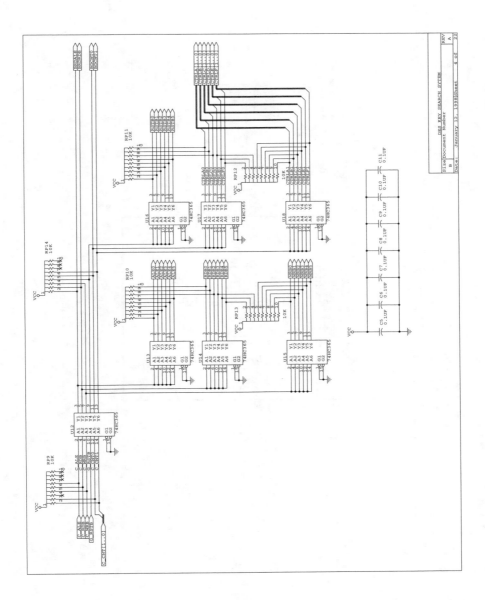

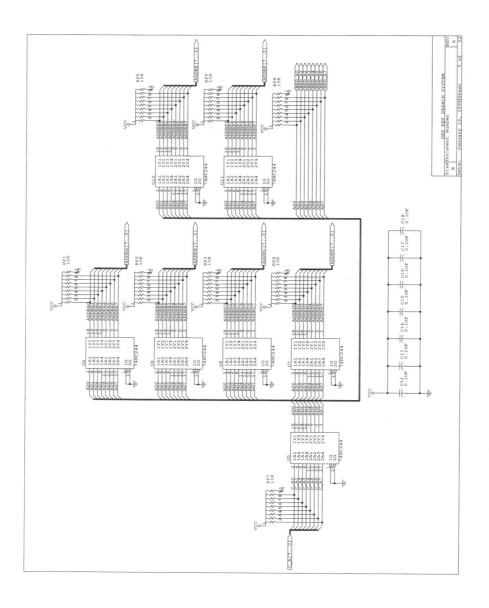

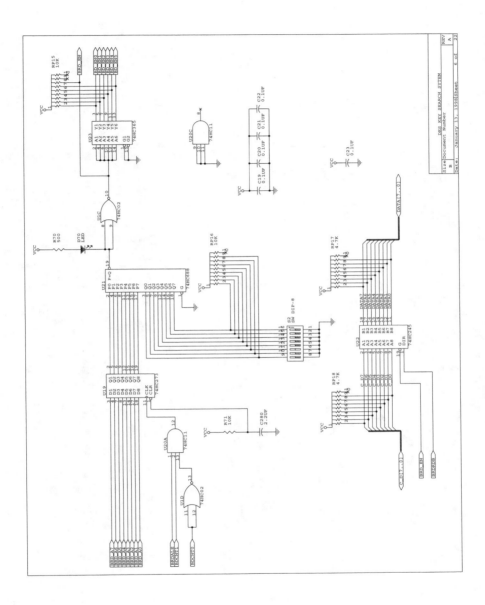

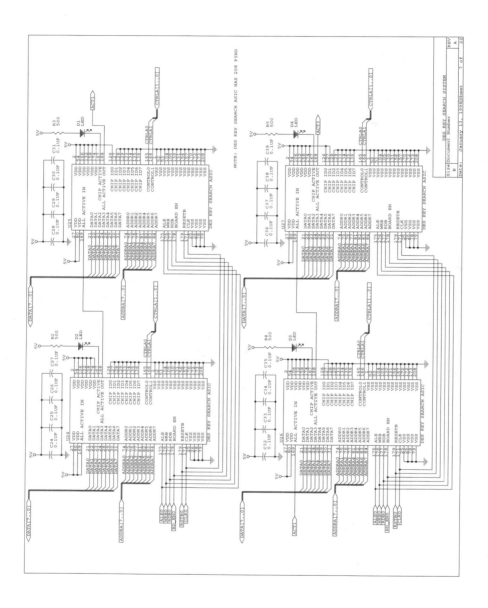

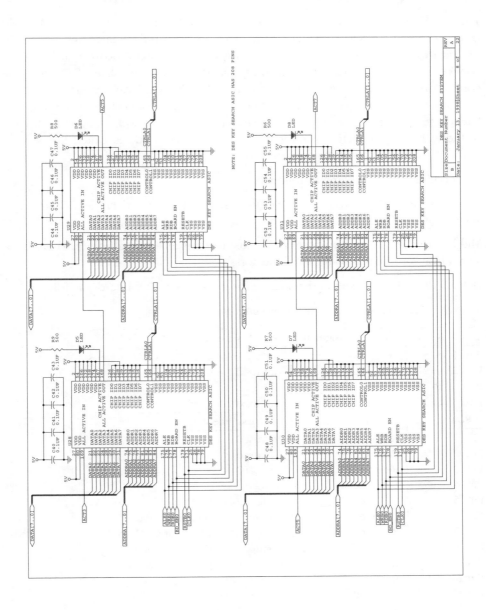

# Sun-4/470 backplane modifications

The first DES Cracker uses several chassis recycled from Sun-4/470 servers to hold its boards. Each chassis contains a card cage, power supplies, fans, and covers. In the card cage there is a backplane, which is a printed circuit board that holds the connectors for each board that can be plugged into the card cage. Each row has connectors for 12 slots numbered from 1 to 12. The card cage is sized for "9U" VMEbus boards, each of which has three large 96-pin connectors. Therefore, the backplane also has three 96-pin connectors per board, called P1, P2, and P3. Each of these 96-pin connectors has three rows of 32 pins inside it, called Rows A, B, and C.

We modified the backplane as follows:

Top Row (P1): No modification. We just use this as a board holder. There is no signal from our boards to these connectors.

Middle Row (P2): No modification. We just use this as a board holder. There is no signal from our boards to these connectors.

Bottom Row (P3): Power and signaling for the DES Cracker boards, as follows:

*Table 8–1: Signal assignments on bottom connectors*

| Row A | Original Assigment | New Assigment |
|---|---|---|
| Pin  1 to 25 | +5 Volts | Supply voltage for DES Cracker chips |
| Pin  26 to 27 | +12 Volts | Not used |
| Pins 28 to 29 | -12 Volts | Not used |
| Pins 30 to 32 | -5 Volts | Not used |
| Row B | Original Assigment | New Assigment |
| Pin  1 | Reserved | Not used |
| Pin  2 | Reserved | Not used |
| Pin  3 | Reserved | Reset  (C_RST) |
| Pin  4 | Reserved | Read  Strobe (C_RDB) |
| Pin  5 | Reserved | Write Strobe (C_WRB) |
| Pin  6 | Reserved | Address Latch Enable (C_AEN) |
| Pin  7 | Reserved | Control_1 (C_CNT1) or C_ADRSELB |
| Pin  8 | Reserved | Control_2 (C_CNT2) or C_CSB |
| Pin  9 | Reserved | Data 7 (C_D7) |
| Pin 10 | Reserved | Data 6 (C_D6) |
| Pin 11 | Reserved | Data 5 (C_D5) |
| Pin 12 | Reserved | Data 4 (C_D4) |
| Pin 13 | Reserved | Data 3 (C_D3) |
| Pin 14 | Reserved | Data 2 (C_D2) |
| Pin 15 | Reserved | Data 1 (C_D1) |

*Table 8-1:  Signal assignments on bottom connectors  (continued)*

| Pin 16 | Reserved | Data 0 (C_D0) |
|---|---|---|
| Pin 17 | Reserved | Address 7 (C_A7) |
| Pin 18 | Reserved | Address 6 (C_A6) |
| Pin 19 | Reserved | Address 5 (C_A5) |
| Pin 20 | Reserved | Address 4 (C_A4) |
| Pin 21 | Reserved | Address 3 (C_A3) |
| Pin 22 | Reserved | Address 2 (C_A2) |
| Pin 23 | Reserved | Address 1 (C_A1) |
| Pin 24 | Reserved | Address 0 (C_A0) |
| Pin 25 | Reserved | GND |
| Pin 26 | Reserved | GND |
| Pin 27 | Reserved | GND |
| Pin 28 | Reserved | GND |
| Pin 29 | Reserved | GND |
| Pin 30 | Reserved | GND |
| Pin 31 | Reserved | +5 V supply to all Interface ICs |
| Pin 32 | Reserved | +5 V supply to all Interface ICs |
| Row C | Original Assigment | New Assignment |
| Pins  1 to 25 | GND | GND |
| Pins 26 to 27 | +12 Volts | Not used |
| Pins 28 to 29 | -12 Volts | Not used |
| Pins 30 to 32 | -5 Volts | Not used |

Row A, pins 1-25 provide the supply voltage for the DES Cracker chips. The supply is normally +5 Volts.

The chips can be run on a lower voltage, to reduce power consumption and heat generation. In that case, two voltages must be supplied. The lower voltage for the DES Cracker chips is supplied on Row A, pins 1-25. +5 volts is supplied to the interface circuitry on Row B, pins 31 and 32. In low voltage operation, Jumper JP1 on each of the DES boards must be removed. If the DES chips are using +5 Volts, then no external power connects to Row B, pins 31 and 32, and Jumper JP1 on each of the DES boards is connected.

## Physical Modifications on P3 Bus (Bottom Row)

The P3 bus (bottom row) of the backplane has 12 slots. Some of these slots are wired to their neighboring slots, forming a bus. In its original Sun configuration, the P3 bus was mainly used for a high-speed memory bus between the CPU board and the memory boards. It was divided into 4 independent groups:

Group 1
    This group has 7 slots (from 1 to 7) which have their Row B's bussed together.

Group 2

This has only slot 8. Its Row B did not connect to any other.

Group 3

This has only slot 9. Its Row B did not connect to any other.

Group 4

This group has 3 slots (from 10 to 12) which have their Row B's bussed together.

We modified the backplane to connect each of these four groups together, so that P3 Row B connects from slot to slot along the whole backplane.

On both slot 1 and slot 12 we added a dual-row header to the P3 connector, Rows B and C (signals and grounds), so that a 50-pin ribbon cable can connect to the bus. These headers allow each chassis to be cabled to the next chassis, and also allow the first chassis to be cabled to a general purpose computer, where the software that controls the DES Cracker runs.

On slot 11, we also added a dual-row header to the P3 connector, Rows A and B (Supply voltage and signals), to let us install termination resistors when no ribbon cable is attached to Slot 12. These protect the integrity of the signals on the bus.

## *PC Interfaces*

The first chassis connects to the controlling computer via a ribbon cable, which attaches to the dual-row header installed on Slot 1. This cable leads to a plug-in hardware card which provides three parallel I/O ports. The software talks to this card, causing it to write commands to the ribbon cable, or read results back from the ribbon cable. The software runs in an ordinary IBM PC, and could be ported to other general purpose computers.

Our project used either of two interface cards. Both are from National Instruments Corporation of Austin, Texas, reachable at http://www.natinst.com or +1 512 794 0100. Their PC-AT bus interface card is called the PC-DIO-24, order number 777368-01. For laptops, a "PC card" (PCMCIA) interface is also available, the DAQCard-DIO-24, order number 776912-01. This card requires the PSH27-50F-D1 cable, with order number 776989-01.

Other parallel interface cards that provide 24 bit I/O could also be made to work.

# *Errata*

This page contains notes about errors detected late in the hardware or software published herein.

## *Chip select for reading*

The DES Cracker chips do not properly tristate their data buffers. When any chip on any board is reading, every other DES Cracker chip drives garbage onto its data pins. The buffer enables were not qualified by the Board Enable and Chip Enable signals. The initial hardware boards were modified to circumvent this by providing individual RDB signals to each chip, qualifying them externally with an FPGA. The correct fix is in top.vhd in the chip VHDL; near the last line, change:

```
DATA <= DATAO when (RDB = '0' and ADDSEL2 = '0') else (others => 'Z');
```

to:

```
DATA <= DATAO when (RDB = '0' and ADDSEL2 = '0' and CHIP_EN = '1')
               else (others => 'Z');
```

This also involves adding CHIP_EN as an output of upi.vhd.

*In This chapter:*
- *Abstract*
- *Introduction*
- *The basic idea*
- *Details of such a machine*
- *Obtained results and remarks*
- *Conclusion*
- *Acknowledgement*

9

# Breaking One Million DES Keys by Yvo Desmedt

*This paper was presented at Eurocrypt 1987 by Yvo Desmedt and Jean-Jacques Quisquater, under the title "An Exhaustive Key Search Machine Breaking One Million DES Keys". We publish it here for the first time, since no proceedings were made. It points out some research directions in parallel brute force codebreaking that are still useful today.*

## Abstract

The DES is in the commercial and industrial world the most used cryptoalgorithm. A realistic exhaustive key search machine will be proposed which breaks thousands of keys each hour, when DES is used in its standard 8 byte modes to protect privacy. Also authenticity protection with DES is sometimes insecure.

## Introduction

The DES is the NBS[*] and ANSI[†] standard for encryption. It has been proposed to become an ISO[‡] standard, under the name DEA1. From the beginning Diffie and Hellman mentioned that one DES key could be broken under a known plaintext attack using an exhaustive keysearch machine.[§] However the design was criticized because practical problems as size and power dissipation were not taken into

---

[*] "Data Encryption Standard", FIPS (National Bureau of Standards Federal Information Processing Standards Publ.), no. 46, Washington D.C., January 1977

[†] "Data Encryption Algorithm", ANSI X3.92-1981, (American National Standards Institute), New York, December 31, 1980

[‡] "Data Encipherment, Specification of Algorithm DEA1", ISO/DP 8227 (Draft Proposal), 1983

[§] Diffie, W., and Hellman, M.E.: "Exhaustive cryptanalysis of the NBS Data Encryption Standard", Computer, vol. 10, no. 6, pp. 74 - 84, June 1977

consideration. Hoornaert* proposed last year a realistic exhaustive keysearch machine, which solved all practical problems. Instead of breaking DES in half a day (as in the Diffie-Hellman machine), the cheap version ($ 1 million) needs maximum 4 weeks to find the key. In practice however companies or secret agencies want to break several keys at once. Indeed for doing industrial espionage, companies want to break as many communications as possible of their main competitors. Secret agencies want to be able to eavesdrop all communications and to follow up industrial developments in other countries which may be used for military purposes. The above machine is unpractical or expensive for this purpose. Instead of using thousands of machines for breaking thousands of keys, one modified machine is enough.

## *The basic idea*

At first sight if one wants to break one million keys with an exhaustive machine one needs one million pairs (plaintext,ciphertext)=(Mi,Ci) and do the job for each different pair. If all these pairs have the same plaintext M, the exhaustive machine can do the same job by breaking all these one million ciphertexts, as in the case it had only to break one. This assumption is very realistic, indeed in letters some pattern as e.g."Yours Sincerely" are common. For all standard† 8 bytes modes a partially known plaintext attack is sufficient. In the case of ECB a ciphertext only attack is sufficient. Indeed the most frequent combination of 8 bytes can easily be detected and used. Evidently more machines can handle more different plaintext patterns. So, a few machines can break millions of keys. The number of different patterns can be reduced by using a chosen plaintext attack!

## *Details of such a machine*

Although we did not built it, in this section sufficient details are given to show that such a machine is feasible. The machine will be based on a small extension of the DES chips used in Hoornaert's machine. We will call the ciphertexts for which one wants to break the key: "desired" ciphertexts. In one machine, each of the (e.g.) 25 thousand DES chips will calculate ciphertexts for variable keys starting from the same 8 byte "plaintext" pattern. The machine has to verify if such a ciphertext is the same as some "desired" ciphertext. If so, it has to communicate the corresponding key to the Key Handling Machine (KHM) and the "number" of the "desired" ciphertext. However each used DES chip generates each second about

---

* Hoornaert, F., Goubert, J., and Desmedt, Y.: "Efficient hardware implementations of the DES", Advances in Cryptology, Proceedings of Crypto 84, Santa Barbara, August 1984 (Lecture Notes in Computer Science, Springer-Verlag, Berlin, 1985), pp. 147-173

† "DES modes of operation", FIPS (NBS Federal Information Processing Standards Publ.), no. 81, Washington D.C., December 2, 1980

one million pairs (ciphertext, key). This gives a major communication problem. Indeed all this information (about 110Mbit/sec.= (56 key bits + 64 ciphertext bits) x 1M DES/sec.) cannot be communicated constantly outside the chip. To avoid this communication problem, the chip will internally exclude ciphertexts which certainly are not equal to a "desired" ciphertext. So only a fraction has to be communicated to the outside world. Hereto the "desired" ciphertexts were previously ordered based on their first 20 bits, which are used as address of the desired ciphertexts. If more than one of these "desired" ciphertexts have the same 20 first bits then one of them will later be transfered to the exhaustive machine. The others will be put on a waiting list. In the exhaustive machine bits of the desired ciphertexts are spread in RAMs, as explained later, using the 20 first bits as address. Each extended DES chip is put on a hybrid circuit together with 4 RAMs of 1Mbit and a refresh controller (see also fig. 1). For each enumerated key the DES chip communicates the 20 first bits of the corresponding generated ciphertext to the RAMs as address. The 4 bits information stored in the RAMs correspond to the next 4 bits of the desired ciphertexts. The RAMs communicate to the modified DES chip these 4 bits. Only if these 4 bits are equal to the corresponding ones in the generated ciphertext, the generated pair (ciphertext, key) is communicated outside the DES chip to a local bus (see fig. 1). So in average the communication rate is reduced, by excluding the ciphertexts which are certainly not desired. About 10 of these hybrids are put on a small PCB. A custom designed chip checks the next 10 bits (the bits 25 till 34) of the ciphertexts using the same idea as for the 4 bits (the bits 21 till 24). Hereto 10 RAMs each of 1Mbit are used, the address is again the first 20 bits of the generated ciphertext. Only if the check succeeds the pair (ciphertext, key) is communicated to the outside world via a global bus. This reduces the communication between the local bus and the global bus with a factor 1000. About 2500 similar PCBs are put in the machine. The last 30 bits of the ciphertext are checked further on. Hereto similar hardware controls several PCBs. Finally a small machine can do the final check. The machine KHM checks the correctness of the key on other (plaintext, ciphertext) pairs or on the redundancy in the language. Once each (e.g.) hour the machine KHM will update the broken keys and put the ones which are on the waiting list into the exhaustive machine (if possible). Suppose that one hybrid cost $80, then the price of $3 million (25,000 x hybrid + custom chips + PCBs + etc) for this machine is realistic.

# *Obtained results and remarks*

The described machine breaks about one million keys in 4 weeks, or in average about 3000 keys each hour. By updating the broken keys better results can be obtained.* Practical problems as buffering, synchronization, MTBF, power dissipation, size, reloading of the RAMs and so on are solved by the author. Optimizations under several circumstances and variants of the machine are possible. In view of the existing rumors that a trapdoor was built in DES by NSA, the feasibility of this machine shows that a trapdoor was not needed in order to break it. Old RAM technology allowed to design similar (or larger) machines which break less keys (e.g. thirtytwo thousand keys). This attack can be avoided if the users of DES use the CFB one byte mode appropriately, or use new modes,[†] or triple encryption with two different keys. DES-like algorithms can be designed which are more secure against the described attack and which use a key of only 48 bit, and which have the same encryption/decryption speed as DES (if used with fixed key).[‡] The protection of the authenticity of (e.g. short) messages with DES is sometimes insecure.[§] These results combined with the above one, shows that the authentication of standardized messages with DES may be worthless. Remark finally that the DES chip used in this machine does not use the state of the art of VLSI. Indeed about only 10,000 transistors are used in it. Megabits RAMs are easily available.

# *Conclusion*

Every important company or secret agency over the world can easily build such a machine. Because it is not excluded that such machines are already in use by these organizations, the author advises the users to be careful using DES. Because the most used modes are breakable, the users have to modify their hard- or software in a mode which avoids this attack. Meanwhile only low-sensitive information can be transmitted with DES. If the authenticity of the messages is protected with DES under its standardized use, short messages have to be enlarged.

---

* Desmedt, Y., "Optimizations and variants of exhaustive key search machines breaking millions of DES keys and their consequences on the security of privacy and authenticity with DES", Internal Report, ESAT Laboratory, Katholieke Universiteit Leuven, in preparation.

† Quisquater, J.-J., Philips Research Laboratory, Brussels, paper in preparation.

‡ Quisquater, J.-J., Desmedt, Y., and Davio, M.: "A secure DES* scheme with < 48 bit keys", presented at the rump session at Crypto '85, Santa Barbara, August, 1985

§ Desmedt, Y.: "Unconditionally secure authentication schemes and practical and theoretical consequences", presented at Crypto '85, Santa Barbara, August, 1985, to appear in the proceedings: Advances in Cryptology (Springer-Verlag, Berlin, 1986).

# *Acknowledgement*

The author is sponsored by the Belgian NFWO. The author is very grateful to F. Hoornaert, IMEC-ESAT, Leuven, and J.-J. Quisquater, Philips Research Laboratory, Brussels, for many suggestions and improvements.

Y.Desmedt
ESAT Laboratory
Katholieke Universiteit Leuven
Kard. Mercierlaan 94
B-3030 Heverlee, Belgium

# 10

# *Architectural Considerations for Cryptanalytic Hardware*

Ian Goldberg and David Wagner
[iang,daw]@cs.berkeley.edu

*This paper was written in Spring 1996. Its performance numbers are several years out of date, and it used what hardware was handy, rather than the best possible hardware for its time. Still, results based on actually building working devices are preferable to much better theories about reality.*

## Abstract

We examine issues in high-performance cryptanalysis, focusing on the use of programmable logic. Several standard techniques from computer architecture are adapted and applied to this application. We present performance measurements for RC4, A5, DES, and CDMF; these measurements were taken from actual implementations. We conclude by estimating the resources needed to break these encryption algorithms.

## Introduction

Large-scale open electronic communications networks are spreading: for example, mobile computing is on the rise, the Internet is experiencing exponential growth, and electronic commerice is a hot topic. With these advances comes a need for robust security mechanisms, and they in turn depend critically on cryptographic protection. At the same time, computer power has been growing at dizzying rates, matching or exceeding Moore's Law. Therefore, in this rapidly changing environment, it is important to assess the strength of deployed encryption algorithms against the tremendous computational power available to potential adversaries.

The best attacks on today's symmetric-key encryption algorithms simply apply massive computing resources to break their security by pure brute force. If a cryptographic algorithm is secure, it will be far too expensive for an attacker to gather the processing power necessary for such a brute-force cryptanalytic attack to succeed. Assessing the security of a cryptographic algorithm against this threat, then, involves surveying the state of the art in cryptanalytic computational power and estimating the investment required to mount this type of attack.

This paper explores the use of programmable logic hardware devices in cryptanalytic applications. Programmable logic attempts to provide much of the premier performance available from custom hardware, while partially retaining the reconfigurability and ease of development benefits found in software.

Our research draws heavily on the computer architecture field. Surprisingly, many techniques, tools, and models for the design of general-purpose processors also proved useful in the specialized domain of cryptanalytic hardware. We investigate the benefits of various forms of parallelism, including pipelining and superscalar architectures. We also examine and identify critical structural hazards and data hazards, as well as the crucial performance bottlenecks. This paper focuses especially on an analogue of the central "CPU time" formula from [20]. By framing the problem from the perspective of system architects, we were able to take advantage of the extensive knowledge base available in the architecture literature.

This paper is organized as follows. The section "Motivation" elaborates on the need for estimates of the performance of cryptanalytic hardware, and the section "Related Work" lists previous work which touches on this project and influenced our approach. Next, the the section "Technical Approach" introduces our experimental methodology and goals. The section "Design and Analysis" describes our design, implementation, and data in depth, providing a detailed technical analysis. Finally, the section "Future" briefly identifies some areas for future research, and the "Conclusion" concludes the paper.

# *Motivation*

There is currently a strong need for a solid assessment of the resources required to break the common cryptographic algorithms. This information is a crucial data point for system designers—they need this information to determine which encryption algorithm is appropriate for their system. The need is only intensifying: weak encryption is becoming the norm, earlier assessments are either incomplete or out-of-date, and steady increases in computing power are threatening the viability of these weak encryption systems.

Security is little more than economics. A cryptographic system is secure when it costs more to break it than the data it is protecting is worth. Accordingly, determining the strength of an encryption algorithm comes down to measuring the cost of the cryptanalytic resources needed to break the system. That explains the basic need for an evaluation of the cryptanalytic performance possible today.

In fact, several recent factors make the need more urgent. Weak encryption is being widely deployed. SSL with 40-bit RC4 is becoming a de facto standard for secure Web channels, largely because of Netscape's support. GSM, a European mobile telephony system, depends for its link-layer security on A5, an apparently weakened algorithm. Export restrictions are largely to blame for the recent preponderance of weak encryption algorithms; they are an unfortunate fact of life at the moment. This intensifies the need for accurate estimates of the true protection these cryptographic algorithms offer. For extremely strong algorithms, it is sufficient to provide order-of-magnitude estimates to show that breaking these algorithms requires absurd collections of resources; but when it is feasible (or barely feasible) to break an encryption algorithm, it becomes extremely important to pinpoint the cost of cryptanalysis accurately.

The section entitled "Related Work" lists several earlier algorithm assessments. DES has received by far the most attention, but we are also greatly interested in the (today all-too-common) case of exportable encryption algorithms. Most of the experience with weak encryption systems has been with software cryptanalysis; yet programmable logic may be the most cost-effective method of assembling computational power for this problem. A recent paper [4] did briefly address the cost-effectiveness of programmable logic, but their estimate appears to be based on flawed assumptions. The one work which investigated the problem most closely [22] was a good start, but it didn't go far enough: their estimates were based on theoretical calculations, instead of real implementations and measurements.

Therefore, there is new ground to cover, and previous work to validate. We will explore the applicability and performance of programmable logic to cryptanalysis of A5, DES, CDMF, and RC4. This paper attempts to provide a solid, rigorous assessment of the economics of cryptanalysis, relying on actual implementations and experimental measurements.

# *Related work*

Previous exploration into exhaustive keysearch has tended to concentrate on either software implementations or custom hardware designs; not much has been reported on FPGA (programmable logic) architectures. We will survey the results available in the open literature.

The first public brute-force cryptanalysis of 40-bit exportable RC4 appeared from the Internet cypherpunks community. (The NSA (National Security Agency) had almost certainly mounted an exhaustive 40-bit search of RC4 long before that, but they're playing their cards close to their chest.) The cypherpunks are a loose-knit community dedicated to exploring the social ramifications of cryptography. To demonstrate the need for more secure encryption, Hal Finney challenged his fellow cypherpunks to break 40-bit RC4 [16]. Soon Adam Back, David Byers, and Eric Young announced [3] that they had successfully searched the 40-bit keyspace with a software implementation running on the idle cycles of several workstations. At the same time, Damien Doligez had also independently finished a succesful sweep of the RC4 40-bit keys [12], with the same software implementation. Not long later, Piete Brooks, Adam Back, Andrew Roos, and Andy Brown organized a distributed effort [5] which used donated idle cycles from many machines across the Internet to finish a second challenge in 31 hours, again using a similar software implementation. The cypherpunks efforts gave us a fairly accurate estimate of the complexity of exhaustively searching the RC4 40-bit keyspace in software.

There have been no reports of any experience with exhaustive keysearch of A5 in the open literature. The details of the A5 algorithm were only recently revealed to the public [1], so it is perhaps not surprising that it has received less attention. Several cryptographers' initial reaction was that there must be a trivial brute-force attack on A5 requiring $2^{40}$ operations [26],[[1] No such attack ever materialized, and it became clear that the matter was not so trivial as initially imagined [26],[2]. The current consensus appears to be that A5's strength is possibly somewhat more than a 40-bit cipher but less than its 64-bit key might indicate.

There have not been any reports on CDMF exhaustive keysearch in the literature, either. On the other hand, CDMF is very similar to DES—it is essentially DES with a reduced 40-bit keylength—so all the research into understanding DES keysearch will apply immediately to CDMF. As we shall see, there has been extensive work examining DES brute-force cryptanalysis.

There have been many studies into the economics of a DES keysearch implementation in custom hardware. (No one has seriously proposed breaking DES via software, as general-purpose computers are orders of magnitude slower at this task than specialized hardware.) The earliest estimate came not long after DES was ratified as a national standard. Whit Diffie and Martin Hellman designed a system containing a large number of custom-designed chips [11]. They estimated that their $20 million architecture could recover a DES key each day. After their paper appeared, great controversy ensued. Some argued that the mean time between failures would be inherently so small that the machine could never work; Diffie and Hellman refuted these objections, although they also increased their cost estimate somewhat [27], p.283. After the controversy died down, the final estimate was that DES would be insecure by the year 1990 [19]. A later paper suggested that a $1 million custom-designed hardware architecture could break DES in 9 days with technology forecasted to be available by 1995 [18]. Another more recent estimate took advantage of an extremely fast DES chip (designed for normal cryptographic use, not cryptanalysis), concluding that a $1 million assembly could search the DES key space in 8 days [31],[13],[14]. Yet another study examined the feasibility of using existing general-purpose content-addressable processors, and concluded that a DES keysearch would take 30 days on them with a $1 million investment [30] Even more writing on the subject of hardware DES keysearch can be found in [25], and some issues in DES chip design can be found in [21,[15],[6].

All these estimates were superseded by a compelling 1993 paper [31] from Michael Wiener. He went to the effort of assembling a very comprehensive design (extending for a hefty 42 pages!) of a custom-hardware DES keysearch machine, including low-level chip schematics as well as detailed plans for controllers and shelving. After a $0.5 million investment to design the machine and $1 million to build it, a DES key could be recovered each 3.5 hours, he argued. (Note the large development cost. This is a unique attribute of custom hardware designs.) His work has remained the definitive estimate of DES keysearch cost since then. On the other hand, we have seen 3 years of steady progress in chip performance and cost since then, and Moore's law remains as true as ever, so Wiener's figures should be adjusted downward accordingly.

This year an ad-hoc group of experts was convened to recommend appropriate cryptographic key lengths for corporate security; their report [4] was very influential. In this larger context, they very briefly surveyed the application of software, reconfigurable logic, and custom hardware to the brute-force cryptanalysis of 40-bit RC4 and (56-bit) DES. We are a bit skeptical about the precise performance predicted for an RC4-cracking chip: they claimed that a single $400 FPGA ought to be able to recover a 40-bit RC4 key in five hours. (Amortizing this over many keysearchs, they determined that each keysearch would cost $0.08, causing some to refer to 40-bit RC4 as "8-cent encryption".) This estimate seems extremely optimistic, as it would require 30 million key trials per second; RC4 key setup requires at least 1024 serialized operations (256 iterations of a loop, with 4 memory accesses and calculations per iteration), so this would represent a throughput of 30 billion operations per second. Even with a dozen parallel independent keysearch engines operating on the chip (which would require serious hardware resources), this would imply clock rates measured in Gigahertz—a rather unlikely scenario! Accordingly, our skepticism helped motivate us to attempt an independent investigation of these issues.

At the other extreme, we are also concerned about gross overestimates of the security of RC4. After several cypherpunks folks demonstrated how easy it is to cryptanalyze RC4 with the idle cycles of general-purpose computers, Netscape had to respond. Their note made several good points—for instance, that export controls were to blame, leaving them no choice but to use weak encryption—but their estimate of the cost of breaking 40-bit RC4 was greatly flawed. The first successful keysearch used idle cycles on 120 workstations for 8 days. Netscape claimed that this was $10,000 worth of computing power, concluding that messages worth less than $10,000 can be safely protected with 40-bit RC4 encryption [9]. Exposing the invalidity of this estimate was another motivating force for us.

One unpublished work [22] has studied in depth the relevance of reconfigurable logic to cryptologic applications. They assessed the complexity of a keysearch of DES and RC4 (as well as many other non-cryptanalytic problems). The main weakness of this aspect of their survey is that several of the estimates relied on theoretical predictions instead of real implementations and experimental measurements. In this paper, we attempt to give more rigorous estimates, paying attention to the architectural and economic issues facing these cryptanalytic applications.

# Technical Approach

## Workloads and Architectures

As we have explained earlier, there is much interest in the security of cryptographic algorithms. The algorithms with short keys (such as A5, RC4, CDMF, and DES) are the most interesting to examine, as their security depends intimately on the state-of-the-art in high-performance computing. Therefore, we concentrate on algorithms to break A5, RC4, CDMF, and DES.

Software implementations running on general-purpose microcomputers have received perhaps the most attention [3],[12],[5]. To achieve maximum performance, though, we must also consider the tradeoffs associated with customizable hardware. We will focus mainly on hardware implementations of cryptanalytic algorithms; we then compare the tradeoffs between the hardware and software approaches.

The most specialized approach involves using ASICs: custom-designed hardware, specially tailored to one particular cryptanalytic application. They require a significant initial investment for design and testing; they also must be produced in mass quantity for them to be economical. Therefore, while probably the most efficient approach for a dedicated cryptanalytic application, ASICs require such a large investment that they are probably only of interest to small governments or large corporations—they are certainly not within reach for a class project!

Fortunately, there is a middle ground between ASICs and software. CPLDs (Complex Programmable Logic Devices) provide reconfigurable logic; they are commercially available at low prices. They provide the performance benefits of customizable hardware in small volume at a more reasonable price. We obtained access to a set of Altera FLEX8000 series programmable logic devices—more specifically, 81188GC232 chips.* These are mounted on a RIPP10 board, which can accomodate up to eight FLEX8000 chips and four 128KB SRAM memory chips.

Therefore, the primary platform of interest was the RIPP10 board with FLEX8000 chips; for comparison purposes, we also investigated several other programmable logic devices, as well as software-driven implementations. The workload consisted of brute-force cryptanalytic applications for RC4, A5, DES, and CDMF.

## The Figure of Merit

It is important to keep in mind what quantities we are trying to measure. Regardless of whether the methodology involves real implementations or synthetic simulations, the ultimate figure of merit is the performance-cost ratio.

Why is the performance-cost ratio the relevant quantity? In general, our cryptanalytic applications are characterized by extreme suitability to parallelization: the process of exhaustive search over many keys can be broken into many independent small computations without penalty. One fast machine will finish the computation in exactly the same time as two machines which are twice as slow. Therefore, the relevant criterion is the "bang-to-buck" ratio, or more precisely, the numbers of trial keys searched per second per dollar.

## Methodology

We used several methods to understand the architectural tradeoffs and their effect on cryptanalytic applications. We first implemented a few sample cryptanalytic algorithms and directly measured their performance on real workloads and actual architectures. Direct measurement is obviously the most desirable experimental technique; unfortunately, we do not have access to every system in existence. Therefore, to forecast the behavior on other platforms, we also used several simulation tools. In both cases, we examine actual applications and real systems.

---

\* We greatly appreciate the kind support of Bruce Koball and Eric Hughes!

## Direct measurement

Doing direct measurements on real systems running real applications is conceptually straightforward (but still labor-intensive in practice!). First, we directly implemented the relevant cryptanalytic algorithms for the Altera FLEX8000 platform. Once this is done, it is easy to do several small time trials to measure performance. Finally, we used technical data sheets [8] and price lists [7],[24] from Altera to assess the cost of the system.

We also implemented the applications in software. Measuring performance is easy; fixing a price on the computation is a bit less straightforward, and we will address that in a later section.

## Simulations

It would be valuable to obtain measurements for a variety of CPLD architectures. As we only have access to the Altera RIPP10 board and FLEX8000 81188GC232 chips, the experimental procedure becomes a bit more involved. Fortunately, our development environment offers compilation, simulation, and timing analysis tools for several programmable logic devices. We therefore compiled the applications for several other chips and calculated predicted performance estimates with the simulation tools.

An important step for any simulation technique is to validate the simulation process. Accordingly, we applied the same simulation and timing analysis procedure to our applications for the FLEX8000 81188GC232; comparing the performance estimates from the simulation with the direct measurements lets us validate our experimental methodology.

# Design and Analysis

## Overview

We begin by setting up a model for analysis and describing several design issues that are common to all cryptanalytic hardware.

For this project, we are assuming the "known plaintext" model of cryptanalysis. In this model, an adversary has an encrypted message (the *ciphertext*), and also a small amount of the original message (the *known plaintext*). He also knows what part of the ciphertext corresponds to the known plaintext. The goal of the adversary is to determine the key necessary to decrypt the ciphertext into the known plaintext. He can then use this key to decrypt the rest of the encrypted message.

Other models of cryptanalysis, such as "ciphertext only" or "probabilistic plaintext" [29] are more complicated to use, but do not require an adversary to have specific knowledge of part of the original message. However, as most messages have some well-known parts (a From header in a mail message, for example), the known plaintext model turns out to be applicable to almost all situations.

For a cryptographic algorithm to be considered secure, there must be no way to determine the decryption key which is faster than just trying every possible key, and seeing which one works (note that this is a necessary, but not sufficient, condition). This method is called *brute force*.

Breaking a cryptographic algorithm by brute force involves the following steps:

For each key in the keyspace

* Perform key setup

* Decrypt the ciphertext and compare it to the known plaintext

As will be seen below, different algorithms spend different amounts of time in the two steps. (For instance, *stream ciphers*—which generate output one bit at a time—allow us to prune incorrect key guesses very rapidly—while *block ciphers*—which operate on a block at a time—require us to generate the entire output block before any comparison is possible. DES and CDMF are block ciphers; A5 and RC4 are stream ciphers.)

We measure the expected number of cycles for each of the two steps for each key, and add them to determine a *Cycles per Key*, or *CPK* value for the algorithm.

Similar to the formula for CPU time found in [20]:

$$\text{CPU time} = \text{Instruction Count} \times \text{CPI} \times \text{Clock cycle time}$$

we have a formula for brute-force searching a keyspace:

$$\text{Search time} = \text{Keys to check} \times \text{CPK} \times \text{Clock cycle time}$$

As with the [20] equation, we ignore CPU time. This is valid because we take care to avoid I/O as much as possible. Cryptanalytic applications are typically compute-bound, so this is an important optimization.

In the above formula, "Keys to check" indicates the number of keys to search; this can simply be the total number of keys that can be used with the algorithm, or, in the event that many chips are being used to simultaneously search the keyspace, it can be some fraction thereof.

"CPK", as described above, is defined to be "KeySetup + Comparison". "KeySetup" is the number of cycles required to load a key into the algorithm's internal data structures, so that the key search engine is ready to produce output. "Comparison" is the expected number of cycles required for the algorithm to produce enough output so that it can be determined whether the key is the correct one. Note that different algorithms divide their time differently between these two parts, as will be seen in more detail below.

"Clock cycle time" is exactly what one would expect; algorithms that attempt to do more complicated work in one cycle will tend to have a higher clock cycle time. This is also the factor that will vary most when using different models of hardware, as faster (more expensive?) chips have smaller gate delays. One important design feature common to all brute-forcing algorithms also affects this factor: how does one cycle through all of the keys in the keyspace? The obvious solution (to simply start at 0, and increment until the correct key is found) turns out to be a bad one, as incrementing a number of even 8 bits causes unacceptably large gate delays in propagating the carry. Tricks such as carry-save arithmetic [20] are usually not useful here, because keys are usually not used by the encryption algorithms as numbers, but rather, as bit strings.

A better solution [31], which uses the fact that the keys need not be checked in sequential order, is to use a *linear feedback shift register* [27], or *LFSR*. An LFSR is a register that can either be *loaded* (to set the register's value), or have its existing value *shifted* (in order to output 1 bit, and to change the register's value). Of the two styles of LFSR, the usual style is called a *Fibonacci LFSR*. To shift a Fibonacci LFSR, simply copy each bit to its neighbor on the right. The original rightmost bit is considered the output. The bit that is shifted in at the left is the parity of some specific subset of the bits (the *taps*) of the register (see Figure 10–1.

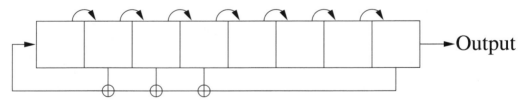

*Figure 10–1: Fibonacci LFSR*

The most important properties of an LFSR are that it has a low (constant) gate delay, and more importantly, if the taps are chosen properly, repeated shifting (starting with any non-zero value) will cycle through every possible non-zero value of the register.

The other style of LFSR is called a *Galois LFSR*, which has the same properties as the Fibonacci LFSR, but is shifted differently. To shift a Galois LFSR, copy each bit to its neighbor on the right, except for the taps, for which the rightmost bit of the register is XOR'd in before the copy is done. The bit that is shifted in at the left is the original rightmost bit, which is also considered the output (see Figure 10–2). The advantage of a Galois LFSR over a Fibonacci LFSR when being implemented in hardware is that a Galois LFSR usually has an even lower gate delay than a

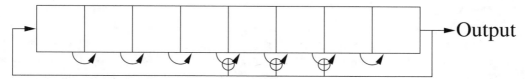

*Figure 10-2: Galois LFSR*

Fibonacci LFSR, resulting in a potentially lower clock cycle time. For this reason, Galois LFSRs are usually used to cycle through the list of possible keys.

In order to take advantage of parallelism, one must be able to distribute the keyspace equitably among the multiple hardware devices. Standard mathematical techniques allow us to easily calculate the value of the shift register after any given number of shifts. From this, we can determine evenly separated starting positions for each device in the search engine.

We will now describe the design issues and analysis that were performed when we implemented various encryption algorithms in programmable logic.

## A5

A5 [1] is the encryption algorithm used in GSM, the European standard for digital cellular telephones. It consists of three Fibonacci LFSRs of sizes 19, 22, and 23 respectively, which are initially loaded with the contents of the 64-bit key. The middle bits of all three LFSRs are examined at each clock cycle to determine which registers shift and which do not (at least two of the three registers shift in each clock cycle). The parity of the high bits of the LFSRs is output after each shift, and this output bitstream is XOR'd with the ciphertext to recover the original message.

This algorithm is quite well-suited for implementation in hardware due to the simplicity of LFSRs; given that it was designed for use in cellular phones, in which limited resources are available, this should not be surprising. The simplicity of the algorithm leaves almost no room for creativity to the implementer.

The resource requirements for A5 are quite minimal; they consist mainly of the 64 flipflops that make up the three LFSRs. In this algorithm, the key setup time is trivial (a single cycle to load the LFSRs with their initial state); the majority of the algorithm consists of comparing the output of the generator (which comes out at a rate of 1 bit per cycle) to the expected output. Since incorrect keys produce essentially random data, the expected number of bits we need to check before rejecting a key is 2. Thus, the total number of cycles per key for A5 is CPK = KeySetup + Comparison = 1 + 2 = 3.

# RC4

RC4 [27] is the encryption algorithm used in, among other things, the Secure Sockets Layer (SSL) protocol [17] used by Netscape and other World Wide Web browsers to transmit encrypted information (such as banking transactions) over the Internet. RC4 is quite a simple algorithm; start with a 256-byte read-only array K that stores the key (repeat the key as often as necessary to fill K), a 256-byte random-access array S, and two 8-bit registers i and j.

To do key setup, start with $j=0$, and do:

```
for i = 0 to 255:
    S[i] = i
for i = 0 to 255:
    j = (j + S[i] + K[i]) mod 256
    swap S[i] and S[j]
```

Once the key setup is complete, set $i=j=0$, and to generate each byte, do:

```
i = (i + 1) mod 256
j = (j + S[i]) mod 256
swap S[i] and S[j]
output S[(S[i] + S[j]) mod 256]
```

The sequence of bytes outputted is XOR'd with the ciphertext to recover the original message.

SSL, one common system that uses RC4, has a small added complexity. Instead of the key being copied into the array K, as described above, it is first processed by the MD5 hash function; the result of the MD5 computation is then copied into K. Our design and analysis does not include MD5, which is quite large, complicated, and includes many 32-bit additions, so readers hoping to break SSL should keep in mind that their performance will be substantially worse than that determined below.

The resource requirements for RC4 are considerable. Most notably, it requires 258 bytes of state (compare 8 bytes of state for A5), 256 bytes of which need to be accessed randomly. Such resources were beyond the capabilities of the programmable logic chips we had available, but fortunately the board on which the logic chips were mounted had 128KB of SRAM accessible to the logic chips via a bus; we stored the array S in this SRAM. Note that the key array K is accessed in a predictable order, so it was not necessary to store it in the SRAM.

Unfortunately, when trying to produce intstruction-level parallelism in the algorithm, the single port to the SRAM becomes a structural hazard. For this reason, it was necessary to serialize accesses to this SRAM. Initially, we expected that going off-chip to access the SRAM would be the bottleneck that determined the minimum clock cycle time; the section entitled "Analysis" below shows that we were incorrect.

We now calculate the "Cycles per Key" value for RC4. Examining the key setup code, it is clear that the first loop requires 1 cycle to initialize i to 0, and 256 cycles to complete, and each iteration of the second loop requires 4 cycles (1 each to read and write S[i] and S[j]), for a total key setup time of 1281 cycles.

Similarly, each byte of output requires 5 cycles to produce (1 each to read and write S[i] and S[j], and 1 to read S[(S[i] + S[j]) mod 256]. The expected number of bytes needed to determine whether the guessed key is correct is:

$$(1 - \frac{1}{256})^{-1} < 1.004$$

so the value of "Comparison" is very near 5. Thus we calculate the total Cycles per Key to be CPK = KeySetup + Comparison = 1281 + 5 = 1286.

## DES and CDMF

DES is the national Data Encryption Standard; it enjoys widespread use by the banking industry, as well as being one of the preferred algorithms for securing electronic communications. DES transforms a 64 bit input block into a 64 bit output by a reversible function which depends on the 56 bit key in a highly non-linear way.

The DES algorithm was designed primarily for efficiency in hardware, and thus has several distinguishing features worth noting. It consists of an initial and final permutation and 16 rounds of main processing, with each round transforming the input bits via a "mix-and-mash" process. Bit permutations are used extensively; of course, they are trivial to do in hardware by simply reordering wires. Each round also contains 8 different "Substitution" boxes (or S-boxes for short); the S-boxes are non-linear functions which map 6 input bits to 4 output bits. S-boxes are not very resource-intensive in hardware: they can be implemented as four 6-input boolean functions, and their small size keeps the gate count reasonable. The key is stored in a shift register, rotated before each round, and exclusive-or-ed into the block during each round. This is also straightforward to implement in hardware.

CDMF (Commercial Data Masking Facility) [23] is a related algorithm which uses DES as the underlying transformation; the only difference is that it weakens the key to meet US export restrictions. CDMF has an effective 40-bit keylength, which is then expanded to a 56 bit DES key by using another DES transformation. Loading a CDMF key requires one initial DES operation, and transforming each 64 bit block requires one DES operation. Therefore an implementation of a DES keysearch application leads easily to a CDMF keysearch engine with half the search rate.

Our DES implementation was forced to be rather minimal to fit in the limited resources available on our chip. We implemented one round of DES, with the appropriate S-boxes and bit permutations. Some extra flip-flops and a state machine allow us to iterate the round function 16 times; there was not sufficient space (i.e. logic gates) available to implement 16 instantiations of each S-box.

The S-boxes are perhaps the most critical component, and we tried several different implementation approaches for them. One natural way to describe each S-box is as a 64-entry lookup table containing 4 bit entries. This might be a good choice if the chip had contained some user-configurable ROM; ours didn't. A similar approach takes advantage of the compiler support for "case" statements, which gets translated into a hardware structure containing a 64-line demultiplexor and or gates expressing the relevant minterms. This structure minimizes gate delay at the expense of space resources. In fact, this structure increased the gate requirements significantly, to the point where the 8 S-boxes alone required more hardware resources than our overworked chip had to offer. The compiler was not particularly helpful at doing space-time tradeoffs to minimize the space requirements, so we ended up optimizing the S-box functions by hand.

The manual optimization we settled on can be viewed as a form of speculative execution. First, note that it suffices to describe how to compute the 6-bit to 1-bit boolean function that calculates one output bit of some S-box. Since the S-boxes behave roughly like they were chosen at random, we don't expect to find any structure in the outputs—i.e. each output will be an uncorrelated non-linear function of the inputs—so this is roughly optimal. To compute such a 6-to-1 function, we first isolate 2 of the 6 input bits as control bits. We do speculative execution with four functional cells; each cell computes the output of the 6-to-1 function under a speculative assumption about the 2 control bits. As there are four possible values of the control bits, the four functional cells enumerate all possibilities. At the same time the functional cells are computing their 4-to-1 function, a multiplexor unit concurrently selects one of the functional cells. The calculation of the 6-to-1 function via speculative execution is depicted in Figure 10-3. This choice of S-box implementation structure is tailored to our Altera FLEX8000 chips: these chips are organized as an array of logic cells, where each logic cell can compute an arbitrary (configurable) 4-to-1 boolean function. For chips with a different organization, some other manual optimization might be more appropriate.

The "Search time" equation for our CDMF implementation is not hard to analyze. One can easily count the CPK by direct inspection of our implementation. We have a finite state machine with 4 states, labelled from **a** to **d**. The cycle-by-cycle breakdown of the "KeySetup" time for one CDMF encryption is as follows:

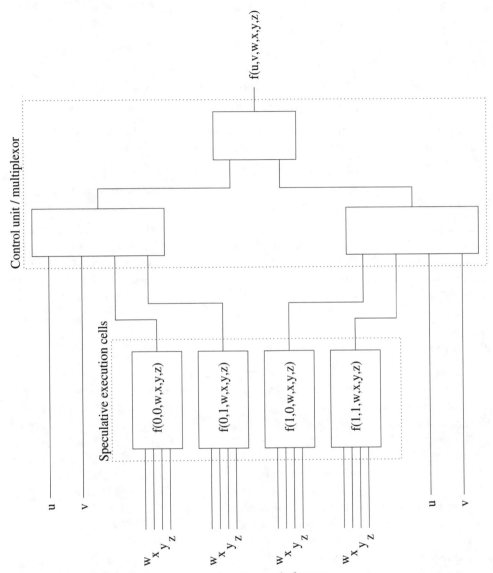

*Figure 10-3: Calculation of a boolean function with 6 inputs*

a. 1 cycle to increment the key and load in the 40-bit CDMF trial key

b. 1 cycle to perform the DES input permutation

c. 16 cycles to perform 16 rounds of encryption

d. 1 cycle to perform the DES final permutation and load in the 64 bit plaintext block

We can see that the "KeySetup" time is 19 cycles. An enumeration of the output generation and comparison stage yields

a. 1 cycle to perform the DES input permutation

b. 16 cycles to perform 16 rounds of encryption

c. 1 cycle to perform the DES final permutation, compare the ciphertext block to the expected value, and return to state **a** if this trial key was incorrect

This means that the "Comparison" time is 18 cycles, so the total CPK is 19+18 = 37. Note that DES encrypts the entire 64 bit block at once, unlike a stream cipher, so we check all of the output bits in parallel.

The hardware resources required by CDMF are reasonable but non-negligible for commercial CPLDs. Our minimal implementation required (the equivalent of) roughly 10000 gates. This is certainly within reach for many newer commercial CPLDs, although there are also many older or less expensive CPLDs which cannot handle the requirements. It is important to keep the entire keysearch engine on one chip; otherwise, inter-chip I/O will severely limit performance.

## *Analysis*

We cross-compiled our cryptanalysis implementations for many different Altera CPLDs, and ran a simulation and timing analysis to measure the maximum applicable clock cycle time. The results are plotted in Figure 10–4 for CDMF, Figure 10–5 for A5, and Figure 10–6 for RC4. Some explanation is in order, as there are a lot of data summarized there. The chip specification (e.g. 81188GC232-3) can be dissected as follows: the 81188 refers to the general family, the 232 specifies a 232-pin package, and the -3 refers to the speed grade (lower numbers are faster). The 81500 is the top of the line Altera FLEX8000 device; the 81188 is a bit less powerful. Chips without the "A" designation were fabricated with an older .8 micron process; the "A" indicates chips that were manufactured with a newer, faster .6 micron process. The figure shows throughput graphed against the initial investment required; the chips with the best performance-to-cost (Y/X) ratio are the best buy. The prices are taken from a very recent Altera price list [7],[24]. As there are discounts in large quantities, we have plotted price points for small quantities with a red line and for large batches with a blue line.

We also measured the performance for the 81188GC232-3 chip directly—it is the only one we had access to. Our measurements agreed closely with the simulated timing analysis, confirming the validity of our experimental methodology.

Measurements for DES are not listed. Nonetheless, they track the CDMF performance figures very closely. CDMF consists of two DES encryptions—one for key setup, and one for output generation—with very little overhead. The DES key-search rates can be derived from Figure 10–4 by simply doubling the CDMF rate. Also, remember that the DES keyspace is $2^{16}$ times as large. Our data indicate that if one wanted a machine which could perform a DES keysearch in a year on average, it would suffice to spend $45,000 to buy 600 of the Altera 81500ARC240-4 CPLDs. (This is a very rough estimate, which does not include overhead such as mounting shelves, etc.)

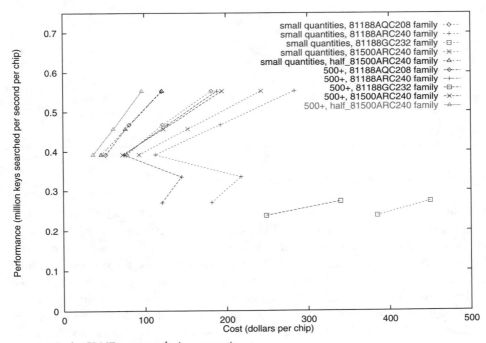

*Figure 10–4: CDMF cryptanalysis economics*

One can note several interesting things from the graph. First, examine the peculiar zig-zag nature of the 81188ARC240 lines. The points are plotted in order of the chip's rated speed grade, from A-6 on the bottom to A-2 on the top. The strange "zag" occurs because the price for a faster A-4 chip drops significantly below the price for the slower A-5. Altera specifies the A-4, A-3, and A-2 as their "preferred" grades for that chip, presumably because there is more sales volume for those speed grades. If you were to build a keysearch engine out of 81188ARC240 chips, you should try to be right at the "hump"—the A-4 speed grade is the best buy for that chip.

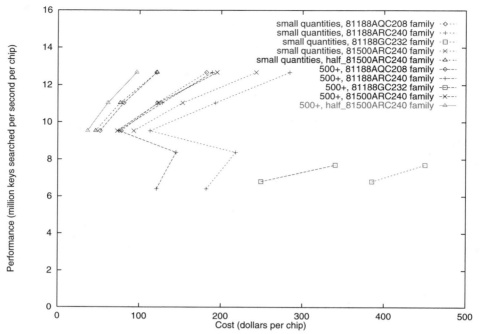

*Figure 10–5: A5 Cryptanalysis Economics*

We have not yet explained the two leftmost dotted lines. The 81500 line of chips contains more hardware resources than the 81188—1296 instead of 1008 "logic elements"—and this extra space should be taken into account when comparing hardware devices. With our A5 and CDMF implementations, there is quite a bit of space left over on the 81500 chip, as it turns out. Therefore, it is natural to ask whether two independent key trial engines might fit on the same chip. We believe (from close examination of the resource usage) that, with A5 and CDMF, there are sufficient hardware resources on the 81500 to support two superscalar keysearch operations. (It would admittedly be a tight fit.) Because of time pressures, we have not actually implemented this. RC4 requires, it seems, too many resources (mainly flip-flops for internal state) to use this strategy. There would be other difficulties with RC4, anyhow—one would probably need a dual-ported SRAM, or two SRAM chips attached to the CPLD (as discussed below).

One might wonder why we proposed taking advantage of extra hardware resources with a multiple-issue architecture, instead of using (say) advanced pipelining techniques. It is worthwhile to recall why advanced pipelining techniques were developed. On a traditional general-purpose computer, programs are typically serialized so highly that if one were to implement several independent simple processors on the same chip, there simply would not be enough tasks to

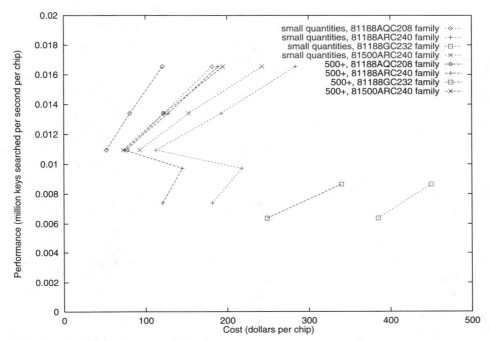

*Figure 10-6: RC4 Cryptanalysis economics*

keep the co-processors busy with useful work. Architects have been blessed with plentiful hardware resources and cursed with the need to speed up single-instruction-stream uniprocessors; this explains the proliferation of sophisticated pipelining methods. (Of course, pipelining does not provide linear speedup with linear increases in hardware resources, like parallelism would, but it is better than nothing!) We are faced with an entirely different situation here. Our cryptanalytic applications encourage virtually unlimited parallelism, so there is no need to look to sophisticated caching schemes for speeds. Achieving parallelism via a superscalar architecture is both simpler and more effective for our purposes.

The projected performance for parallelized 81500 A5 and CDMF keysearch is indicated on the plots with a green and block dotted line, labelled "half_81500ARC240 family", with the unit price halved to indicate its factor-of-two multiple-issue nature. (We could have doubled the performance instead, but that would have made the graph harder to read, so for ease of comprehension and comparison we chose to halve the cost instead.)

We discussed in class why the future of high-performance computing lies in massively-parallel collections of low-end processors (say, Pentiums), instead of in specialized advanced CPUs. One major reason is that Pentium processors are sold in such large quantities that tremendous economies of scale apply, and specialized processors simply cannot compete with the low-end's ever-increasing perfor-mance-cost ratio. We can see that an analogous situation applies here as well. The graphs show that, for our applications, upgrading to a higher speed grade is almost never worth the increased cost. (Two notable exceptions—the "hump" in the 81188ARC240 plot, and the benefits of using a 81500 with enough hardware resources to implement two keysearch engines on-chip—have already been dis-cussed.) Within each family, the least expensive chip turns out to yield the best performance-to-cost ratio; spending twice as much money on a higher-grade chip in the family never results in twice the performance. On the other hand, upgrading to a more recent "A" designated family—one fabricated with a newer .6 micron process—is a worthwhile move. Altera has listed the "A" chips as their preferred technology, and presumably there is more sales volume for devices on their pre-ferred list (though it might be hard to separate cause from effect here). These charts don't tell the whole story. Altera is as we write starting to release a new advanced line of reconfigurable logic devices, the FLEX10K architecture. In recom-mending the 81188 and 81500 devices, we gain extra price-performance benefits by staying a bit behind behind the bleeding edge. Exploiting parallelism with low-end devices is a win for our applications.

We have not yet discussed the impact of software in relation to the hardware per-formance measurements. Software is a bit trickier to evaluate and compare to the other measurements, as it is not clear how to compare the price of a software solution to a hardware approach. While hardware devices would typically be pur-chased with one application in mind, often a certain amount of idle cycles on gen-eral-purpose computers is available "for free". Nonetheless, software and hardware approaches typically won't be in serious competition: the extra expense of hard-ware is usually not justified until "free" software implementations on general-pur-pose computers are unacceptably slow.

*Table 10–1:　Typical software performance on cryptanalytic applications*

| Algorithm | Keys searched per second |
|---|---|
| RC4 | 21900 |
| CDMF | 29800 |
| DES | 41300 |
| A5 | 355000 |

Table 10–1 lists the performance of brute-force keysearch applications, as mea-sured on a Pentium P100 machine. Of course these figures will vary widely from computer to computer. For example, we estimate that we could perform a dis-tributed RC4 40-bit keysearch in a weekend or so, and a CDMF 40-bit keysearch in about a night or two, by using idle cycles on the hundreds of general-purpose computers we have access to as Berkeley computer science graduate students.

Many other organizations also have large numbers of computers which are idle much of the time. Many employees and students thus have access to spare computational power which may be harnessed for cryptanalysis, at essentially zero cost. Compare this to Netscape's estimate that amassing enough processing power to break 40-bit RC4 would cost roughly $10,000. For much less than this, one could probably convince a starving graduate student to lend out access to the necessary computer account. In any event, if Netscape were willing to pay $10,000 for the amount of computing power required to break 40-bit RC4, some enterprising student could easily form a extremely profitable business model.

Given a distributed system of general-purpose computers, one can easily compute the maximum rate of 40-bit keysearching possible in idle cycles by assuming that most machines are idle at least half of the time and using estimates such as those in Table 10-1; achieving better performance than this calls for hardware. We can see from Table 10-1 that our hardware implementations of CDMF, DES, and A5 keysearch are orders of magnitude faster than software; this is not surprising, as these encryption algorithms were designed for efficiency in hardware.

RC4, by contrast, was designed to run efficiently in software, and indeed, as can be seen by comparing Figure 10-6 and Table 10-1, RC4 performs about twice as well in software than on programmable logic. The primary reasons for the large search time on programmable logic are that RC4 has a large "Cycles per Key" value, and a large "Clock cycle time" value: as seen above, the total CPK for the RC4 algorithm is 1286; far larger than the 3 for A5 or the 37 for CDMF. The large clock cycle time stems from the fact that the algorithm contains a number of register additions; as discussed above, these can produce very large gate delays. Unfortunately, changing the additions to LFSRs (as was done above), or using tricks such as carry-save arithmetic, is not appropriate for RC4, as can be seen by examining the algorithm.

Another blow to implementing RC4 efficiently was the particular hardware architecture we had. The programmable logic devices we used were not large enough to store the necessary 256-byte state array on-chip, so we were forced to store them in the external SRAM. However, the algorithm utilizes the SRAM every cycle, so the number of simultaneous RC4 trials we can compute is limited by the number of ports to SRAM that we have available. Unfortunately, on the RIPP10 programming board, not only is the SRAM single-ported, but each SRAM is shared by *two* logic chips. Thus on a fully-populated board with eight logic chips and four SRAMs, we can only perform four simultaneous RC4 trials. Redesigning the programming board to include a port to SRAM for each simultaneous RC4 trial would save some overhead (wasted space on the board), but would not increase the relatively poor performance to cost ratio shown above.

One advantage of software is that the development process is significantly easier. By reusing code (from cryptographic libraries available on the Internet, for example), we prototyped RC4, A5, CDMF, and DES software keysearch applications in a total time of under an hour. In contrast, our programmable logic design and implementation effort took roughly 4 weeks to complete.

Programmable logic has similar advantages over custom-hardware. Development and design would be still more time-consuming and costly for a custom-hardware approach, such as an ASIC. Furthermore, such an ASIC can only be used for one limited algorithm. Programmable logic is more flexible—the hardware devices can be reused for cryptanalysis of many different encryption algorithms with little extra effort. Apparently AccessData, a business that specializes in recovering lost data (i.e. cryptanalysis) for the corporate and law enforcement industries, prefers programmable logic over custom hardware for exactly these reasons [28].

Let us summarize what the charts recommend to one in need of cryptanalytic computational power. RC4 keysearches appear to be most efficiently performed in general-purpose distributed systems. Performing a single isolated 40-bit CDMF keysearch is perhaps best done with distributed software, if time is not of the essence and there are sufficient general-purpose computational resources easily available. For CDMF and A5 keysearch in anything more than that extremely minimal setting, though, reconfigurable logic is the most appropriate solution of the technologies that we examined. Of the devices we surveyed, the Altera 81500ARC240-4 device is the most appropriate and economical choice for cryptanalytic applications; for instance, a \$15,000 initial investment buys about 200 of these chips, allowing one to perform on average one CDMF keysearch every hour. The cost scales linearly, requiring approximately $10^8$ dollar-seconds for a complete CDMF keysearch; that is, an initial investment of X dollars allows one to search the entire CDMF keyspace in $10^{8/X}$ seconds, while the average time to find a key is half that. In addition, we provisionally estimate that about \$45,000 of CPLD hardware could perform a DES keysearch in a year, as calculated above. Table 10–2 summarizes some of these calculations. It takes into account the economies of scale associated with buying many logic devices, and is based on the average-case (not worst-case) search time; the worst-case figure would be twice as large. No figures for A5 are included, because at the moment, there is no consensus among cryptographers as to the size of the keyspace [26].

*Table 10–2: Estimating the cost of cryptanalysis: a summary*

| Algorithm | Investment for average keysearch time of | | | | Architecture components |
|---|---|---|---|---|---|
| | 1 year | 1 week | 1 day | 1 hour | |
| RC4 | $0 | $0 | - | - | 100 general-purpose computers |
| CDMF | $0 | $0 | - | - | 100 general-purpose computers |
| CDMF | $93 | $93 | $745 | $15,000 | Altera 81500ARC240-4 CPLDs |
| DES | $45,000 | - | - | - | Altera 81500ARC240-4 CPLDs |

# Future work

Due to time and resource limitations, we were only able to examine the Altera FLEX8000 series of programmable logic devices. An obvious extension of this work would be to examine other kinds of devices, such as the new Altera FLEX10K series, or devices from other vendors such as Xylinx. Additionally, it would be worthwhile to examine the technology trends in programmable logic, to determine how they compare to those for general-purpose hardware.

We leave it as an open problem to the reader to actually construct a fully operational DES keysearch engine.

# Conclusions

We found that RC4 cryptanalysis is most effectively implemented in software. Since RC4 was specifically designed for efficiency on general-purpose computers, it is not entirely surprising that programmable logic fares so poorly. We showed that the estimate in [4] (which inspired the term "8-cent encryption" for 40-bit RC4) is over-optimistic and unrealistic. On the other hand, Netscape's $10,000 estimate was far too large.

Programmable logic devices are very efficient at CDMF cryptanalysis. We estimate that an initial investment of $745 buys enough programmable logic to recover one CDMF key each day; this shows that CDMF is practical to break. Moreover, DES is nearly practical to break; a cryptanalytic engine to do a DES keysearch each year can be built with roughly $45,000 of programmable logic.

Several architectural techniques from the design of general-purpose processors were useful in this project. Adding parallelism, identifying structural and data hazards, identifying performance bottlenecks, and other techniques helped maximize the performance of our design. The cryptanalytic analogue to the "CPU time" equation from [20] was surprisingly useful, lending structure to our analysis.

We also identified several important aspects found only with cryptanalytic applications on programmable logic. In this application, superscalar parallelism is more effective than pipelining. Also, register additions can often be a limiting bottleneck for programmable logic—we avoided them where possible, and suffered large performance hits elsewhere.

By considering architectural issues both common to general-purpose processors and unique to programmable logic, we examined the feasability of using commodity logic devices for cryptanalytic applications.

## Acknowledgements

This work would not have been possible without the assistance of a number of people. We would like to thank Eric Hughes and Bruce Koball for providing the hardware and software. We would also like to thank Clive McCarthy and Stephen Smith, both of Altera, for their generous support.

## Availability

This paper, and other related materials, are available on the World Wide Web at `http://www.cs.berkeley.edu/~iang/isaac/hardware/`.

## References

[1] Ross Anderson, A5, June, 1994
Post to `sci.crypt` newsgroup. Available on the Internet as `http://chem.leeds.ac.uk/ICAMS/people/jon/a5.html}`,

[2] Ross Anderson, personal communication, April, 1996

[3] Adam Back, Another SSL breakage . . . , August, 1995
Post to `cypherpunks` mailing list. Available on the Internet as `http://dcs.ex.ac.uk/~aba/ssl/`.

[4] Matt Blaze and Whitfield Diffie and Ronald L. Rivest and Bruce Schneier and Tsutomu Shimomura and Eric Thompson and Michael Wiener, Minimal key lengths for symmetric ciphers to provide adequate commercial security: A report by an ad hoc group of cryptographers and computer scientists, Business Software Alliance, January, 1996
Available on the Internet as `http://www.bsa.org/policy/encryption/cryptographers.html`

[5] Piete Brooks, Hal's second challenge, August, 1995
Available on the Internet as `http://www.brute.cl.cam.ac.uk/brute/`.

[6] Albert G. Broscius and Jonathan M. Smith, "Exploiting Parallelism in Hardware Implementation of the DES," in *Advances in Cryptology: Proceedings of CRYPTO*

*'91*, Springer-Verlag, 1992, pages 367-376

[7] Altera Corporation, Altera components North America price list, May, 1996

[8] Altera Corporation, Altera home page, 1996
Available on the Internet as `http://www.altera.com/`

[9] Netscape Communications Corporation, Key Challenge, 1995
Available on the Internet as `http://www.netscape.com/newsref/std/key_challenge.html`

[10] Wei Dai, Speed benchmarks, 1996
Post to cypherpunks mailing list. Available on the Internet as `http://www.eskimo.com/~weidai/benchmarks.txt`

[11] Whitfield Diffie and Martin E. Hellman, "Exhaustive Cryptanalysis of the NBS Data Encryption Standard, *Computer* 10:6, June, 1997, pages 74-84.

[12] Damien Doligez, SSL challenge—broken, August, 1995
Post to cypherpunks mailing list. Available on the Internet as `http://pauillac.inria.fr/~doligez/ssl/`,

[13] H. Eberle and C. P. Thacker, "A 1 Gbit/second GaAs DES Chip," in *Proceedings of the IEEE 1992 Custom Integrated Circuits Conference*, IEEE, May, 1992, pages 19.7/1—4.

[14] Hans Eberle, A High-Speed DES Implementation for Network Applications, Technical Report 90, DEC SRC, September 1992.

[15] R. C. Fairfield and A. Matusevich and J. Plany, "An LSI Digital Encryption Processor (DEP)," in *Advances in Cryptology: Proceedings of CRYPTO '84*, 1985, Springer-Verlag, pages 115—143

[16] Hal Finney, SSL RC4 Challenge, July, 1995
Post to cypherpunks mailing list. Available on the Internet as `http://www.rain.org/~hal/sslchallong.html`

[17] A.O. Freier and P. Karlton and P.C. Kocher, SSL Version 3.0, 1995
Internet-Draft `draft-freier-ssl-version3-00.txt`, work in progress

[18] Gilles Garon and Richard Outerbridge, "DES Watch: An Examination of the Sufficiency of the Data Encryption Standard for Financial Institution Information Security in the 1990's," *Cryptologia* XV(3), July, 1991, pages 177-193.

[19] Martin E. Hellman, "DES will be totally insecure within ten years," *IEEE) Spectrum*, 16:7, July 1979, pages 32-39

[20] John L. Hennessy and David A. Patterson, *Computer Architecture: A Quantitative Approach*, Morgan Kaufmann Publishers, Inc., San Francisco, 1996, 2nd edition

[21] Frank Hoornaert, Jo Goubert, and Yvo Desmedt, "Efficient hardware implementation of the DES," in *Advances in Cryptology: Proceedings of CRYPTO '84*, 1985, Springer-Verlag, pages 147-173

[22] Eric Hughes and Bruce Koball, "Cryptography and the Altera FLEX 81188," Unpublished manuscript, December, 1994

[23] D.B. Johnson, Sm.M. Matyas, A.V. Le, and J.D. Wilkins, "Design of the Commercial Data Masking Facility Data Privacy Algorithm," in 1st ACM Conference on Computer and Communications Security, ACM Press, 1993, pages 93-96

[24] Clive McCarthy, Personal communication, April, 1996

[25] Robert McLaughlin, "Yet Another Machine to Break DES," *Cryptologia* XVI:2, April, 1992, pages 136-144

[26] Michael Roe, Personal communication, April, 1996

[27] Bruce Schneier, *Applied Cryptography*, John Wiley and Sons, New York, 1994, 2nd edition

[28] Bruce Schneier, Personal communication, April, 1996

[29] David Wagner and Steven M. Bellovin, "A probable plaintext recognizer," Unpublished manuscript, September, 1994

[30] Peter C. Wayner, "Content-Addressable Search Engines and DES-like Systems, in *Advances in Cryptology: Proceedings of CRYPTO '92*, 1993, Springer-Verlag, pages 575-586,

[31] Michael J. Wiener, "Efficient DES Key Search," in *Advances in Cryptology: Proceedings of CRYPTO '93*, Santa Barbara, CA, 1994, Springer-Verlag.

# 11

# *Efficient DES Key Search — An Update by Michael J. Wiener*

An exciting moment in the history of DES was reached in June 1997 when a group coordinated by Rocke Verser solved RSA Data Security's DES challenge by exhaustive key search on a large number of computers. This result was useful because it served to underscore in a public way how vulnerable DES has become. However, it may also have left the false impression that one cannot do much better than attacking DES in software with a large distributed effort. The design of DES is such that it is fairly slow in software, but is compact and fast when implemented in hardware. As a result, using software to attack DES gives poor performance compared to what can be achieved in hardware. This applies not only to DES, but also to most other block ciphers, attacks on hash functions, and attacks on elliptic curve cryptosystems. Avoiding efficient hardware- based attacks requires the use of algorithms with sufficiently long keys, such as triple-DES, 128-bit RC5,[*] and CAST-128.[†]

In this article we assess the cost of DES key search using hardware methods and examine the effectiveness of some proposed methods for thwarting attacks on DES.

Michael J. Wiener, Entrust Technologies, 750 Heron Road, Suite E08, Ottawa, Ontario, Canada K1V 1A7

This article first appeared in RSA Laboratories' Autumn 1997 Cryptobytes newsletter; it is reprinted with permission from the author and RSA Data Security, Inc.

[*] R. Rivest, "The RC5 Encryption Algorithm", Fast Software Encryption — Lecture Notes in Computer Science (1008), pp. 86-96, Springer, 1995.

[†] C. Adams, "Constructing Symmetric Ciphers Using the CAST Design Procedure", Designs, Codes and Cryptography, vol. 12, no. 3, pp. 283-316, Nov. 1997. Also available as "The CAST-128 Encryption Algorithm", RFC 2144, May 1997.

# Advancing Technology

The best known way to attack DES is to simply try all of the possible 56-bit keys until the correct key is found. On average, one expects to go through about half of the key space. In 1993, a design for an exhaustive DES key search machine including a detailed chip design was published.* A $1 million version of this machine used 57600 key search chips, each capable of testing 50 million keys per second. Overall, the machine could find a DES key in, on average, three and a half hours.

About four and a half years have passed since this design was completed, and according to Moore's Law, processing speeds should have doubled three times in that period. Of course, estimating in this fashion is a poor substitute for the careful analysis and design effort that went into the earlier design. The original chip design was done in a 0.8 micron CMOS process, and with the geometries available today, it is possible to fit four instances of the original design into the same silicon area. In keeping with the conservative approach to estimates in the 1993 paper, we assume here that the updated key search chip's clock speed would increase to only 75 MHz from the original 50 MHz, making the modern version of the chip six times faster for the same cost. It is interesting to note that just 21 of these chips would give the same key searching power as the entire set of computers used by the team who solved the DES challenge.

Today's version of the $1 million machine could find a DES key in, on average, about 35 minutes (one-sixth of 3.5 hours). This time scales linearly with the amount of money spent as shown in the following table.

| Key Search Machine Cost | Expected Search Time |
|---|---|
| $10,000 | 2.5 days |
| $100,000 | 6 hours |
| $1,000,000 | 35 minutes |
| $10,000,000 | 3.5 minutes |

Note that the costs listed in the table do not include the cost to design the chip and boards for the machine. Because the one-time costs could be as high as half a million dollars, it does not make much sense to build the cheaper versions of the machine, unless several are built for different customers.

This key search engine is designed to recover a DES key given a plaintext-ciphertext pair for the standard electronic-codebook (ECB) mode of DES. However, the machine can also handle the following modes without modification: cipher-block

---

* M. Wiener, "Efficient DES Key Search", presented at the Rump session of Crypto '93. Reprinted in Practical Cryptography for Data Internetworks, W. Stallings, editor, IEEE Computer Society Press, pp. 31-79 (1996). Currently available at `ftp://ripem.msu.edu/pub/crypt/docs/des-key-search.ps`.

chaining (CBC), 64-bit cipher feedback (CFB), and 64- bit output feedback (OFB). In the case of OFB, two consecutive plaintexts are needed. The chip design can be modified to handle two other popular modes of DES, 1-bit and 8-bit CFB, at the cost of a slightly more expensive chip. Fewer chips could be purchased for a $1 million machine causing the expected key search time to go up to 40 minutes for all modes, except 1-bit CFB, which would take 80 minutes, on average.

# Programmable Hardware

The costs associated with chip design can present a significant barrier to small-time attackers and hobbyists. An alternative which has much lower start-up costs is the use of programmable hardware. One such type of technology is the Field Programmable Gate Array (FPGA). One can design a circuit on a PC and download it to a board holding FPGAs for execution. In a report in early 1996,* it was estimated that $50000 worth of FPGAs could recover a DES key in, on average, four months. This is considerably slower than what can be achieved with a chip design, but is much more accessible to those who are not well funded.

Another promising form of programmable hardware is the Complex Programmable Logic Device (CPLD). CPLDs offer less design freedom and tend to be cheaper than FPGAs, but the nature of key search designs seems to make them suitable for CPLDs. Further research is needed to assess whether CPLDs are useful for DES key search.

## Avoiding Known Plaintext

The designs described to this point have relied on the attacker having some known plaintext. Usually, a single 8-byte block is sufficient. One method of preventing attacks that has been suggested is to avoid having any known plaintext. This can be quite difficult to achieve. Frequently, data begins with fixed headers. For example, each version of Microsoft Word seems to have a fixed string of bytes that each file begins with.

For those cases where a full block of known plaintext is not available, it is possible to adapt the key search design. Suppose that information about plaintext is available (e.g., ASCII character coding is used), but no full block is known. Then instead of repeatedly encrypting a known plaintext and comparing the result to a ciphertext, we repeatedly decrypt the ciphertext and test the candidate plaintexts against our expectations. In the example where we expect 7-bit ASCII plaintext, only about 1 in 256 keys will give a plaintext which has the correct form. These

* M. Blaze, W. Diffie, R. Rivest, B. Schneier, T. Shimomura, E. Thompson, and M. Wiener, "Minimal Key Lengths for Symmetric Ciphers to Provide Adequate Commercial Security", currently available at http://www.bsa.org/policy/encryption/cryptographers.html.

keys would have to be tried on another ciphertext block. The added logic to handle this would add just 10 to 20% to the cost of a key search chip.

Even if we only know a single bit of redundancy in each block of plaintext, this is enough to cut the number of possible keys in half. About 56 such blocks are needed to uniquely identify the correct key. This does not mean that the run-time is 56 times greater than the known-plaintext case. On average, each key is eliminated with just two decryptions. Taking into account the cost of the added logic required makes the expected run-time for a $1 million machine about 2 hours in this case.

## Frequent Key Changes

A commonly suggested way to avoid key search attacks is to change the DES key frequently. The assumption here is that the encrypted information is no longer useful after the key is changed, which is often an inappropriate assumption. If it takes 35 minutes to find a DES key, why not change keys every 5 minutes? The problem with this reasoning is that it does not take exactly 35 minutes to find a key. The actual time is uniformly distributed between 0 and 70 minutes. We could get lucky and find the key almost right away, or we could be unlucky and take nearly 70 minutes. The attacker's probability of success in the 5-minute window is $5/70 = 1/14$. If after each key change the attacker gives up and starts on the next key, we expect success after 14 key changes or 70 minutes. In general, frequent key changes cost the attacker just a factor of two in expected run-time, and are a poor substitute for simply using a strong encryption algorithm with longer keys.

# Conclusion

Using current technology, a DES key can be recovered with a custom-designed $1 million machine in just 35 minutes. For attackers who lack the resources to design a chip and build such a machine, there are programmable forms of hardware such as FPGAs and CPLDs which can search the DES key space much faster than is possible using software on PCs and workstations. Attempts to thwart key search attacks by avoiding known plaintext and changing keys frequently are largely ineffective. The best course of action is to use a strong encryption algorithm with longer keys, such as triple-DES, 128-bit RC5, or CAST-128.

# 12

# *Authors*

## *The Electronic Frontier Foundation*

Electronic Frontier Foundation
1550 Bryant Street, Suite 725
San Francisco CA 94103 USA
+1 415 436 9333 (voice)
+1 415 436 9993 (fax)
http://www.eff.org
info@eff.org

The Electronic Frontier Foundation (EFF) is a nonprofit public-interest organization protecting rights and promoting liberty online. It was founded in 1990 by Mitchell Kapor, John Perry Barlow, and John Gilmore.

The Foundation seeks to educate individuals, organizations, companies, and governments about the issues that arise when computer and communications technologies change the world out from under the existing legal and social matrix.

The Foundation has been working on cryptography policy for many years. It was a significant force in preventing the adoption of the "Clipper chip" and its follow-on "key escrow" proposals, and continues to advocate for wide public availability and use of uncompromised and unbreakable encryption technology. EFF is backing the lawsuit in which Professor Daniel Bernstein seeks to overturn the United States export laws and regulations on cryptography, arguing that the First Amendment to the US Constitution protects his right to publish his cryptography research results online without first seeking government permission. EFF's research effort in creating this first publicly announced DES Cracker, and the publication of its full technical details, are part of EFF's ongoing campaign to understand, and educate the public about, the social and technical implications of cryptographic technology.

EFF encourages you to join us in exploring how our society can best respond to today's rapid technological change. Please become an EFF member; see `http://www.eff.org/join/`.

## John Gilmore

John Gilmore is an entrepreneur and civil libertarian. He was an early employee of Sun Microsystems, and co-founded Cygnus Solutions, the Electronic Frontier Foundation, the Cypherpunks, and the Internet's "alt" newsgroups. He has twenty-five years of experience in the computer industry, including programming, hardware and software design, and management. He is a significant contributor to the worldwide open sourceware (free software) development effort. His advocacy efforts on encryption policy aim to improve public understanding of this fundamental technology for privacy and accountability in open societies. He is currently a board member of Moniker pty ltd, the Internet Society, and the Electronic Frontier Foundation.

John leads the EFF's efforts on cryptography policy, managed the creation of the DES cracker, and wrote much of the text in this book.

John can be reached at the email address `gnu@des.toad.com`; his home page is `http://www.cygnus.com/~gnu/`.

## Cryptography Research

Cryptography Research
870 Market Street, Suite 1088
San Francisco, CA 94102 USA
+1 415 397 0123  (voice)
+1 415 397 0127  (fax)
`http://www.cryptography.com`

Cryptography Research is Paul Kocher's San Francisco-based consulting company. Cryptography Research provides consulting, design, education, and analysis services to many leading firms and start-ups. Kocher and the company are widely known for their technical work and research, including the development of leading cryptographic protocols (such as SSL 3.0), cryptanalytic work (including the discovery of timing attacks against RSA and other cryptosystems), and numerous presentations at major conferences. To reach Cryptography Research please write to `info@cryptography.com`.

Cryptography Research managed the hardware and software design for the DES cracker, and wrote the chip simulator and the driver software.

Paul Kocher, Josh Jaffe, and everyone else at Cryptography Research would like to thank John Gilmore and the EFF for funding this unique project, and AWT for their expert hardware work!

# Paul Kocher

Paul Kocher is a cryptographer specializing in the practical art of building secure systems using cryptography. He currently serves jointly as President of Cryptography Research (http://www.cryptography.com) and Chief Scientist of ValiCert (http://www.valicert.com). Paul has worked on numerous software and hardware projects and has designed, implemented, and broken many cryptosystems. Paul can be reached via e-mail at paul@cryptography.com.

# Advanced Wireless Technologies

Advanced Wireless Technologies, Inc.
3375 Scott Blvd, Suite 410
Santa Clara, CA  95054 USA
+1 408 727 5780  (voice)
+1 408 727 8842  (fax)
http://www.awti.com

Advanced Wireless Technologies, Inc. (AWT) is dedicated to providing Application-Specific Integrated Circuit (ASIC) and board level design solutions for high tech industries at highest quality and lowest cost. AWT's design philosophy is to reduce product development cost/risk and recurring cost. AWT employs a thorough design flow from system architecture to system integration and test.

AWT was founded in 1993. Its engineering team is composed of a highly qualified, tenured employee base, including technical management staff. The employees are knowledgeable, motivated, highly competent, and have from 3 to 25 years of experience in system engineering, chip design, and complete subsystem design.

AWT offers digital ASIC/Gate Array and Board design services to support customers' specific requirements. The company can participate in any development phase from specifications definition to design implementation and prototype testing.

In addition to providing engineering services AWT has developed leading products for use in the communications industry. AWT's standard products include IP Cores,

ASICs, and board level products in the fields of demodulation, forward error correction, and encryption/decryption.

AWT designed and built the hardware for the DES Cracker, including the custom ASIC, logic boards, and interface adapters. If you're interested in purchasing a DES Cracker unit, contact AWT.

AWT invites you to visit at `http://www.awti.com` or call +1 408 727 5780 for your specific engineering needs.

# Titles from O'Reilly

## O'REILLY™

# International Distributors

## UK, EUROPE, MIDDLE EAST AND NORTHERN AFRICA (EXCEPT FRANCE, GERMANY, SWITZERLAND, & AUSTRIA)

**INQUIRIES**
International Thomson Publishing Europe
Berkshire House
168-173 High Holborn
London WC1V 7AA
United Kingdom
Telephone: 44-171-497-1422
Fax: 44-171-497-1426
Email: itpint@itps.co.uk

**ORDERS**
International Thomson Publishing Services, Ltd.
Cheriton House, North Way
Andover, Hampshire SP10 5BE
United Kingdom
Telephone: 44-264-342-832 (UK)
Telephone: 44-264-342-806 (outside UK)
Fax: 44-264-364418 (UK)
Fax: 44-264-342761 (outside UK)
UK & Eire orders: itpuk@itps.co.uk
International orders: itpint@itps.co.uk

## FRANCE

Editions Eyrolles
61 bd Saint-Germain
75240 Paris Cedex 05
France
Fax: 33-01-44-41-11-44

**FRENCH LANGUAGE BOOKS**
All countries except Canada
Telephone: 33-01-44-41-46-16
Email: geodif@eyrolles.com
English language books
Telephone: 33-01-44-41-11-87
Email: distribution@eyrolles.com

## GERMANY, SWITZERLAND, AND AUSTRIA

**INQUIRIES**
O'Reilly Verlag
Balthasarstr. 81
D-50670 Köln
Germany
Telephone: 49-221-97-31-60-0
Fax: 49-221-97-31-60-8
Email: anfragen@oreilly.de

**ORDERS**
International Thomson Publishing
Königswinterer Straße 418
53227 Bonn, Germany
Telephone: 49-228-97024 0
Fax: 49-228-441342
Email: order@oreilly.de

## JAPAN

O'Reilly Japan, Inc.
Kiyoshige Building 2F
12-Banchi, Sanei-cho
Shinjuku-ku
Tokyo 160-0008 Japan
Telephone: 81-3-3356-5227
Fax: 81-3-3356-5261
Email: kenji@oreilly.com

## INDIA

Computer Bookshop (India) PVT. Ltd.
190 Dr. D.N. Road, Fort
Bombay 400 001 India
Telephone: 91-22-207-0989
Fax: 91-22-262-3551
Email: cbsbom@giasbm01.vsnl.net.in

## HONG KONG

City Discount Subscription Service Ltd.
Unit D, 3rd Floor, Yan's Tower
27 Wong Chuk Hang Road
Aberdeen, Hong Kong
Telephone: 852-2580-3539
Fax: 852-2580-6463
Email: citydis@ppn.com.hk

## KOREA

Hanbit Media, Inc.
Sonyoung Bldg. 202
Yeksam-dong 736-36
Kangnam-ku
Seoul, Korea
Telephone: 822-554-9610
Fax: 822-556-0363
Email: hant93@chollian.dacom.co.kr

## SINGAPORE, MALAYSIA, AND THAILAND

Addison Wesley Longman Singapore PTE Ltd.
25 First Lok Yang Road
Singapore 629734
Telephone: 65-268-2666
Fax: 65-268-7023
Email: daniel@longman.com.sg

## PHILIPPINES

Mutual Books, Inc.
429-D Shaw Boulevard
Mandaluyong City, Metro
Manila, Philippines
Telephone: 632-725-7538
Fax: 632-721-3056
Email: mbikikog@mnl.sequel.net

## CHINA

Ron's DataCom Co., Ltd.
79 Dongwu Avenue
Dongxihu District
Wuhan 430040
China
Telephone: 86-27-3892568
Fax: 86-27-3222108
Email: hongfeng@public.wh.hb.cn

## ALL OTHER ASIAN COUNTRIES

O'Reilly & Associates, Inc.
101 Morris Street
Sebastopol, CA 95472 USA
Telephone: 707-829-0515
Fax: 707-829-0104
Email: order@oreilly.com

## AUSTRALIA

WoodsLane Pty. Ltd.
7/5 Vuko Place, Warriewood NSW 2102
P.O. Box 935
Mona Vale NSW 2103
Australia
Telephone: 61-2-9970-5111
Fax: 61-2-9970-5002
Email: info@woodslane.com.au

## NEW ZEALAND

Woodslane New Zealand Ltd.
21 Cooks Street (P.O. Box 575)
Waganui, New Zealand
Telephone: 64-6-347-6543
Fax: 64-6-345-4840
Email: info@woodslane.com.au

## THE AMERICAS

McGraw-Hill Interamericana Editores, S.A. de C.V.
Cedro No. 512
Col. Atlampa 06450
Mexico, D.F.
Telephone: 52-5-541-3155
Fax: 52-5-541-4913
Email: mcgraw-hill@infosel.net.mx

## SOUTH AFRICA

International Thomson Publishing
South Africa
Building 18, Constantia Park
138 Sixteenth Road
P.O. Box 2459
Halfway House, 1685 South Africa
Telephone: 27-11-805-4819
Fax: 27-11-805-3648